THE REAL SHAKESPEARE

THE REAL SHAKESPEARE

Retrieving the Early Years,
1564–1594

ERIC SAMS

YALE UNIVERSITY PRESS
NEW HAVEN AND LONDON · 1995

Set in Meridien by Best-set Typesetter Ltd., Hong Kong
Printed and bound in Great Britain by Biddles Ltd., Guildford and Kings Lynn

Library of Congress Cataloging-in-Publication Data

Sams, Eric.
    The real Shakespeare : retrieving the early years, 1564–1594 /
Eric Sams.
        p. cm.
    Includes bibliographical references and index.
    ISBN 0-300-06129-3 (hbk.)
    ISBN 0-300-07282-1 (pbk.)
    1. Shakespeare, William, 1564–1616. 2. Shakespeare, William,
1564–1616—Childhood and youth. 3. Dramatists, English—Early
modern, 1500–1700—Biography. I. Title.
PR2903.S26 1995
822.3'3—dc20
[B]   94–27876
                                                                        CIP

A catalogue record for this book is available from the British Library.

semper ad manes fratrum

Contents

viii   *Contents*

Acknowledgements

I AM GRATEFUL to my family and friends for all their timely assistance and encouragement. In particular I am indebted to the scholarship and acumen of Clifford Broadbent, Hayat Mathews and Jon Mills. The London Library was, as ever, indispensable. A special word of thanks is due to my publisher Robert Baldock, who played an essential part throughout; and I was fortunate in having the help of Candida Brazil, an exemplary editor.

Foreword

SHAKESPEARE WAS A Stratford butcher's eldest son, whose father took him away from school to help in hard times. When the boy 'kill'd a Calfe, he would doe it in a high style, & make a Speech' (Aubrey *c*. 1681). He married at eighteen, and soon left for London, where he successfully acted and wrote popular plays (Rowe 1709). So said his first biographers, after due enquiry. Their modern successors treat all such testimony as 'gossip' (Schoenbaum 1975, 14, 59, 60, 82, 87, 111, etc.) or 'stories' (Honigmann 1982, 82, 1985, 2) or 'quite wrong' and 'muddled' (I. Wilson 1993, 59–61). So much for the prose stylist and antiquary John Aubrey, and his enquiries among Stratfordians, and his friends the Davenants, who were Shakespeare's godsons. So much for the Poet Laureate and playwright Nicholas Rowe, and his collaborator the actor Thomas Betterton, who had visited Stratford. They were writing decades after Shakespeare's death. Modern authorities somehow know better, several centuries later still. They have only to hear of a pantomime called 'Killing the Calf', played at Court in 1521, to know that this must have been what Aubrey and his yokel informants meant, without realising it (Schoenbaum, Wilson, idem, Powell 1985, etc.); never mind common sense, or counter-evidence, or the absence of any reason to suppose that Shakespeare had ever heard of 'Killing the Calf' (Sams 1985e, 1987b).

In this refractory frame of mind, only twentieth-century theories stand any chance of being believed; and indeed these are solemnly hailed, by the selfsame authorities, as infallible gospel. Thus Alexander's 1929 notions of 'memorial reconstruction', the editorial equivalent of 'Killing the Calf', are acclaimed as 'demonstrated' (Schoenbaum 1975, 123) and treated as truth (Honigmann 1982, *passim* in a book dedicated to Alexander's memory). Ian Wilson (1993, vii , 169), like all modern experts (such as Taylor 1988, 111), avowedly bases his dating of the plays on the same notions. He is as sure as Schoenbaum that the Bard cannot conceivably have been a butcher. John Shakespeare was allegedly apprenticed as a glover; so, no doubt, was young William; but stringent regulations kept the two trades apart (Schoenbaum 1975, 14, 60). And of course 'we need not doubt that Shakespeare received a grammar-school education' (ibid., 50); indeed, at sixteen he was better educated in Latin literature than many a modern classics graduate (Wells 1986, xiv). However, he was a late developer who wrote nothing for the next twelve years (the so-called

'Lost Years', Schoenbaum 1975, 77f), and then started with sophisticated comedies of upper-class life.

Thus speak the experts, with one voice. But how do they know so much more and so much better than their sources, 400 years later? They don't. On the facts, Shakespeare's father was not only a glover but a farmer, hide-dresser and wool-dealer, who would naturally undertake his own slaughtering. The alleged regulations and apprenticeships are merely imaginary, like the lost years and the late development and the post-graduate Latin. Such inventions surely spring from neo-Baconian social and intellectual snobbery: only the most mysterious and exalted of back-grounds is good enough for our national poet and his commentators. Hence the accepted theories of 'memorial reconstruction', 'derivative play', 'collaboration' and so forth (XXXI–XXXIII), which preserve him from any taint of inferior writings, even those that proudly announce his name on their title-pages. These fantasies are passed off as fact in all current major editions (Arden, Cambridge, Oxford, Penguin, etc.), biographies (Schoenbaum, Rowse, Levi, I. Wilson, etc.), dictionaries (Oxford, Chambers) and reference books (Wells 1978–85, Jackson 1986, Taylor 1988, Boyce 1990, etc.) published and sold by reputable presses throughout the world. Thus thousands of Shakespeare's lines have been misdated or lost, together with at least a decade of his career.

It is time to give him his life and works back. This entails a fresh start from the facts. The first need therefore is a check-list of sixteenth- and seventeenth-century sources, set out in date order (by month or day if known, otherwise by year) on pp. 197–226. Space and format restrict it to 205 items in the present volume, ending in 1594; a sequel is in preparation. Meanwhile that date is a convenient cut-off point. *Venus and Adonis* had been published as Shakespeare's in 1593, but it was not until the following year that his work as both poet and playwright appeared in print, with the publication of *The Rape of Lucrece* and (anonymously, as usual then) the earliest canonical play, *Titus Andronicus c.* 1589. By that time, he had made his name in the London theatre and book world; the factual foundations were already laid.

They stand far aloof from every modern literary edifice ever erected. Take for example the forgotten comedy *The Taming of A Shrew*, also published anonymously in 1594. Editors from Alexander (1926) on have asserted that this was a 'memorial reconstruction' by 'actors' of *The Taming of the Shrew*. *Ex hypothesi* that play was not only written but acted and available for 'reconstruction' in good time for 1594; so it must be dated very early. But the copious contemporary records offer no support for any such notions. On the contrary, there is no evidence that anyone even so much as hinted at *The Shrew's* existence until after 1600, and it remained unpublished until the 1623 Folio, seven years after its author's death. Thus the very first check reveals fatal flaws. The next test is equally elementary. What does 'memorial reconstruction' entail? The two plays are plainly variations on the same theme, with many similarities (XXV). But their words are totally different. It follows from modern theory that professional Tudor actors, in Shakespeare's own company, had forgotten *every single line* of the popular and masterly play they had recently performed and were trying hard to remember. In the effort to do so they magically constructed a new play by mistake, with a different location, plot and characters.

This is not just ordinary nonsense, but obvious and outrageous nonsense. Yet it has been accepted and announced by every specialist editor (Hibbard, Morris, Oliver, Thompson) in all main current editions (Penguin, Arden, Oxford, New Cambridge) of *The Shrew*. Why were such manifest falsehoods ever invented, let alone believed? Why are they printed and distributed by learned presses and left uncorrected year after year, to be taught and learned worldwide?

One of the authorities concerned has offered an answer. 'Textual critics are the unacknowledged civil servants who promulgate and administer [Shakespeare]. Editors are the pimps of discourse. . . . Editorial controversy, like all other forms of discourse, is an instrument of power . . .' (Taylor 1988, 7). Further (Taylor 1990, 321),

> OUP can afford to experiment, because its risky innovations are subsidised by its safe market leaders. The Oxford editors, too, can afford to experiment, because they know that the global power and prestige of OUP will be mobilized in support of their experiments. Their shocking edition is empowered by and, in turn, empowers, the multinational business interests of Oxford University Press. . . .

Experimentation is thus admittedly marginal. Power, prestige and profit are central. They radiate out to the entire scholarly community, past and present, who thus in turn become accepted authorities by knowing and believing and repeating what their predecessors or colleagues have said. In an ideal world, that would work well. In practice, it entails the ceaseless dissemination of irresponsible nonsense. In that interest, whole populations (including the earliest actors, administrators, audiences, biographers, booksellers, commentators, critics, printers and publishers) are written off as knaves or fools or both, while the personal opinions of modern literary academics (about graphology, Latin, law or shorthand for example, as well as style) are trumpeted as truth.

One prime purpose of this book is to expose and if possible reverse such pretensions, thus bringing Shakespeare back to the general public and scholarship back to its collective senses. But that will still be only a starting step. There is a long new road to travel; and it begins in the sixteenth century. The scholarly world took a wrong turning early this century and is now far out of sight and earshot. Its assumptions are so arcane that most Shakespeare-lovers have never heard of them. So I have to explain in more detail what our present authorities are asserting before trying to refute them. In what follows, I shall tackle the two tasks together. For both purposes I shall rely on direct quotation. My main source will be the Oxford University Press Shakespeare publications, especially their *Documentary Life* 1975 (Schoenbaum), *Complete Works* 1986 (ed. Wells and Taylor) and *Textual Companion* 1988 (Taylor). These are the best-known and most influential. If they are as mistaken and misleading as I aver, then so *a fortiori* are all other extant editions, series, reference books and biographies, in hundreds of respects including their dates and texts. If nothing is done, these same mistakes will be taught and learned, published and sold, as infallible facts, worldwide, for ever.

I am sorry that so many literati feel that debate with or within Academia is itself academic, or useless, as that word has come to mean. My own position is passionately opposed to that viewpoint. I believe that Shakespeare needs to be validated and defended against his detractors and disintegrators. To offer only one example among thousands: the British Library labels and libels its precious copy of *Hamlet* 1603 as a 'Bad Quarto', deriving from an unauthorised reproduction from memory by one or more of the actors. This must surely be true, the official concerned has courteously explained (Barr 1991), because Gary Taylor says so. But Taylor says so (1988, 398) secure in the knowledge that 'it is now generally agreed', after 'the evidence for this conclusion has been discussed in detail by Duthie (1941), Jenkins (1982) and Hibbard [the Oxford editor of the separate volume] (1987)'. Brian Vickers (1993) also shares and reasserts this belief, which he feels was 'irrefutably confirmed' by Duthie (1941) and Hart (1942).

But what if it is false, as in the case of the *Shrew* and the *Lear* plays – both also 'confirmed' by the same Duthie, in 1943 and 1949 respectively, and wrongly on each count (on his own 1960 admission in the latter case)? Then the world is deprived of an early play 'by William Shakespeare', as the *Hamlet* 1603 title-page proudly proclaims. And this epitomises the choice to be made: modern literary opinion, or past documentary evidence?

The latter needs to be as fully documented as possible, for purposes of study and comparison. From the appended check-list, therefore (pp. 197–226), no substantive source has been wittingly excluded. Nor should any of its items be rejected or disparaged *a priori*. In particular none of it deserves to be dismissed as mere 'mythos', 'gossip', 'lore' or 'legend', or 'too early for Shakespeare', in the style of Chambers (1930 ii, 186, 238–302, etc.) followed by Schoenbaum (1975, 59, 82, 87, 111, 115, etc.). Such bias is barren. As Bentham says (1825, 226) 'let us not judge on authority; let us seek reasons'.

This approach is unprecedented. No doubt it will also be called undiscriminating and old-fashioned. But such epithets might be better applied to present professional practice, which has created catastrophic confusion for most of this century – for example by dismissing the Shakespeare masterpiece *King Lear* 1608 as a mere 'memorial reconstruction' by pirate-actors, as Taylor confesses (1988, 509). The prime point has to be hammered home; no one really knows any different, or any more, or any better, than the documentary data on which this book is based.

They have been set out with a copious use of literal quotation so as to convey the flavour of the relevant sources without imposing any need for specialist knowledge. Explanatory notes have been added [in square brackets] wherever the context requires, together with extensive cross-references (in round brackets, with serial numbers in **bold** type) to facilitate verification. The list begins before 1509, with the earliest known reference to any of Shakespeare's ancestors, and ends in 1594, the key date already defined. It includes every known item of relevance to Shakespeare, whether overt, covert or putative, which occurred within that time and still remains on record to this day.

This total tally of 205 provides the basis for a new approach to the life and works (cited for convenience of reference from the Spevack Concordance, based on the Riverside Edition). The works are also occasionally invoked as biographical evidence. Shakespeare, like other great masters, excavates raw material from his own life and times, which is then processed into art. But untreated traces are also left lying on the surface. *Love's Labour's Lost* for example is replete with deliberate allusions, whether historical, literary or personal. Similarly the Earl of Essex's Irish expedition is no more relevant to *Henry V* (V Chorus 30–34) than his capture of the galleon *San Andres*, renamed *Andrew*, to *The Merchant of Venice* (I.i.27), or the war of the theatres to *Hamlet* (II.ii.336f), or the death of Marlowe to *As You Like It* (III.iii.15, v.81–2). Such references therefore had powerful personal significance for Shakespeare; and he offers many other such examples including cross-reference to his own works. As Mozart quotes *Figaro* in *Don Giovanni* and Wagner *Tristan* in *Die Meistersinger*, so *Henry V* ends (Ep. 9–14) with a sly allusion to the plays about King Henry VI, 'which oft our stage hath shown', while *Hamlet* (III.ii.103f) looks back to *Julius Caesar*. Similarly the Sonnets *passim* and *The Merry Wives of Windsor* Act I are supercharged with subjective feeling – *pace* their modern editors, such as Kerrigan (1986) and Craik (1989) respectively.

But the general reader knows that life and works are best studied together, because of their logical and aesthetic links. First, art without an artist has never yet been observed. Secondly, 'In practice, since the precise interpretation of works of art is no easy matter, such knowledge [of the artist's life] will give us a valuable context of understanding: it will show us what to look for' (Sparshott 1963, 31). Shakespeare's personal allusive procedures exemplified above, and exemplifiable by scores of other instances, mirror his myriad creative facets. We may not see them or interpret them all correctly, but that is no reason for closing our eyes and minds to them.

This applies equally to all other known or putative sources of information about Shakespeare. The allusions in Greene's 1592 *Groats-worth of Witte* are manifest and undoubted. *Pace* the academic consensus, it would surely be astounding if so outstanding a poetic and dramatic genius had not started young and become well-known by his twenty-ninth year. So whatever looks like another such allusion, pro or con, may well be one. One essential principle in Shakespeare studies, though enunciated in the particular context of authorship studies three decades ago and neglected ever since, surely has universal and permanent validity, thus: 'Intuitions, convictions and subjective judgements generally, carry no weight as evidence. This no matter how learned, respected or confident the authority' (Schoenbaum 1966, 178).

However, some subjectivity may be unavoidable, because the conspectus of extant evidence, as defined and deployed here, needs extension by processes of inference, which are perforce personal and hence fallible. But any rational factually based inference must be preferable to rigid preconvictions, especially those which have come to be counted as 'scholarship' and hence sacrosanct. Yet these remain apparently ineradicable, even when their illogicalities and errors are pointed out (as for example by Sprinchorn 1994 in his controversy with Jenkins and Vickers about *Hamlet* 1603), and even when their eradication would open new and fertile fields of research.

A striking example is the unshakeable belief that the Shakespeares called their only son 'Hamnet' (Rowse 1973, Schoenbaum 1975–91, Wilson 1993, Nye 1993, Freeman 1993, Wells 1994, Bearman 1994, etc.). Of course that sadly short-lived lad (1585–96) was called Hamlet. This name came from Stratford on Avon, not Denmark (whose prince is called Amlodh or Amleth in all the sources). So which Stratfordian wrote the early play of *Hamlet* that Nashe mentioned in 1589? And why does it exist in three very different versions, published in 1603, 1604 and 1623? As soon as Shakespeare is allowed to have been a real person in a real world he will be seen as an early starter and a reviser; and an early start needs to be made on revising all his modern editions, biographies and reference books.

I

The Country Background

SHAKESPEARE'S BACKGROUND WAS an illiterate Catholic peasant homestead. But the facts are rarely faced; orthodox belief focuses on secular sophistication. Peasantry has come to connote boorish poverty; toilers and tillers are often despised, despite their provision of daily bread for all. That dependence was even greater in Tudor times. According to the College of Arms in 1596, the ancestral Shakespeares were landholders (1). Richard Shakespeare, the poet's grandfather, remained a tenant farmer all his life, as attested in the archives of Snitterfield near Stratford. He was fined for keeping his cattle on the common pasture (5, 24) and for neglecting to ring his swine (24); he was ordered (6) to mend his hedges; he was bequeathed (8) a team of oxen by a fellow-yeoman. Like other Tudor farmers, he would raise his cattle for milk and ploughing, and slaughter them and other livestock for meat and raw materials, including wool and leather for clothing, bedding, shoes, gloves and harness. His two sons, John (4) and Henry (70), would naturally have learned and continued all such trades, in the tradition of the times, and for centuries before and since. So would their eldest son or nephew William in his turn.

The Shakespeares had leased their land from a branch of the Arden family, which could trace its descent from the Saxon era. One of its members had been High Sheriff of Warwickshire before the Norman Conquest, and another in 1438; a third attained that office in 1575 (Halliday 1964, 36). The Ardens of Wilmcote near Stratford are not known to have attained any such distinction. But Thomas Arden owned estates in that vicinity; and he had prospered sufficiently to acquire further holdings in Snitterfield (2) jointly with his son and heir Robert Arden (3), who built a house and raised a family there. In about 1557 Robert's young daughter Mary Arden (7) married (16) his tenant Richard Shakespeare's son John, then in his later twenties (4), who had moved some years earlier to Stratford (10). There their eldest son William (35) was born in 1564; and until he left for London some twenty years later, his family life and livelihood lay entirely in the land. By then he had married Anne Hathaway (15), sister of one local farmer and daughter of another (117), with two other local farmers as witnesses (119).

That was his small community, his narrow circle, his daily round. Not only both his grandfathers and his father- and brother-in-law were farmers; so were his uncles Henry Shakespeare (70, 108, 142), Edmund

Lambert (86, 94, 104, 157) and Alexander Webbe (68). His step-grandmother Agnes Arden née Webbe (105) was a farmer's (Alexander's) sister, a farmer's daughter and a farmer's (John Hill's) wife and widow (9) on the Arden estate; and in her will she left a cow to her son John Arden, Shakespeare's cousin once removed. Indeed, Shakespeare's own mother Mary née Arden had inherited land already tilled and crops already sown (14), while his own father John was not only a farmer's son and heir but was also himself explicitly recorded as 'agricola', a farmer (26). The 'gutters' he had been fined for neglecting (22) were no doubt the channels or watercourses needed for farm irrigation; their communal use justified a corporate concern for their proper upkeep. He too was fined in 1561 and 1562 for neglecting his hedges, both in Stratford (28) and in his home village of Snitterfield (30), where he had inherited a share of his father's land and presumably also of the livestock. Hedging, like ditching, belongs among the corporate disciplines of husbandry; the frequent fines imposed on the Shakespeare family suggest that they were overworked and short-handed. Even after John had leased out his Snitterfield land in 1562 he still had substantial holdings in Stratford, and he acquired a further tenancy at Ingon Meadow in 1568 (50).

He first appears in the historical record when fined one shilling (10) for keeping a dunghill at the Henley Street house in Stratford, now known as the Birthplace. No doubt he thereby contravened the municipal sanitary bye-laws; but he is thus confirmed as a farmer. Four years later (12) he bought a croft [a piece of enclosed ground used for farming purposes, whether tillage or pasture], and also sued for the detention of a sizeable quantity of barley (13) which presumably represented his own sowing, threshing, harrowing, reaping, harvesting and storing. It would also account for the dunghill; as the contemporary Tudor farmer Thomas Tusser (1573) often notes, the cultivation of barley demanded manure all the year round. In February, he counselled, 'place doong heapes alowe/ more barlie to growe'; and further applications after harvest time were warmly recommended.

Thus throughout Shakespeare's formative years, the family background was one of unremitting toil on the land. His father John is clearly identified or confirmed as a farmer. In 1575 when William was eleven, and again in 1579, John was still recorded as 'yeoman' in legal documents (73, 97). These influences permeate all Shakespeare's writing and thinking, in ways derived from each of his father's special trades, later to be examined in more detail. But the vital general point is that his main imagery derives directly from intimate observations of birds and beasts, seasons and crops, tending and hunting, killing and eating. He writes and thinks like a countryman, and in particular like a farmer versed in animal husbandry and folk lore. Proverbs, a countryman's wisdom, come easily and naturally to his mind; and they are likely to refer to the weather, which forms and frames the farming life. What is called his bawdry is often a countryman's plain thought and speech, the naming of parts. He knows about human and animal reproduction as it were from the inside.

His norms of reference are thus those of his own monarch contemplating abdication and a return to rural roots:

> So many hours must I tend my flock . . .
> So many days my ewes have been with young,
> So many weeks ere the poor fools will ean,
> So many years ere I shall shear the fleece. (*3 Henry VI*, II.v.31f)

This shepherd's calendar is presented as real time, moving with the seasons in an unhurried *tempo ordinario*. Sheep-farming is the paradigm of mortal life.

It would have figured among the poet's earliest recollections, as a staple part of the family trade. That fact was among the many recorded by Rowe, and corroborated by real evidence a century later (**54**) as well as in archive documents from 1568 onwards. In that year John Shakespeare entrusted no less than five hundredweight of wool (**49**) to a putative customer who lived some sixty miles away. So heavy and so crucial an investment strongly suggests immediate personal involvement; prima facie that wool came from his own flock. Despite his severe initial setback the business expanded into further buying and selling (**54, 61**) on an even larger scale, together with substantial loans of money to a sheep-farmer (**55**) and a woolshop built into the birthplace premises (**54**).

The successful wool-stapler, i.e. a merchant who buys from the producer and sells to the manufacturer, would be well advised to keep his own sheep, at least in the earlier stages of his enterprise. No wonder then that Shakespeare knew from his earliest years which was 'the tainted wether* of the flock/Meetest for death', and instantly related that idea to a further country metaphor: 'The weakest kind of fruit/Drops earliest to the ground' (*Merchant of Venice*, IV.i.115–16).

He also took a special and informed interest in the bizarre Bible story of sheep-breeding (ibid., I.iii.71f), where Antonio and Shylock both speak as simple shepherds. The gracious shearing scene in *The Winter's Tale* is introduced by a rustic who says 'Let me see: every 'leven wether tods [every eleven sheep yield two stone of wool], every tod yields pounds and odd shilling; fifteen hundred shorn, what comes the wool to? . . . I cannot do't without counters' (IV.iii.31f).

Those rural accents sound authentic, indeed heard at first hand. They lend the language a new directness and significance. John Shakespeare sold timber, among other commodities. One countryman rough-hews timber ends, and his workmate shapes them to fit a particular function;

---

* Cf *Edmund Ironside* 'sheep/tainted'(1296–7).

thus they depict the human and the divine, according to Hamlet: 'There's a divinity that shapes our ends/Rough-hew them how we will' (V.ii. 10–11).

The best analyses of Shakespeare's instinctive imagery (such as Whiter 1794, Spurgeon 1935, Fripp 1938, Armstrong 1946) rightly identify his essential sources as the life of the English countryside, its fields and gardens, flora and fauna, sports and pastimes. These ideas recombine kaleidoscopically; in the history plays for example the realm itself is commonly a cultivated enclosure and its enemies are fierce wild beasts or destructive pests. The first oppressed characters observed by the young Shakespeare were domesticated animals. Mere literary metaphor would make slaves resent their servitude as oxen the yoke. The country poet's eye perceives beasts as people, and conversely. England itself becomes a farm, as in *Richard II* (II.i.60). On this animal farm the populace are livestock (the common herd), and the rulers or pretenders are predators. The slaughter and sacrifice of innocent victims yields a new and intense imagery, suffused with suffering.

Characteristic image-clusters have been isolated; one centre from which they regularly radiate is some aspect of animal life, whether dogs* (Whiter 1794, 138–45, Spurgeon 1935, 195–9) or birds such as kites, eagles, geese or jays (Armstrong, 11–90). These fingerprints provide clear but neglected clues to the authorship of anonymous or disputed works, such as *Edward III* (Everitt 1954, Wentersdorf 1960) or *Edmund Ironside* (Everitt 1954, Sams 1985b, 1985f) which contain exactly such images and clusters. Similarly the study of *1–3 Henry VI* in the same light 'suggests that we should be suspicious of the radical opinions which dismiss these plays as by another hand' (Armstrong 1979, 198).

---

* Described by Spurgeon as 'the idea of flatterers' expressed in 'a rather curious set of images', defined as 'dog or sugar or melting', any one of which 'almost invariably . . . gives rise to the whole series': cf *Edmund Ironside* 'sugared' (1185), 'flatter' (1187), 'distilléd . . . drops' (1188), 'Cerberus' (1189). The symbolism of crow (1362–3), falcon (480–82), peacock (282–4), yoked oxen (114–15), etc. is equally typical.

II

Reading and Writing

THESE EARLY QUASI-PICTORIAL sense-impressions may have been all the more intense and colourful for the absence of printed books, which could have played no part in the home background or the parental consciousness. Shakespeare's father must have been in some sense numerate; he not only ran his own business but also rendered Stratford accounts (32, 34, 40, 43). But he was in no sense literate. He and his wife Mary both regularly signed important documents with a mark. She attested thus to the sale of her inherited lands (97); he to the same transaction, as previously to his appointment as affeeror (23), his presence as a court witness (27), his reappointment as petty constable (23), the authenticity of his first annual mayoral account (32) and later his own sale of the Henley Street land in 1597. His second set of accounts (34) remains unsigned; so does each of the many other recorded proceedings to which he was a party. On the evidence of documents by the dozen, over the forty-five-year span 1556–1601, Shakespeare's parents could not write their own names.

These facts fail to conform with literary preconception; but they are entirely unsurprising. There were no girls' schools. John and Henry Shakespeare were farmer's boys who lived more than three miles from Stratford; and no grammar school is recorded there until 1553, when John was some twenty-four years old. Not only William's parents but his daughter Judith also signed with a mark, even in 1611, when she was twenty-six years old, as witness to the sale of her future mother-in-law's house.

Of course their own handicap may have made John and Mary Shakespeare all the more determined that young William should be properly educated. Before he was seven, and no doubt much earlier, he would qualify for the local school by learning to read. The best book to learn from was the best book in the world, namely the Bible. The likeliest place to find one in Stratford was either the church or the school. There is no direct evidence that the Bible was taught at the latter in the 1560s. But the church may well have been used for preparatory classes; Malvolio was 'cross gartered . . . like a pedant that keeps a school i' the church' (*Twelfth Night*, III.ii.74–5). In any event churchgoing was compulsory; the young Shakespeare would be instructed in his catechism by the local curate, who could doubtless recognise a promising pupil. So *a fortiori* could the local schoolmasters; and the archives (Fripp 1926) record a payment of three pounds authorised by John Shakespeare during 1564 and 1565 to an assistant named Allen for 'teaching the children', presumably on an extracurricular basis in kindergarten or primary classes.

Whoever the teachers were, their work abides. The plays and poems are running over with scriptural allusions, both overt and covert, from sources including the Apocrypha, the non-canonical books of the Old Testament found in the Latin Vulgate but excluded from most Protestant Bibles in Shakespeare's lifetime. Many such references may have derived from ordinary church services; but some surely stem from early reading of the Bible as a set book or primer.

Among much assumption, two statements stand firm. First, Shakespeare cites far more scripture than any other contemporary writer. Many of his references are very detailed and specific; some necessitate specialist knowledge for their full appreciation. Thus 'there is hardly a phase of the story [of Adam and Eve] that has been missed' (Noble 1935, 42), a fact not apparent to the laity. Again, the complex and arcane Bible story of sheep-breeding, already mentioned, is expertly expounded in *The Merchant of Venice* (I.iii.71f) and 'not only does Shylock add the concluding verse of the chapter as to the blessing that attended Jacob but Antonio refers to the succeeding chapter' (Noble 1935, cf Genesis 30:31–43; 31:9).

Secondly there is a striking preponderance of allusion to Genesis, the first book of the Old Testament, and Matthew, the first of the New. The clear inference is that those were the first books studied; they served as primers in every sense. Shakespeare sometimes misquotes them; no doubt he was so steeped in those sources that he felt able to rely on his memory, which could be fallible. Thus he repeatedly claims, e.g. in *Richard II* (IV.i.169–70), that Judas betrayed Jesus with a cry of 'All hail', though in fact only Jesus himself, never Judas, is recorded as having spoken those words. Perhaps the phrase was remembered from one of the miracle plays, some of which were still performed in the Midlands during Shakespeare's formative years. But in an age of devout Protestantism built on Bible texts, it would rightly be reckoned culpably solecistic to place the words of Jesus in the mouth of Judas, especially when a stage player thereupon identifies himself with Christ.*

Writing skills were also no doubt acquired equally early, at five or six years old. They too were an essential qualification for admission to the Tudor grammar school; and Shakespeare's 'father bred him . . . for some time at a free-school' (82). Penmanship was also an investment; it could

---

* As also in *Edmund Ironside*: 'Edricus: All hail unto my gracious sovereign! [*bis*] Edmund: *Judas*, thy next part is to kiss my cheek and then commit me unto *Caiaphas*' (1643–5). That entire text is permeated with scriptural thought and allusion, including clear echoes of Genesis (2039f) and Matthew (1640f).

soon be put to profitable and practical use. Paper was expensive in Tudor times; but goosefeather quills and sheepskin parchment, with oak-galls for making ink, would not be lacking in a country community, and least of all in families which lived by animal husbandry.

III

The Family Home and Trades

SHAKESPEARE'S MOTHER MARY is named in documents about her legacy (14), her property (85, 94, 157), and her burial in 1608. She is also documented in her first-born son; her genes, no less than his father's, are part of his genius. It is therefore fitting that, although his poetic imagery derives mainly from husbandry, housewifery in the form of 'daily indoor life' comes next (Spurgeon 1935, 45). He has 'an unusually large number of images drawn from the daily work and occupations of women in a kitchen and living room' (ibid., 114); in particular his 'interest in and acute observation of cooking operations are very marked all through his work' (ibid., 119). And 'one occupation, one point of view, above all others, is naturally his, that of a gardener; watching, preserving, tending and caring for growing things, especially flowers and fruit'; hence his visualisation 'of matters human as of growing plants or trees', which is 'ever present in his thought and imagination, so that nearly all his characters share in it' (ibid., 86), especially in moments of stress and emotion.* These two terrains unite in the kitchen-garden and the orchard.

The paternal domain ranged far wider, but was no less rooted in the land. John Shakespeare's trades of butcher (83) and whittawer (67), and his description as 'agricola' (26), tenant farmer (50), substantial landowner (50, 85) or 'yeoman' (73, 97) all fit together, like his work as a glover (11, 55, 140, 183), wool-dealer (54, 61) and moneylender (55), over many years. There is no reason to assume a plurality of life-styles, and still less to invent a labour-dividing society of Happy Families in Merrie England. Like father like son was a sound enough maxim in Tudor times, and John Shakespeare was a Jack-of-all-trades; their presence in the plays† will be documented in detail (VIII). William himself would later be described as a Johannes Factotum. He would have known from boyhood, and as the eldest son would be expected to inherit and continue,

---

* All as in *Edmund Ironside*, including Spurgeon's examples of sugaring (1185) and distilling (1188), while the villainous King Canute displays knowledge of replanting and pruning as well as strong feelings about countrymen (129–35) and traitors (606–13).

† As in *Edmund Ironside*, ladder (76), hammer (266), axe (610), whetstone (1162), etc.

the family trade of animal husbandry with all its land, livestock, sidelines and by-products. John Shakespeare rose thereby from the dunghill (**10**), via the petty office of ale-taster (**17**) to constable (**20**), juror (**21**), borough treasurer (**29**), contributor to local charity (**37**), witness to and member of the corporation (**38, 39**), alderman (**41**) and finally mayor and president of the council and court of record (**47, 48**), later appointed to visit London and report on Parliamentary matters affecting Stratford on Avon (**64, 65**). All this entailed an eminence (**46, 57, 58, 62**) so exalted that he felt entitled to claim a coat of arms (**76**) while still only in his thirties. But at that very moment, with a proper sense of timing and drama, he fell into penury (**78, 82**) for reasons to be investigated later (VII). Thus '. . . vaulting ambition . . . o'erleaps itself/And falls on the other side' (*Macbeth*, I.vii.27–8). In text after text, his son observes the turn of Fortune's wheel and the whirligig of time.* Among the calamitous consequences (**85, 94, 97**) was the mortgaging of the land and property which had been bequeathed to Shakespeare's mother and which he in turn would one day have owned as part of his patrimony. No wonder that he evinces a special interest in the law of contract (Knight 1973). The illegal or inequitable loss of land, by a father to a usurper, is a leitmotif in the plays (VII).† So is the concept of flattery‡ considered as an evil lever for prising possessions away from their rightful owner; this novel notion too is surely another intuitive response to early personal experience.

Other paternal trades and traits from the same early period included money-lending, illegality and litigiousness. None is commonly mentioned by biographers or critics, but all three were surely immediately influential. John Shakespeare was not only adept at bailment (**44**) and valuation (**178**) but also at usury (Razzell 1990); he broke the law by charging much more than the standard rate of interest (**55**). This is linked to his other illicit or contentious activities (**18, 67, 150**) by the business of wool-dealing; he was indicted for selling too much wool (**61**) as well as for asking too much interest on the substantial sums he lent to a sheep-farmer. The young Shakespeare must have been perfectly aware of this aspect, among others, of the family business, which involved much dealing with money and merchandise, together with extensive travel in the Midlands and as far as London. It would be natural for him too to take an inordinate interest, in one sense or another, in inaugurating and attaining his own expertise. *Timon of Athens* is full of financial reference; relevant allusions abound throughout the plays and poems. Loans are levers of power as well as forces for enterprise. In 1599, John Shakespeare would go to law about a bad debt (again in the wool trade) incurred over thirty

---

* As in *Edmund Ironside* (768–71).
† Also found in *Edmund Ironside*; forfeiture of 'thy father's land' as a bad debt (1789–95).
‡ See also *Edmund Ironside* (*passim*).

years earlier (**49**). Such bad debts (**42, 63**) were an affront to an entrepreneurial society; they marred the market and thus undermined the economy. Shakespeare himself would later sue for default, no doubt from the same convictions. But he too could delay repayment of borrowed money and be pursued for overdue taxes. Further, he himself was also named and known and consulted as a moneylender; the Quiney correspondence of 1598 (Halliday 1964, 400) is revealingly explicit on that point. Shakespeare was also a close friend of the money-lending Combe brothers (ibid., 100–101); and the teasing tone of his supposed epigrams, genuine or not (Chambers 1930, ii. 140), at least shows that his name and abilities were closely associated with that trade, of which his high intelligence would make him master and no mere Jack. All this is entirely conformable with his later identification as a noverint or legal copyist (XI); and with the assumption that this trade went hand in hand with money lending (Freeman 1967, 3) for convenience in executing conveyances and other binding contracts for repayment or repossession. The theme of Shakespeare's financial dealings and entrepreneurship has been ably expounded and developed (Honigmann 1982); it harmonises well with the accusations of 'usury' from Greene and Nashe, and indeed sounds like a main cause of that long altercation, documented in detail below (XVI).

IV

Religion

RELIGION IS OFTEN the first influence on young artists, because their work is drawn directly from the shared beliefs and values of their community. Drama derives from ritual and myth; poetry expresses heightened and exalted feelings, such as those that religion inspires. So the dramatic poet's personal credo will enshrine his deepest convictions about life and its meaning.

The young Shakespeare's earliest emotions and experiences were enshrined in the language and teaching of the old Catholic faith. The Mass itself may be seen as a dramatic ritual, cognate with the stage masque; thus the appearance of Hymen in *As You Like It* (V.iv.107f) with 'still music' and of Iris, Ceres and Juno in *The Tempest* (IV.i.59f) with 'soft music' are intended as intimations of a divine presence. Shakespeare turns to music and dumb shows* whenever words fail him, which is surprisingly often; such meanings and messages are remote and numinous. The Chorus in *Henry V* is a priestly officiant celebrating the stage events. Statues and images have mystical significance, as at the climax of *The Winter's Tale* (V.iii) where Hermione lives again amid '*Music*' and its verbal overtones of 'holy' . . . 'magic' . . . 'gods' . . . 'sacred'. Robes and vestments, sacrifices and vessels, shriving and sanctification, the rites of birth, death and marriage are all constant and insistent themes. So is the relation between father and son, often invested with universal significance. The imagery of the Bible is also the fact of the farm, where the blood of the lamb was shed literally.

But Shakespeare evinces a special revulsion at the idea of drinking blood, which throughout the plays connotes vindictive savagery, as in 'this quarrel will drink blood . . .' (*1 Henry VI*, II.iv.133) or 'now could I drink hot blood . . .' (*Hamlet*, III.ii.390). This seems to be a personal aversion.† In other aspects, butchery is not only a necessary act but a quasi-religious observance. Aubrey's claim (83) 'that when he kill'd a Calfe he would doe it in a high style, and make a Speech' plainly implies artistic fervour and its ritual significance. That interrelation is a topic still scarcely touched upon. Perhaps it is seen as too subjective, too uncertain.

---

*   Cf the final invocations of bliss in *Edmund Ironside*: 'music . . . heavenly' (2011–6) 'dumb shows' (2133).
†   Also found in *Edmund Ironside* (1685, 1989).

Shakespeare may well have rebelled against his Catholic background; his 1616 will certainly begins with a Protestant preamble (Rowse 2/1988, 240). But there is no consistent evidence for the further far-reaching claim (idem) that 'he died as he had lived, a conforming member of the Church of England'. On the contrary; the plays are often Catholic in spirit as well as letter (Milward 1973). They are also free-thinking and even pagan, especially in the later years. The 1649 epitaph on Shakespeare's daughter Susanna is explicit.

> Witty above her sexe, but that's not all,
> Wise to salvation was good Mistris Hall.
> Something of Shakespeare was in that, but this
> Wholy of him with whom she's now in blisse . . .
>
> (Halliday 1964, 446)

The careful distinctions drawn between the poet and his pious son-in-law, and also between that and this, former and latter, seem designed to instruct posterity that something of Susanna's intelligence though nothing of her piety was inherited from her father. But her piety was perhaps Puritan, like her husband's; there is no reason to dispute that Shakespeare was not only a cradle Catholic, but a death-bed one also. As Richard Davies reported *c.* 1700, 'he died a Papist'. His uncle Henry Shakespeare was excommunicated in the 1570s (Halliday 1964, 34); his grandfather Robert Arden left an expressly Roman Catholic will (14). His mother Mary, named after the Queen of Heaven as well as the then Queen of England, married John Shakespeare during that brief but bloody reign (1553–8). Their union itself plainly implies that they were co-religionists; a shared faith is still one of the very highest correlative coefficients among married couples (Diamond 1991, 86). Their first-born was baptised according to the Roman rite (19), in what was in effect still a Catholic country. Furthermore, John Shakespeare left a Catholic confession of faith (IV, IX), even more explicit than his father-in-law's.

The pendulum of persecution swung with a vengeance in the reign of Elizabeth. In 1592 John Shakespeare was twice arraigned (172, 181), among many others, as a recusant, i.e. one who 'refused obstinately to resort to the church'. Three of their names later surfaced from his son's retentive memory – Bardolph (*1–2 Henry IV*), Fluellen and Court (*Henry V*). In 1606, Shakespeare's elder daughter Susanna was cited for failure to receive communion; so were his close friends Hamlet and Judith Sadler, after whom he had named his twins (136). When his younger daughter Judith married in 1616, she and her husband Thomas Quiney were cited to a church court for failing to secure the required Protestant marriage licence; Thomas was excommunicated and so presumably was Judith herself, though no such specific record survives. In 1640 to 1641, one Nicholas Shakespeare was listed as a recusant at Budbrook, Warwickshire.

There is some counter-argument against the family's Catholic background. Could a Catholic John Shakespeare have suffered the priest who in 1558 had baptised his first child (19) to be ousted from Stratford only two years later (25)? Could a Catholic have countenanced the required defacing of images in Stratford Church in 1564, when John Shakespeare was chamberlain (34), or the dispersal of its copes and vestments and the destruction of its rood screen as Papist idolatry in 1571 when he was lord mayor (56)? On such scores, history is silent; and even if John Shakespeare was too, that may mean only that he was no saint and no hero, not that he was no Catholic. There is evidence (IX) that he did not see himself as a martyr either; his all too explicitly Catholic will was found hidden in the roof of his house.

A more substantive objection is that no Catholic could have attained such exalted municipal offices (47, 53, 56) in an era of Protestant persecution. It is true that as mayor of Stratford, John Shakespeare would in theory have been required to take the oath of supremacy, vowing fealty to Elizabeth and forswearing the Pope. But he might well have viewed any such vow, if indeed it was enforced, as invalid in the sight of heaven. His son's plays, for whatever reason, are insistent on the subject of oath-taking* to the point of obsessiveness; many different characters share the trait of meditation on the validity of vows, and the apportionment of allegiance among conflicting claims.

But ordinary prudence and local toleration prevailed among the populace throughout the realm. Religious persecution, though zealous, was sporadic; thus in 1579 John Cottam was appointed as Stratford schoolmaster despite his Catholic affiliations (99). Perhaps John Shakespeare was well liked locally. The sole extant memorandum of him, jotted down by Thomas Plume *c.* 1657, sounds most agreeable: 'a merry Cheekd old man – that said – Will was a good Honest Fellow, but he durst have crackt a jeast with him at any time'.

Again, it has been represented that the real reason for his prolonged absence from church, as previously from the council chamber (81, 100, 109, 122), was his 'fear of process for debt'. But those marginalia (172, 181) were only suggestions ('we suspect' . . . 'it is said'), not (*pace* Schoenbaum 1975, 39) clear statements; and in those days Catholicism and poverty, so far from being exclusive alternatives, were often cause and effect. Besides, the documentary evidence is surely conclusive, even without invoking John Shakespeare's specific profession of Catholic faith. His name first appears on a list of recusants (172) prepared following an anti-Catholic edict of autumn 1591 under which a massive fine of twenty

* As also in *Edmund Ironside*, 677, 2060.

pounds was imposed for each month of non-attendance at the Protestant services. This was in addition to an earlier imposition of a shilling fine for non-attendance either on a Sunday or a holy-day (Halliwell-Phillipps 1887 ii, 397). So any recusant was liable to debt and arrest, by definition. The above-mentioned marginalia may have meant to imply that the debt was secular, perhaps as a praiseworthy attempt to defend freedom of worship or preserve friends from persecution and penury. But the preamble (not found in Schoenbaum idem) to the September 1592 list could hardly be more explicit: 'The seconde certificat of the Commission-ers for the Countie of Warwicke touching all such persons as have been presented to them, or have been otherwise fownde owt by the endevoire of the sayd Commissioners, to be Jeshuites, seminarye preestes, fugitives or recusantes within the sayd countie of Warwick, or vehementlye sus-pected to be sutche, together with a true note of so manye of them as are allreadye indicted for thear obstinate and willfull persisting in their recusancy . . .' (Fripp 1926–9, 159). Foremost among these com-missioners was the zealous local anti-Catholic Sir Thomas Lucy, whose signature appears on every page of this return. The Mrs Wheeler named as a Catholic 'now conformed' at the foot of the list was the wife and mother respectively of the two John Wheelers at its head; its third name is John Shakespeare.

Whether or not the poet wholly shared the family religion, it was surely a powerful and detectable influence. The most perceptive commentators on such subjects will be Catholics or ex-Catholics themselves (e.g. Milward 1973, Levi 1988). The textual evidence is extensive; thus (*pace* Schoenbaum 1975, 50) 'a month's mind' in *The Two Gentlemen of Verona* (I.ii.134) entails the Catholic sense (OED 1) of a memorial Mass a month after death, whether literal or figurative. 'The fools of time/Which die for goodness, who have lived for crime' (Sonnet 124.14) prima facie relates to Catholicism considered as good religion yet bad politics. The ghost of Hamlet's father, a pagan monarch in all that play's sources, is not only a good Catholic but actually quotes from the Catholic will of Shakespeare's father (IX). Shakespeare's own epitaph on his gravestone, in words which he himself composed (Dowdall 1693) and 'orderd to be cutt', according to an anonymous seventeenth-century source (Chambers 1930, ii, 261), is often chided for poor poetry; but it is more a plea than a poem, and it implores the unbroken rest of a whole body:

> Good frend for Iesus sake forbeare
> to digg the dust encloased heare!
> Blest be the man that spares these stones
> and curst be he that moves my bones.

His widow's epitaph, probably composed by his puritanical Latinist son-in-law Dr John Hall, suggests, in its cheerful acceptance of the removal of tombstones, a direct and deliberate counter to such superstitions. Nevertheless, the poet's absolute prohibition was respected, despite the wish of his widow and his daughter to be buried with him (Dowdall 1693); they would know the strength of his feelings. These are somewhat corroborated by the tradition of the horror inspired in him by the repository of bones near Stratford church, 'so many that they would load a great number of waggons' (Hall 1694), and the association of that grisly charnel-house with the Ghost in *Hamlet* (Gildon 1694, 1710), where 'canonised bones, hearséd in death/Have burst their cerements' (I.iv.47–8).

Cursed, in Shakespeare's view, was he who moved anyone's bones; and those moved bones' ex-owners were in desperate straits. Perhaps 'all those bodies and all those heads/Shall join together at the latter day' (*Henry V*, IV.i.136–7); but a prudent believer would not count on it. The plays evince a special distress at the thought of being dead yet unburied; hence the poignancy of 'my poor corpse, where my bones shall be thrown' (*Twelfth Night*, II.iv.62). The venomous Tamora is not only deprived of ritual observance but thrown 'forth to beasts and birds to prey' (*Titus*, V.iii.198), as a fitting posthumous punishment. On the sea-bed, the 'dead bones that lay scattered by' enhance the dread of Clarence in his nightmare (*Richard III*, I.iv.33), with its strange notion of gems gleaming in drowned soldiers' empty eye-sockets,* with the same distress at the fate of unburied bones. The later Shakespeare matures and mellows; the fears are transformed into magic; the eyes become pearls and the bones coral (*The Tempest*, I.ii.398–9).

But even that mystical metamorphosis is the epitome of eeriness. Such feelings may well derive from the absorbed precepts and practice of the old faith, which to this day lays more stress on the importance of intact and undisturbed earth burial than other forms of Christianity. The memorandum (Davies *c.* 1700) that Shakespeare 'hath a monument on which he lays a heavy curse upon anyone who shall remove his bones' instantly proceeds to add 'He dyed a papist', which sounds more like a logical corollary than a mere afterthought. It is surely meant to convey that the sacrament of extreme unction was duly administered in accordance with the old faith. Hence perhaps also Shakespeare's apparent preoccupation with ritual preparation for death, which concerns even those who are sworn enemies of the living body in question. Thus the villainous Catesby's dictum is not necessarily ironic or cynical, ''Tis a vile thing to die, my gracious lord/When men are unprepared† and look not for't' (*Richard III*, III.ii.62–3).

---

* Cf *Edmund Ironside* 1101–2, where soldiers are 'drowned in brinish tears like jewels in the bottom of the sea'.

† As also in *Edmund Ironside* (1775–8), where Canute worries that his hated foe Edmund is 'unprepared for death', not 'fit to go to God'.

The plays are equally insistent, not to say obsessed, with the ritual solemnity and significance of weddings, which are habitually invested with a Latin-derived dignity of language.* Shakespeare's own wedding of 1582 may well have been celebrated according to the then forbidden Roman rite (XIII).

---

* See also *Edmund Ironside*: 'celebrate . . . solemnity' (444–58).

V

School and Latin

IN THE PLAYS, small boys are often pert and precocious, like little Macduff, who much apostrophises his mother* (*Macbeth*, IV.ii.33, 37, 45). Tudor society had little time for childhood; life-spans were short, and children were seen as undeveloped adults. But the first Elizabethan age aspired to extend education; and the new grammar schools, like the old universities, provided some free places for promising pupils. Among the beneficiaries were the English Renaissance dramatists. All attended their local school; most proceeded to the higher degree. Indeed, there are only two known exceptions, namely Kyd and Shakespeare; and that fact helps to identify them as the grammar-school or 'Grammarian' butts of the University Wits (XVI).

Kyd had at least completed his course at Merchant Taylors'. Shakespeare would have become eligible for Stratford Grammar School at seven (60), and no doubt attended it, as Rowe testifies (82), whether regularly or not, for some time. But on the same evidence, with copious corroboration (82), the boy was prematurely removed thence at about twelve or thirteen years old, because his impoverished father needed his help at home. Perhaps his attendance had always been sporadic; perhaps he was not reluctant to leave. His references to schools and schooling in the plays are uniform in their distaste, e.g. 'creeping like snail unwillingly to school' (*As You Like It*, II.vii.147), 'as willingly as e'er I came from school' (*Taming of the Shrew*, III.ii.150), 'towards school with heavy looks' (*Romeo and Juliet*, II.ii.157). The modern view of the well-educated Shakespeare (e.g. Wells 1986, xiv) assumes full-time attendance at a school where 'there would be little but Latin' (Chambers 1930, i, 10–11). All the actual evidence says, on the contrary, but little Latin. Even the trivial anecdotes about Shakespeare, true or invented, with their puns on 'latten' [metal] christening spoons (Chambers 1930, ii, 243, 247), depend for their point upon his lack of Latin, from which (since the grammar schools existed to teach Latin grammar) a lack of education follows as the inescapable inference. Even his friends and admirers are constrained to agree; his 'small Latin and less [i.e. almost no] Greek' are mentioned by Ben Jonson (82) as part of a loving eulogy, not as an

---

* As does little Edward in his one *Edmund Ironside* line (1465).

'accusation' (*pace* Wells 1986, xiv). The claim that Jonson meant 'small in comparison with my own' is offensive to him and without foundation in fact. Of course he meant what he said; and everyone else who spoke on the subject said the same, for centuries. The point must have had much pith.

Shakespeare's well-evidenced and intense emphasis on the first books of both the Old and the New Testament (II) permits the further inference of interrupted studies, just as Rowe avows and Aubrey confirms ('little Latin'), each after due enquiry among Stratfordians (82). Analogous assurances continue in unbroken sequence. The classicist Richard Farmer (1767) concluded that Shakespeare had some schoolboy Latin '. . . but his *studies* were most demonstratively confined to *nature* and *his own language*'; in other words, he studied no Latin to speak of, and hence could not have been in prolonged and regular attendance at Stratford Grammar School, though this is no doubt the 'free-school' at which 'his father bred him for some time' before being withdrawn thence to help at home (82). He was left with enough Latin to qualify 'in his younger years' as a 'schoolmaster in the country' (112), as Aubrey adds on the cited authority of the actor Beeston, whose father was a colleague of Shakespeare's. But this need have entailed no more than being better than a beginner, and thus keeping ahead of the class, or of one pupil (XVIII).

On any objective assessment the historical consensus must prevail. As George Chalmers says (1810, 4), 'It is indeed a strong argument in favour of Shakspeare's illiterature, that it was maintained by all his contemporaries, many of whom have left on record every merit they could bestow on him, and by his successors, who lived nearest to his time, when "his memory was green"; and that it has been denied only by [those] who could have no means of ascertaining the truth'. Carlyle (1842) bluntly called him 'the Stratford Peasant', with much justification (I). In the mid-nineteenth century, Shakespeare was described as 'self-schooled' in a famous sonnet by Matthew Arnold, who was a professional inspector of schools as well as a great critic. Halliwell-Phillipps draws the same sensible inferences from the same evidence (1887, i, 51f) and concludes that when Shakespeare left school, at about thirteen, he must have been 'destitute of all polished accomplishments'.

Of course he must have known some Latin, even by that early age; it was after all the language of his family's religion, and there is evidence that he learned more at school. *Love's Labour's Lost* (IV.ii.95) quotes from a Tudor text-book, the *Bucolica* of Battisto Spagnuoli of Mantua. The little local lad, helpfully identified as William, whose elementary Latin is catechised in *The Merry Wives of Windsor* (IV.i) was evidently acquainted with Lyly's *Grammar* of 1568. But that scene was designed to show how Latin declensions and conjugations can conceal a multitude of lewd allusions, which are duly descanted upon by the bawdiest playwright of his age. He was no doubt precocious in that respect also. The notion that he, alone among country boys, had been 'shielded from contact with some of the grosser and more indecent terms in the English language' (Wells 1973, 192) belongs to the legend of the genteel Shakespeare, late developer and cultivated young classical scholar. This has now become the accepted icon on the strength of one sole tome (Baldwin 1944) which purported to prove that Shakespeare was intimately familiar with Latin and indeed Greek literature.

Professor Baldwin's own subject was English literature. Actual classical scholars take a very different view, derived from their own detailed and precise knowledge. Thus J. Thomson (1952, 154) says, with unstated but unmistakable reference to Baldwin's supposed parallels between the canon and the classics: '. . . it seems to me that a judge, not excited by his own discoveries, would decide on the evidence that Shakespeare was but a perfunctory reader of the classics, and that like most of us who are not Latin scholars he used translations when they came to hand, and only turned to the originals when his interest or curiosity was aroused. I ask this question; how could a man who read Ovid's Latin with ease and pleasure, bear to read Golding instead?'. Shakespeare's frequent recourse to Golding's translation of the *Metamorphoses* has often been demonstrated; Thomson's pertinent enquiry remains unanswerable. Sixty years earlier, A.E. Housman, the greatest Latinist of his time and a most memorable poet and critic, had already deplored (1892, 10–12) Shakespeare's 'lack of the classics' and analysed the unfortunate results of that manifest lacuna in a great poet who exceeded all others in the richness of his natural endowment but lacked worthy models to guide him.

Without such models, the early plays draw on classical tags and allusions for decoration, ably documented by Anders (1904) and Thomson (1952). But these sometimes seem to misconstrue or diverge from their sources. Thus in *Titus Andronicus* Hecuba runs around madly in Troy (IV.i.20–21; cf also *Hamlet*, II.ii.505), the Cyclops are conflated with the Giants (*Titus*, IV.iii.46–7, 50–51), and Cerberus is enchanted by Orpheus (ibid., II.iv.51).* All these may derive from Ovid, with whose original Latin texts Shakespeare certainly became fully familiar. But there is no reason to resist the obvious implication that he was self-taught in these respects as in so many others; his innate linguistic genius would naturally include an elective affinity for languages and their literature. None of this contradicts his early lack of classical learning, which brands him as a 'Latinless author', a rare and identifiable sub-species of Tudor poet and dramatist, remorselessly gunned for by Nashe and Greene from 1589 onwards (XV, XVI).

---

* All three notions are also implied in *Edmund Ironside* (1477–80; 660, 1048–9; 1189) which freely draws on Ovidian stories and characters *passim*, e.g. Cadmus (425).

VI

The Early Theatre

THE FUTURE DRAMATIST, for all his genius, had to discover drama. The creative child, however brilliant, remains a child of its time. If Shakespeare the butcher-boy killed calves 'in a high style, and made a speech' (83), in the 1570s, he had no doubt seen a play or pageant in which slaughter was enacted on the stage, whether of tyrants by heroes or of the innocents by Herod. The Stratford archives contain no account of any theatrical company or performance until the summer of 1569, when Shakespeare was five years old (52). Now, that was the year in which John Shakespeare became 'the Queenes officer & cheffe of the towne' (53). Can this be mere coincidence? The substantial sums payable to players had to be authorised and disbursed by the local council; and the father of a great playwright may well have evinced a special interest in and feeling for staged entertainment. Further, the Queen's players were required to perform first for the mayor in private session, who was empowered to censor or license them (Halliday 1964, 23); and this presumably applied to all touring troupes, by municipal fiat.

Their repertory is rarely recorded. But printed texts survive. The earliest known example is *Gorboduc*. Though the point is seldom specifically made, this tragedy by Thomas Norton and Thomas Sackville, written *c.* 1560 and published in September 1566, is the manifest source of Shakespeare's lifelong style and idiom. His indebtedness is demonstrably as great as Schubert's to Zumsteeg and Zelter in the *lied* genre. In each instance the pupil so far surpassed his masters and models as to create a new and durable art-form from the modest materials and patterns of his far less memorable predecessors.

Gorboduc is the first known play written in the Shakespearean medium of blank verse, i.e. unrhymed iambic pentameter, with the basic pattern of five feet (each consisting of an unstressed followed by a stressed syllable) in each line. For example it begins 'The silent night that brings the quiet pause . . .'. This is an English equivalent for the five-stressed Latin line of Seneca, who wrote violent dramas of power and passion, murder and madness. His tragedies were first translated into English *c.* 1560. The new English drama they inspired retained their stage devices of Chorus and Prologue (typically spoken by a vengeful Ghost who initiates the action). It treated the same themes, but transposed them from classical mythology into a modern human world. It also added ideas from other sources, such as dumb show, a mimed representation of the action often accompanied by music. This was imported from Italian drama of the period. The resulting rich mixture provided a sophisticated entertainment, suitable for staging with masque and pageantry. Thus *Gorboduc* was performed at the Inner Temple in January 1562 and before Queen Elizabeth herself at her Whitehall court later that same month.

But that play and its successors also embodied the popular English theatrical traditions of mediaeval stage entertainments, which Shakespeare had surely seen during his Stratford boyhood. They assumed two distinct forms. The Miracles dramatised saints' lives; the Mysteries, Bible stories. Each had evolved from church rituals celebrated by priests, in Latin, into market-place enactments by members of craft guilds, in English. Scores of performances are recorded in local archives throughout the country between 1300 and 1600. Benjamin Britten's *Noye's Fludde* is among the most familiar of modern exemplars. Many of the ancient texts still survive, such as the cycles presented at York, Wakefield, Chester and (nearest to Stratford) Coventry. Morality plays developed from the Mysteries; they were essentially sermons in dramatic form, with such characters as Good Deeds and the Devil. Marlowe's *Dr Faustus* continued that tradition; Bunyan's *Pilgrim's Progress* has preserved it. Its main exemplar in Tudor times was *Cambises*, by Thomas Preston, published *c.* 1570. This includes the Morality character Ambidexter* or Vice, as a commentator, together with crudely violent Senecan tragedy and rustic comedy.

In later years, Shakespeare would show his awareness of all these works and genres in such allusions as:

> Like to the old Vice . . .
> who with dagger of lath
> in his rage and his wrath
> cries ah, ha! to the devil . . . (*Twelfth Night*, IV.ii.124f)

or 'O'erdoing Termagant; it out Herods-Herod' (*Hamlet*, III.ii.13–14).

He not only mentions Seneca by name (*Hamlet*, II.ii.400) but deliberately draws on the revenge-play genre for *Titus Andronicus c.* 1589, the earliest of his canonical works. For these reasons among others he is prima facie the Senecan playwright lampooned by Thomas Nashe, and hence (as common sense confirms) the author of the early *Hamlet*, also *c.* 1589. Nashe's jibe at 'English Seneca' may also aim at those who need translations; and ten of those tragedies (113) had been available in English since 1581. No doubt English Senecan drama in blank-verse form had been among Shakespeare's earliest experiences. He also seems to recall the lavish entertainments (71) presented to Queen Elizabeth by the

---

* Invoked in the Senecan tragi-comedy *Edmund Ironside*, together with Chorus and dumb show (330, 963f, 2033).

Earl of Leicester at Kenilworth, twelve miles north-east of Stratford, in 1575. John Shakespeare, as an eminent burgess and recent lord mayor, had good title to be present; perhaps he took his eleven-year-old eldest son to see the show and the sights. These too survive in an eye-witness archival account (Laneham *c.* 1575). A water-pageant on a lake in the castle grounds depicted the myth of Arion, the lyric poet and musician, borne singing on a dolphin's back.

As the sea-captain says of the shipwrecked Sebastian, 'like Arion on the dolphin's back,/I saw him hold acquaintance with the waves' (*Twelfth Night*, I.ii.15–16). More vividly and specifically, as Oberon tells Puck,

> . . . once I sat upon a promontory
> And heard a mermaid, on a dolphin's back
> Uttering such dulcet and harmonious breath
> That the rude sea grew civil at her song
> And certain stars shot madly from their spheres
> To hear the sea-maid's music.*
> (*Midsummer Night's Dream*, II.i.149f)

Oberon then proceeds to pay a special tribute to the Virgin Queen, perhaps with a further recollection of the same royal occasion and its resplendent pageantry. He had seen:

> Flying between the cold moon and the earth
> Cupid all armed. A certain aim he took
> At a fair vestal thronéd by the west,
> And loosed his love-shaft smartly from his bow. . . .
> [But] the imperial votaress passéd on,
> In maiden meditation, fancy-free. (ibid., 156f)

In addition there were local pageants written and acted by the townspeople, which could include scenes from traditional plays but were mainly designed as secular entertainment. An example (**127**) is recorded in the Stratford archives for Whitsun 1583. The young Shakespeare may well have taken part in just such a performance. As Julia tells Sylvia,

> At Pentecost,
> When all our pageants of delight were played,
> Our youth got me to play the woman's part
> And I was trimmed in Madam Julia's gown . . .
> And at that time I made her weep a-good
> For I did play a lamentable part.

---

* Cf *Edmund Ironside*: 'Muses . . . breathe . . . dulcet and melodious harmony (1174–5).

Madam, 'twas Ariadne passioning
For Theseus' perjury and unjust flight;
(*Two Gentlemen of Verona*, IV.iv.158f)

Perhaps the same local sources inspired the show of the Worthies in *Love's Labour's Lost*, where Judas jostles Hercules in a conflation of genres (V.ii.587f). Similarly the ritual shooting of arrows with messages in *Titus Andronicus* (IV.iii), or the chorus, dumb show and parade of knights with mottoes in *Pericles* (II.ii), among many other examples, recall early experience of staged entertainments. And of course the constant traffic of theatre troupes to and from Stratford and indeed throughout the Midlands and the south must have exerted an immense influence on any born playwright and actor, especially one whose propensity to ritual and rhetoric were long remembered from his earliest days as a butcher-boy (VIII). That assorts well with later impressions of 'tragical speeches' and tirades 'terribly thundered' (XVI). Tudor theatrical records are now at last being thoroughly researched; but enough facts have always been available to show that Shakespeare in Stratford, throughout his formative years, was exceptionally well placed to profit from frequent and repeated exposure to the staging and performance of English vernacular drama. From 1569 onwards, when he was five years old and his father became the leading citizen of Stratford, the recorded visits and remunerations there and in the vicinity were as follows:

1569   Queen's 9/-, Worcester's 1/- (**52**)
1573   Leicester's (led by Burbage) (**66**)
1575   entertainments for Queen Elizabeth at Kenilworth, no doubt presented by Leicester's (**71**)
1575   Warwick's 17/- (**72**)
1576   Worcester's (**77**)
1576–7   Leicester's 15/-, Worcester's 3/4 (**79**)
1577   Leicester's 25/- (**80**)
1579   Strange's (**91**)
1579   Countess of Essex's (**95**)
1580   Derby's (**106**)
1581–2   Worcester's, Berkeley's (**115**)
1582–3   Berkeley's, Chandos's (**124**)
1583   a local troupe 13/4 (**127**)
1583–4   Oxford's, Worcester's (with Alleyn, **123**), Essex's (**130**)

Thus for the entire fifteen years of Shakespeare's boyhood and young manhood the best theatre companies in the realm performed in Stratford and also its environs such as Coventry, only some twenty miles away and readily reachable on horseback. Of course he had full opportunity to sample stage entertainments, realise his own talents and consider his own contributions. If the eleven-year-old William could attend performances at Kenilworth, in accordance with the evidence already cited, he could certainly later travel to London about his father's business, whether in his father's company, or on his own. Of course he would have visited the home-town, provincial and London theatres as often as possible, from his earliest years. Like the young Mozart, he was not only a prodigy at composition and performance (as Aubrey testifies, **83**), but a potentially high wage-earner. That must surely have been much in his mind, and his father's, when the Shakespeare family fell on hard times.

VII

Poverty

IN ABOUT 1576, John Shakespeare's fortunes began to decline from manifest affluence to apparent penury. In 1578 he transferred seventy acres of land, to raise cash (85); in the following year he mortgaged his wife's estate, William's patrimony (94), and also sold her interest in her inherited property (97), again for cash. Perhaps his farming had failed. Livestock could always perish from disease, crops from frost or storm; and these are recurrent images in the works. But what actually threw a permanent and protracted blight on the family fortunes, also causing 'the narrowness of [John's] circumstances' and William's withdrawal from school c. 1576 (82)? Thereafter, the eminent civic dignitary John Shakespeare suddenly ceased to attend Stratford council meetings (78, 81, 89, 100, 109, 128) save on one occasion (122) when he supported a friend's candidature for the mayoralty. By 1578 he was in such stringent financial straits that he was officially exempted from modest local taxes (84, 87, 92). In the same year he was again sued for a thirty-pound debt (88) presumably unpaid since the first application five years earlier (67). Meanwhile there were more mouths to feed. Joan and Margaret, the first two children of John and Mary Shakespeare, had died in infancy (19, 31, 33), conformably with the high mortality rate of the times. But the parents, together with their first-born son William, survived the virulent outbreak of plague that ravaged Stratford in 1564 (36); and their second and third sons Gilbert (45) and Richard (69) and their third and fourth daughters Joan (51) and Anna (57) were born in 1566, 1574, 1569 and 1571 respectively. Anna died at eight (93); another child, Edmund, was born in 1580 (102). In that same summer, John was fined the swingeing sum of forty pounds for failing to keep the peace towards the Queen and her subjects (107). In 1582 he craved sureties against notable Stratfordians 'for fear of death and mutilation of his limbs' (116). In 1586 he was deposed as alderman for his persistent absences (139). By that time he had missed some fifty meetings. His colleagues on the council had plainly been sympathetic, indeed indulgent, towards his troubles; but even friends and fellow-Catholics had their own constraints and limitations. Others were plainly hostile. Many further court actions (142, 150) followed in 1587 and 1588. Thereafter the archive records dwindle. But even as late as 1597 John and Mary Shakespeare declared themselves to a London high court, on oath, as being 'of very small wealth and very few friends and alliance'.

The sudden chronic indigence from which the Catholic John Shake-speare certainly suffered, apparently for some twenty years (despite any dutiful support from his successful son), started soon after the first emissaries of Rome reached the Midlands in 1575, eager to reclaim Prot-estant England for the old faith. So any signs of poverty or isolation may well imply that he was paying for his faith in every sense. One estate sold by John Shakespeare (**94**) belonged to his Catholic wife Mary; there was a common cause. Of course the English Catholics generously supported the Jesuit missions with money as well as hospitality. Further, Catholics had been subject to uncompensated seizure of property since the 1570 Papal Bull excommunicating Elizabeth I. Such punitive measures and other persecutions steadily increased; so too, thus encouraged, did public Protestant hostility. In response to the mission of 1580–81, the Mass was proscribed and heavy fines were imposed on those who claimed that they could not in conscience attend the official services. 'The object of this legislation was to outlaw and ruin the Catholic community' (Waugh 1935, 109); and in the case of John Shakespeare it may well have succeeded. The decline of his family fortunes has been closely charted (Schoenbaum 1975, 36–40; Thomas 1985; Razzell 1990). Whatever his financial failures or setbacks, he would also be vulnerable to extortion and blackmail on charges of disloyalty and indeed treason in an era when England was under threat of invasion by Spain, whence an actual attack by the Armada followed in 1588. This was also the year of John Shake-speare's maximum harassment by lawsuits for debt and damages (**150**).

His son's intense innate patriotism, as expressed for example in John of Gaunt's famous speech* about England (*Richard II*, II.i.40f), would have created inner conflicts about Catholicism, especially in times of national crisis; hence such admonitions as 'if England to itself do rest but true' (*King John*, V.vii.118), with their clear connotations of fifth-column treachery. Such hostile feelings would have been exacerbated if the paternal poverty was caused by Catholicism. Its effects wrought deep wounds, the works suggest. 'To recover of us by strong hand/And terms compulsatory those foresaid lands/So by his father lost,' is a cause of war in *Hamlet*; paternal culpability is needlessly stressed only a few lines later: 'those lands/Lost by his father . . .' (I.i.102–4, ii.23–4); cf also 'Twere pity they should lose their father's lands' (*3 Henry VI*, III.ii.31) by dispos-session. That linkage of land and loss rankled deeply, for a decade (**143**, **144**, **157**). *Pace* Shakespeare's modern editors (e.g. Kerrigan 1986), there is no need to disbelieve him when he says that Fortune provided badly for him, and that he was poor and despised (Sonnet 111.1–4, 37. 10). He

---

* Paralleled throughout *Edmund Ironside*: 'this little world' (15), 'Jews, stubb-orn' (145) 'this realm of England' (818), 'this land . . . fortress' (1019–20), 'paradise' (1458) 'this little isle' (1897) etc., and 'we conspire with [foreigners] against ourselves' (375–80), 'thy father's land/I seize upon' (1793–5), etc.

certainly became rich and respected, as it were in reaction. Hence perhaps such typical utterances as '. . . a true-born gentleman . . . no flatterer' (*1 Henry VI*, II.iv.27, 31) with concomitant contempt for 'dunghill grooms' (ibid., I.iii.14).* This looks like the driving force which in 1596 renewed his father's quest (76) for a family coat of arms, and retained or devised the motto 'non sans droict', not without right, with its plain implication of entitlement by ability if not by birth. Any feelings of resentment and deprivation would have been vastly aggravated by the menial and degrading employments imposed by poverty.

---

* See also *Edmund Ironside*, where even before the Norman Conquest 'base-born grooms', 'each dunghill brat' and 'flatterer' vied with 'true noble gentlemen' (235–8).

VIII

Butchery and By-Products

WHATEVER THE CAUSE of John Shakespeare's financial and social decline, there is evidence of its effect; his eldest son left school at about thirteen to help on the home farm. There is no reason (*pace* Schoenbaum 1975, 60, Powell 1985, I. Wilson 1993, 60) to doubt this boyhood experience in the traditionally familial butcher's trade. He was 'apprenticed to a butcher' (**83**); he was withdrawn from school to work for his penurious father (**82**), whose own general farming experience and skills, like his specialist trades, must have included butchery and who is twice called a butcher by John Aubrey (**83**). Apart from his Stratford informants, Aubrey was well acquainted with Shakespeare's godson William Davenant, and was also a close friend and Wiltshire neighbour of Davenant's brother Robert (Tylden-Wright 1991, 78–9), who later became a parson. Both those brothers, in their childhood, had often seen Shakespeare at their Oxford home. Further, the Spiritual Testament of John Shakespeare, now lost, occasioned a noteworthy comment, which has been cited thus (Schoenbaum 1971, 80) from an unspecified source in the popular press of February 1790: 'This testament is no farther remarkable than in proving that John Shakespear was a Butcher, and that he bequeathed all his acquirements in that profession to his son William.' That comment must surely relate to some specific relevant reference in a text no longer extant.

Common sense also confirms that John Shakespeare, as a Tudor farmer, yeoman, wool-merchant, glover and dresser of hides and skins, was also a butcher, on all five counts (Sams 1985c). Of course an eldest son would lend a hand, at need, then as now, in slaughtering and skinning as in shearing; the young Shakespeare, constrained to kill a calf, might well do so 'in a high style, and make a speech', just as Aubrey says. A later English biographer adds that 'it would, in fact, be rather like him' (Rowse 2/1988, 27). The neighbours would naturally reminisce about the early theatricality of Stratford's most famous son, and pass the story on to their own children. This special way of suiting 'the action to the word, the word to the action', as Hamlet advises the players (III. ii. 17), epitomises the budding actor and playwright in a scene of assassination. When Brutus killed Caesar in the Capitol 'it was a brute part of him to kill so capital a calf there'; thus Polonius is mocked by Hamlet (III. ii. 106). The puns are playful, but the subjects are serious. The effect on a sensitive child of killing a calf can readily be imagined. Such deeds must be done, but with dignity and sympathy; as Brutus says of 'the most unkindest cut of all': 'alas, Caesar must bleed . . . let's kill him boldly but not wrathfully' (*Julius Caesar*, II.i.170–72). The sympathy would include empathy if, as Aubrey implies, the boy was given the young cattle to kill. That detail has verisimilitude; it takes a grown man's strength to pole-axe an ox. But calves though more amenable are also more appealing, as Shakespeare recalls in many a memorable image. No wonder he 'ran from his master to London' (**125**); and repugnance is a reason for dating that departure early. On the evidence, the eldest son's young hand was subdued for a time to what it worked in, including blood.

The poetic feelings also ran rich and deep. In the plays and poems, butchery is unpredictably associated with fathers* and family feuds. Thus such lines as 'The father rashly slaughtered his own son,/The son, compelled, been butcher to the sire' (*Richard III*, V.v.25–6) seem to derive from some strong source of dissension. So do 'The butcher sire that reaves his son of life' (*Venus and Adonis*, 766), again in a context of 'home-bred strife', and the 'father that hath killed his son' and cries 'how butcherly' (*3 Henry VI*, II.v.78, 89). All these deep feelings seem to flow from the same wound; the private wound, which is deepest (*Two Gentlemen of Verona*, V.iv.71).

Shakespeare has a whole rich vocabulary of blood,† as varied and detailed as the Eskimo words for snow. He knows how it forms into gouts (*Macbeth*, V.i.46), or spouts in dismaying profusion (*Troilus and Cressida*, IV.v.10), or drips, 'drop by drop' (*1 Henry IV*, I.iii.134); how it follows the withdrawn knife (*Julius Caesar*, III.ii.178), how it could temper clay (*1 Henry VI*, III.i.311) or make paste (*Titus*, V.ii.187) or manure the battle-field (*Richard II*, IV.i.137), how it grows sticky (*Macbeth*, V.ii.17), and how it darkens on coagulation while a 'watery rigol' or clear serum separates from the black clot (*Rape of Lucrece*, 1743–5). As we have seen, he also has a strange obsession about blood-drinking, which disgusts him. But his imagination flows with rivers (ibid., 1736f) or even a sea of blood (*1 Henry VI*, IV.vii.14). He knows at first hand how

> the butcher takes away the calf,
> And binds the wretch, and beats it when it strays,
> Bearing it to the bloody slaughter-house . . .
> And as the dam runs lowing up and down,
> Looking the way her harmless young one went . . .
>
> (*2 Henry VI*, III.i.210f)

---

* Cf *Edmund Ironside*: 'fathers' (723, 725), 'butchery' (728).

† Cf *Edmund Ironside*, where fathers are callous about the killing of their sons: 'blood of our own blood' . . . 'for us they shed their blood' (250, 279); '[I] will shed . . . drop by drop' (132); 'manuréd with carcases/And made a sea with blood' (1898–9); in lines 881f the Thames turns into blood.

This tone of touched concern is made more meaningful by its own matter-of-factness. Such sights are made to seem as familiar as they are painful; 'lay on like a butcher' (*Henry V*, V.ii.141) invites us to imagine them for ourselves. They become premises for simple syllogisms, as the next scene in *2 Henry VI* shows: 'Who finds the heifer dead and bleeding fresh/And sees fast by a butcher with an axe,/But will suspect 'twas he that made the slaughter?' (III.ii.188). Man in general is seen as part of nature, which is red in axe and knife as well as tooth and claw. We freely slaughter, maim and mutilate all animals, human and other. The modern sanitisation of Shakespeare has led to disputes about *Titus Andronicus*, which is notorious for its horrendous hacking of hands* and tearing of flesh. But those characteristics are surely more authenticating than otherwise. Shakespeare's repeated descriptions of carnage in the language of the shambles ('butchered', 'slaughtered' and so on), often for the first time in English, according to the OED, and with typical symbolism according to Spurgeon (1935, 227–8), together with his awareness of 'the uncleanly savours of the slaughterhouse' (*King John*, IV.iii.112), and of how 'a barrow of butcher's offal' looks when dumped in a basket (*Merry Wives of Windsor*, III.v.5), and of the clean look of a sound sheep's heart (*As You Like It*, III.ii.423), and so forth, serve to corroborate his close involvement with that trade.

Tudor butchers dealt in hides and skins as well as meat. In 1573 John Shakespeare was recorded as a whittawer (**67**), that is one who softens hides and skins by dressing them with alum and salt to facilitate their manufacture into saddles, harnesses and other leather goods, including parchment. Such processes were well known to both Hamlet and Horatio: 'parchment [is] made of sheepskins . . . and of calves'-skins too' (V.i.112–13). This follows directly from thoughts about lawyers and the ownership of land. Similar associations occur in *2 Henry VI* (IV.ii.78f), where the rebel leader Jack Cade complains 'Is this not a lamentable thing that the skin of an innocent lamb should be made parchment? That parchment, being scribbled o'er, should undo a man? . . . I did but seal once to a thing, and I was never mine own man since.' He intends to 'kill all the lawyers', in revenge. He makes a start by hanging a clerk, 'with his pen and inkhorn around his neck', for such grave offences as the ability to 'write and read and cast accompt', and sign his name, instead of having 'a mark to thyself, like an honest plain-dealing man'. Handwriting, and its equipment of quill, parchment and inkhorn (**II**), are persistently associated with animals as their source and the law as their subject throughout the plays and poems.†

---

*   Cf *Edmund Ironside* with the same on-stage display and use of axe, block and knife, and the same sick pun on 'handle' (602; *Titus*, III.ii.29); also 'butchery' (*Edmund Ironside*, 728), 'slaughtering . . . slaughtered' (1864, 1873).
†   Cf *Edmund Ironside*: 'paper . . . inkhorn' (1148), 'feathers . . . pens' (1173) 'write . . . accuse . . . be a witness' (1193–4).

Those works are also redolent of raw materials, as E.A. Fripp (1938, i, 79–80, cited by Schoenbaum 1975, 61) has documented in detail, thus:

William Shakespeare refers to the hides of oxen and horses, to calf-skin, sheep-skin, lamb-skin, fox-skin and dog-skin, deer-skin and cheveril . . . He knew that 'neat's leather' was used for shoes, sheep's leather for a bridle. The poet was aware that horsehair was used in bowstrings and 'calves' guts' in fiddle-strings. He notices leathern aprons, jerkins and bottles, the 'sow-skin bowget' or bag carried by tinkers, and he comments humorously on the capacity of tanned leather to keep out water. He alludes to 'flesh and fell', to the 'greasy fells' of ewes. and, with evident pleasure, to the lamb's 'white fleece'. He knew that the deer's hide was the keeper's perquisite, and we may believe that his father made purchases from the keepers round Stratford. References to cheveril (kid-skin) are much to the point. On account of its softness and flexibility it was used in the making of finer qualities of gloves. Shakespeare speaks of 'a wit of cheveril, that stretches from an inch narrow to an ell broad'. This is technical language, borrowed from his father's business. He mentions a 'soft cheveril con-science', capable of 'receiving gifts' if the owner will please to stretch it; and 'a cheveril glove . . . how quickly the wrong side may be turned outward' [to change the meaning of a sentence].

That epithet occurs only those three times, in *Romeo and Juliet* (II.iv.83), *Henry VIII* (II.iii.32) and *Twelfth Night* (III.i.12). Those plays span some twenty years. Yet the image and its meaning remain the same; slippery thinking is deprecated. Even with gloves, the hand leaves fingerprints of style and attitude; and the process of association is as unflattering to glovemaking as to butchery (VIII). Both used knives; thus Dame Quickly, who asks of Slender in *The Merry Wives of Windsor*, 'Does he not wear a great round beard like a glover's paring knife?' (I.iv.21).

Such allusions are often very near the bone and the knuckle; raw material in every sense. The butchery was basic, in art as in life.

IX

John Shakespeare's Catholic Testament

JOHN SHAKESPEARE'S SPIRITUAL Testament (111; full text in Schoenbaum 1975, 41–3) is even more explicitly Roman Catholic than the will left by his late father-in-law Robert Arden (14); indeed it is entirely an elaborate profession of faith, not a legal testamentary disposition at all. It assumes that all the testator's 'dear friends, parents and kinsfolks' are Catholics too. It was translated from the Italian of Cardinal Carlo Borromeo, with whom the Jesuits Edmund Campion and Robert Parsons spent a week in his Milan residence en route for England (Reynolds 1980, 64) on their special mission to reaffirm the old faith. In June 1581 Rome was informed that 'Father Robert wants three or four thousand or more of the Testaments, for many persons desire to have them' (De Groot 1946, 88). Reynolds (1980, 99) interprets that request as a reference to versions of the Vulgate. But it surely meant the Borromeo *Testament*; and the repeat order was surely fulfilled.

That text was regarded by Elizabeth's government as the illicit and defiant profession of a forbidden faith. An English translation reached John Shakespeare, presumably by way of the 1581 Campion mission, which included Warwickshire in its itinerary. He duly subscribed to it, by specific attestation; so his name appeared fourteen times in a document, now lost, once in the possession of Edmund Malone and published by him as genuine (1790, i/2, 161–2, 330–31). There is no reason to doubt its authenticity. On the contrary; the existence of *The Contract and Testament of the Soule* (Borromeo 1638), a quite different English translation (reproduced in Schoenbaum 1975, 44–5) of the same Italian text, serves to validate the version given by Malone. This transcribed a handwritten document placed between the rafters and the tiling of John Shakespeare's Henley Street house in Stratford. There it was discovered in 1757 by repairers in the employ of Thomas Hart, a direct descendant of Shakespeare's sister Joan. Hart had inherited the property from his father George Hart (1636–1702) to whom Shakespeare's granddaughter Elizabeth, Lady Bernard née Hall, had bequeathed it on her death in 1670. The document's credentials are thus more than creditable.

The original manuscript contained blank spaces to be filled in by the testator's signature or mark. It was presumably copied from a printed English translation supplied by the Jesuit fathers, who already in 1580 had access to a clandestine press in London (Reynolds 1980, 88). Who was trustworthy enough, at a time of bitter religious persecution and punishment, to undertake such copying or insertions? Some Shakespeare, surely. But John and Mary were both illiterate. Their eldest son and heir was sixteen or seventeen years old at the material time. It is thus doubly regrettable that the document in question was missing from Malone's posthumous papers.

But at least its likeliest source is well documented. The Jesuit missionary priests led by Campion stayed with the Catholic Sir William Catesby at his home some twelve miles from Stratford (Bowden 1899, 66; Milward 1973, 21; Schoenbaum 1975, 46). Catesby, who was related by marriage to the Catholic Ardens, the family of Shakespeare's mother (Bowden idem), was arrested and imprisoned for harbouring Papists.

One of the priests, Robert Parsons (1546–1610), went into hiding and escaped; his later writings are a significant source of further reference to Shakespeare and the Catholic connection (Sams 1993d, 183). Campion (1540–82) was caught, tortured and executed after a sham trial. So were many other priests, including Thomas Cottam (1549–82), brother of the Stratford headmaster (99). Some local or diocesan influence sanctioned the appointment of Catholics, or their kinsfolk and sympathisers, to such public posts although that was forbidden by law. Perhaps some cleric in the Worcester diocese (which then included Stratford) had remained tolerant of the old faith. The appointment of the Catholic Simon Hunt to the Stratford headship in 1579 (59, 75) is ascribed to the Bishop of Worcester, then the staunch Anglican John Whitgift, who as we shall see (XIII) is named in other Shakespearean connections.

On any assessment there were many faithful hands eager to provide John Shakespeare with his copy of the Borromeo *Testament*; the supplier closest to home was John Cottam (X). A likely time and occasion for its concealment occurred in 1583, when a search was made in Stratford and the environs for the accomplices of the deranged Catholic John Somerville, who had ridden armed to London, allegedly to assassinate Queen Elizabeth. He was captured and killed; the task of seeking out his accomplices was laid on the Stratford landowner Thomas Lucy, who was traditionally famous for his persecution of Shakespeare (XII). This Somerville had married Margaret Arden, a Catholic cousin of Shakespeare's mother Mary Arden (Chambrun 1957, 48f). Other Ardens hanged or burnt for alleged complicity included Edward Arden, the head of the clan. He in turn was apparently related to the Jesuit Father Robert Arden who was a friend and correspondent of Edmund Campion (Reynolds 1980, 55).

All Shakespeare's kinsmen on both sides of the family would have had good reason to hear the whole sad Somerville story, and fear for their own safety in those times of terror. As the government was informed, 'the papists in [Warwickshire] do greatly work upon the advantage of clearing their houses of all shows of suspicion' (Milward 1973, 21, Chambrun idem). The document in the rafters is thus a doubly powerful testimony to John Shakespeare's faith. It could easily have been burnt, and so could he.

Among the best witnesses to its genuineness is Shakespeare himself. Its text silently surfaces from his own subconscious in *Hamlet*. The Ghost seems to have studied its contents with some care. 'I John Shakespeare doe protest that I will also pass out of this life, armed with the last sacrament of extreme unction: the which if through any let or hindrance I should not be able to have, I doe now also for that time demand and crave the same' (item IV); further, 'I may be possibly cut off in the blossome of my sins' (item I). Hamlet's father was in fact 'Cut off even in the blossoms of my sin./Unhouseled, disappointed, unaneled' (I.v.76–7), i.e. without the eucharist or extreme unction or any other due preparation, which it is now too late to demand or crave: 'No reckoning made, but sent to my account/With all my imperfections on my head.' Hamlet himself shares the same belief; he refuses to kill his stepfather at prayer, preferring to await 'some act/That has no relish of salvation in it' (III.iii.92) so as to ensure perdition.

John Shakespeare's Catholic testament committed not only his soul but his body into the 'most holy hands' of God, and not to 'the earth whereof it is made' in the customary invocation. So any subsequent disturbance would have seemed blasphemously sacrilegious. No wonder Hamlet is distressed that 'thy canonised bones, hearséd in death/Have burst their cerements' (I.iv.47–8); hence perhaps his own horror at such thoughts, as already discussed (IV). The principle of earth burial awaiting personal resurrection into eternal bliss is among Tudor Catholic dogmas imported into pagan Denmark. Thus the Gravedigger in *Hamlet* claims that the houses he makes will last till doomsday (V.i.59), with their occupants undisturbed; a priest certifies that Ophelia will be lodged in the ground till the last trumpet (V.i.229–30). The Ghost is often said to inhabit Purgatory (McGee 1987, 27–46); and it certainly complains of being 'confined to fast in fires/Till the foul crimes done in my days of nature/Are burnt and purged away . . .' (I.v.iif).

This may contain a recollection of Seneca's *Thyestes*. The Ghost's further grievances about fasting, fires and a prison house, as well as its foreshadowings of revenge, demonstrate its direct descent from the ghost of Tantalus "snatching with famished mouth at vanishing food" . . . "let me return to my prison house . . . let me stand in a stream of fire"' (Sams 1988c, 22). However, the allusions to Catholic Purgatory, also explicitly incorporated in the Borromeo *Testament*, are plain enough; and this dogma played no part in Protestant theology except to be derided as rank superstition.

All Shakespeare's allusions to Roman literature in *Hamlet* could have been deliberate; but those to Roman Catholicism were surely inadvertent, at a time when such affiliation was still unlawful as well as unsafe. John Shakespeare died in 1601, at about the time when this version of *Hamlet* was being written. As its hero says (I.ii.184): 'My father – methinks I see my father.'

X

Lancashire

ROMAN APOSTASY WAS tantamount to treason, for which the doom pronounced by Elizabeth's Lord Chief Justice ran thus:

> You must go to the place from whence you came, there to remain until ye shall be drawn through the open City of London upon hurdles to the place of execution, and there hanged and let down alive, and your privy parts cut off, and your entrails taken out and burnt in your sight; then your heads to be cut off and your bodies divided into four parts, to be disposed of at her Majesty's pleasure. And God have mercy on your souls.

It would be prudent for any member of a Catholic family in Warwickshire in the early 1580s, when persecution was rife there, to seek sanctuary elsewhere. In this same period, William Shakespeare was to fall foul of the anti-Catholic zealot Sir Thomas Lucy (XII), who in 1581 'was appointed Commissioner with truly inquisitorial rights to investigate' his Stratford neighbours (Chambrun 1938, 97). This same Lucy would use those powers against Shakespeare's kinsmen (IX) including his father John. Further, it was prima facie in 1581, during the Jesuit mission of Campion and Parsons, that John Shakespeare acquired and signed his Spiritual Testament, the possession of which was a danger to the entire family (IX).

They would all have agreed that young William and his conspicuous talents should be preserved from harm if at all possible. But the presence of Lucy made Stratford on Avon especially dangerous for him. So where might he have sought refuge? In his younger years, according to John Aubrey (112), he had been a schoolmaster 'in the country', presumably as distinct from Stratford itself. This may well have meant a private tutor. Moneyed Catholic families customarily protected their children thus from the Protestant teachers appointed to almost all the grammar schools. In 1581, Stratford was an exception; the schoolmaster there then was John Cottam, who was a likely source of the Spiritual Testament signed by John Shakespeare (IX). As Ernst Honigmann has discovered (1985, 5, 15), Cottam's home at Tarnacre (to which he later retired) was only some ten miles from Lea, the estate of the Catholic Houghton family.

There, also in 1581, history records a William Shakeshafte. Alexander Houghton's will made in that year reads:

yt is my mind & wyll that . . . Thomas Houghton of Brynescoules my brother shall haue all my Instrumentes belonginge to mewsyckes & all manner of playe clothes yf he be minded to keppe & doe keppe playeres. And yf he wyll not keppe & manteyne playeres, then yt ys my wyll that Sir Thomas Heskethe Knyghte [another Catholic recusant] shall haue the same Instrumentes and playe clothes. And I most hertelye requyre the said Sir Thomas to be ffrendlye unto ffoke Gyllome & William Shakeshafte nowe dwellinge with me & eyther to take theym vnto his Servyce or els to help theym to some good master, as my tryste ys he wyll.

It seems clear from the rather touching tone of this last request that both Gillom and Shakeshafte were very young at the time, and employed as actors and musicians.

These duties were in no way incompatible with tutoring. On the contrary, Shakespeare himself confirms that a schoolmaster's duties included musical instruction:

> And for I know she taketh most delight
> In music, instruments and poetry,
> Schoolmasters will I keep within my house
> Fit to instruct her youth. (*Taming of the Shrew*, I.i.92f)

Cf also '. . . offer me disguised in sober robes/To old Baptista as a schoolmaster,/Well seen in music, to instruct Bianca' (ibid., I.ii.131). That sense of 'schoolmaster' as applied to a private tutor (OED Ie) continued to be cited from 1510 to 1654. It may have been the usage intended by Aubrey's named informant, the actor William Beeston (d. 1682), who would in turn have heard about it from his father Christopher Beeston (fl. 1598–1637), an actor colleague of Shakespeare's in the Chamberlain's company.

In developing the earlier theory (Baker 1937, Chambers 1944) that 'William Shakeshafte' was a sobriquet for the young Shakespeare, Honigmann points out (1985, 18) that a number of Shakespeare's later colleagues, including boy-actors, were singers and instrumentalists. It is worth adding here that the character Studioso in the 1605 *Parnassus* trilogy, who is colourably identifiable with Shakespeare (XVIII), not only sings and plays the fiddle but is called 'schoolmaster' and teaches Latin to a boy.

'Shaft' for 'spear' sounds forced at first. Yet, as other documents demonstrate, the Shakespeare family name was variable in form as well as spelling. Thus Shakespeare's grandfather recognisably figures in the Snitterfield records as 'Shakstaff' (5) if not 'Shakeshaft', which is the usual Lancashire form of that surname group. All three forms still survive. The hypothesis that William Shakespeare sought refuge from Protestant persecution in Warwickshire, under an alias, among the Catholic Houghtons of Lancashire is not implausible, especially given that the

Stratford schoolmaster at the material time, John Cottam, came from a Catholic family in the same neighbourhood as the Houghtons. He would be well placed to recognise and recommend the intellectual abilities of young William, and also to appreciate the very real dangers attached to Catholic affiliation. His own brother, the priest Thomas Cottam, was arrested in June 1580, arraigned with the Jesuit Edmund Campion in 1581 and executed in May 1582.

Again, and quite independently, the Catholic sympathiser who annotated the copy of Hall's *Chronicles* 1550, and is identified by Alan Keen as Shakespeare (by way of textual parallels with canonical plays), had also been traced (Keen and Lubbock 1954, 34) to a family closely related by marriage to the Houghtons and the Heskeths. Keen further reports (ibid., 49–50) a long-standing tradition, independently elicited and cited by Honigmann (1985, 34), that Shakespeare had been employed at Rufford Hall, the home of the Heskeths, as if 'Shakeshafte' had indeed moved on there as Houghton had hoped. The Tudor tapestry at Rufford Old Hall depicting the fall of Troy is also worth comparing with the description of the same scene in 'a piece of skilful painting' (*Rape of Lucrece*, 1366f).

Other aspects of the Houghton-Hesketh background need further dispassionate study; see for example Broadbent (1956) on Lancashire topography and Honigmann (1985) on the connections between the Houghtons and the Lancashire epigrammatist John Weever and between the Lancashire Catholics and the Lord Strange, in whose theatre company Shakespeare may have served in the early 1590s (XIV), shortly before it became a source of recruitment for the Chamberlain's Men. It is damagingly negative to ignore or even dismiss (G. Smith 1963, 16) any such possibilities, especially while the graphological and other links between the Catholic annotator and the young Shakespeare remain uninvestigated by any professional authority (XXXVI). Keen and Lubbock, as Ernst Honigmann says in his preface (1985, vii), 'have not had the acclaim they deserve'.

XI

The Law-Clerk

A BETTER-ATTESTED EMPLOYMENT possibility has very often been mooted (most recently in Sams 1993e); the young Shakespeare worked as a lawyer's clerk. This was first proposed by the Shakespeare editor and biographer Edmund Malone (1790, i/1.307) as a direct inference from the legal knowledge so lavishly displayed throughout the plays and poems. As a barrister, Malone was well placed to distinguish technical detail from mere general allusion. He adjudged that Shakespeare 'was employed, while he yet remained at Stratford, in the office of some county attorney'. The equally well-qualified archivist, palaeographer and Shakespeare specialist Edgar Fripp (1929, 135–6) independently offered the same interpretation of the same evidence; 'his familiarity with country-law is among the main hallmarks of his workmanship'; so 'we may conclude . . . that he served his articles in a lawyer's office . . .'. Similarly F.E. Halliday, who also devoted his life to Shakespeare studies, offers his own sensible and strong argument (1961, 57) that 'if Shakespeare did begin his career . . . as an articled clerk to an attorney, it would account for his remarkable knowledge of the law, legal terms and procedure . . . his knowledge seems to be . . . ingrained; the point need not be laboured, for there are few scenes in Shakespeare without some legal reference or other'.

Yet the young law student's readily recognisable features, like the butcher's (VIII) and the deer-poacher's (XII) and the ostler's (XIV), have been obliterated by snobbish assumptions; in this case, that if Shakespeare was connected with the law he must have been a leading legal luminary, not a lowly clerk, even in his youth. Thus Samuel Schoenbaum (1975, 87) approves an ancient Aunt Sally argument: had Shakespeare been a fully-fledged lawyer (nothing less can be envisaged) and 'occupied a desk in some Warwickshire solicitor's office', he must have signed documents in that capacity. But no such documents have ever been discovered despite ceaseless search; ergo, the massive evidence, and indeed the entire question, can safely be set aside.

For the opposite *non sequitur*, namely that the playwright was so obviously a lawyer that he could not possibly have been Shakespeare, see Mark Twain (1909, 14–15, 100–101). The rational choice avoids frying-pan and fire, eschewing both Bacon and bias, but sticking to the facts. On this showing, Shakespeare learned a lot about the law in his youth and then or later worked as a legal penman. The extant evidence is stronger for London than for Stratford legal affiliations; but the later links support, though they may not entail, the earlier.

On the facts, in the first place, John Shakespeare was a local law officer (**20, 21, 41, 48**), whose illiteracy must often have proved a grave handicap; he needed advice and assistance from friends or family. In times of hardship or persecution, young William's writing skills could not only make money but also save expense or safeguard security in the preparation or copying of legal records, or indeed illegal documents such as his father's testament (IX) or perhaps his own marriage-bond (XIII). In times of prosperity, he could lend a hand in drafting and penning an application for a family coat of arms (**76**). His school Latin would help in acquiring the legal Latin in which all such contracts and claims were commonly couched.

He was surely a 'snapper-up of unconsidered trifles' (*Winter's Tale*, IV.iii.26); his good brain would readily master technical data; and he had the law thrust upon him in his boyhood, in contexts that are worth setting out in some detail. His father John had fallen foul of the law from the dunghill days (**10**) onwards; so had John's brother Henry (**108, 142**); so had their father Richard before them (**5, 6, 24**). John Shakespeare remained a litigant throughout his long life. His eldest son William in turn figures in legal records with comparable frequency, whether as property-owner, witness, legatee, profit-sharer, debtor, (non)-taxpayer, vendor in Stratford, purchaser in Stratford and London, defendant, plaintiff or testator. Even as a child, he might well have been aware of his father's legal tangles and perplexities in debt and distraint (**55, 61, 67**), or of the documents and details pertaining to the purchase or sale of family land (**50, 74**) or the technicalities of will-making and executorship (**68**). In adolescence he would certainly have had an interest, in every sense, in his parents' disposal of the family land and property.

Given that both his mother and his father were illiterate, and signed their names with marks, it would be no more than ordinarily prudent on his part to study and indeed if possible prepare the relevant documents (e.g. **85, 94, 97**). He is specifically recorded as having been present at the relevant later debates (**144**) and a named party to the ensuing acrimonious lawsuits (**157**), which were revived (no doubt at his own instigation and expense, since his parents were still 'of very small wealth') in 1597, when he was thirty-three. Already at half that age his intelligence and maturity would have been helpful at the meeting about the land with his uncle by marriage Edmund Lambert (**104**) and at later family conclaves. Again in 1580, he would surely have heard why his father failed to attend the London court of Queen's Bench, with consequent heavy fines (**107**). At eighteen, he would have been privy to the legal implications of his father's suit against Ralph Cawdrey and others

(116), and also his father's citation as a witness before a London court in what was presumably the same quarrel with the Lamberts about the family lands (121). Similarly, William would have been well aware of his father's clashes with the law in 1586 to 1588 (138, 142, 150). Applications for coats of arms argue acquaintance with the laws of heraldry. A Catholic family background, finally, would promote knowledge of the religious laws proscribing popery, under heavy penalties including fines, dispossession, imprisonment, even torture and death. The regulations governing church attendance in particular would be an immediate concern. All this and very much more is apparent from the plays and poems, where legal references famously proliferate whether as technicalities or metaphors (e.g. 'set thy seal manual on my wax-red lips *Venus and Adonis*, 516). The histories for example very often rehearse the law of succession or entitlement, as the motive forces of the plays and indeed of history itself; loss of paternal lands (VII) is a recurrent theme.

There is an even closer connection. Shakespeare's signature, authenticated by professional specialists (Knight 1973, Dawson 1942 and 1992), appears on the Folger Library copy of a 1568 legal textbook *Archaionomia*, a selection by the distinguished Tudor lawyer William Lambarde from pre-Conquest regnal statutes, mainly those of King Canute,* in Anglo-Saxon and Latin. A later hand has supplied an address: 'Mr. Wm Shakespeare Lived at No. 1 Little Crown St. Westminster NB near Dorset Steps St. James's Park'.

This textbook's topics include land tenure; Shakespeare would surely be studying that subject, in good time before the family case was heard (without any recorded result) at Westminster in 1589. On any analysis there is an immediate independent inference that the owner and inscriber of a legal textbook was studying law. But so strong is the inexplicable bias against any such association that even those commentators who support the signature feel able to call *Archaionomia* 'an odd choice for Shakespeare's library' (Schoenbaum 1981, 109, following Dawson 1942, 97, 'a strange volume indeed for his library'). It seems it is

---

* All as in the history play *Edmund Ironside*. The holograph, certified as Shakespeare's writing by the documents expert Charles Hamilton (30 June 1986), is penned in a legal style (blocked margins, standard abbreviations) and hand strikingly similar to the 1579 document recording the sale of land by John and Mary Shakespeare (XXXVI). Its characters talk in such terms as 'for a manual seal receive this kiss' (439), 'approve his title naught', 'deliver me possession', 'forfeiture . . . copyhold . . . rent-run' (1791–2), 'equity' (1825), a concept devised by Lambarde and first described in his *Archion* 1591. The cruel mutilations prescribed as penalties by King Canute in *Archaionomia*, and underlined by the owner of the copy signed 'Shakespeare', are actually practised in this play, where also 'thy father's land' is 'seized upon . . . for want of tribute-paying long since due' (1793–5).

for modern commentators, not Shakespeare himself, to decide what books he ought to own and read. Note too that even in his youth he has to be imagined as a library-owner, far too grand for a mere bookshelf, as well as a high-level lawyer if one at all. Of course he need never have risen higher than a part-time clerk; in London at least he was certainly otherwise engaged. But in the real world of Tudor times where even Shakespeare was once a needy beginner, he surely studied law.

Many commentators, including some who are both legal and literary specialists (notably Knight 1973) have reached that same conclusion via many different approaches. The sole yet insuperable obstacle on this road is modern prejudice, which claims that the barrister Malone merely 'conjectured' (Schoenbaum 1975, 87) his expert inferences, and treats Lord Chief Justice Campbell in such terms as 'fantasy' and 'idyll' (Schoenbaum 1971, 2/1991, 333). The legal expert Nicholas Knight fares no better: he 'tends to lose sight of the fact that the Chancery litigants in the nineties were John and Mary Shakespeare, not their son William' (Schoenbaum 1981, 108). But again it is Schoenbaum himself who has lost sight of the facts. Thus he wrongly states (1975, 77) that 'from 1585 . . . until 1592 . . . the documentary record presents a blank', which overlooks the 1589 family lawsuit (157) altogether. He then turns a blind eye to William's undeniable interest and involvement as eldest son and heir to the property in question.

But Shakespeare's legal connections are completely confirmed by other experts on grounds that are quite distinct from the content of the plays and poems, and hence offer further powerful support. Three experienced palaeographers (E. Thompson 1916, Everitt 1954, Hamilton 1985) have said that Shakespeare's handwriting, in the other six signatures as well as in *Sir Thomas More*, offers plain evidence of legal training. So does the terminology of his own last will and testament, on the testimony of Lord Chief Justice Campbell. But all this is also swept aside by Schoenbaum, who ignores Thompson, continuously scoffs at Everitt, and actually accuses Campbell of 'tampering with the rules of evidence' (1971, 333, 533). The same authority claims that Shakespeare's will was written by 'Francis Collins' perhaps with some help from 'his clerk' (1975, 242; 1977, 297–9).

Shakespeare's earliest definite datable association with legal procedures and documents is his demonstrable awareness of the 1580 Stratford inquest verdict on the drowned Katherine Hamlett (98, 101), with the legal and religious implications later recalled and incorporated in *Hamlet* (Sams 1988c, 14, 19). That play was first mentioned by Nashe in 1589; he says it was written by a noverint or lawyer's clerk. He coined that term in that context for that purpose; it is the first word of the typical preamble of Tudor legal documents, including the 1579 contract for the Shakespeares' sale of land: 'Noverint universi per praesentes', let all men know by these presents. Robert Greene, in his own famous attack on

Shakespeare and his like, calls them 'buckram* gentlemen', also meaning law-clerks or noverints.

Here then is the evident explanation of how, as Mark Twain pithily puts it (1909, 14–15, 99–101), Shakespeare came to be so 'limitlessly familiar with the laws, and the law-courts, and law-proceedings, and lawyer-talk, and lawyer-ways', from experience not books. Of course an intelligent and ambitious law-clerk would study law most diligently; of course such knowledge would then permeate his other writings, as terminology or imagery. Fripp (1926–9, xlix–l) enumerates 150 examples, many highly technical, in *The Comedy of Errors* alone. Not only the plays but the Sonnets (XX) are crammed with legal references and allusions, far more so than any comparable oeuvre in any period or language. Naturally, too, Shakespeare learned to write a legal hand (155) as well as his own normal secretary script. And only anti-biographical prejudice could fail to admit a possible personal significance in such passages as 'I once did hold it . . . / A baseness to write fair, and labour'd much/How to forget that learning, but, sir, now/It did me yeoman's service', with its natural transition from penman back to yeoman (*Hamlet*, V.ii.33f), just as in the earlier link (III) between parchment and sheep or calf-skin, which arises from thoughts about lawyers and the ownership of land.

Even the Gravedigger (ibid., V.i.9f) shows detailed technical knowledge of the unpublished arguments recorded in the case of Hales v. Pettit 1560 (Trinity term 3. Eliz. Rot. 921), while the Prince himself claims astonishing skills in forging legal documents with the help of a signet seal (*Hamlet*, V.ii.31f, 49f). More plausibly, the law-clerk, scrivener or noverint in *Richard III* is well acquainted with the inordinate time taken to prepare an original official document (the 'precedent') and copy it out in large clear letters ('engross' it) for the purposes of public proclamation:

> Here is the indictment of the good Lord Hastings
> Which in a set hand fairly is engrossed
> That it may be today read o'er in Paul's.
> And mark how well the sequel hangs together:
> Eleven hours I have spent to write it over . . .
> The precedent was full as long a-doing . . . (III.vi.1–6)

Perhaps this was one of Shakespeare's own roles?

---

* The secretary Nimble in the anonymous play *Woodstock, c.* 1590, which has been cogently attributed to Shakespeare (Robinson 1988), is called a 'buckram scribe' (Everitt 1965, 259–60); the same path is predicted for him as that already followed by his master who 'did become a plodding clerk,/From which I bounced, as thou dost now, in buckram,/To be a pleading lawyer'.

XII

Lucy and his Deer

PURITANS AND OTHER Protestants had their own private tutors, like Catholics (X), also as a defence against dangerous heresies. Between 1545 and 1547 the Stratford worthy Sir Thomas Lucy (1532–1600) had been tutored by the Puritan John Foxe (1516–87), whose fierce anti-Catholic doctrines he enthusiastically espoused and practised (IV, IX, X). Foxe's *Book of Martyrs* (1563), a prime source of sectarian strife, was well known to Shakespeare, who later based his reprobate Falstaff on its Wycliffian martyr Sir John Oldcastle, thus giving lasting offence to many pious souls (Sams 1993d).

Lucy's lifelong persecution of Catholics is copiously documented from the early 1580s, the period of young Shakespeare's well-attested deer-poaching escapades. By then, popery had become more perilous than ever, because of the 1581 Jesuit mission (IX, X). In this same year, Lucy was appointed 'to put down abuses in religion'. In this interest he denounced many Catholics, including the Ardens, near relatives of Shakespeare's mother Mary née Arden, who were executed in 1583 (Chambrun 1957, 11, 27, 47). In November 1584 Lucy was elected Member of Parliament for Warwickshire (132). Among his earliest contributions to the common weal was a petition for the execution of his fellow-member Dr Parry, who had protested against Queen Elizabeth's anti-Catholic measures. Lucy warmly recommended the devising of special punishments suitable for so evil a villain. His actual words are worth recording:

> Forasmuch as that villainous traitor Parry was a member of this house in the time of some of his most monstrous, horrible and traiterous conspiracies that her Majesty vouchsafe to give licence to this house to proceed to the devising and making of some law for his execution after his conviction as may be thought fittest for his so extraordinary and most horrible kind of treason. (Chambrun 1957, 55–6)

Similarly the Cardinal enquires about the villainous Gloucester: 'Did he not, contrary to form of law,/Devise strange deaths for small offences done?'; and the interrogation is taken up more directly by York: '. . . you did devise/Strange torments for offenders, never heard of' (*2 Henry VI*,

III.i.58–9, 121–2); in other words 'some never-heard-of torturing pain'*
(*Titus*, II.iii.284–5).

It was also contrary to law that Parry's conviction was taken for
granted, like Edmund Campion's, in advance of the trial and in the
absence of evidence. Poor Parry's parliamentary privilege was duly
rescinded; in March 1585, he was done to death in Westminster, help-
lessly protesting his innocence to the last. Soon thereafter, Lucy
denounced the priest William Hartley, who was hanged in 1588 'nigh
the Theator' in Bishopsgate, where Shakespeare was then working
(Chambrun 1957, 27, 81). Four years later, Lucy would be the chief
signatory on two documents indicting John Shakespeare for non-
attendance at the prescribed Protestant church services (172, 181).

Lucy was also a zealous protector of his own property rights, which his
persecutions helped to extend; thus in 1584 he appropriated the Fulbrook
estate of a Catholic exile (133). In the following year, he continued his
public services by promoting a bill for the better preservation of game; in
1610, his son prosecuted deer-poachers. From first to last, the various
sources (125, *passim*) record hatred and ill-usage ('whipt . . . Imprisoned/
. . . lawyer . . . proceed against him/prosecuted . . . bitter . . . Prosecution/
bitter . . . vindictive/persecutor . . . anger . . . inexorable/prosecution/
prosecution/confined') culminating in banishment and exile ('fly his
Native Country/ . . . forc'd him out of his Country/. . . obliged to leave his
Business and Family/. . . and shelter himself in London/drove him to
London . . . /obliged him to quit . . . his native place/obliged him to quit
Stratford'). Most of these sources are separate; and their unanimity as
well as their substance is redolent of the religious persecution to which
Lucy devoted much of his life. Indeed, the earliest source, the brief notes
penned by the Protestant divine Richard Davies, seems to imply a dis-
approving connection between 'stealing venison . . . from Sr. Lucy [sworn
enemy of Catholics] who had him oft whipt' to 'He dyed a Papist' (i.e. as
he had lived).

As Fripp says (1938, i, 80), 'we may believe that [Shakespeare's] father
made purchases [of deer-hide] from the keepers round Stratford'. Indeed
we may; that commodity was among the main raw materials of his trades,
as Schoenbaum himself points out (1975, 14): 'he tawed the hides of
deer . . . he made and sold not only gloves but all manner of soft leather
goods . . .'. And what happened in hard times, when John lacked ready
money and the family had extra mouths to feed, as for example when
William in his turn became a husband and father?

Other trespassers might have been forgiven by the landed gentry, even
for deer-stealing; but not the lower-class Catholic Shakespeares, dressers
of hides and skins, including deer-hides. They, conversely, would have

---

* Cf *Edmund Ironside* 'some new never-heard-of torturing pain' (1276).

had a special incentive to flush any coverts owned or claimed by the odious Lucy, rather than other local lands. He thought papists fair game; and no doubt that was how they, from the other side of the fence, saw the Lucy venison.

Those who mislike Shakespeare the butcher-boy or 'the Deerslayer... a picturesque relation deriving, one expects, from local Stratford lore' (Schoenbaum 1975, 78) sometimes rely on 'scholars who demonstrated that Lucy had at the time neither park nor deer' (Holderness 1988, 11) although no such demonstration has ever been, or could ever be made (*pace* M. Eccles 1961, 73; Craik 1989, 7). In fact the already powerful tradition which, as even its detractors agree, derives from four separate sources (Schoenbaum 1975, 83) is strengthened still further by its derivation from Stratford sources including the Lucy family; and the Fulbrook estate is named by two separate writers (Jordan 1790, Ireland 1795), and possibly implied by others (Cooper 1788, Scott 1828), who were unaware of Lucy's annexations.

Not only deer but hares and rabbits would also provide food for the family and fur for its trade; and Shakespeare was also rated a rabbit-killer (**125**). His lines on hare- and boar-hunting (*Venus and Adonis*, 673–708, 877–924) show experience as well as empathy; so do his images from falconry and archery* (Spurgeon 1935, 31, 104). The young Tudor country bowman would acquire and use his skills for hunting, rather than the butts. Shooting skills would have been assiduously practised, from boyhood. As Bassanio tells Antonio,

> In my schooldays, when I had lost one shaft,
> I shot his fellow of the self-same flight
> The self-same way, with more adviséd watch,
> To find the other forth; and by adventuring both
> I oft found both. I urge this childhood proof . . .
>
> (*Merchant of Venice*, I.i.140f)

Shakespeare displays his practical knowledge of deer-hunting in dozens of detailed allusions,[†] often drawn from personal observation (Madden 1897 and Spurgeon 1935, 102f). Illicit deer-killing by bow and arrow is specifically cited in the canon. As Demetrius rhetorically enquires of his brother, 'What, hast thou not full often strook [= struck] a doe/And borne her cleanly by the keeper's nose?' (*Titus*, II.i.93–4).

Above all, the details of the deer-hunt are deliberately incorporated into *The Merry Wives of Windsor*; and it cannot be mere coincidence that the name and the arms and other details of the Lucy family are plainly identified for all to see and hear. Unless the play's opening theme related directly to the killing of deer that Lucy claimed to own, it would be

---

*   As in *Edmund Ironside* 'lofty pitch' (480–81), 'thou hit'st the mark I level at' (1906), etc.
†   Cf *Edmund Ironside*: 'get the wind to compass them' (1706).

sheerly incomprehensible. Then or now, the audience must be in the know.

Shallow:	Sir Hugh, persuade me not. I will make a Star Chamber matter of it. If he were twenty Sir John Falstaffs, he shall not abuse Robert Shallow, Esquire.
Slender:	In the county of Gloucester, justice of peace and Coram.
Shallow:	Ay, cousin Slender, and Custalorum.
Slender:	Ay, and Ratolorum too. And a gentleman born, master parson, who writes himself Armigero – in any bill, warrant, quittance or obligation, Armigero.
Shallow:	Ay, that I do, and have done any time these three hundred years.
Slender:	All his successors gone before him hath done't; and all his ancestors that came after him may. They may give the dozen white luces in their coat.
Shallow:	It is an old coat.
Evans:	The dozen white louses do become an old coat well. It agrees well, passant. It is a familiar beast to man, and signifies love.
Shallow:	The luce is the fresh fish. The salt fish is an old coat.
Slender:	I may quarter, coz?
Shallow:	You may by marrying.
Evans:	It is marring indeed, if he quarter it.
Shallow:	Not a whit.
Evans:	Yes, py'r lady. If he has a quarter of your coat, there is but three skirts for yourself, in my simple estimations. But that is all one. If Sir John Falstaff have committed disparagements unto you, I am of the Church, and will be glad to do my benevolence to make atonements and compromises between you.
Shallow:	The Council shall hear it. It is a riot.
Page:	. . . I thank you for my venison, Master Shallow.
Shallow:	. . . I wished your venison better – it was ill killed.
Shallow:	[Falstaff], you have beaten my men, killed my deer and broke open my lodge.

(*Merry Wives of Windsor*, I.i.1–35, 80, 82, 111–12)

The manifest autobiographical content (*pace* Craik 1989) was well known three centuries ago:

Amongst other Extravagances, in *The Merry Wives of Windsor*, [Shakespeare] has made [Falstaff] a Deer-Stealer, that he might at the same time remember his *Warwickshire* Prosecutor, under the Name of Justice *Shallow*; he has given him very near the same Coat of Arms which *Dugdale*, in his Antiquities of that County, describes for a Family there, and makes the *Welsh* Parson descant very pleasantly upon 'em.' (Rowe 1709)

Already in *2 Henry IV* (III.ii) Justice of the Peace Shallow personifies the injustice of war. Like Lucy, he cold-bloodedly despatches harmless people to mutilation or death; he is presented as a liar and a fool; and he is unobtrusively identified as a luce [= pike] or Lucy when Falstaff calls him 'the old pike'. The deer incident died hard. But the retaliatory hits are scored without overt malice; Shallow in both contexts is delineated almost endearingly.

Such personal allusions were dear to the dramatist who slyly advertises his own *Henry VI* plays at the end of *Henry V* (Ep. 9–14). In the *Merry Wives* context cited above, Falstaff has features of a self-portrait. The dialogue recreates Stratford enmities and encounters of the 1580s. Sir Thomas Lucy's denunciatory impulses were inherited by his son, who took the Draconian action that Shallow threatened, and denounced deer-stealers to the Star Chamber. In Queen Elizabeth's day, that dreaded court was reponsible directly to her. It had special jurisdiction over offences of riot, the word that Shallow uses. It also arraigned heretics, who were treated as traitors.

Shakespeare's Lucy died in 1600, just before this version of *Merry Wives* was written. Perhaps its function was cathartic. Like Robert Shallow, Sir Thomas Lucy as High Sheriff of Warwickshire from 1586 (Halliday 1964, 91) was also 'Justice of Peace' and '*Custalorum*' (i.e. *custos rotularum*, Keeper of the Rolls). Lucy's ancestors, too, had been armigerous for 300 years. They shared the same coat of arms, namely a dozen white pikes or luces (almost a homophone of 'louses' in Midland speech). An illustration in Dugdale's *Warwickshire* shows the three Lucy luces in four quarterings, hence the 'dozen' of the text.

Considered in these contexts, the 'Ballad' made 'upon' Lucy (125) may well be 'probably the first Essay of [Shakespeare's] Poetry' (Rowe 1709). The punning and quibbling verses recorded in Stratford by Professor Barnes (125), with their word- and idea-play on deer/dear, covetous/covet/covert and horns/wife sound quirkily characteristic. Other versions retain the jest lousy/Lucy and knowingly describe him as 'a parliemente member, a justice of peace'. All this (*pace* Craik 1989, 7) surely anticipates rather than echoes the *Merry Wives* scene. There, the deer was killed for a feast, the keeper was assaulted and the lodge broken open, conformably with the traditions (125) about venison on marriage-tables (Phillips 1818) and confinement in the keeper's lodge (Ireland 1795). The accounts also accord in their overtones of sectarian hatred, expressed in the play by Parson Evans's spirited offer of mediation from 'the Church' with any necessary 'atonements' (*Merry Wives*, I.i.32–3), exactly as if religion were among the bones of contention. So it surely was.

XIII

Marriage and Departure

ON 27 NOVEMBER 1582, a clerk recorded the issue of a marriage licence to Shakespeare and 'Annam Whateley de Temple Grafton' (**118**). A bond dated the next day (**120**) states his intention to marry 'Anne Hathewey of Stratford'. Unless he had changed his mind and his affections overnight, these were one and the same person, in Latin and English. There is no doubt that the bride's name was Hathaway, a fact established, for example, by Thomas Whittington's will in 1601.

This permits the inference (Gurr 1971) that Sonnet 145 was Shakespeare's earliest surviving poem, because of the apparent pun on that name in its penultimate line (italics added):

> Those lips that love's own hand did make
> Breathed forth the sound that said 'I hate'
> To me that languished for her sake.
> But when she saw my woeful state,
> Straight in her heart did mercy come,
> Chiding that tongue that ever sweet
> Was used in giving gentle doom,
> And taught it thus anew to greet:
> 'I hate' she altered with an end
> That followed it as gentle day
> Doth follow night, who, like a fiend,
> From heaven to hell is flown away.
> 'I hate' from *hate away* she threw
> And saved my life, saying 'not you'.

'Hate away' in the Midlands speech of the time would be pronounced 'Hattaway' (the name survives in that form also), just as Shakespeare was pronounced and often spelt 'Shakspere'. The pun also suggests that the medial 'h' of Hathaway was commonly elided in country parlance.

This is the sole octosyllabic sonnet. It has often been rejected as 'unauthentic' (e.g. Pooler 1918, Mackail 1930) because the early style remains unrecognised. Others accept these lines as genuine, yet feel free to dismiss them as 'trivial', 'unimportant', and 'feeble childishness' (Ingram and Redpath 3/1978, 334). Its acceptance entails serious rethinking of the 'late start' stance. Once this obstacle is overcome, the early years will surely be seen as the apt field for pastoral poetry such as the lament of the love-lorn shepherd in No. 17 of *The Passionate Pilgrim* ('My flocks feed not, my ewes breed not,/My rams speed not'). The youthfully elated No. 12 ('Crabbed age and youth cannot live together') is also about a shepherd. No. 18 shares the iambic quadrimeter of Sonnet 145: 'When as thine eye hath chose the dame/And stalled the deer that thou shouldst strike . . .' which reads like another Hathaway poem from the same period of deer-killing and courtship; indeed the two procedures are punningly equated by the dual idea of deer and dear, as also in 'dear deer' (*1 Henry VI*, IV.ii.54) and the anti-Lucy lampoons attributed to the young Shakespeare (**125**; XII).

There are no allusions to 'Whateley'. Perhaps this was a mere mistake; the name had already appeared in another case, a dispute involving one William Whateley, before the same court on the same day. Temple Grafton was a village five miles west of Stratford, where no church register survives; it may well have been the venue of the ceremony itself, of which no record remains (and which accordingly could not have taken place in Stratford). It has been claimed (Fullom 1862) that by local tradition Shakespeare married Anne Hathaway at Luddington, near Temple Grafton, where some of the Hathaway family lived (Malone 1821, ii, 116). However, no marriage record remains, perhaps because the ceremony was Catholic, as the priest arguably was (I. Wilson 1993, 57). The significance of the extant documentation has been much disputed, and many aspects of this marriage will remain veiled. But there are clear inferences to be drawn. There is no evidence that the Hathaways were Catholics; but the Shakespeares were, and the two families had been linked in friendship and loyalty (**44**) some sixteen years before they were united by marriage. Roman ceremonies were often cautiously left undocumented for fear of reprisal. Such prudence might have motivated the much-debated and still unexplained legal document (**119**) formally exempting the Bishop of Worcester (whose diocese included the Stratford area) from liability in respect of any irregularity in the marriage arrangements (Halliday 1964, 210; details in Schoenbaum 1975, 62–3, Chambers 1930, ii. 41f and Gray 1905). That bishop was the ardent Anglican John Whitgift, later Archbishop of Canterbury, who was a stage censor in 1589 (**161**) and the licenser (uniquely in the history of Shakespeare publications) of *Venus and Adonis* in 1593 (**186**).

There is no evidence of any closer link between poet and prelate at any time; and the 1582 marriage arrangements remain mysterious in their elusive hints of secrecy, confusion and haste. The bride's pregnancy provides one possible reason; Susanna Shakespeare was born six months after the ceremony (**126**). Chambers (1930, 51) suggests that 'John Shakespeare's financial straits may have motived secrecy'. So may his Catholic convictions. William, though his eldest son, was only eighteen and hence still a minor, under parental authority; and persecution and prosecution could well be necessary or sufficient causes of flight.

The canonical plays contain allusions to (a) whirlwind wooings, (b) a bride's pregnancy, (c) a disparity of ages, (d) the urgency of marriage arrangements, (e) the sacred solemnity of wedding rites, and (f) the especially intense sadness of separation soon after the ceremony.

Those ideas* need not be interrelated; but they arise associatively in Shakespeare's mind as if from deep personal feelings. On (a), the key passages include *Titus Andronicus* (I.i.238–75, 315–37) and *1 Henry VI* (V.iii.45–195). Item (b) combines with (e) in Prospero's solemn homily:

> . . . take my daughter; but
> If thou dost break her virgin-knot before
> All sanctimonious ceremonies may
> With full and holy rite be ministered,
> No sweet aspersion shall the heavens let fall
> To make this contract grow; but barren hate,
> Sour-eyed disdain and discord shall bestrew
> The union of your bed with weeds so loathly
> That you shall hate it both. (*Tempest*, IV.i.14f)

Perhaps Shakespeare later regarded his own marriage as over-hasty and its age-discrepancy (item c) as inadvisable. His wife was some eight years his senior, as he could hardly have failed to reflect when writing the lines: 'let still the woman take/An elder than herself; so wears she to him,/So sways she level in her husband's heart' (*Twelfth Night*, II.iv.29–31). The feeling is more apparent than the reasoning, as if the counsel came more from experience than reflection.

The urgency of the ceremony (item d) is apparent in the *Titus* and *1 Henry VI* passages and often elsewhere, e.g. *The Taming of the Shrew* (II.i. 287). But even in such contexts the sanctity of marriage and the nobility of its rituals (item e) are ceaselessly hymned, in lordly language. Thus *The Tempest* devotes an entire masque with music 'a contract of true love to celebrate', and again for good measure 'to celebrate/A contract of true love' (IV.i.84, 132–3). In his peroration, Prospero expresses his '. . . hope to see the nuptial/Of these our dear-beloved solemnized' (V.i.309–10). From the earliest canonical plays onwards, the same solemn organ-tones are sounded, with the same orotund Latinate polysyllables, as though the poet were invoking and evoking the Roman rite. The reader or spectator is meant to imagine pageants and processions in the mind's eye: 'Ascend, fair queen, Pantheon . . ./There shall we consummate our spousal rites' (*Titus*, I.i.333, 337). As in that context, there is often a named destination:

---

* Well represented in *Edmund Ironside*: (a) 405–88, (d) 444, 475, (e) 458, (f) 1288–9, plus a mention of irregularity by a complaisant bishop (448).

'I'll over then to England . . . /And make this marriage to be solemnized'*
(*1 Henry VI*, V.iv.167–8) or '. . . at Saint Mary's chapel presently [i.e.
straightaway]/The rites of marriage shall be solemnized' (*King John*,
II.i.538–9). Other favourite ritual vocabulary includes 'ceremony' or 'ceremonial', as in: 'when the priest attends/To speak the ceremonial rites of
marriage' (*Taming of the Shrew*, III.ii.5–6), 'a nuptial ceremony' (*A Midsummer Night's Dream*, V.i.55) or 'celebrate' or 'celebration', as in: 'it is the
celebration of his nuptial' (*Othello*, II.ii.6) and 'there, my queen/We'll
celebrate their nuptials' (*Pericles*, V.iii.80). But despite all the solemnity,
the wedding is often followed by an enforced flight† of the groom from
the bride, as in: 'an hour but married . . . and like me banishéd' (*Romeo
and Juliet*, III.iii.67), or 'I will from hence today' (*Cymbeline*, I.i.80) as
Postumus says just after his marriage to Imogen. And he adds with great
feeling, '. . . Should we be taking leave/As long a term as yet we have to
live/The loathness to depart would grow. Adieu!' (ibid., 109).

All this permits the inference that Shakespeare left his own wife for
London soon after his own marriage in 1582. There are also documentary
reasons for dating his departure to that year, for example Aubrey's assurance that he came to London at about eighteen, the age that Shakespeare
had attained in April 1582. That period would be further confirmed if the
wedding or the flight were causally connected with the deer-stealing
escapades. These are regularly recorded as occurring very early in Shakespeare's life. They are a young man's offences; whipping (**125**, Davies) is
a young man's punishment, and he was a 'young Fellow' at the time
(**125**, Rowe). As we have seen (XII) the association persists in tradition
and in Shakespeare's own mind; thus the first scene of *Merry Wives of
Windsor* begins with 100 lines about deer-poaching, followed by the
entrance and formal introduction of Anne Page, the promise of a 'hot
venison pasty to dinner' and the talk of her marriage (I.i.170–81, 205).
Further, a pregnant bride and a brawling deer-poacher might be recalled
in Shakespeare's own ruefully ironic recollections of salad days in the
country, thus, in the words of 'an old shepherd': 'I would there were no
age between ten and three-and-twenty, or that youth would sleep out the
rest: for there is nothing in between but getting wenches with child,
wronging the ancientry, stealing, fighting' (*Winter's Tale*, III.iii.58f).

There are also close causal links among deer-stealing, pregnancy and
marriage, namely mouths to feed and trades to pursue. Young William
must have felt responsible for supporting and sustaining his own new
family as well as the old. He was helping at home; his parents were poor

---

*   Cf *Edmund Ironside* 'I intend to be/Espoused tonight with all solemnity' (457–
8), and with urgency.

†   As in *Edmund Ironside*, again with urgency: 'we will straight to church and
celebrate/The duties which belong to marriages' (444–5) and 'the late-
espouséd man/Grieves to depart from his new-married wife' (1288–9).

(VII); his surviving siblings Gilbert, Joan, Richard and Edmund were sixteen, thirteen, eight and two years old respectively. He had no home of his own; worse still, his patrimony of a house and land had been mortgaged (**94, 97**). As the eldest son, and now a husband and father in his own right, he was already, at eighteen, a main provider and breadwinnner in hard Tudor times. His tasks thus included the provision of raw materials, meat and skins, for the family's food, clothing and trades; in a word, deer.

As to the connection between deer-stealing and flight, the testimony is clear and copious (**125**). He had to 'fly his Native Country' (Davies); he was 'forc'd out of his Country' and 'oblig'd to leave his Business and his Family in *Warwickshire* . . . and shelter himself in *London*' (Rowe); his deer-stealing 'drove him to London' (Oldys); he was 'obliged to quit . . . his native place' (Ireland); 'obliged him to quit Stratford' (Fullom).

There are additional reasons for dating the exodus early. Sir Thomas Lucy, the prosecutor of poachers, was also the persecutor of papists, and the early 1580s were their most perilous period. The Stratford parish clerk and sexton quoted by Dowdall (**125**) says that Shakespeare ran to London while still an apprentice, i.e. as a very young man. No doubt country matters (**90**) would soon pall; he could hardly have considered them his permanent career. Further, his 'being naturally inclined to poetry and acting', with an innate 'high style' in role-playing and speech-making from boyhood (**83**), confirms the commonsense perception that such a genius would seek fulfilment in the best possible place, namely London theatreland, at the earliest possible moment. He was already well aware of theatre and its attractions, including its remuneration, in Stratford and the environs and perhaps also already in London (VII). The ostler's trade in London, the next reported transition, would also be a young man's occupation; so would the next reported step of call-boy to the company (XIV). Again, the country player and playwright openly lampooned by Greene, in a book (**179**) famous only for its attacks on Shakespeare, is said to have been active in the theatre world for at least seven years, which would give a date of 1585 or earlier if applied to the young Stratfordian. Besides, country boys of all epochs have traditionally left home, impelled by 'Such wind as scatters young men through the world/To seek their fortunes' (*Taming of the Shrew*, I.ii.50). Stratford was after all within four days of London, even on foot, and half that on horseback; the roads and routes were well known to touring theatre companies, and inns cost only a penny a night. Of course Shakespeare would return as soon as he could to see his wife and their little daughter Susanna in 1583; he was certainly there in the spring of 1584 (**131**), and would naturally wish to see his twins Hamlet* and Judith, born in February 1585 (**136**). But common

---

* Not 'Hamnet', *pace* Schoenbaum 1971, Nye 1993, Wells 1994, etc.; see XXII.

sense and copious evidence, from every source, combine to contradict the 'late developer' of academic fiction and substitute the early developer of historical fact and everyday reality, who fled to London in the early 1580s, 'to his great Advancement' . . . 'among the Players . . . he became the Great Genius we read him . . .' (**125**). There he 'had an oppertunity to be wt he afterwards pro'vd; his departure 'happily prov'd the occasion of exerting one of the greatest *Genius's* that ever was known in Dramatick Poetry' (**129**).

XIV

Theatre, Work and Company

SO WHERE, HOW and with what company was Shakespeare first employed? 'The playhouse' (129) in the early 1580s points to either Burbage's Theatre or Laneman's Curtain, the first purpose-built public playhouses in the world. Their Shoreditch sites, not far north of Liverpool Street station, were chosen as being just outside the jurisdiction of the City authorities, who exercised strict control over players, repertory, performances and premises (such as the Boar's Head in Aldgate). Of the two, the Theatre is prima facie the more likely. It was and remains by far the more famous. Its classical Greek name soon became a synonym for such premises everywhere, in all languages. Aptly, the first recorded use of 'a theatre' as a generic term occurs in *Richard II* (V.iii.23), which helps to confirm the Theatre as Shakespeare's first choice.

Like the rest of his early career, it has been lost and forgotten, although in 1598 when its lease expired it literally became the Globe, after the transportation of its timbers across the Thames to Bankside. Its original builder, James Burbage (*c.* 1530–97), was the father of Richard Burbage (*c.* 1568–1619), named in the 1623 Folio as one of the 'Principal Actors' in Shakespeare's plays. This long-lasting and cordial relation, documented from 1594 (203) and continuing until Shakespeare's death and after, with a memorial bequest in his will, may have begun much earlier. Leicester's Men had performed in Stratford from 1573 onwards (66), for over a decade; James Burbage had been among them at that first recorded appearance.

The Shoreditch Theatre certainly housed Shakespeare. One of his only two recorded acting roles, the Ghost in *Hamlet*, was seen there (Lodge 1596, 56). From 1583, it was the London base of the newly-formed Queen's Men, with whom he had separate and strong historical links (VI). What work could he have found there, as a needy new-married country boy, while waiting for his various talents to be discovered? The Theatre happened to have its own adjacent slaughterhouse, where a butcher's apprentice would be useful. It was then approached across fields (then as now known as Finsbury), and hence on horseback, so that stabling facilities would be as essential as a car park today. The modern genteel Bard could not possibly have been an ostler; but the actual historical Shakespeare certainly could. Indeed, *pace* Schoenbaum (1975, 111–12), this occupation would be the obvious outlet for the skills and experience of a yeoman's eldest son in search of a living in the London theatreland of the 1580s.

Here too is a good reason why Greene (179) could unkindly call Shakespeare a 'groom', namely that he was known to have been one. Again the corroboration is unanimous: commentators stress 'serviture', 'mean Rank', 'poor boy', 'without money and friends', 'extreme end of ruin . . . very low degree of drudgery' (129) and so forth. The historical documents specifically associate Shakespeare's family with sheep and cattle, and him personally with calves, deer and rabbits. Of course he also knew how to ride and handle horses; and his sharp 'naturall witt' would have been well whetted by experience of the family business. No doubt he was indeed 'taken notice of for his diligence and skill', and 'conspicuous for his care and readiness' (129).

The plays and poems are eloquent about his detailed technical knowledge of horses,* their appearance and behaviour (*Venus and Adonis*, 260f), their tending (*1 Henry IV*, II.i), their breaking and training (*Henry VIII*, V.iii.55–66) and their complaints in every sense, whether diseases (*Taming of the Shrew*, III.ii.48f) or distresses (Sonnet 50). Just as in other animal contexts, the unmistakable tones of sympathy are the more persuasive and poignant for being uttered by the inflictor of pain or discipline. The imagery is equally characteristic (I); rebels are like unruly mounts who must be managed (*Henry VIII*, idem). In other contexts, the horse is not only a thing of beauty but a source of inspiration. Thus the Dauphin's Pegasus, 'pure air and fire' (*Henry V*, III.vii.11f), adored like a mistress, is also the latent image of 'The poet's eye, in a fine frenzy rolling/Doth glance from heaven to earth, from earth to heaven' (*Midsummer Night's Dream*, V.ii.12–13). The prancing horses seen in the mind's eye 'printing their proud hoofs i' th' receiving earth' (*Henry V*, Prologue 27) also resemble the artist, in equine equivalents for painting pictures or writing poems. Similarly the unconstrained colt's elated kicking of heels is a favourite metaphor of freedom as well as mere wilfulness (e.g. *Richard II*, II.i.70). Other horses, though more pedestrian, are no less lovingly observed: 'though patience be a tired mare, yet she will plod' (*Henry V*, II.i.24). And in the Sonnets 50 and 51 the steed becomes a character in the drama.

Then what was the next 'very mean employment' of the young theatre 'serviture' after he had been 'taken notice of' by the players and ⬅'recommended . . . to the house', the 'higher and more honourable employment within doors' on promotion from ostler (129)? Malone (1790, i.67) tells of a stage tradition (134) that Shakespeare became a call-boy or prompter; and this would be the natural next step up from the beginner's bottom rung. The boy actor who was employed to revise the

---

* All as in *Edmund Ironside*: 'reinéd with a marking-stall [martingale] . . . curb . . . bridle' (151–2).

defective plays of his seniors soon after his arrival in London, conversely, was always a figment of literary wish-fulfilment fantasy.

The house call-boy would be a perfect post for the aspiring young actor-playwright: it offers priceless experience in the management of exits and entrances and the learning of lines. Perhaps the favourite device of ending a scene with a rhymed couplet*, which would serve to alert an actor to an imminent entrance, was the young Shakespeare's idea?

As a prompter he would have a perfect opportunity in read-through and rehearsal, and as a stand-in at need, to display his native talents (83). Acting was the next logical stage. As a 'handsome well-shap't man' (Aubrey *c.* 1681) the young Shakespeare may well have created, in his own first playhouse the Theatre, the effect described in *Richard II* (V.ii.23–6):

> As in a theatre the eyes of men
> After a well-graced actor leaves the stage
> Are idly bent on him that enters next,
> Thinking his prattle to be tedious.

There is no report that he was ever a really outstanding performer; but his combined talents as actor-playwright would have been an asset to any Tudor company. He, conversely, with his well-attested diligence and acumen, would surely have sought to serve the leading troupe of the 1580s, the élite Queen's company. Membership offered unprecedented prospects of court performance, and perhaps even royal protection and preferment. The Queen's Men, recruited by her own command as 'a companie of players for her Maiestie' (Halliday 1964, 397–8), appeared at court in its very first season, 1583 to 1584, and presented plays to the paying public at the Shoreditch Theatre. The nineteen-year-old Shakespeare was not named among the dozen Queen's Men licensed by the City Corporation on 28 November 1583 to play 'at the sygnes of the Bull in Busshopesgate streete and the sygne of the Bell in Gratious [= Gracechurch] streete and nowheare els within this Cyttye'. But these early recruits included the famous comedian Richard Tarleton (XVII), who died in 1588. He is colourably claimed to have contributed to Hamlet's recollections of Yorick (V.i.184f); his jests (Sams 1988c, 38) are quoted in the 1603 first edition of that play, in a passage accepted as authentic by one modern edition (Spencer 1980, 276); an early version of *Hamlet* is mentioned in 1589 (160). Tarleton is called 'one of the first actors in Shakespeare's plays' in an eighteenth-century woodcut (Pitcher 1961, 175).

* See also *Edmund Ironside*: 'What after happens, with your patience/The entering actors gives intelligence' (1016–17), which cues the next entrance and soliloquy.

Shakespeare too had been a touring actor. As he says in Sonnet 110: 'Alas, 'tis true I have gone here and there/And made myself a motley to the view'. He confirms that he was poor and ignorant at first, and regrets that Fortune '. . . did not better for my life provide/Than public means which public manners breeds'.

Sonnet 153 may well contain a reference to early itineraries. It is a makeweight *pièce d'occasion*, out of the main sequence, like the 'Hathaway' Sonnet 145 and perhaps almost as early, in the same typical style of punning and word-play. The lines printed as 'I sick withall the helpe of bath desired/And thether hied a sad distemperd guest' would make good sense if 'bath' were capitalised. To the historian, this explanation is self-evident (Rowse 1964, 317); to the literary editor, embarrassing (Kerrigan 1986, 387). But that spa was already well known then for the medicinal properties of its hot springs. The Queen's Men visited the town on tour in 1588; according to Sidney Lee (7/1915, 82) 'Shakespeare's company' were there in 1587.

In the same season, the Queen's Men had performed at Stratford on Avon. Earlier that year, their leading serious actor William Knell had been killed in a duel; so they had a vacancy. 'Before leaving Stratford, had they enlisted Shakespeare, then aged twenty-three, as their latest recruit?' (Schoenbaum 1975, 90). No, not unless all the evidence for his far earlier departure is ignored, and he was content to be a farmer's (and butcher's) boy for ten years or more. He is far more likely to have gone to Stratford in 1587 as a Queen's Man than to have joined them there. His abilities and advancement might well have already put him in a position to propose Stratford as a staging-post, and one where he could surely count on a warm welcome and indeed a favourable fee authorised by his alderman father, whose civic duties included the payment and supervision of travelling troupes (VI). In fact the Queen's Men received twenty shillings (141) in 1587, the highest amount ever recorded as paid in Stratford to any one company. The further outlay of sixteen pence to repair a broken bench suggests overcrowded attendance and payment *pro rata*; perhaps the town had turned out in force to see its native son's success?

There is additional evidence that Shakespeare was a Queen's Man in the 1580s. The crucial facts are commonly left unmentioned (as in I. Wilson 1993) or incomplete and inaccurate (as in Schoenbaum 1975, 125 and 1977, 165). Shakespeare drew on the texts (not necessarily just his 'memory') of at least five (not 'three') Queen's plays from the 1580s (not 'old') as raw material (not just 'plot-sources') for his later and far more highly polished artefacts (VI). The earliest such work on record is *Felix and Philiomena*, written *c.* 1584 and acted before Elizabeth by her own company at Greenwich (135) in January 1585. This play is lost; but its plot was presumably based on Montemayor's tale of Felix and Felismena (1542 in Spanish, 1578 in French translation) which Shakespeare used in

The Two Gentlemen of Verona. Another early Queen's play of the 1580s, *The True Tragedy of Richard the Third,* was the source of certain ideas in *Richard III.* There is no reason to dismiss the former as 'probably a reported text' (Halliday 1964, 504); however poorly printed (Malone Society, 1929), it represents an original work by a Queen's dramatist. *The Famous Victories of Henry the Fifth,* written by 1587 and registered in 1594 (197), was also a Queen's play, well known to Shakespeare. Again its regular rejection as 'memorially reconstructed' (e.g. Taylor 1982, 4) has no basis but bias. Like two other popular Queen's plays of the same early period, *The True Chronicle History of King Leir* and *The Troublesome Reign of King John* (169, 170), it was drawn upon by Shakespeare for his own later versions of the same themes.

Of course the obvious inference from his close textual familiarity with such early plays, often before their publication, and his detailed use of them for his own prestige and profit, affords very much more than 'mere speculation' (Schoenbaum 1975, 125). Firstly, Shakespeare is thereby identifiable as an actor or a writer, or both, for the Queen's Men. The plays themselves, moreover, prima facie figure among his own early popular works (XXXIII), mentioned explicitly or implicitly by his earliest biographers (137), yet now just as ignored or forgotten as the theatre or the company for which, or the capacity in which, he worked for some ten or twelve years before being named and registered in the Lord Chamberlain's London company which he joined during 1594 – the year when 'the Queenes players . . . broke & went into the contrey to play' (Halliday 1964, 398).

XV

The Battle of the Books

THE YOUNG SHAKESPEARE'S early success with popular plays (137) would predictably provoke admiration or jealousy from fellow writers. So whatever can be colourably construed as a reference to him from the early 1580s onward may well be just such a reference. At least there are no reasons for rejecting any apparent allusion automatically, as 'too early'; and the relevant archives remain full of fierce rivalries and resentments that echo down the decades. No doubt 'it is difficult for us to realise the interest which, in the far more limited circle of Elizabethan writers and readers, such a quarrel could arouse' (McKerrow 1966, 65). But Shakespeare was certainly among the named and known belligerents in this battle of the books, and envy of him was among its main causes. His main direct enemy was Robert Greene (1558–92), whose young protégé Thomas Nashe (1567–c. 1601) collaborated with Christopher Marlowe (1564–93) in playmaking. In 1592, Greene famously called Shakespeare names including 'Shake-scene' (179); three years earlier, Nashe's preface to a novella by Greene (160) had attacked ex-grammar-school boys, naming Thomas Kyd (1558–94) and the author of *Hamlet*. Nashe also satirised the critic and scholar Gabriel Harvey (c. 1545–1630), who furiously fought back against both him and Greene. Harvey was a friend of the great poet Edmund Spenser (c. 1522–99). In 1592 the playwright and editor Henry Chettle (c. 1560–c. 1607) warmly defended Shakespeare and disparaged Marlowe, who was claimed by Greene as an ally, together with Nashe and the playwright George Peele (c. 1557–96) and perhaps Thomas Lodge, who also collaborated with Greene in playmaking.

Greene, Nashe, Marlowe and Lodge are thus linked by active collaboration; together with Peele, and the novelist and playwright John Lyly (c. 1554–1606), they constitute the so-called University Wits (V). The first three studied at Cambridge, the others at Oxford, and Greene at both. But the education of Thomas Kyd, as of Shakespeare, had stopped short at grammar school; and in this they were unlike every other known playwright of their period. Kyd was associated with Marlowe for a time (they shared a patron) but testified against him in 1593, identifying him as the source of lewd and blasphemous utterances (Freeman 1967, 29–30).

These facts draw clear lines for battle: Wits versus Grammarians. The former's enemies would be the latter's friends, and conversely. Of course fortunes and allegiances might fluctuate; but the neutral observer would expect to find Shakespeare and/or Kyd additionally attacked by Marlowe and/or Lodge as well as by Greene and Nashe, and defended by Harvey and/or Spenser as well as by Chettle (whose educational record is unknown). Alone among them, Shakespeare was also a known actor. So if any book of the period satirises a provincial lack-Latin actor-playwright who was already active and successful in the 1580s, then its intended butt was prima facie Shakespeare; and identifiably so to the book's readers, or the shafts would lose all point and miss their mark. That conclusion would be even clearer if the satirist were Robert Greene himself, the writer who is remembered chiefly if not solely for his attack on Shakespeare. And there, in the same book that contains that attack, stands just such a character, portrayed from and indeed to the life (179). Four hundred years later, his features are lost in the mists of 'late development' and 'late start'. Yet this unflattering likeness is clearly drawn on the same lines as the historical Shakespeare.

The book in question, *Greenes Groats-worth of Witte, boughte with a million of Repentance*, is usually regarded as a datable unity. In fact, as its long title implies and its editor Chettle confirms (182), it was a miscellany compiled from Greene's posthumous papers and published within four months of his death on 3 September 1592. Any of it might have been penned at any earlier period. In particular the famous attack on Shakespeare is so closely paralleled (XVI, Appendix) in Nashe's 1589 Preface to Greene's *Menaphon* as to suggest that earlier date for the former. The main *Groats-worth* component is clearly a *roman à clef*; its picaresque hero Roberto unsubtly represents Robert Greene. So who is the nameless X whom he meets on his travels, and dislikes? As depicted by Greene, X is besotted by his own insipid ideas, and in love with his own loud voice, which has 'terribly thundered on the stage'. He thus sounds very like a study, or understudy, for the leading player who was 'in his own conceit the only Shake-scene in a country'. By 1592 or earlier, X has served a seven-year theatrical apprenticeship on the stage, at the same period as the historical (though not the literary) Shakespeare. Although avowedly an author, X is forced to confess that he is a parasite on scholars (i.e. better playwrights, namely the University Wits) just as Greene complained about 'the only Shake-scene'. Although avowedly an actor, X is made to disparage members of his own profession as 'puppets', a word Greene also uses in jeering at 'Shake-scene'. This versatile and successful actor-author is servile, as befits a 'peasant' or 'rude groom', as Greene called 'Shake-scene'. He seems to have a yokel's accent, which is presumably why his voice sounds 'nothing gracious' to the sophisticated cosmopolitan Greene. Furthermore, X lacks education in general and Latin in particular, exactly as Shakespeare was regularly described. He trots out the tag *tempora mutantur*, and is depicted as pathetically nonplussed by it. He tugs his forelock to Greene the classics graduate: 'I know you know the meaning of it better than I.' Then he maladroitly tries to translate it, like a provincial schoolboy being taught a lesson: 'thus I conster [= construe] it, its otherwise now'. This tag may be another identity disc, like Nashe's 'Hamlet' or *'tempus edax rerum'* [time is voracious of all things, i.e. all-consuming] (XXIII, XXVI) from Ovid's Metamorphoses (XV. 234). It is not found in any accredited or attributed Shakespeare play. But its only known source is Harrison's 1577 *Description of Britain* which forms part of Holinshed's *Chronicles*, the most famous of all Shakespeare's source-books, and a work on which he was the only dramatist to draw extensively.

Again, Greene's X is over-pleased with his own rhymed jingles, like one of the 'rhyming mother-wits' ridiculed by Marlowe in *Tamburlaine*. He has written old-fashioned moralities, and also acted in more modern drama. He was famous for certain roles, such as Delphrigus and the King of the Fairies. At least the latter looks identifiable, as Oberon in Greene's own play *The Scottish Historie of James the Fourth*, of unknown date and not published until 1598. That would certainly have added extra irony to the encounter, and extra significance to the famous phrase 'Puppets . . . that spake from our mouths' and would mean that Shakespeare had profited by performing in plays by Greene himself, and those of other University Wits. In short, X has turned his multiple talents to whatever was required; the complete parvenu and entrepreneur, or Johannes Factotum. Thus he is able to affect dress and manners above his station, like the beautified crow and 'painted monster' he is; and he dares to patronise his betters, like the 'upstart' he is. These are, furthermore, exactly the tones and the tactics earlier employed by Greene's ally Nashe to put down the author of *Hamlet*.

Such sharp and repeated digs surely expose the root causes of all the quarrels. A rustic actor of the 1580s has also prospered prodigiously in the 1605 tract *Ratsei's Ghost*, where he is similarly characterised not only as mean and miserly ('feed upon all men . . . let none feed upon thee' etc.), but also as uncaring for 'them that before made thee proud with speaking their words upon the stage'. This too, like the 1600 to 1601 Parnassus plays and other sources, refers to past events and ancient quarrels still vivid in the literary world; again the charges of profiting and indeed profiteering from superior playwrights are exactly those that Greene brings against 'Shake-scene' and Nashe against the author of *Hamlet*. Finally, X is reported as asserting, apparently in all good faith, that he could make the gifted Greene just as rich as he. In fact, Greene died poor, sick, bitter and, in his own estimation, duped and exploited. Hence perhaps his enduring hatred, which also apparently surfaces in his *Groatsworth* fable of the Ant and the Grasshopper, and his label 'usurer', a trade well known to Shakespeare as his father's (III) if not indeed his own.

Schoenbaum objects (1975, 115) that X cannot well be Shakespeare, because the plays mentioned, *Man's Wit* and the *Dialogue of Dives*, 'belong to the pre-Shakespearean drama'. But only Shakespeare then, not

Schoenbaum now, could possibly know what was pre-Shakespearean. Nor is Greene, six years the older of the two, 'clearly represented as junior' (idem). Nor in any event would that pose the least difficulty, for the reason that Schoenbaum himself gives: the episode 'must be at least partly fanciful'. Further, Shakespeare saw himself, and as a weatherbeaten countryman and itinerant player presumably looked, much older than he was (cf 'beaten and chopped with tanned antiquity', Sonnet 62. 10). The common sense of the historian Rowse (1973, 51f) and others is far preferable; here prima facie (179) is Shakespeare's early stage career seen and distorted through the envious eyes of Greene.

A corrective lens brings the picture into sharp focus. Greene unwittingly portrays X as kind and thoughtful to the point of wishing others to share his own success and prosperity as a playwright. His acting and writing of morality or miracle plays in the 1580s adds new perspective to their manifest influence upon the young Shakespeare (VI). So does his declamation of the twelve labours of Hercules (also favourite topics in the canon). Indeed, according to Greene, X was among the very earliest writers of modern English drama, on the road with the Queen's Men in the 1580s. Further, X had dominated that drama, as one who 'for seven yeares space was absolute Interpreter to the puppets' [= actors]. Greene recorded those words in or by 1592 from his own clear recollection of an earlier encounter with the actor-playwright X, whose successful career had then already lasted seven years. So if X = Shakespeare, that career must have started in the early 1580s (XIV); and Dryden was indeed right to call him 'the father of our dramatic poets' and to apostrophise him thus:

> Untaught, unpractised, in a barbarous age,
> Thou founds't not, but created first, the stage.
>
> (Prologue to *Troilus and Cressida*, 1679)

XVI

Wits and their Butts

Marlowe

FROM THE MODERN 'late start' viewpoint, the University Wits won not only the battle of the books but the entire literary campaign. They are now typically hailed as 'the group of playwrights who, in the 1580s, transformed the native didactic interludes and shapeless chronicle histories into real plays by giving them dramatic form and inspiring them with vigorous action and the energy of their poetry' (Halliday 1964, 510). They are named (XV) as Marlowe, Greene and Nashe (from Cambridge) and Lyly, Lodge and Peele (from Oxford). Shakespeare (removed prematurely from Stratford grammar school) is supposed to have stayed silent until his late twenties, by which time Greene and Marlowe were dead and the rest wrote little, so he 'entered into his inheritance with no important rival in the field' (Halliday idem).

But what if he had begun in the 1580s, and thus created the stage, as Aubrey and Rowe imply and Dryden asserts? The dramatist best placed to transform shapeless plays would be one who had written them, like Greene's X, and then developed as an artist; the dramatist best known for form, action and poetry is Shakespeare, who was also an assiduous reviser. And who would be more likely to bridge the aesthetic and social gap than a self-taught writer who had to acquire his own classical models, as great critics from Dryden to Housman have characterised Shakespeare? All the many manifestos from the University Wits, conversely, aim to discourage the climb up from popular to serious art and indeed to kick away the ladder. Among the earliest and most outspoken was Marlowe's attack on his rival predecessors in the prologue to *Tamburlaine, c.* 1587, which begins thus:

> From jigging veins of rhyming mother-wits*
> And such conceits as clownage keeps in pay,
> We'll lead you to the stately tent of war
> Where you shall hear the Scythian Tamburlaine
> Threaten the world in high astounding terms . . .

---

* Cf *Edmund Ironside* 1149: 'Trust a mother-wit'.

In other words, Marlowe announces the advent of a new high-class drama designed to replace the current low-class shows, which often included actual jigs and other antics. In the earlier 1580s, such popular entertainments were provided by the Queen's Men, whether in town or on tour, with Shakespeare apparently among them. Marlowe, after taking his Cambridge M.A. in 1587, went to London and served their competitors the Admiral's Men, formed *c.* 1585. Any target he attacked, whether company or writer, might be expected to retaliate in kind. The only known direct counter occurs in the Queen's Men's play *The Troublesome Reign of King John, c.* 1588. Although no longer than average, it was printed as two separate parts in frank imitation of *Tamburlaine*; and its prologue begins with an overt rejoinder and rebuke to Marlowe, addressed to groundlings rather than graduates:

> You that with friendly grace of smoothéd brow
> Have entertained the Scythian Tamburlaine
> And given applause unto an Infidel
> Vouchsafe to welcome, with like courtesy,
> A warlike Christian and your countryman.

This sounds affable enough on the surface. Deeper down, it harbours resentment. 'An Infidel' may hit back at Marlowe himself, who was a reputed atheist. Another popular play of the later 1580s, *The Taming of A Shrew*, deliberately burlesques *Tamburlaine* and *Dr Faustus* by quotation and parody.

Greene

It was also in about 1587 that Greene first attacked a fellow playwright, in his *Farewell to Folly* (**146**). He flouts at the anonymous play *Faire Em*, which he typically identifies by quotation, not by name. His readers are assumed to know the work and its writer. Greene spitefully says that the passages in question constitute 'simple abusing of Scripture. In charity [*sic*] be it spoken, I am persuaded the sexton of St. Giles without Cripplegate would have been ashamed of such blasphemous rhetoric. But not to dwell in the imperfection of these dunces, or trouble you with a long commentary of such witless coxcombs, Gentlemen,' etc. Blasphemy was a serious crime as well as a mortal sin, so these are grave indictments. But they are also baseless, as textual study shows. Which playwright had already so enraged the Protestant Greene, by 1587, as to provoke so savage an onslaught?

In his *Penelope's Web* (**146**), also published in 1587, Greene writes: 'they which smiled at the *Theatre* in Rome [= London] might as soon scoff at the rudeness of the *scoene* as give a Plaudite at the perfection of the action'. In other words, the acting at the Shoreditch Theatre (XIV) was good but the staging and writing crude. Greene then refers to those who 'pass over my toys with silence', i.e. fail to appreciate his own plays, or worse still reject them for performance. Perhaps he had eagerly written and submitted a play, as X had suggested to him (XV) only to have it passed over in silence? Clearly there has been some such slight; and this rivalry rankles.

So does the criticism of his own work, which is the main *casus belli* in these battles. Greene says so in his *Pandosto*, published in 1588, which castigates those who 'seek with their slanderous reproaches to carp at all, being often-times most unlearned of all' (151). So his plays have again been rejected, even by his social and intellectual inferiors. Again, these were presumably not ordinary playgoers but one or more fellow playwrights. Their lack of education is doubly deplorable, being so totally atypical; all the rest were University Wits, whose work these upstarts dare to denigrate. Worse still, their adverse judgements had apparently proved influential in practice; so they were in a position of some power, perhaps as advisers to a theatre company. Again Greene's attack is personal, directed against one or two people, whose identity his readers were meant to recognise.

In *Perimedes the Blacksmith* (151), also in 1588, Greene mentions one of the mottoes that he often appended to his title-pages, and complains that 'two gentleman poets . . . had it in derision', through the agency of actors on the London stage. The motto in question was the first three words of Horace's dictum that 'omne tulit punctum qui miscuit utile dulci', he gains every vote [i.e. all praise him] who unites what is useful with what is pleasant. Such fulsome and public self-praise surely invited derision. Again, among much obscurity, Greene's hatred for two playwrights still blazes. His description of them as gentlemen is surely intended ironically. He brands them as 'mad and scoffing poets', and their work 'impious instances of intolerable poetry', again with the same charge of irreligion. Their clearest criticism had been 'that I could not make my verses jet upon the stage like the fa-burden of Bow-bell, daring God out of heaven with that atheist Tamburlaine'; in other words, his own 1587 play *Alphonsus, King of Arragon*, intended to rival *Tamburlaine*, had been rejected by these two playwrights as mere imitation Marlowe.

The same cauldron of resentment continues to simmer in Greene's next published work, the bland romantic novella *Menaphon* (160), registered in August 1589. It contains no overt literary feuding. But its preface, by the young Thomas Nashe, is a savage satire on certain unnamed but readily identifiable writers. This preface quotes from *Menaphon*, as if that work too had continued the same campaign of calumny; and indeed it is no mere romance, despite appearances. Greene's shepherd Doron is despised as a mere countryman plain and simple, just like the actor-playwright X encountered in *Groats-worth*. The two characters share the same traits, such as self-satisfaction and mock-modesty, in similar turns of phrase. 'How like you this Dittie of mine own devising, quoth *Doron*?'; 'Was this not prettie for a plain rime extempore?' asks X, who also self-disparagingly offers 'such simple comfort as my ability may yield'; cf 'As well as I can, answered Doron, I will make description . . .'. The 'countrey Author' X 'can serve to make a pretie speech'; the shepherd Doron's eclogue is 'stufft with prettie Similies and far-fetched metaphors', which will later form the gravamen of Greene's charge against the 'Shake-scene' with his typical 'tiger's heart' line in a similarly exaggerated style. Doron's other poetic efforts entail inept Latin allusions, classical personifications and juxtapositions of the exotic with the everyday. An actual style is being cruelly parodied as pretentious, and an actual person gratuitously insulted as a rustic clown. Doron, Greene slyly tells his readers, had a brother called Moron; the whole family are as simple-minded as their own sheep.

Greene's autobiographical *Never Too Late*, published in 1590, includes yet another attack on actors, again in the course of a feigned comparison between the theatrelands of modern London and of ancient Rome. There too, actors were allegedly 'mean men, greedy of gains' who 'grew rich and insolent'. One in particular is referred to as 'Roscius', after his Roman predecessor; but the reader is left in little doubt that a latterday London celebrity is aimed at. The Greene character cries 'Why *Roscius*, art thou proud with *Esops* crow, being pranct [= pranked] with the glorie of others feathers? Of thyself thou canst say nothing . . .'. This actor too wears 'costly roabes', like the £200 of playing apparel owned by Greene's actor-playwright X (**179**). No doubt this attack is aimed at specialist actors such as Edward Alleyn, who made a fortune; but affluent actor-playwrights were clearly included.

Finally comes the famous overt attack on 'Shake-scene' in the so-called *Groats-worth of Witte* edited by Henry Chettle (**182**) after its author's death in 1592. That year was a terminus, not a date of composition. Greene's trains of thought consistently ran on the same lines and took a long time in transit. There is no evidence that he penned this lampoon 'on his death-bed' (Halliday 1964, 196, among many others), or for the equally tall tale that his demise was directly due to a surfeit of Rhenish wine and pickled herring in the previous month (again often taken for fact, e.g. by Schoenbaum 1975, 114). On the contrary, though the evidence seems to have passed unnoticed, Greene was surely dying of his self-confessed syphilis. He is outspokenly specific about his life-style in the 1580s and its sequelae: 'the loathsome scourge of lust tyrannised in [my] bones' . . . 'for my adultery, [I suffer] ulcerous sores'. He explicitly likens his own lot to that of George Peele, who was 'driven (as my selfe) to extreme shifts'; Peele died four years later, 'of the poxe' according to Francis Meres in *Palladis Tamia* 1598. Syphilis was a scourge of artists in London as in other European capitals, from the fifteenth century to the twentieth. Its victims rarely retained their creative skills until their dying day. Greene had surely been incubating his disease, like his grudge, for some years.

On any assessment, his expressions 'Shake-scene', 'upstart Crow' and 'Johannes Factotum' need not denote a Johnny-come-lately. On the contrary; the playwright thus described must surely have been already successful. He was an upstart in the social sense of parvenu (OED A sb. 1), who had risen to prominence from mean beginnings. The implied 'Jack of all trades but master of none' would be an effective thrust at an adversary known or thought to have been a moneylender (III), a butcher (VIII), a schoolmaster (X), a law-clerk (XI), a deer-poacher (XII), an ostler (XIV), a call-boy (XIV), a translator and a pamphleteer (XVI, Nashe, *infra*) as well as an actor and a playwright, all by 1589.

What Greene says, finally, accords so closely with his own tones and terms from 1587 onwards, and those of his younger crony and protégé Nashe in 1589, as to leave little room for doubt about the close consultation between those two, in a common cause. From his first intervention onwards, Nashe speaks in his master's ventriloquising voice, as recorded in the Appendix to this section. Already in 1589, Nashe had access to Greene's opinion in Greene's words, whether spoken, printed or written, which is another reason for assigning the latter's attack on 'Shake-scene', like the former's on the author of *Hamlet*, to 1589 rather than 1592. If so, Greene's unkind parody of the Shakespeare line 'o tiger's heart wrapped in a woman's hide', which he must have heard spoken on the stage, might entail a date of *c.* 1588 for the play concerned, namely *The True Tragedy of Richard, Duke of York* (XXVII).

Nashe

Nashe's 1589 Preface to *Menaphon* (160) offers just the same insults and gibes as Greene (italicised in the following summary so as to bring out their family resemblance as shown in the Appendix to this section). Certain playwrights, says Nashe, are so *blasphemous* that they 'repose eternity in the mouth of a player', and so *uneducated* that they have almost no 'learning in their skull'. They are also *actors* ('vainglorious tragedians') who have soared so far above their station that they act as *critics*; they 'will take upon them to be the ironical censors of all'. Yet they are shamelessly *lower-class* (their art comes from 'a serving-man's idleness') and populist, *passim*. By implication, this class of person writes comedies; Greene had noted and hated the smiles among the audience at the Shoreditch Theatre. By Nashe's direct statement, they also write Senecan tragedies, such as a play called *Hamlet*. Nashe affects to deplore such *plagiarism*, from Ovid and Cicero among other sources, especially in its reliance on English translation by those who *lack Latin*. His satirical shafts would be pointless unless they could be seen to strike home on actual targets. But all literary London would know the grammar-school playwrights and their Senecan plays of the 1580s, full of vengeance and violence, such as Kyd's *Spanish Tragedy* and Shakespeare's *Hamlet* and *Titus Andronicus** (163, 175, 192).

Everyone could also see and hear Nashe acting as Greene's spokesman or mouthpiece. The former's satire on London literary life, addressed to 'The Gentlemen Students of Both Universities', is so obviously alien to Greene's bland pastoral style in *Menaphon*, which it purports to introduce, that their collusion is clear from the first.

In 1589, Nashe had just come down from St John's, Cambridge, which he eulogises in his preface. It was also Greene's college. Their relation of mentor and protégé is confirmed in other writings; thus Greene's *Groatsworth* advises his young friend, playfully named 'Juvenal' after the Roman satirist, to be less savage in his onslaughts, while Nashe in *Strange News* 1592 loyally defends the dead Greene against the enraged attacks of Gabriel Harvey. Nashe would be permitted to make his first appearance in print under Greene's aegis on condition that he aired Greene's grievances. In fact his 1589 Preface not only echoes the earlier Greene sources already cited (XVI) but also cites the actual text of *Menaphon* as if this too had special polemical significance, about which he was well placed to know. Thus his jeer at playwrights who 'think themselves more than initiated in poets immortalitie, if they but once get *Boreas* [= god of the north wind] by the beard, and the heauenlie bull by the deaw-lap' is borrowed from Greene's naive rustic shepherd Doron, whose poetic pretensions and lack of classical learning produce comically far-fetched comparisons between earthy reality and heavenly ideals. 'Wee had, answered *Doron*, an Eaw amongst our Rams, whose fleece was as white as the haires that grow on father *Boreas* chin, or as the dangling deawlap of the siluer Bull . . .'. The Boreas phrase is cited from *The Taming of A Shrew*: 'Whiter than . . . the . . . icy hair that grows on Boreas' chin' (I.ii.150). In the Senecan play *Titus Andronicus* the constellation Taurus is handled like a real bull (IV.iii.70–72), which collides with Aries the Ram. Nashe links Boreas' beard with the bull by 'and', as if the same hand were applied to both.

Nashe also cites, as an equally readable identity tag, *tempus edax rerum*. That phrase was far less famous and familiar then than now; and the Sonnets, with their scores of Ovidian allusions including 'devouring time' (19.1) were mostly still unwritten in 1589 and remained unpublished for another twenty years. But Tudor theatre-goers would already have heard those Latin words spoken on the stage in a popular play, namely *The Troublesome Reign of King John*, among many other such references. The same *Metamorphoses* line (XV.234), linked with its continuation, is heard

---

* The only other evident example is *Edmund Ironside*.

in *The Taming of A Shrew*: 'the teeth of fretting time may ne'er untwist' (III.vi.75). Only one Tudor poet was ever explicitly identified with such diction: as the well-informed classicist Francis Meres noted in 1598, 'the sweete wittie soul of Ovid liues again in' Shakespeare.

Nashe also supplies an ineptly homely translation of *tempus edax rerum*, 'where's that will last always?', just as Greene's X had crudely construed *tempora mutantur* as 'tis otherwise now'. These Latinless dunces, whose education stopped at grammar-school level, even misunderstand their own pretentious allusions; so the University Wits seek to suggest. Nashe sarcastically calls them 'deep-read Grammarians'. Yet they dare to 'vaunt *Ovids* and *Plutarchs* plumes as their own . . . in disguised arraie' and indeed adapt 'whole sheetes and tractates *verbatim* from the plentie of *Plutarch* and *Pliny*', as well as draining Seneca dry. All these are nowadays well known as Shakespeare's special sources; only bias forbids him to have found them as early as 1589. In fact, *Titus Andronicus c.* 1589 is deeply indebted to both Seneca and Ovid for its plot and incident, and it not only quotes the latter's *Metamorphoses* (IV.iii.4) but brings that actual volume on stage as a named property (IV.i.41). Pliny the Elder wrote the comprehensive *Historia Naturalis*; Plutarch's *Lives of the Noble Greeks and Romans* was translated from the Greek in 1579; Shakespeare was demonstrably indebted to both sources (Anders 1904, 36, 40) in his Folio plays, and his knowledge of Ovid and Seneca was acquired and used very early.*

Not only *Titus c.* 1589 but the lost 1589 *Hamlet* derives from Seneca. That is the whole point of Nashe's accusation; and his reference to 'tragical speeches . . . if you intreat him fair in a frosty morning' manifestly defines the first scene of *Hamlet* ('tis bitter cold', I.i.8) and the Senecan ghost whose search for revenge (as in *Thyestes*) initiates the action. In those words, indeed, Nashe may well be alluding more directly to Shakespeare, whose best-remembered role was the same Ghost in the same play (Rowe 1709). 'English Seneca' may also be intended as a direct description of the playwright, which would again serve among the necessary means of satirical identification, with the secondary meaning that the playwrights thus pilloried borrow from the 1581 translation of Seneca's tragedies (113) because their own small Latin would not stretch that far. Of course Nashe does not really mean that they are wholly illiterate in Latin; if so, they would not be worth attacking at all. The point is their mere smattering.

This is succinctly suggested in Nashe's further gibe that such playwrights as the author of *Hamlet* 'take up choice of words by exchange' in *Tullies Tusculane*. That source, the *Tusculan Disputations* of Marcus Tullius

---

* Items of Plinian natural history (vipers 167, basilisks 1652, etc.), allusions to Ovid (Deucalion and Pyrrha 180–83, Cadmus 425, etc.) together with a reference to and a quotation from Plutarch (777, 1555–6) all occur in the Senecan play *Edmund Ironside*.

Cicero, was known to Nashe in 1589; in his *Anatomy of Absurdity* published
in that year, he quotes from the introduction to its first dialogue which
concerns life after death. Its focal point is Cicero's dictum (VI.14) that in
logic as in eschatology entities must either exist or not: 'id aut esse aut
non esse', *anglice* 'to be or not to be,* ay, there's the point', as the 1603
First Quarto puts it. Cicero has just mentioned (V.10) the 'iudices' or
judges of the underworld Minos and Rhadamanthus, and Hamlet fears to
be 'borne before an everlasting judge'.

Nashe says that such plagiaristic playwrights of the late 1580s would
also 'borrow invention of *Ariosto*', whose *I Suppositi* was a source of *The
Taming of A Shrew*; no other Shrew play was then known. Once again,
such writers are denounced for their pretentious style; they 'think to
outbrave better pens [such as Marlowe's, and Greene's] with the swelling
bumbast of a bragging blank verse'. They also suffer from 'the ingrafted
overflow of some kilcow conceipt'. This is the first recorded use of the
contemptuous epithet 'kill-cow'; it would certainly suit the only playwright ever described as a butcher-boy who killed cattle (VIII). He and his
like also 'bodge out a blank verse with ifs and ands'; and the trick of
beginning consecutive lines of verse with the same unimportant word
characterises both Kyd and the young Shakespeare. In the former's *Spanish Tragedy*, four consecutive lines begin with 'And' (II.i.122–5) and three
with 'If' (III.xiii.99–101; cf also ibid. 14, 16, 18); in a passage of *Titus
Andronicus*, eleven lines (including groups of three, three and two con-
secutively) begin with 'And' (IV.i.87–108).†

Nashe's writers are impecunious; they 'feed on nought but the
crummes that fal from the translators trencher'. So they are the 'trivial
translators' with whom Nashe ironically offers to 'talk a little in friendship', in other words berate them on Greene's behalf. It can hardly be
coincidence that when Chettle comes to defend Shakespeare against
Greene (**182**) he drags in a laborious reference to 'two very sufficient [=
competent, capable] Translators'. Nashe's targets in 1589 'intermeddle
with Italian translations' and publish them as 'pamphlets', i.e. slim quarto
volumes, as he also described Greene's *Groats-worth*. He has earlier complained of 'the Italionate pen' and borrowings from Ariosto's countrymen. In 1588, Kyd published a translation of Tasso's *Padre di Famiglia*
entitled *Householder's Philosophy*; *Tarleton's News out of Purgatory*, which has
been attributed to Shakespeare (Everitt 1954, 30), draws on Italian
sources.

Nashe's victims can also understand French; they 'spend two or three
howers in turning over' dubious books in that language. Kyd translated

---

* Cf Nashe's 1591 allusion, in his preface to Sidney's *Astrophel and Stella*, to the
  style of those writers who 'sit taboring five years together nothing but "to be,
  to be" on a paper drum'.
† Cf *Edmund Ironside*, where lines 525–6 and 528–9 also begin with 'And'.

Garnier's *Cornelia*, and Shakespeare used Belleforest's *Histoires tragiques*
for *Hamlet* among other plays. To visit the booksellers in the 'inner parts
of the city' [i.e. St Paul's], Nashe explains, his playwrights 'make a
peripateticall path', i.e. they lived some distance away; the Folger Library
copy of the legal textbook *Archaionomia* (152), signed 'Wm. Shakespeare'
(XI, XXXV) bears a Westminster address (153). Until recently, says
Nashe, their main trade was that of lawyer's copy-clerk or scrivener
('*Noverint* . . . whereto they were born'). This sufficiently identifies Kyd,
who was indeed a scrivener by trade, like his father (Freeman 1967, 2),
and whose handwriting shows signs of legal training (Greg 1925, 1, XV).
But it also applies, with ample sufficiency for the satirist's purpose, to
Shakespeare (XI), whose father was a law officer for a time, and whose
known handwriting has been identified by accredited experts (e.g. E.
Thompson 1916, 1923) as inscribed in the style of a trained law-clerk.
Furthermore, Nashe is speaking of the author of *Hamlet*, and calling him
a noverint, a category found in Westminster, near the law-courts, where
Nashe himself later locates them in *Pierce Penniless*. In 1589, Shakespeare
and his parents were jointly pursuing, through a Westminster law-court,
a claim for rights in land and buildings that had once been Shakespeare's
patrimony.

Nashe further implies that his detested playwrights share lodgings,
where he has seen them together, or otherwise discovered their practice
of starching their beards most curiously and writing by candlelight, as if
they were employed during daylight hours and wrote their despised plays
or frequented their shady City booksellers in the evening. If the diminutive Nashe thus visited them at candle-time, that would explain why
Shakespeare caricatured him in turn as the miniature Moth in *Love's
Labour's Lost*.

Nashe's victims also ignorantly 'thrust *Elisium* into hell, and have not
learned . . . the iust measure of the Horizon without an hexameter'. In
Kyd's *The Spanish Tragedy*, the Senecan ghost describes the Elysian fields as
his abode; the equally early play *Locrine*, attributed to 'W.S.' on its title-
page, and the collection of tales from Italian sources *Tarleton's News out of
Purgatory*, both locate Elisium in the vicinity of hell. The reference to
'horizon' seems to mean that the poets concerned cannot pronounce or
scan the word properly, and Shakespeare certainly stresses the first syllable in *3 Henry VI* (IV.vii.81) as in its earlier version *The True Tragedy of
Richard, Duke of York c.* 1589.

Nashe is pillorying more playwrights than one, as his repeated plurals
insist; and not all his allusions can now be elucidated. But so detailed a
description could hardly apply to more than two writers. Tudor readers
would readily recognise them, as they would Chettle's explicit 'two . . .
translators'. On the evidence, they are Shakespeare and Kyd. By direct
inference, they roomed and worked and wrote together in the later
1580s; no wonder there are such close textual affinities between *Hamlet*
and *The Spanish Tragedy* (Jenkins 1982, 97f).

Nashe continues to repeat, often in the same language, the 1589 Greene-inspired accusations about ignorant upstart peasants who progress through various base employments (including law-clerking) to undeserved prosperity as actors and authors, while remaining dependent upon their betters in either of those last two guises, because they are mere parasites and parrots. These charges, already copious and explicit in the 1589 *Menaphon* Preface (**160**), are supplemented in the 1589 *Anatomy of Absurdity* (**149**), and are prolonged and often intensified after Greene's death, in the 1592 *Pierce Penniless* and the 1593 *Terrors of the Night*.

Henry Chettle, in his *Kindhart's Dream* (1592), offers a compelling but neglected explanation for this. He imagines Greene calling for revenge from beyond the grave, like a Senecan spectre or the ghost in *Hamlet*. That appeal is addressed to 'Pierce Pennilesse', which was the name that Nashe gave himself in his 1592 satire thus entitled. Chettle had no known quarrel with either of them, and no reason to misrepresent or exaggerate their feelings. Yet he tells us how Greene wished to exhort Nashe, in strong terms, thus: 'Awake (secure boy) reuenge thy wrongs, remember mine: thy adversaries began the abuse, they continue it: if thou suffer it, let thy life be short in silence and obscuritie, and thy death hastie, hated, and miserable'.

As if in obedience to this injunction, Nashe's *Pierce Penniless* is indeed aimed at exactly the same targets as before. Furthermore, it again identifies Shakespeare, by the same Greene-Nashe technique of quoting his work, with which the theatre-going public would be perfectly familiar. The authorship of *1 Henry VI* for example has been disputed or disintegrated only by modern editors (e.g. Taylor 1988, 217), not by readers or audiences of any era. In the 1590s, all literary London would know who wrote the play in which brave Talbot was described, in words which Nashe cites verbatim as 'the terror of the French' (I.iv.42). Nashe grudgingly acknowledges this patriotric evocation of a historical hero. But he begins by renewing his accusations of plagiarism: 'for the most part [the subject of plays] is borrowed out of our English Chronicles'. Then he shows a scholar's scorn for the mass audiences ('ten thousand spectators at least, at several times') and their naive empathy ('in the tragedian that represents [Talbot's] person, [they] imagine they behold him fresh bleeding!'). Extant documents (**173**, **174**, **176**) confirm the packed houses, and the accuracy of Nashe's attendance figures; at a penny per place, *1 Henry VI* would indeed have been seen, at the Rose Theatre between March and May 1592, by some 10,000 spectators, including Nashe, whose comments were written and registered by August of the same year (**177**). He is silent about the play's inherent poetic or dramatic merits, by which he was presumably just as unimpressed as he was by the 'tragical speeches' in *Hamlet*, or as Greene was by the 'tiger's heart' style of *True Tragedy*. But the facts confirm that the author of *1 Henry VI* had good cause to consider himself 'the only Shake-scene in a country'. That name might even have been meant literally. No doubt the same scene shook when the cannon was fired ('here they shoot', I.iv.69); rival plays and competing play-wrights were among the casualties.

Nashe instantly follows his allusion to *1 Henry VI* by parallel praise of the pageantry in *The Famous Victories of Henry V*, as if that too was by Shakespeare. It is not thus recognised now. But the play that has 'Henry the Fifth represented on the stage, leading the French king prisoner, and forcing both him and the Dolphin to swear fealty', is (*pace* Taylor 1984, 4) surely *Famous Victories*, which has been cogently claimed as early Shakespeare (by Pitcher 1961; see also Sams 1993d, 183).

On any assessment, Nashe continues to aim at Shakespeare, in a continued campaign unmitigated by Greene's death. The satirist's readers, then as now, have to understand the occasion for these firework displays; otherwise the squibs fizzle out. Above all they have to know who is being guyed. And the victims are, predictably, the same straw men in *Pierce Penniless*, written in 1592, as in *Menaphon* three years earlier.

Who are 'these men' against whom the two main Wits, singly or collectively, so tirelessly fulminate? Their categories are clear-cut. 'They' are (a) law-clerks, who (b) lack education in general, and (c) Latin in particular, despite attendance at (d) the local grammar school, where 'they' had 'some little sprinkling of Grammer learning in their youth' (*The Terrors of the Night* 1594). 'They' are also (e) suspiciously popish and indeed (f) Italianate, as betrayed by (g) the very cut of their beards. 'They' are also (h) usurers. But above all 'they' are (i) authors, and in particular (j) poets, (k) playwrights, and (l) pamphleteers, as well as (m) influential critics and (n) actors, though 'they' began as (o) provincial peasants, and are thus (p) upstarts. 'They' are also (r) in need of advice. Nashe adds new categories: 'they' are (s) reckless young rogues (t) supported by (u) their country fathers who though impoverished (v) come to London (w) in search of gentility, and indeed a family motto (x) which 'they' also seek (y) in the interest of (z) their own patrimony and their own incongruously high social status.

Of course Nashe is writing a general satire on Tudor society at large. But it cannot be coincidence that *Pierce Penniless* identifies Shakespeare, as the playwright of *1 Henry VI*, and also castigates *twenty-six* other categories, singly or in combination, to which Shakespeare certainly or arguably belonged, in passages that cluster in separate parts of *Penniless* (pp. 54–75, 92, 112–17, 139–40: here and below the Nashe page numbers are those of Steane 1972).

(a) law-clerks.
The Devil himself 'is as formal as the best scrivener of them all . . . To Westminster Hall I went, and made a search of enquiry [for the Devil] from the black gown to the buckram bag [i.e. from the higher to the lower ranks of lawyers] (p. 57); cf Greene 1592, 'these buckram gentlemen' [such as Shakespeare].

(a, b) lowly law-clerks who are also (i) authors.
'Not a base ink-dropper, or scurvy plodder at *Noverint*, but nails his asses' ears on every post, and comes off with a long *circumquaque* to the gentlemen readers' [an exordium in a published book] (p. 140).

(a, b) poorly educated law-clerks who are also (h) usurers.
'a scrivener [is] better paid for an obligation [a loan] than a scholar for the best poem he can make . . .' (pp. 53–4); cf Greene 1592, 'usurer', and Nashe's 1589 reference in *Menaphon* (160) to grammar-school boys who are no better than usurers: 'Grammarians who [have] no more learning in their skull than will serve to take up a commodity', which is a technical term of usury (OED 7b) first cited from Greene 1590.

(a, c) lawyers who, amazingly, lack Latin.
'a number of needy lawyers . . . that would go near to poison [people] with false Latin' (pp. 60–61).

(a, j, x) lawyers and poets as the best advocates for honours.
'how much better it is . . . to have an elegant lawyer to plead one's cause . . . for a gentleman to have his honour's story related . . . by a poet than a citizen' (p. 92): cf also 'gave their upstart fathers titles of gentry' (p. 64). John Shakespeare's application for arms was certainly supported by his son, who could be called a lawyer as well as a poet.

(a, l) lawyers who are also pamphleteers.
'such of you as frequent Westminster Hall [the main legal centre, where the Shakespeares' suit was heard in 1589], let them be circumspect what dunghill papers they bring hither; for one bad pamphlet is enough to raise a damp that may poison a whole term' (p. 139: cf 'the trade of Noverint . . . their twopenny pamphlets' (Nashe *Menaphon*)).

(a, o, p, u) lawyers whose fathers were mere peasants.
'the common lawyers (suppose in the beginning they are but husbandmen's sons)' (p. 75).

(c, i) authors who, incredibly, lack Latin.
'Alas, poor Latinless authors, they are so simple they know not what to do . . .' (p. 92); cf 'could scarcely latinise their neck-verse, if they should have need' (p. 474).

(d, e, r, s) grammar-school boys popishly affected and in need of advice.
Religion is among the causes of this war. Nashe and Greene were both anti-papist propagandists. The writers that Nashe derides as 'idle wits' (*Anatomy* 1589) were sent 'to shrift to the vicar of S. Fooles, who instead of a worser may be such a Gothamist's [= village idiot's] ghostly Father [Catholic confessor]'. This seems to hit at the same strange dependence as that already pilloried by Greene in his *Farewell to Folly* (146), who rails at a writer who 'cannot write true Englishe without the help of Clearkes of parish Churches', alias 'the sexten of Saint Giles', who may well also be

Nashe's 'vicar of S. Fooles'. In *Pierce Penniless* 'they' 'contemne Arts [=
scholarship] as vnprofitable, contenting themselues with a little Countrey
Grammer knowledge, god wote, thanking God with that abscedarie Priest
in Lincolnshire, that he neuer knewe what that Romish popish Latine
meant'; cf also 'deep read Grammarians' (Nashe *Menaphon*).

(f, g, j, p) Italianate eccentrically-bearded upstart love-poets.
'The nature of an Upstart . . . he will sonnet a whole quire of paper in praise
of . . . his . . . mistress . . . All *Italianato* is his talk, and his spade peak [cut of
beard] is sharp . . .' (p. 64) cf 'intermeddle with Italian translations . . .
having starched their beards most curiously . . .' (Nashe *Menaphon*).

(m) influential critics.
'shallow-brained censurers' (p. 112), cf the 'upstart reformers of art' that
'will take upon them to be the ironical censors of all' (Nashe *Menaphon*);
and 'others will flout and over-read every line with a frump, and say "tis
scurvy"' and 'pass over my toys [plays] in silence' and 'carp at all', as
Greene complained in 1587 and 1588.

*(o, p, s, t, u, v, w, z) peasant upstarts concerned with their patrimonies and supported
by impoverished country fathers in London, all in search of gentility.*
'swears . . . that ne'er a such peasant as his father or brother shall keep him
under', 'ungrateful peasants [raised] from the dunghill of obscurity' (p. 54),
'carterly upstarts, that outface town and country in their velvets, when Sir
Rowland Russet-coat, their dad . . . hath much ado, poor penny-father, to
keep his unthrift elbows in reparations. Marry, happy are they (say I) that
have such fathers to work for them while they play . . . [and] consume
their patrimonies' (p. 55) (cf 'spending that in their velvets which was
raked up in a russet coat . . . having lewdly spent their patrimony', p. 471),
'learning, that gave their upstart fathers titles of gentry' (p. 64), 'The Nature
of an Upstart' (p. 64), 'The Pride of Peasants sprung up of Nothing . . .
upstart gallants . . . without desert or service are raised from the plough to
be checkmates with princes' (p. 69), 'men by their mechanical [labouring]
trades . . . come to be . . . gentlemen and . . . burgomasters' (p. 70), 'drawn
up to the heaven of honour from the dunghill of abject fortune . . .' (p. 71),
'Drudges, that have no extraordinary gifts of body or mind, filch themselves into some nobleman's service' (p. 71), 'peasants that come out of the
cold of poverty, once cherished in the bosom of prosperity, will straight
forget that ever there was a winter of want' (p. 72); cf also 'every mechanical mate' (Nashe *Menaphon*) and Greene's 1592 use of this same Aesop
allusion in his fable of the Ant and the Grasshopper, also with overtones of
financial unfairness (Honigmann 1982, 2f). Again, 'upstart' and 'peasant'
also famously figure in Greene's attack on Shakespeare.

(x) a family motto.
'without mustard . . . not without mustard, good Lord, not without mustard' (p. 67). When that phrase was used by Ben Jonson in 1599, it was

taken to be a parody of the motto included in the coat of arms that Shakespeare had applied for on his father's behalf in 1596: 'non sanz droict'. So it is interpreted still (Chambers 1930, ii, 202). Perhaps Nashe knew of John Shakespeare's earlier application for arms (76), *c.* 1576, which prima facie proposed the same motto.

There are many more links and cross-references that elude closer classification; thus the mélange of love poetry, sonnets, Catholicism, Italianate influences, a nobleman's service and hobnobbing with royalty could hardly fail to remind readers of Shakespeare's sojourn with the young Earl of Southampton, who was seeking favour with his sovereign. Nor need Nashe's references to the Queen's Men, and the players Tarleton, Alleyn, Knell and Bentley (pp. 85–6, 116) be other than deliberate allusions to the ambience he is aiming at. He describes 'the puling accent' of 'one's voice that interprets to the puppets' (p. 69); cf the ungracious voice of Greene's playwright who had been 'absolute interpreter to the puppets' for seven years. Among the 'base men' that now had 'wealth at command' was 'an hostler' (p. 53); cf Greene's jibe at Shakespeare as a 'rude groom'; and the Spaniard now suffers from 'kill-cow vanity' (p. 73), as the actors and playwrights in 1589 allegedly affected 'some kill-cow conceit'. Further, Nashe claims that the 'cobbler's crow, for crying but *Ave Caesar*', is better esteemed than rarer birds (p. 70). This image too is drawn direct from Greene (*Never Too Late*, 1590), who there applies it to a certain successful actor he knows. Again the upstart crow is seen in clumsy flight and heard in raucous caw.

Nashe continues the same campaign in his *Terrors of the Night*. This was registered on 30 June 1593 (188) but remained unpublished until the following year; 'a long time since hath it lain suppressed by me', as Nashe explains in his preface. He adds that it had already circulated in manuscript, so 'I thought it as good for me to reap the fruit of my own labours, as to let some unskilful pen-man or Noverint-maker starch his ruff and new spade [cut] his beard with the benefit he made of them . . .' Here is the same accusation of profiting from the work of others that Greene levels at Shakespeare in *Groats-worth*, combined with the same attack on law-clerks, with the same curious personal references to starching and the cutting of beards as Nashe had made about Shakespeare and Kyd in 1589.

Literary London would look forward to further retaliation. Its source provides the final evidence of Nashe's intentions. Shakespeare counter-attacked, good-humouredly enough, in *Love's Labour's Lost*, where the tiny young visitor by candlelight, who had looked down on such 'candle-stuff' as *Hamlet*, is pinned down and exhibited as 'Moth'. The modern emendation of that name to 'Mote', in defiance of both the Quarto and the Folio texts (e.g. in Kerrigan 1982, Wells 1986), is typically remote from any reality, like comparable convictions about the abstract nature of the play itself. All lay spectators and readers can appreciate the autobiographical and historical elements in *Love's Labour's Lost* as in so many other works, with the corollary that what seem to be topical or personal allusions may well be exactly that. Nashe is plainly presented, and his style parodied, by Moth. As soon as he appears on stage he is called 'Juvenal', which is the name Greene gave him in *Groats-worth*. Before long Moth announces that green is the best of complexions (I.ii.80–82). Just as Nashe had punned on Kyd, and Greene on Shakespeare, furthermore, so *Love's Labour's Lost* puns endlessly on *penny, person, pierce* and *purse*, thus sufficiently identifying *Pierce Penniless*. Those well-documented ripostes are discussed by Ernst Honigmann (1982, 68) who explains such personal references by 'the fact that Nashe was widely thought to be the author or part-author of Greene's *Groats-worth*' or else that 'Nashe was known to be the dead Greene's closest literary associate' and hence somehow involved in the attack on 'Shake-scene'. But this may miss the mark by miles. Of course Shakespeare and everyone else would have known perfectly well that Greene wrote *Groats-worth*, exactly as its title-page says and as Nashe and Chettle explicitly and independently confirmed. If Shakespeare fired directly back at Nashe the reason was that Nashe had directly shot at him. So if Shakespeare 'had reason to think himself injured by' Nashe in the autumn of 1592, just after the publication of *Pierce Penniless*, as Honigmann argues, there is no reason at all to resist the obvious inference that Shakespeare's armour, and amour-propre, had been pierced by the personalities of that same satire.

The attackers so far reviewed and self-identified are three University Wits closely linked by collaboration in playwriting: Greene with Nashe ('young Iuvenall . . . that lastly with mee together writ a Comedie', 179) and also in many a joint or linked satirical passage (Appendix); and Nashe with Marlowe (*Dido, Queen of Carthage*, published under both their names in 1594). Greene also invokes Nashe and Marlowe in *Groats-worth*, and warns them against the dangers of being plagiarised (XXXII) by Shakespeare: never tell him what you are writing, he says maliciously.

Lodge

But there is a fourth, who should certainly be mentioned, namely Thomas Lodge, who collaborated with Greene on *A Looking Glass for London and England*. His assistance would surely also be solicited in satirising Shakespeare, and indeed he may well be one of those also instanced in *Groats-worth*, in the phrase 'two more that both have writ against' Shake-scene and his sort. In fact, Lodge wrote in his *Wit's Miserie*, published in 1596, about a devil 'as pale as the vizard of the ghost who cried so miserably at the Theatre, like an oyster-wife, *Hamlet, revenge!'*. That was surely intended as an affront to the author and actor of that role, who was appearing at the Shoreditch theatre where he and his company worked. Furthermore, Lodge's volume of poems, *Scilla's Metamorphosis*, published in 1589, probably provided Shakespeare with hints for *Venus and Adonis*; and his prose romance, *Rosalynde: Euphues Golden Legacy* (1590), was to be the source of *As You Like It* (Halliday 1964, 284).

Peele

Another University-trained dramatist, George Peele, was also invoked by both Greene and Nashe. His style and phraseology were so thoroughly absorbed by Shakespeare, e.g. in the first act of *Titus Andronicus*, that one respected modern editor felt sure, and indeed maintained as a fact for twenty years, that Peele must have written it (J. Wilson 1948). Peele was liked as well as admired by his contemporary colleagues, and he refrained from any overt intervention – unless perhaps the following couplet from his *Edward I* (164), where a new-crowned king is admonished thus to pay homage, was ironically intended:

> Shake thy speres, in honour of his name
> Vnder whose roialtie thou wearst the same.

Lyly

John Lyly was the oldest (born *c.* 1554) of the University Wits. He made no identifiable allusion to Shakespeare, pro or con; but he had cause to, not only as an ally and associate of Nashe and Greene but because *Love's Labour's Lost* is deeply indebted to the elegantly patterned style of his *Euphues*. Perhaps Ben Jonson is hinting at these and other examples of influence in his First Folio encomium about 'how farre thou didst our Lily out-shine/Or sporting Kid, or Marlowe's mighty line'.

However this may be, there is no doubt about the long and hard-fought battle of the books, with ammunition as bright and distinctive as tracer bullets and star-shell, all aimed from the same entrenched positions over the same range, for the duration of hostilities throughout this seven years' war. Furthermore, the same enemy camps are lit up for all to see, even among the obscure allusions of the Parnassus plays (XVIII) and *Willobie his Avisa* (XIX), soon to be considered. First, however, the archives are examined for signs of support from the enemy's enemies, notably Gabriel Harvey and his friend Edmund Spenser.

Appendix: Nashe-Greene Parallels 1589–93

Nashe	Greene
M Preface to *Menaphon* by 1589	N *Never Too Late* by 1590
A *Anatomy of Absurdity* by 1589	G *Groats-worth* by 1592
S *Strange News* by 1592	
P *Pierce Penniless* 1592	
T *Terrors of the Night* by 1593	

Players 'carried their fardles [baggage] on footback' (M)	The player 'was fain to carry' his 'fardle a footback' (G)
'A company of' players . . . with *King of Fairies . . . Delphrigus*' (M)	The player was 'famous for Delphrigus and the King of Fairies' (G)
'To the Gentleman Students' (M)	'To my fellow scholars' (G)
'George Peele . . . *primus verborum artifex* goeth a step beyond all that write' (M)	[Peele] 'in some things rarer, in nothing inferior' [to other writers] (G)
'they might have anticked it' (M)	'those anticks garnished in our colours' (G)
'vaunt Ovid's and Petrarch's plumes as their own . . . borrow invention of *Ariosto . . . verbatim* from . . . Plutarch and Pliny' (M)	'beautified with our feathers' (G)
'tricked up . . . fools with their feathers' (M)	'the glory of other's feathers' (N)
'the Kidde in *Aesop*' (M)	'upstart crow' (G) 'Aesop's crow' (N)
'they that obtrude themselves unto us as the authors of eloquence' (A) 'idiot art-masters, that intrude themselves to our ears as the alcumists of eloquence, (mounted on the stage of arrogance) think to outbrave better pens with the swelling bumbast of a bragging blank verse' (M)	'supposes he is as well able to bombast out a blank verse as the best of you' (G)
'These upstart reformers of arts' (M)	'upstart crow' (G)
'run through every art and thrive by none' (M)	'Johannes Factotum' (G)

'an hostler' (P)'

'apish devices . . . the ape's folly' (M)

'interpreter of the Puppits' (S)
'puling accent . . . like . . . one's voice
that interprets to the puppets' (P)

'Grammarians . . . that could scarcely
latinise their neck-verses' (M)
'a little country grammar knowledge'
(A)
'some little sprinkling of
Grammer learning in their youth' (T)

'the trade of *Noverint* [lawyer's clerk]
whereto they were born' (M)
'the buckram bag' (P) ['worn by
lawyers' clerks', Steane 1972, 57]

'a scrivener . . . paid for an
obligation' (P) [= a loan]

'rude groom' (G)

'those apes' (G)

'it seems to me your voice is
nothing gracious . . . absolute
interpreter to the Puppets' (G)

'rude grooms . . . peasants'
'a country author' (G)

'these buckram gentlemen' (G)

'usurer' (G)

These are only a few samples from the profusion of such parallels, which still await detailed analysis. They explain *inter alia* why Greene's *Groats-worth* was attributed by some Tudor readers to Nashe himself. But this is expressly rebutted by Chettle: 'I protest [*Groats-worth*] was all *Greenes*, not mine nor Maister *Nashes*, as some unjustly haue affirmed.' Nashe's own later rejection of the same notion (*Pierce Penniless* 1592) was memorably vehement: 'Other news I am advertised of, that a scald [= scurvy] trivial lying pamphlet, called Greene's *Groats-worth of Wit*, is given out to be of my doing. God never have care of my soul but utterly renounce me if the least word or syllable in it preceded from my pen, or if I were in any way privy to the writing or printing of it.' That solemn Christian oath on pain of damnation surely confirms that Nashe had no hand in *Groats-worth*, though Greene no doubt had a voice in the Preface to *Menaphon*, and was likely to have been the senior partner and instigator throughout.

XVII

Allies

Harvey

THE SCHOLAR, CRITIC and barrister Gabriel Harvey was educated at Cambridge. In 1570 he became a fellow of Pembroke Hall, where he formed a lifelong friendship with Edmund Spenser. Harvey hated Greene and Nashe, who had mocked him unmercifully, in print, as an upstart pedant – for such varied offences as being the son of a mere rope-maker, and applying classical rules to English prosody. He might well have sympathised with Shakespeare, as a fellow victim of such assaults. No such reference is known, however, until about 1598, when Harvey made a marginal note that 'the younger sort takes much delight in Shakespeares Venus, & Adonis; but his Lucrece, & his tragedie of Hamlet, Prince of Denmarke, haue it in them, to please the wiser sort'. This surely refers to the 1589 version criticised by Nashe (XVI) in which Shakespeare had played the Ghost at the Shoreditch Theatre and in the provinces, including Cambridge, as the 1603 Quarto title-page says – the same role that Greene's collaborator Lodge had scoffed at (XVI). In the same note, Harvey lists both Spenser and Shakespeare among 'owr florishing metricians'. The former must have been aware of the latter's published poems and plays, and of the Wits' feud against Harvey. As a renowned and revered leading light on the London literary scene, and an out-spoken public critic and indeed satirist of such circles, he must surely have taken sides.

Spenser

And indeed there is excellent evidence to that effect. Rowe (1709) says that 'Men of the most delicate Knowledge and polite Learning' have admired Shakespeare, and 'amongst these was the incomparable *Mr. Edmund Spencer*, who speaks of him in his *Tears of the Muses*, not only with the praises due to a good Poet, but even lamenting his absence with the tenderness of a Friend'. But these striking words remain unmentioned even by Honigmann (1985, 2) who accepts Spenser's allusion as auth-entic; Rowe in 1709 is reckoned too late to be sound on Shakespeare. For the opposite bias, see Chambers (1930, ii, 186) followed by Halliday (1964, 469) et al.: 'even [May 1590] is too early to make a reference to Shakespeare, as conjectured [*sic*] by Rowe, at all plausible'. But Rowe is a better witness than any modern commentator. Thus he was proved right about the Shakespeare family wool business, as even his detractors admit (Schoenbaum 1975, 79, followed by Honigmann idem and 1982, 89); and he may well have had independent confirmation about the Spenser allusion, since it is far from self-evident and he states it as a fact.

Spenser (*c.* 1552–99) lived mainly in Ireland. But part-copies of his *Faerie Queene* were known in his native London by 1587 (Honigmann 1982, 74–5; Maley 1994, 47), and he returned there for an audience with Queen Elizabeth at the end of 1589 (Maley 1994, 52–3). His poetic description of the London stage, in *The Teares of the Muses* (registered in December 1590), was couched as a complaint by Thalia, the muse of Comedy, about the current neglect or abuse of her genre. He singles out one comedian and one writer of comedy as praiseworthy exceptions (166). At the time, only one famous comedian was 'dead of late', namely Richard Tarleton (148), in September 1588. He had joined the Queen's Men in 1583; his much mourned demise five years later soon led to their decline. He would have been well known to Shakespeare, as a close colleague; his links with Yorick in *Hamlet* are well documented (XVI). So prima facie Tarleton was 'our pleasant *Willy*'. Then who was the 'gentle Spirit', still alive but in retreat? They both belong to us, Spenser assures his readers; though one alas has gone, we still have the other. Thus a great poet, without feigning or condescension, announces his personal pride and pleasure in the achievements of both. He also sets a lasting fashion with his many *mots justes*. 'Gentle' became accepted as the typical epithet for Shakespeare's personality, like 'honey and sweet nectar' for his poetic style. These would be astonishing epithets for an unknown and forgotten writer of comedy in the late 1580s. But they are exactly the terms in which Shakespeare was described, for decades. Ben Jonson calls him 'gentle' twice in the 1623 First Folio, in the portrait's caption as well as the famous long eulogy'. For both Meres (1598) and Weever (1599) he is 'honey-tongued'. Chettle (1603) talks of his 'honied muse', while Barnfield (1598) describes his 'honey-flowing vein'; the equivalent 'mel-lifluous' is applied to him by both Meres (1598) and Heywood (1635). The unknown C.B. (1614) identifies Shakespeare's 'nectared veines' of style, 'drunke by thirstie men'. These allusions range over five decades; their source is surely this Spenser poem *c.* 1590. They all distil the essence of Shakespeare as a poet universally savoured as 'sweet', whether directly as in the Parnassus play or obliquely as in Thomas Bancroft's phrase 'thy muse's sugared dainties' (1639). What is thus singled out to be especially savoured is surely the characteristic lyric component of his style, which figured among the first personal features discernible in his work, and thus may well help in identifying his apocrypha. It had emerged by the end of the 1580s,* just as Spenser implies and the Greene-Nashe duo confirms.

Spenser adds, in the allusive tones of Tudor times, that his admired writer of comedy has temporarily withdrawn from the London scene. Even as early as *c.* 1590, furthermore, the 'gentle spirit' is being noted and discussed as a well-known writer, not an actor. Spenser's readers are expected to recognise him from a description of his style, and he is praised for his pen. The phrase 'idle cell' may suggest a rural retreat, whether one of the regular returns to Stratford or perhaps a sojourn at Southampton or its young Earl's other estates. Shakespeare is known to have withdrawn from playwriting *c.* 1590 to write the two great narrative poems dedicated to his patron (**167**).

If there is other evidence, conversely, that a Tudor author absented himself from the London scene after the death of Tarleton in 1588 until about 1590, then that author may well have been Shakespeare. So it is perhaps significant that the anonymous popular pamphlet *Tarleton's News out of Purgatory*, registered for publication on 26 June 1590, begins thus:

> Sorrowing, as most men doo, for the death of Richard Tarlton . . . the wonted desire to see plaies left me . . . he was a mad merry companion, desired and loved of all, amongst the rest of whose wel wishers myselfe, being not least, after his death I mourned in conceite, and absented myself from all plaies . . . yet at last, as the longest sommers day hath his night, so this dumpe had an end: and forsooth upon Whitson monday last I would needs to the Theatre [i.e. the Shoreditch playhouse thus named] . . .

The reason given for absence is admittedly different from Spenser's, who says that the 'gentle spirit' sought to escape mockery. But this too fits Shakespeare in 1590; the author of the early *Hamlet* had been openly mocked by Thomas Nashe in 1589. Nor are the two explanations in any way incompatible. Further, there are independent grounds for attributing *Tarleton's News* to Shakespeare (Everitt 1954, 30f). Later in 1590 appeared *The Cobbler of Caunterburie, Or, An inuectiue against Tarltons News out of Purgatory*, which offers a frank imitation of the earlier work's format, namely separate stories linked by a central character and situation, as in Boccaccio or Chaucer respectively. But the text of *The Cobbler* certainly announces its title-page intention to collect stories and 'set them out . . . as an inuective against *Tarlton's Newes out of Purgatory*', which is disparaged as 'a foolish toy' with which 'I haue found fault, and therefore I haue attempted to amend it, not in the correcting of his worke, but in setting out one more pleasant, and more full of delightful tales for all mens humours'. Halliwell, the Victorian editor of *Tarlton's Newes* (1844, 108) comments: 'Notwithstanding this egotistical opinion, the *Newes out of*

---

* As occasionally in *Edmund Ironside* (e.g. 2010f).

Purgatory is altogether a far more amusing work, and better written than the *Cobbler of Canterbury.*'

The latter seems to have been written by Greene. At least he tells us that it was attributed to him, and he carefully refrains from denying the charge directly (*Vision*, 1593). And *The Cobbler* ends with a sly allusion to the excellence of Greene's prose. His consistent victim and supposed inferior was Shakespeare, whom Nashe had accused of thrusting Elysium into hell and plagiarising French and Italian sources. The *Newes* describes a 'broad and fair' passage 'over a green vale' into hell, and draws on Ronsard and Boccaccio, as well as parodying Greene's poetic style. All this skirmishing characterises the same camps in the same campaign.

Other lines in Spenser's poem about literary life in London *c.* 1590 also help to confirm the contending parties. He deplores the theatre's 'vgly Barbarisme' and 'brutish Ignorance' from 'the deep Abysme/Where being bredd, he light and heauen does hate'. These sound very like descriptions of *Tamburlaine* and *Dr Faustus c.* 1587–8, while the further references to 'scoffing Scurrilitie' and 'rhymes of shameless ribaudre' assort well with, respectively, the religious pamphleteering known as the Marprelate controversy (**154**) and the obscene verses called *The Choice of Valentines*. Thomas Nashe had contributed to the former and written the latter; his satirical style is well described as scoffing scurrility. It seems then that Shakespeare, according to Spenser's information, had resolved to withdraw from the theatre scene in 1590 rather than endure public mockery from Nashe, already notorious for his invective and obscenity. And even in 1590, it seems, to be pro-Shakespeare was to be anti-Nashe.

But Shakespeare's absence from the scene was neither permanent nor unduly prolonged. Before long, his reappearance is signalled by Spenser in a further poem about London literati, *Colin Clout's Come Home Again* (written *c.* 1591 and published, perhaps after revision, in 1595):

> And there though last not least is *Aetion*,
> A gentler shepherd may no where be found:
> Whose *Muse* full of high thoughts inuention,
> Doth like himself heroically sound.

This poet too is gentle, and a pastoral lyricist ('shepherd' OED 1b, first cited from Spenser), like Greene's rhyming shepherd Doron, who shared John Shakespeare's trade of sheep-farming. Yet the muse of Spenser's writer is also heroic, as his name sounds. Again, all Tudor readers and playgoers would recognise him without further prompting, or else Spenser has failed in his prime purpose of communication. Shakespeare wrote heroic history and tragedy as well as comedy; among all known Elizabethan or indeed Jacobean playwrights, only one actual name sounds heroical, and that is the most famous of all. Only the 'too early' blinkers could have lost sight of so unique and commanding a figure, emerging in the 1580s.

XVIII

The Parnassus Plays

AMONG THE MOST inexplicably neglected key documents of Shakespeare's age are the so-called Parnassus plays, an anonymous dramatic trilogy (cited here from the latest edition, Leishman 1949) of which the third part was acted in 1601 by students of St John's College, Cambridge and published in 1606 (pp. 8–9). All three plays were presumably performed in that same venue, which was the *alma mater* of both Greene (d. 1592) and Nashe (d. 1601); so the first two at least were written within the latter's lifetime, and perhaps played in his presence. He is directly depicted in them as Ingenioso, and his portrait is 'essentially a friendly one' (Steane 1972, 19); so their anonymous author was on Nashe's side, and hence ranged against Shakespeare, whom playgoers and readers would hence expect to see satirised. As already noted (XVI), Nashe himself had been taken to task in *Love's Labour's Lost*, in retaliation for his *Pierce Penniless* of 1592. So it would then be the turn of the Greene-Nashe University faction to counter-attack against the mere grammarians Shakespeare and Kyd. St John's would obviously offer a safe base for such an operation.

In the Parnassus plays, Shakespeare is named, quoted and parodied. Their theme is the Universities versus The Rest, Gown v. Town, Gentlemen v. Players, in the field of dramatic and poetic literature. This *casus belli* is clearly declared by the Chamberlain's Men Richard Burbage (*c.* 1568–1619) and William Kempe (*c.* 1564– *c.* 1607), who are caricatured as illiterates (p. 337): 'Few of the vniuersity pen plaies well . . . Why heres our fellow *Shakespeare* puts them all down . . .'

These works (exhaustively expounded in Leishman's introduction, pp. 3–92) are allegories aimed to amuse academics. 'Parnassus' stands for University status. Several other authors, such as John Marston and Nashe, are also mentioned by name. In addition, certain characters in the play are clearly related, by deliberate and identifiable quotation, to actual known personalities; not only is Ingenioso recognisable as Thomas Nashe but Furor Poeticus as John Marston, and Luxurio as Gabriel Harvey. Similarly the courtier Gullio is not only a character in the play but a series of palpable hits at Shakespeare's patron, the Earl of Southampton, who was also a graduate of St John's; his substantial donation of books is still treasured there. Presumably he was not among the audience; in 1601 he was in prison under sentence of death for his part in the Essex conspiracy.

On all this evidence it seems manifest (though not to scholars, including Leishman) that Philomusus and Studioso, who appear in each of the three plays, also represent well-known writers. Indeed, how could they fail to, as the central characters around whom the entire trilogy revolves? As Leishman perceives (p. 55), some of Nashe's views, as expressed in his Preface to *Menaphon*, 'though written in 1589, probably still expressed the feelings of most University men at the time of the Parnassus plays'. This also applies to that preface and those plays *passim*; their actual themes are the manifest artistic and intellectual supremacy of graduates over grammarians, as playwrights or poets. If Harvey and Nashe and Southampton are portrayed, at a time when (after 1592) Greene was dead, in a re-enactment of the Battle of the Books, with the same uniforms and weapons, then surely the only other known participants, the mere grammarians Kyd (the 1589 Kidde in Aesop) and Shakespeare (the 1589 author of *Hamlet*, alias the 1592 upstart 'Shake-scene') must also be present. So the protagonists Philomusus and Studioso, who are depicted as earnest aspirants to university education from the first page of the first play, *The Pilgrimage to Parnassus* (p. 95), are prima facie rather likely to embody elements of of Kyd and Shakespeare.

They duly attain the heights of learning and art; Parnassus was traditionally the mountain sacred to the Muses. But having come down with B.A. degrees, in *The First and Second Part of the Return from Parnassus*, they come down in the world. Meanwhile they 'runne through every arte and thrive by none', as Nashe said of Kyd and Shakespeare in 1589, like a typical factotum, as Greene said of Shakespeare *c*. 1592. Their trades include noverint-making (like the historical Shakespeare and Kyd) and schoolteaching (like the historical Shakespeare). Finally they finish up as shepherds, which (we are to understand) was always the lowly level appropriate to such peasants.

These identifications are enhanced by a scene in which both Studioso and Philomusus are invited, after a mock audition by the characters who are called after two real-life Chamberlain's Men, Burbage and Kempe, to join that company, which Burbage, Kempe and Shakespeare had in fact inaugurated in 1594 (203). Studioso is later (p. 350) made to inveigh against the players, calling them 'mimick apes' and 'glorious vagabonds' that 'carried erst their fardels [baggage] on their backs' and 'with mouthing words that better wits have framed/They purchase lands, and now Esquiers are named'.

But all this is surely aimed straight at Shakespeare himself. It repeats Greene's ancient accusations against him. By 1596, he had a coat of arms and the title of 'Gentleman', and he purchased lands. The reference to fardels is a deliberate echo of the lampoons already published by Nashe and Greene (XVI Appendix); it was the despised category of actors that 'carried their fardels on footback' (Nashe 1589) or 'was fain to carry his fardle a footback' (Greene 1592). Such knowing allusions also confirm

Nashe himself, though much more congenially, as the fiercely satirical Ingenioso (p. 71f). The diminutive Nashe-Moth character in *Love's Labour's Lost* is not only addressed as 'Juvenal' in that play (Greene's name for Nashe) but also alluded to as 'ingenious' (I.ii.27) or 'pretty ingenious' (III.i.58), and amusingly allotted the part of Hercules in a pageant (V.ii.583). In the Parnassus plays, Nashe-Ingenioso enters 'with Juvenal in his hand', and quotes from its Latin text; he then mentions Hercules (pp. 225–6). Earlier, he also quotes verbatim from Nashe's *Pierce Penniless* (pp. 125–6). Further, Ingenioso is made to mention '*Thomas Nash* . . . whose muse was armed with a gagtooth [= projecting tooth] and his pen possesst with *Hercules* furies'. Nashe had a projecting tooth and wrote about '*Herculean* fury' (p. 245). Ingenioso-Nashe, true to his type-casting, deliberately mimics and mocks the early Shakespeare style, thus: 'Faire Venus, queene of beutie and of loue,/Thy red doth stayne the blushing of the morn,/Thy snowie neck shameth the milke-white dove' etc. (p. 192). Such lines would be readily recognisable to Tudor readers as a sharp parody of Shakespeare, whether in actual phraseology ('milk-white dove', *The Passionate Pilgrim*, 9, 3) or characterisation and idiosyncrasy (the red-white contrasts that begin *Venus and Adonis*, first published in 1593 and reprinted in the following year; **186, 196**).

Similarly the character Gullio, the conceited young courtier who raves 'Ile worshipp sweet Mr. Shakespeare, and to honoure him will lay his *Venus and Adonis* under my pillow', has far too much in common with Southampton to be anything other than a deliberate lampoon designed to be recognised as such by the St John's cognoscenti. Leishman identifies Gullio's allusions to service under the command of Essex in the expeditions against Spain and Portugal in 1597, and Ireland in 1599 (p. 176) and is also disposed to accept Ingenioso-Nashe's 'wanton lines to please lewd Gullio' (pp. 75, 206) as a reference to Nashe's *Choice of Valentines*, written to beguile the wanton young Henry Wriothesley. But there is much more, unmentioned by Leishman, such as Gullio's love of finery (p. 179), his penchant for Italian sayings (p. 189), his devotion to poetry (pp. 189–90) in Latin, French, Spanish and Italian, his refusal to marry (pp. 179, 188) and his verbatim quotations from *Romeo and Juliet* (pp. 183–4) and from *Venus and Adonis* (pp. 183–5), the poem dedicated by Shakespeare to his patron Southampton. And even the ultra-cautious Leishman agrees that recognisable Southampton traits appear in the Gullio portrait (p. 82).

Studioso and Philomusus are no less visible and recognisable. First, they are forced to confess that Nashe was right about them in his preface to *Menaphon*. There he had scornfully dismissed writers who 'run through every art and thrive by none', and explained that two such writers are 'Kidde' and the author of *Hamlet*, i.e. Kyd and Shakespeare. Now, as Studioso admits to his friend Philomusus, here we are again 'running through every trade, yet thrive by none' (p. 262). The quotation is deliberate and significant.

Later, Philomusus confirms to Ingenioso-Nashe, personally, that 'We haue run through many trades, yet thrive by none' (p. 360). These are plain pleas of guilty to Nashe's accusations. His victims' memories are a little hazy; they remember 'art' as 'trade'. But that is no doubt what Nashe meant to say about them; they belong among the lower orders. They recognise themselves from that description, without difficulty; but their pseudonyms have effectively disguised their allegorical identity for the last four centuries.

As the leading autodidact of his own or any age, and especially one subject to strong Italian influences both literary and personal, as Nashe too had pointed out (XVI), Shakespeare would be well named and readily recognisable as Studioso. His first words in the first Parnassus play are 'I loue to hear loue play the oratoure'* (p. 96). That repetition and image characterise the early Shakespeare style. 'Play the orator' occurs in *1 Henry VI* (IV.i.175), *Richard III* (III.v.95) and twice in *The True Tragedy of Richard Duke of York* (Morgan edn, pp. 310, 769), the Quarto version of *3 Henry VI*. Studioso proceeds to emulate the young Shakespeare's naive classical personification ('frostie Boreas', p. 131; 'breath of Boreas',† p. 196: the figure that both Greene and Nashe select as a target in *Menaphon*). Studioso also scoffs (p. 146) at Greene's maxim *omne tulit punctum*, which Greene complained (XVI) had been 'held in derision' by two playwrights, one of whom was prima facie Shakespeare (so perhaps Kyd was the other?). Studioso, further, next mentions (p. 146) Greene's bragging self-description in *Groats-worth* as *Magister utribus utriusque Academicae*, and then the phrase *Opus* and *Usus*, both used by Nashe in *Pierce Penniless*. Later, Studioso also resorts to the young Shakespeare's alliteration and repetition‡ ('groves grow green . . . too too unkind', p. 157) and his nature-similes, such as 'with swallow-wingéd speed' (p. 110) or 'swift as a swallow' (p. 165): cf *Richard III*, 'swift and flies with swallow's wings' (V.ii.23) or *Titus Andronicus*, 'run like swallows o'er the plain' (II.i.24). Studioso further alludes ('king of a molehill', p. 350) to the cruel mockery of Richard in *True Tragedy* (Morgan edn, p. 429). He also contrasts shrubs with cedars (p. 171), as in *Titus Andronicus* (IV.iii.46).

But these are only a few sample links. Studioso speaks *passim* in parodies of Shakespeare, with plentiful allusion to the early symbolism of human predicaments in terms of beasts, birds and plants,§ such as the nipping of buds or flowers by frost, which Caroline Spurgeon (1935, 91)

---

*   Cf *Edmund Ironside*, e.g. 'become an orator' (1301).
†   Cf *Edmund Ironside*, 'Aeolus' boist'rous northern breath [i.e. Boreas]' (1347).
‡   Cf *Edmund Ironside*, 'dealt the dole of death' (997); 'too too long' (1294).
§   Again as in *Edmund Ironside passim*: had Caroline Spurgeon known this obscure text she could not have failed to note how 'this unwelcome news/Nips like a hoary frost our springing hopes/And makes my fearful soldiers hang their heads' (742–4).

after careful search declared characteristic of his work and his alone:
'nipte the blossoms of our buddinge springe' (p. 122), 'my bloominge
flowers . . . Are now quite nipped with the chillie froste' (i.e. 'the breath
of Boreas', p. 196). A typical Studioso speech begins thus:

> So oft the Northen winde with frozen wings
> hath beate the flowers that in our garden grewe,
> throwne downe the stalkes of our aspiring youth,
> so oft hath winter nipt our trees' fair rinde
> that now we seeme noughte but two bared boughes,
> scorned by the basest bird that chirps in groaue. (p. 251)

Yet again, Boreas figures as a physical human presence, active among
the typical flora and fauna. The alliteration of 'wind/wings', 'bared/
boughs/basest/bird' is equally typical. The manifest mockery even sounds
specific, as if the Parnassus author had seen some sonnets in the manuscript circulation mentioned by Meres in 1598 ('his sugred Sonnets
among his private friends'); cf the conjunction of 'boughs', 'bare' and
'birds' in Sonnet 73(3–4).

Another obvious candidate for stylistic parody is the stichomythia, of
which the early Shakespeare and the Kyd of *The Spanish Tragedy* were
both so fond. Studioso and Philomusus often finish their colloquies with
a flourish by exchanging rhymed one-liners.* So Philomusus predictably
represents Kyd, who had already been linked with Shakespeare by Nashe
in 1589.

At the end of one such session, Philomusus obligingly confirms that he
and Studioso stand for the two playwrights who were attacked by the
University Wits. He complains (p. 253) of 'the hidebound bretheren of
Cambridge and Oxford, or any of those Stigmaticke masters of Arts, that
abused vs in times past . . .'. Nashe's mentor Greene, ringleader of the
abusers, vaunted being Master of Arts in both universities, a phrase
already burlesqued by Studioso (p. 146). Furthermore, Studioso and
Philomusus obligingly concede yet another point that Nashe scored
against Shakespeare and Kyd in 1589. He then advised them both, none
too politely, to give up writing altogether; indeed, he felt that they should
never have left 'the trade of *Noverint* [law-clerking] whereto they were
born'. Shakespeare's father was a law officer; Kyd's was a scrivener, like
both sons. Studioso and Philomusus too are both scriveners, i.e. law-
clerks, a category rare in Tudor literature, especially as a pair of close
colleagues. When they are forced by penury to leave Parnassus,
Philomusus hopes on behalf of both (p. 142) that, 'some scriueners stall/
Will yealde some harboure to our wandringe heades'.

---

* As also often in *Edmund Ironside*, notably in the prose interchanges between
  Edricus and Stitch (e.g. at 1135–40).

Studioso, like Shakespeare, has other strings to his bow. He not only fiddles but sings; and he has yet another trade, namely schoolmaster. He is addressed by that title, and he teaches Latin (p. 169f), which may have been meant as yet more mockery. However, John Aubrey would later write, on good authority, for the first time on record, that Shakespeare 'understood Latine pretty well; for he had been in his younger yeares a schoolmaster in the countrey'; and such duties commonly included music-teaching (cf *The Taming of the Shrew*, as cited in X). Studioso's tutoring and servant duties are indeed located 'in the country', where he deplores his dull environment of 'country fields' and 'country moss' (p. 165). He is also portrayed as addicted to puns and quibbles – again exactly like Shakespeare.* 'Cross or pile?' [= tails or heads] inquires his sportive pupil, and receives the reply 'Why cross, my wagg (for thinges goe cross with me) . . .'. But it turns out to be pile, greeted with 'Well may it pile [= rob] in such a pilled [= beggarly] age.' The boy claims his debt: 'I must have 4 counters of youe.' His master rejoins 'Full many a time fortune encounters mee/More happie they that in the Counter [= prison] be.' To the Boy's sally 'Youle pay them I hope', Studioso rejoins 'Fortune hath paide mee home, that I may pay.' And so on (p. 170f). All the St John's scholars must have enjoyed the skit on Shakespeare the master-punster, still universally seen as such to this day.

Philomusus-Kyd can also be equated with characters attacked by Greene and Nashe. He says that he is 'double benefisde with my Sextonship and my clearkeshippe' (p. 167); and this is no doubt intended as a clear clue to his allegorical identity. Studioso contracts to meet him once a week (p. 167) as if he has something to learn from the clerk-sexton and is indeed taking regular lessons. This recalls Greene's words already cited from *Farewell to Folly*: 'he that cannot write true Englishe without the helpe of Clearkes of parish Churches will needes make himself the father of enterludes [= popular stage plays]'. Greene then complains of the alleged abuse of scripture in one such play (*Faire Em*), and proceeds 'In charitie [*sic*] be it spoken I am perswaded the sexten of Saint Giles without Creeplegate would have been ashamed of such blasphemous Rhetoricke.' So Greene's clerk-sexton is presumably himself a playwright as well as a tutor or mentor, just like Philomusus-Kyd. Nashe complained in his *Anatomy of Absurdity* (1589) that 'when as lust is the tractate of so many leaves, and loue passions the lavish dispence of so much paper' – again the same attack on a love-poet – 'I must needes send such idle wits to shrift to the vicar of S. Fooles, who in steede of a worser may be such a Gothamists ghostly father [= the spiritual confessor of such a village idiot].' So some high-churchman of a London parish (Saint Giles, alias Saint Fools) is acting as adviser to a personage despised as a

---

* Again as in *Edmund Ironside passim*, often quite elaborately: the blood of 'my father Sveyn runs in [my] veins' (130–31) etc.

peasant; and all this belongs to a strong satire on two main identifiable characters.

They are indeed categorised from the outset. As they toil upwards to Parnassus, in search of learning and art, they meet Ingenioso-Nashe coming down. He strongly advises against their pilgrimage; he says he has heard tell how a whole 'companie of ragged vicars and forlorne schoolmaisters' had been seen descending from Parnassus. In other words, there is no room for any more such riff-raff, who 'as they walked scrached their unthrifty elbows and often put their hands into their unpeopled pockets . . .' (p. 125); thus they shared not only their professions but their penury with the churchman Philomusus-Kyd and the schoolmaster Studioso-Shakespeare, the dramatists described by Nashe in 1589 as shifting companions who fail to thrive from any of their activities. In case anyone should doubt these identifications, Ingenioso-Nashe, when he parts from Philomusus and Studioso, says 'Farewell, and take heed I take you not napping twentie years hence in a viccars seate . . . or els interpreting *Pueriles Confabulationes* to a companie of seauen yeare old apes.'

Once accept that 1589 was not 'too early' for Shakespeare, as it certainly was not for Kyd (1558–94), and the playwrights occupy centre stage as Studioso and Philomusus respectively, the main characters of a three-part dramatic entertainment set in that same past epoch and describing the same quarrel, often in the same words.

These tripartite encounters, real or imaginary, are also designed to set the time and place as well as the mainspring of the Parnassus plays' action. Nashe came down from Cambridge to London in 1589, and then first came in contact with Kyd and Shakespeare, whether by name or in person. Both would be already well known *c.* 1590 as the authors of the Senecan dramas *The Spanish Tragedy* (156) and the early *Hamlet** and hence as the joint targets of Nashe's 1589 attack. Before long, Shakespeare would be further famous for his *Titus Andronicus* (159, 175, 184, 190) as well as his narrative poems, frequent allusions to which confirm the time of the Parnassus plays' action as the earlier 1590s, when he was known above all as a love-poet. Thus the critic Iudicio complains about Shakespeare, by name, 'Could but a graver subiect him content/without loues foolish lazy languishment' (p. 244). The same seductive subject-matter was also explicitly ascribed to Shakespeare by Francis Meres, who in 1598 called him 'the most passionate among us to bewaile and bemoane the perplexities of Loue'.

In London, only one dramatist was ever seen as a love-poet and peasant from a Catholic background (IV, IX–X, XII–XIII), later a member of an overtly Italianate circle, again just like the subject of Nashe's satires,

---

*   Cf the equally Senecan *Edmund Ironside*.

All this was the inevitable butt of scorn and censure in an officially anti-papist England. So there is prima facie some special significance in Studioso's sudden and astounding declaration, at the end of the second Parnassus play (p. 213), that: 'To Rome or Rhems Ile hye, led on by fate,/ Where I will ende my dayes, or mende my state'.

As Leishman explains (idem), this refers to two notorious colleges for the instruction of English Catholics: 'their chief purpose was to train priests to be sent into England'. Both were denounced as nests of treason in Elizabethan times; the accusation of attendance at either would still have been a very grave charge even after the accession of James I in 1603. It was from the Roman college that Edmund Campion had begun the ill-fated mission for which he was tortured and executed. This was also the likeliest source of the Catholic testament signed by Shakespeare's father and hidden in the rafters of the Henley Street birthplace (IX). The Rheims college was equally abhorrent to the English authorities for what they saw as its seditious activities. Missionaries from both sources were in the direst jeopardy throughout the 1590s.

Even though Studioso is depicted as returning disconsolate from each expedition, the Parnassus playwright is deliberately seeking to discredit and indeed ostracise the real-life original of that character, who is again selected to announce the return as well as the departure, in the lines

> Nor Rome nor Rhemes, that wonted ar to giue
> A Cardinall cap to discontented clarkes
> That haue forsooke their home-bred thatched roofes
> Yielded us any equal maintenance.

Those words are the continuation of the speech quoted above, about the nipping northern wind, which is among the plainest parallels and parodies of Shakespeare in any of the three Parnassus plays (p. 251). The jeering reference to clerks and thatched roofs confirms the country (and perhaps also the legal) background.

There is no direct evidence that Kyd was ever a churchman of any persuasion; most details of his life are lost. But his scrivener father Francis had been a churchwarden at St Mary Woolnoth's in Lombard Street, not far from Cripplegate, for two years, 1575 and 1576 (Freeman 1967, 4). Skilled penmen were 'sought after . . . for church offices requiring a clear hand' (ibid., 3); Thomas Kyd was a devout Christian who had 'contemplated a poem on the conversion of St. Paul' (ibid., 37). He had indeed taken the trade of noverint whereto he was born, just as Nashe had unkindly commented. Shakespeare too wrote a trained legal hand (155). The two Parnassus scriveners, one of whom is a schoolmaster, also qualify as the two 'translators' of whom Nashe specifically complained in 1589 that they spent hours in reading dubious French books. Studioso-Shakespeare airs his French with a 'Non' (p. 250) while Philomusus-Kyd speaks of their 'shredds of French'.

These identifications add special spice to the Parnassus audition scene. It is still an amusing idea to reverse roles, testing Studioso-Shakespeare on a line from Kyd's *Spanish Tragedy* (p. 341) and Philomusus-Kyd on two lines from Shakespeare's *Richard III* (p. 343). Here is a rich seam for further exploitation. The entire mine, long ago sealed off, could be profitably reopened on the basis that Studioso stands for the poet who in the Sonnets traced his transition from ignorance to learning and in 1593 vowed to 'take advantage of all idle hours' until he had 'honoured [Southampton] with some graver labour' than *Venus and Adonis*. Again the quotations and cross-references may well throw further light on other early works, from which the highly literary Parnassus playwright makes Studiosus quote as though the words were that character's own. Thus one of the phrases that occurred in the early *Hamlet* (Arden, 1608) was 'there are things called whips in store'; and Studioso, in his typical early-Shakespeare speech already cited above, about flowers nipped by frost and Boreas (p. 196), observes that Fortune 'hath more whipps in store'. Further, Studioso's image of the whetting of tongues (p. 123) is echoed, and his phrase 'it grieves my vexed soul' (p. 261) is quoted verbatim, from *Edmund Ironside*; so is the pun 'a vaine veine'* (p. 185), announced with admiration ('prettie y faith') by Gullio-Southampton, the Shakespeare enthusiast and verbatim quoter.

---

* 'Disloyal and ungrateful Sycophant/It grieves my vexed soul to think on thee' (1620–21); 'report shall never whet her tongue/Upon Canutus to eternize thee' (1912–13); 'In vain [four times] . . . In vain – what a vain vein my master is in!' (1669).

XIX

Willobie his Avisa

ONE OTHER CAMPAIGN in the 1590s war against Shakespeare remains to be considered. The anonymous verse novella *Willobie his Avisa* of 1594 contains coded but readable references to Shakespeare and apparently also to the sonnet story, long before the 1609 first publication of those poems. But they and their background were already well known in the 1590s. Two of them (Sonnets 138 and 144) had found their way into *The Passionate Pilgrim* of 1599. Others (e.g. Sonnet 128) exist in early manuscript versions (Kerrigan 1986, 441f). Some had circulated in such copies, as Meres confirmed in 1598 with his published reference to Shakespeare's 'sugared sonnets among his private friends'; and also no doubt *eo facto* among his enemies, and those of his young patron Henry Wriothesley, the 3rd Earl of Southampton, who had made many.

One of those enemies wrote or inspired the scurrilous *Willobie his Avisa* (**202**). Its many ramifications have never been successfully unravelled, despite spirited attempts (notably Harrison 1966, De Luna 1970; the latter source, as the more readily available, is cited here). But the Tudor public would readily recognise it as a versified *roman à clef*. So did the Tudor authorities. In 1599, the Stationers' Register decreed '*Willobies* Adviso to be Called in', i.e. seized and suppressed. Nevertheless a fourth edition 'corrected and augmented' appeared in 1605. No doubt the death of Elizabeth in 1603 had effected the difference. The personal motto of that Virgin Queen was *Semper eadem*, always the same; the ostentatiously virtuous heroine of *Willobie* signs five of her epistles either 'Alwaies the same, *Avisa*', in unusually large and heavy black type (p. 175) or 'Alway the same, *Auisa*' (pp. 188, 190, 210, 224). She discusses her unassailable virtue with various frustrated wooers and pursuers, chief among whom are 'Henrico Willobego, Italo-Hispalensis', also known as 'H.W.', and his 'familiar friend W.S.' This identification of the heroine Avisa is powerfully urged by De Luna (pp. 1–43). She and her suitors clearly correspond to actual personages and their circumstances; otherwise the publication itself, as well as its official suppression, would lack all point. As the 'Epistle to the Reader' is at pains to explain (p. 123), 'there is some thing of trueth hidden vnder this shadow', and more specifically 'there is some thing vnder these fained names and showes that hath bene done truely'. No doubt for example the third suitor, 'D.B. A French man', embodies the Duke of Brabant, just as De Luna proposes (p. 61f).

But an allegorical courtship of the Virgin Queen is fully conformable with the identification of 'H.W. Italo-Hispalensis', the fifth suitor, as Henry Wriothesley the 3rd Earl of Southampton, especially when he is advised on wooing by 'W.S.', the 'old player'. The young Earl was an assiduous if often unsuccessful courtier of his sovereign; and Shakespeare himself, as a leading member of theatre companies under her direct personal patronage, was her much humbler servant. Further, the Sonnets themselves famously describe Shakespeare as old (62.10 'tanned antiquity', 138.10 'I am old') and also, separately, confirm that he is a player (110. 2 'made myself a motley to the view'; 111.4 'public means').

It is true that 'H.W.' is first introduced as 'Henrico Willobego', which certainly recalls Henry Willobie, the ostensible author (p. 120f). The pseudonyms were intended to tease; they had to be recognisable to Tudor readers yet sufficiently disguised to escape any penalties. One purported identification is thus self-refuting.

> *Henrico Willobego* is designed simply [*sic*] ... to give a major clue to the identity of this 'split-personality', for when this name is translated into English and further 'rendered' etymologically, we discover that it means: 'Henry' – 'Ruler of an enclosure, or private property' and 'Willobie' (or 'Willoughby') – 'Near the willows'. In other words, the fifth 'suitor' is the 'Ruler' of an enclosure, or private property 'near the willows'. That so specific [*sic*] a description can point to two men simultaneously is less remarkable when we realize that it is the *same* 'private property' in both cases: Wanstead House in Essex.

On this basis, with the further information that 'Essex county is a marshy section of England, and willow trees abound there', 'H.W.' is unmasked as a composite picture of the Earls of Leicester and of Essex, successive owners of the same allegedly well-willowed Wanstead mansion (De Luna pp. 82–3).

No doubt Shakespeare, who is accepted as 'W.S.' (Harrison 1966, *passim*, De Luna 106–7), was associated with the Earl of Essex, to whom, as his sovereign's commander-in-chief, he pays a personal tribute in *Henry V* (V. Chorus 30–34). But the 'H.W.' with whom that W.S. would be instantly linked by readers in 1594 was Henry Wriothesley, 3rd Earl of Southampton (and close associate of the Earl of Essex) to whom, by that name, William Shakespeare had just publicly dedicated *Venus and Adonis*, by far the best-loved and most popular poem of its time. Nor was that same W.S. ever thus bonded to any other H.W., or indeed anyone else at all, ever; and the same bond was again signed and sealed between the same parties on the title-page of *The Rape of Lucrece*, to which as to Shakespeare himself the satire *Willobie his Avisa* makes the first known allusion ever to appear in print (p. 128). Not only are readers told that '*Shake-speare*, paints poor *Lucrece* rape'; the heroine Avisa herself is called *Lucres-Avis*, on the same page. These deliberate allusions are gratuitous and pointless unless the character 'W.S.' is indeed William Shakespeare; so the young 'H.W.' who sought his advice on wooing was surely young Henry Wriothesley (b. 1573).

But he, like the other courtiers of Elizabeth and courters of Avisa, was dauntingly rebuffed. His obstinate Catholicism was not endearing to his sovereign, that fiercely determined defender of the Protestant faith. In the early 1590s he was in difficulty or disgrace at court because of his Roman and other Italian connections, his complicity in the escape to France of the Danvers brothers (who were wanted for murder), his illicit wooing of the Queen's maid of honour Elizabeth Vernon, and other such misdemeanours. Perhaps Shakespeare himself had suffered royal disfavour, as *Willobie* may intend to imply by saying that W.S. 'not long before had tryed the curtesy of the like passion' (p. 190). He himself must have been well known to Elizabeth from court performances; he would surely have wished to please and impress her, and there is traditional testimony to his success (Chambers 1930, ii, 266, 300–301). At the same time, 'Avisa' may also represent a very different character, namely the so-called Dark Lady, whose favours the poet shared with his fair friend (Sonnets 41.9; 144.13–14 etc.). On this interpretation, which has been the subject of much speculation, Avisa's categorisation as 'chaste and constant' would be intended as ribald irony.

On any analysis, *Willobie*'s conjunction of 'H.W.' with 'W.S.', together with many hints and allusions to Shakespeare and his works as well as insistent stage metaphors ('play his part', 'loving comedy', 'new actor', 'old player', 'Tragedy', pp. 190–191) must have been seen as significant in the current 1590s context of deliberate attacks on Shakespeare by Greene and Nashe, and the apparent defences of him by Spenser. He was the 'W.S.' already well known on the London scene as a player and writer, the 'Shake-scene' of Greene's *Groats-worth* in or before 1592, two years earlier than *Willobie*.

That lampoon's 3,100 lines, mostly written in jogtrot iambic pentameter verses, rhyming ababcc, took time to write; and the complete work was ready for registration at the beginning of September 1594. So its inception may perhaps have preceded the publication and even the May 1594 registration (195) of *The Rape of Lucrece*, in which event the writer of *Willobie* had private knowledge of work in progress. He could rely on many of his readers to trace the various parallels implied by the initials 'H.W.' and 'W.S.' throughout more than 1,000 lines, by far the longest section of the satire. The young Southampton's sustained rejection of Lady Elizabeth de Vere, the bride chosen for him by his guardian Lord Burghley, and his wooing of the Queen's maid of honour Elizabeth Vernon, later Wriothesley, would be notorious at court and in the city. Every reader of *Willobie* could see that 'H.W.' (quite unlike Essex) was described as very young ('if years I want', 'a headlong youth', p. 205, and 'a yong man', indeed a 'boye', p. 212), a bachelor (Avisa urges him to 'marry with some honest wife', p. 206), who insists on staying single for the foreseeable future ('I will not marrie', p. 213, until Avisa's husband dies, however far off that day may be, and 'let setled heads/Inthrall their necks to wedlocke bande', p. 207).

That last phrase, like 'headlong youth', confirms that 'H.W.' himself was anything but settled, as well as reluctant to marry (cf Sonnets 1–17). His traits, again mirrored in the Sonnets (XX) include not only facial effeminacy but a self-confessed tendency to 'trickling teares, like rivers' (p. 196) and weeping in general (pp. 212, 215, 223). Avisa says she is 'loth to see your blobered face/And loth to heare a yong man cry', as 'you weepe and waile' (p. 212). She later becomes 'half angry to see such passionate follie, in a man that should have gouerment', at 'seeing the tears trill downe his cheekes' (p. 216). The poet of the sonnets is more indulgent: 'Ah, but those tears are pearl which thy love sheds' (35.13); but he is surely describing the same rather uncommon trait. Similarly the 'pathetical fancy' and 'passionate follie' of H.W., who was 'not able by reason to rule the raginge fume of this phantasticall fury' (p. 216), and was first encountered in 'a fantastical fit' (p. 190), are entirely congruent with Lady Bridget Manners's 1594 description of Henry Wriothesley: 'yonge and fantastycall' and easily 'carried away' (Akrigg 1968, 182).

In addition, 'H.W.' seems to be a lawyer, for all his beardless youth and emotional instability. Avisa tells him (p. 203) that 'Though you haue bin at common schoole/And enterd plaints in common place;/Yet you will proue your selfe a foole.' Here 'plaints' are surely statements addressed to a court of law (OED 3). Henry Wriothesley had been admitted to Gray's Inn at fifteen, in 1589 (Akrigg 1968, 31). The Sonnets teem with legal metaphor *passim*.

Many of these parallels also apply to the hero of *Venus and Adonis*, written at much the same time. Young Adonis too had a 'hairless face' (487), with only a 'tender spring upon [his] tempting lip' (126); he was 'more lovely than a man' (9); he says 'I know not love' (168). Here is 'H.W.' as well as Henry Wriothesley, both equally recognisable to all instructed readers: 'thou art thy mother's glass' (Sonnet 3.9), 'a woman's face with nature's own hand painted' (Sonnet 20.1), 'for a woman wert thou first created' (Sonnet 20.9), 'but that thou none lov'st is most evident' (Sonnet 10.4). And the Sonnets of course describe just such a triangular relationship as outlined in *Willobie*, where W.S. 'not long before had tryed the curtesy of the like passion' (pp. 190–91) (cf. Sonnets 40, 41, 42, etc.). Given that this allusion is indeed direct and intentional, and that Avisa shadows the Dark Lady as well as Elizabeth I, here for the first time is a definite date. W.S. was 'now newly recovered', i.e. the Dark Lady infatuation so memorably recorded in the Sonnets was over by 1594, so that most of them must have been written by then.

The scurrilous *Willobie*, the gutter press of its day, also offers broad hints of even graver scandals. 'H.W. being sodenly infected with the contagion

... the secresy of his disease ... W.S. ... was now newly recovered of the like infection ... wound ... weak and feeble ... Phisitions [physicians] ... a plaster, if not to heal, yet in part to ease his malady' (pp. 116–17); these ostensible metaphors of passion are surely deliberate references to the cause and course of venereal disease. This is confirmed by canto lx (p. 208), which both by quotation and by textual reference directs the reader's attention to the passage in Proverbs (5:3ff) warning men against the harlot ('her feet go down to death, her steps take hold on hell') and the mortal malady she harbours ('lest ... thou mourn at the last, when thy flesh and body are consumed'). For this topic too the Sonnets provide textual warranty, in the line 'till my bad angel fire my good one out' (144. 14), meaning 'until my friend catches a venereal infection from my mistress' (Kerrigan 1986, 60). *Willobie's* prose introduction to his 'H.W.' and 'W.S.' story (pp. 190–91) promises further salacious innuendo about 'the vnrewly rage of vnbrydeled fancy, hauing the raines to roue at liberty [running of the raines = a genito-urinary discharge, as in gonorrhoea] with the dyuers & sundry changes of affections & temptations, which Will, set loose from Reason, can deuise, &c.' This final phrase also suggests an awareness of the sexually explicit sonnets with their frank puns on 'Will' (e.g. Sonnets 135, 136) and their definition of physical affections and temptations in such terms as 'past reason hunted' (129.6) and 'flesh stays no further reason' (151.8).

And though the Sonnets explicitly disclaim any homosexual intent (20.12–14) they just as clearly express Shakespeare's fervent love for a beautiful and beardless young man many years his junior. The Earl of Southampton himself may well have 'passed through homosexual phases'; on the evidence, 'nothing would be less surprising' (Akrigg 1968, 181–2). The author of *Willobie* confronts this topic too, again with gratuitous irrelevance to his ostensible theme. His annotations to the 'H.W.' sections (e.g. p. 198) are anything but marginal: 'Idleness the mother of all foolish wannesse [pallor] ... Dauid being idle fell to strange lust [i.e. his love for Jonathan, in this context] ... Noblemen gentlemen and Captaynes by idlenesse fall to all kynd of vices.' One kind had already been singled out for special mention and condemnation in the opening canto, which sets the scene for all that follows:

> Our English soile, to Sodoms sinke
> Excessiue sinne transformd of late,
> Of foule deceite the loathsome linke,
> Hath worne all faith cleane out of date,
> The greatest sinnes mongst greatest sort,
> Are counted now but for a sport. (p. 135)

Perhaps this insistent emphasis on the idea of being idle derives from a knowledge of the Sonnets, where (61.5–7) the loved one's spirit is supposed to have been sent 'far from home, into my deeds to pry/To find out

shames and idle hours in me'. Many other *Willobie* allusions condemn
unchastity and adultery, another prime Sonnets topic (cf. 152.3, 'in act
thy bed-vow broke'); and there are hints of illicit pregnancy in the
apparently irrelevant annotation 'Gen. 38.24. Whoremongers burnt',
with its coded reference to Tamar, who 'hath played the harlot, and also,
behold, she is with child by whoredom. And Judah said, Bring her forth,
and let her be burnt.'

In case anyone doubted the intended multiple meanings and failed to
identify the 'noblemen' and 'gentlemen' in question, the writer of *Willobie*
is careful to provide further clues to the young Earl of Southampton,
including the names 'Henrico' and 'Harry' and the description 'Italo-
Hispalensis'. Henry or Harry Wriothesley was well known for his
affiliations with Catholicism (then associated with the enemy Spain, and
its hated Armada) and his fluency in Italian, inculcated by his language
teacher John Florio (often said to have been guyed by Shakespeare as
Holofernes or Don Armado in *Love's Labour's Lost*). Many of the Italian
mottoes quoted in *Willobie*, usually at the end of cantos, for no clear
reason and with no clear relevance, are to be found in the *Giardino di
Recreazione*, a collection of Italian sayings published by Florio in 1591. He
was a member of the Earl's household from 1594 or earlier.

There are, finally, even clearer clues to 'W.S.', whose early poetic
imagery and style is mocked by *Willobie* in 1594 just as maliciously as by
Greene and Nashe in earlier years, and by the *Parnassus* plays later. Thus
'W.S.' is made to say, sententiously, that

> The smothered flame, too closely pent,
> Burns more extreame for want of vent . . .
> So sorrowes shryned in secret brest,
> Attainte the hart with hotter rage,
> Then griefes that are to frendes exprest,
> Whose comfort may some part asswage. (p. 120)

Poetry-lovers of the period would surely recognise so plain a parody of
works already in print, such as *Venus and Adonis* 1593:

> An oven that is stopp'd . . .
> Burneth more hotly . . .
> So of concealed sorrow may be said
> Free vent of words love's fire doth assuage (331f)

or *Titus Andronicus* 1594: 'Sorrow concealed, like an oven stopp'd,/Doth
burn the heart to cinders where it is'* (II.iv.36–7). Similarly the further
assurance from 'W.S.' that 'She is no Saynt, She is no Nonne,/I think in
tyme she may be wonne' is also indebted to *Titus Andronicus*: 'She is a

---

* Cf *Edmund Ironside*: suppressed sorrow 'breaketh forth like hidden fire' (1517).

woman, therefore may be woo'd,/She is a woman, therefore may be won'* (II.i.82–3). 'H.W.' implausibly adds that 'The raging Lyon neuer rendes/The yeelding pray, that prostrate lyes' (p. 197). Here he may be alluding to *Edward III*: 'The lion scornes to touch the yeelding prey' (1806). That play is often attributed to Shakespeare (most recently by the Oxford editors Wells and Taylor, 1990); it might well have been written and performed by 1594, though not registered until late 1595.

'H.W.' also knows a garden decked 'With Couslips and with Eglentine,/ When wofull Woodbyne lyes reject' (p. 219), an unusual triple bouquet found again in *A Midsummer Night's Dream* (II.i.10, 15, 251, 252), sometimes said (e.g. Rowse 1965, 87) to have been performed at the marriage of Sir Thomas Heneage to Henry Wriothesley's widowed mother, the Countess of Southampton, on 2 May 1594, though not published until 1600.

There are other indications that the author of *Willobie* had privileged knowledge about the Southampton-Shakespeare relation, and the latter's works including those still unpublished in 1594, such as the Sonnets. Their readers could detect *Avisa* echoes; thus the youth addressed as 'Musick to heare, why hear'st thou musick sadly' (Sonnet 8.1) looks close kin to 'H.W.' who announces that 'I did once . . . musicke loue/Which . . . now I greatly hate' (p. 196). His 'cloud' that 'eclipst my bliss' and consequent question 'can change of ayre complexions change?' (p. 191) may recall that 'clouds and eclipses stain' the sun, whose 'gold complexion' is 'often . . . dimmed' (Sonnets 35.3; 18.6). Further, the whole of *Willobie* is written in six-line stanzas of iambic tetrameter rhyming ababcc, the form of 'Whenas thine eye hath chose the dame', published as Shakespeare's in *The Passionate Pilgrim, c.* 1599. There is no reason at all (*pace* Prince 1960, 169; Roe 1992, 54f.; etc.) to doubt that ascription; on the contrary these fifty-four lines were prima facie written by the young Shakespeare, long before *Willobie* 1594, and may well have circulated in manuscript like the Sonnets. That could explain the undeniable parallels between them and the forty-two lines of counsel obligingly supplied by 'W.S.' in *Willobie* (pp. 194–5; cf Roe 1992, 283). The shared theme is advice on how to woo and win a woman, which 'W.S.' assesses as 'a matter very easy to be compassed & no doubt with payne, diligence & some cost in time to be obtained' (p. 191). Thus the old married friend advises young 'H.W.', just as the *Passionate Pilgrim* poem proposes: 'Take counsel of some wiser head/Neither too young nor yet unwed.'

Willobie provides other pointers to the sonnet story and its chief male characters, who also figure in the *Parnassus* plays, where each exhibits the same basic characteristics during the same period. There too, Wriothesley in his Gullio guise is expressly presented as an over-emotional poetaster

---

* Cf *Edmund Ironside*: it is 'like a woman to be won with words' (1303).

who refuses to marry and is addicted to flowery Italian phraseology, just like 'H.W.'; there too Shakespeare is quoted and parodied.

The introduction to *Willobie his Avisa* 1594, though teasingly attributed to one 'Hadrian Dorrell', an Oxford man, specifically ascribes the text ('written with his own hand') to 'my very good frend and chamber fellow M. Henry Willobie, a yong man, and a scholler of very good hope' who has 'departed voluntarily to her Maiesties service'. Here too, therefore, are University Wits attacking Shakespeare. One known Henry Willobie was a young scholar at Oxford in 1594. At that time (Halliday 1964, 530), his elder brother's wife's sister was married to the Oxford graduate and Stratford resident Thomas Russell (1570–1634), who was a friend of Shakespeare's and indeed the overseer and a beneficiary of his will. Furthermore, as De Luna says, 'whether or not Shakespeare knew this young satirist personally, in all likelihood he at least knew his father, for in 1591 Thomas Russell 'joined with his friend Henry Willoughby the elder of Wiltshire in a bond dated in that year' (M. Eccles 1961, 117). So this same Henry Willobie or Willoughby was close enough for inside knowledge yet detached enough for satire.

Willobie remained popular; its meaning and message, however opaque now, must have been more transparent then. Perhaps not by coincidence, its fifth edition was published in the same year as the Sonnets, 1609,* while its sixth and last issue appeared in 1635, after a very long interval, in good time for the second edition of the Sonnets in *Poems* 1640. That latter volume contained a verse eulogy of Shakespeare by Leonard Digges (1588–1635), Thomas Russell's stepson by his second marriage, who had special knowledge and appreciation of Shakespeare and his work.

---

* Perhaps those publications rekindled interest in the University Wits' feud against lower-class law-clerks who dared to write poetic drama; the next year saw the publication of the anonymous play *Histriomastix, Or the Player whipt*, written in an age where 'every Scriveners boy shall dippe/Profaning quills into Thessaliaes spring'; one character speaks of a knight who 'shakes his furious Speare'.

XX

The Sonnets

THERE IS FURTHER corroboration, in the coherence of dates and circumstances, that the Sonnets began *c.* 1590 as exhortations to young Henry Wriothesley, 3rd Earl of Southampton (1573–1624). He too was the son and heir of a staunchly Catholic family, in a branch related by marriage to that of Shakespeare's mother, the Ardens.

That point is rarely mentioned, for all its relevance. The genealogy cited (Bowden 1899, 66) from the outstanding Shakespeare scholar Richard Simpson runs essentially thus: Edward Arden of Parkhall near Stratford married the aunt of Lady Catesby of Stratford, whose daughter's husband was Sir Henry Browne, whose sister Mary became Countess of Southampton and mother of Shakespeare's wealthy young patron. So their meeting was not necessarily a matter of mere chance or coincidence.

The 3rd Earl had been a precocious Cambridge undergraduate, who was writing essays in Latin by his thirteenth year. After taking his degree at sixteen, in 1589, he enrolled as a law student at Gray's Inn. In that same year, Shakespeare was called a law-clerk or legal copyist ('Noverint') by Thomas Nashe (XI). The Sonnets are redolent of the law in line after line, as if that were a common language linking poet and patron. Other connections include the fact that a version of *The Comedy of Errors*, which derives directly from a Latin source (Plautus, *Menaechmi*), was performed at Gray's Inn in 1594.

These important legal affiliations regularly remain unremarked, especially by the 'biography need not impinge' school of editors (Kerrigan 1986, 169). But commentators who themselves possess legal expertise offer assured guidance, thus: 'The language . . . alone undeniably evidences [Shakespeare's] considerable learning in the law', and indeed 'there is scarcely a sonnet which fails to contain a legal reference' (Knight 1973, 75, 78), much as one might expect if a law-clerk indited them to a law student. Their opening advocacy of marriage begins with 'heir' and 'contracted' (1.4–5), proceeds to 'succession' (2.12) and 'stop' [estop] (3.8) and expands into 'legacy', 'bequest', 'audit', and 'executor' (4.2–3, 12–14).

Shakespeare needed a patron under whose aegis he could improve his own neglected education, especially in the classics; the poetry of the early 1590s, notably the two long narratives dedicated to the expensively educated Southampton, already well known as a patron of poets and lover of the theatre, serves to confirm that this is what he had found. Both poems derive directly from Latin sources. *Venus and Adonis* flaunts an epigraph from Ovid, which may well have a personal significance and on any interpretation says that the poet is now inspired by the classics and has abjured popular art. Both *Venus* and *Lucrece* bear inscriptions written in a tone of deep indebtedness as well as service. The former's wording 'I . . . vow to take advantage of all idle hours, till I have honoured you with some graver labour' sounds like a promise to try really hard and do better next term, addressed to a tutor as well as a patron.

It is surely a sincere personal utterance, in the poet's own voice. His self-accusations of 'ignorance' and lack of learning (e.g. in Sonnet 78) are no doubt comparative, even rhetorically exaggerated; but treating them as merely poetic (Kerrigan 1986, 272), i.e. as falsehoods, devalues rather than elucidates the poetry and may also misplace a pivotal point in the poet's development.

The academic approach digs even deeper pitfalls. Thus it bears sole responsibility for all the decades of confusion about the famous inscription prefixed to the first edition of the Sonnets, as follows:

> TO. THE. ONLIE. BEGETTER. OF.
> THESE. INSVING. SONNETS.
> Mr. W. H. ALL. HAPPINESSE.
> AND. THAT. ETERNITIE.
> PROMISED.
> BY.
> OUR. EVER-LIVING. POET.
> WISHETH.
> THE. WELL-WISHING.
> ADVENTVRER. IN.
> SETTING.
> FORTH.
>
> T.T.

Editors always agonise about the theoretical meaning of 'begetter', thus promoting their own personal priorities. Typically, the most admired of academic textbooks on the topic (Ingram and Redpath 1964, closely followed by Kerrigan 1986, 168) begins its exegesis by asking 'What is a begetter?' and deciding that it must mean 'inspirer' not 'procurer' because that is the meaning they infallibly infer from their studies of the Oxford English Dictionary. But practical questions in real life are about actions not words, and people not definitions. All the Sonnet editors know that the 'T.T.' of 1609 was the publisher Thomas Thorpe. So 'Mr. W.H.' can hardly be the inspirer of the Sonnets. What publisher ever ventured to dedicate a book to its author's supposed inspirer? But Shakespeare is regularly treated as remote from ordinary reality; hence such assertions (Kerrigan 1986, 168) as 'it is virtually certain that' Mr. W.H. inspired the

Sonnets. One book (Muir 1979) goes so far as to call the 'fair friend' (104.1) 'W.H.' throughout. Yet such notions are not only baseless but counterfactual. The dedicatee is 'the onlie begetter', while the Sonnets have at least two inspirers: 'Two loves I have, of comfort and despair' (144.1). The other is the notorious Dark Lady, who has not been identified, despite the repeated and confident assurances of Dr Rowse (most recently in 1989, 32ff). There are however firm and extensive grounds to support the general conclusion that the young man to and for whom most of Sonnets 1 to 126 were written was indeed the young Henry Wriothesley, the 3rd Earl of Southampton. Even those who eschew biography (e.g. Kerrigan 1986, 11, 168–9, 221) can see clearly enough that he is by far the most plausible addressee, though their own interest ceases at that point.

Here are the ordinary reader's reasons for that identification. First, *Willobie his Avisa* (XIX) is a topical satire of 1594 about young H.W., the old player W.S, and their lady-love. This triangle is visibly congruent with the well-known names of the player-poet William Shakespeare and his patron Henry Wriothesley (as printed in the 1593 and 1594 dedications to *Venus* and *Lucrece*) and also with the story told in the Sonnets. Those poems address a noble (titled) young patron notable for his 'beauty, birth, . . . wealth and wit' [i.e. learning], which 'entitled in thy parts do crownéd sit'; thus abundance and glory are conferred upon the poet (37.5, 7, 10, 12). He speaks to his young lord in terms of triple 'duty' and indeed 'vassalage' (26.1, 2, 4, 5), and also of devoted love, in the most famous and admired volume of love poetry ever written. By the simple principle of economy, the recipient of those lines was the only known patron that Shakespeare ever had, to whom he had inscribed his only published poems in explicit terms of both duty and love; namely the rich, young, handsome, high-born patron of Shakespeare and other poets, the Earl of Southampton. Each of Shakespeare's dedicatory epistles culminates with the words 'in all duty'; the second adds a further reference to the writer's duty and says, most memorably, that 'The love I dedicate to your Lordship is without end . . . What I have done is yours, what I have to do is yours, being part in all I have devoted yours'. Love indeed, and vassalage too; Shakespeare lays his life and his works, past, present and future, at his young lord's feet. But modern editors of the poems remain unaffected by this amazing and moving statement (Prince 1960, M. Evans 1989), which at best is merely 'more personal' than that of *Venus* (M. Evans 1989, 207). So much for love without end. When modern editors of the Sonnets reach No. 26, which begins 'Lord of my love, to whom in vassalage/Thy merit hath my duty strongly knit' and ends with further assurances of present and future love, they find only 'a common idiom in dedications' (Ingram and Redpath 1964, 66) or even 'the commonplace literary language of courtly love' (Kerrigan 1986, 207). So much for Shakespeare.

But ordinary readers can soon see that the language as well as the thought and attitude of the poems' dedications is clearly cognate with the style and content of the Sonnets; thus the *Venus* dedication impugns 'idle hours' (like 61.7). Nor need it be coincidence that Thorpe's 1609 dedication of the sonnet volume wishes 'all happiness', as Shakespeare wished Southampton with *Venus and Adonis*.

Next, Sonnets 1 to 17 enjoin a young man to marry and have children, as if gently chiding him for a reluctance or refusal to do so. They thus tell us how the sequence began, in every sense. There is no a priori reason to suppose that any of its 154 components is misplaced. But the initial theme requires an explanation; the Tudor commoner would hardly presume to advise his noble patron about anything at all, let alone procreation, unless licensed or indeed engaged to do so. Young Henry Wriothesley was in grave disfavour from 1590 onward for refusing to marry his childhood sweetheart Lady Elizabeth de Vere, contrary to the wishes of his widowed mother the Countess of Southampton and his guardian Lord Burghley, Lady Elizabeth's grandfather. *Venus and Adonis*, inscribed to the same young man, is also full of similar arguments for marriage and progeny, again in the same language; cf 'Thou wast begot, to get it is thy duty./ Upon the earth's increase why shouldst thou feed/Unless the earth with thy increase be fed?' (168–70) and 'From fairest creatures we desire increase/. . . Thou . . . diest unless thou get a son/. . . You had a father, let your son say so' (Sonnets 1.1; 7.14; 13.14). This is the theme of the first seventeen sonnets, a self-contained group which would be aptly addressed to a seventeen-year-old youth, such as Southampton in 1590. In that year he was both fatherless (the 2nd Earl had died in 1581) and handsome: he strikingly resembled his mother, who had been a renowned beauty. Hence perhaps the preterite in 'you *had* a father' and the touching tribute of 'Thou art thy mother's glass, and she in thee/ Calls back the lovely April of her prime' (3.9–10).

The young lord of the Sonnets is accused of narcissistic self-love (1.6) and said to be even more beautiful than Adonis (53.5); in the poem Venus rebukes Adonis himself as a Narcissus (161). A Latin poem called *Narcissus* by John Clapham was dedicated to the young Earl of Southampton in 1591; its eponymous hero, who lives in England under the rule of a Virgin Queen, dies because of self-love. Clapham was the secretary and biographer of Lord Burghley, Southampton's guardian (Akrigg 1968, 33; A. Smith 1977). Of course the poem was aimed at its dedicatee in every sense, with the plain implication of sexual immaturity if not ambivalence. At nineteen years of age, in 1592, the young Earl was still beardless. As John Sanford then described him, in a Latin poem celebrating the Queen's visit to Oxford, 'his mouth scarcely yet blooms with tender down', adding that he was rich and outstanding in beauty and learning (*Oxford Historical Society*, viii, 1887, cited in Akrigg 1968, 35–6).

Shakespeare says the same about Adonis: 'the tender spring upon thy tempting lip/Shows thee unripe' (127–8); the image appears in the Sonnets: 'Thou art thy mother's glass' (3.9), 'A woman's face with Nature's own hand painted/Hast thou, the master-mistress of my passion/. . . For a woman wert thou first created' (20.1–2, 9) and 'you in Grecian tires are painted new' [as Helen of Troy] (53.8); and similarly in *A Lover's Complaint*: 'Small show of man was yet upon his chin;/His phoenix down began but to appear' (92–3). The patron's physical beauty of hair as well as feature is repeatedly attested, e.g. 'beauty/beauteous/beauty' (4.2, 5, 13) or 'buds of marjoram had stol'n thy hair' (99.7). 'Southampton's hair, a golden auburn in his portraits, curled naturally' (Rowse 1964, 205). This may well be one of the meanings implied in the Ovid quotation prefixed to *Venus and Adonis*: 'flavus Apollo' is a golden-wavy-haired sun-god, master of the Muses and patron of poets.

In the Sonnets, the young patron returns his poet's devotion ('thy sweet love'; 'dear friend', 29.13; 30.13 etc.) and also possesses 'wealth' (37.5). Only one person is on record as having helped Shakespeare financially, namely the wealthy young Earl of Southampton, with a gift of £1,000, a sizeable sum (about £100,000 in modern money). This is often asserted to be unthinkable, and to the loveless or the ungenerous no doubt it is. But even in crassly commercial terms it would be cheap at the price, especially with two great narrative poems thrown in, complete with personal dedications. The gift was cited by Rowe in 1709 on the authority of Sir William Davenant, who certainly knew Shakespeare personally. It was in 1594, furthermore, that Shakespeare needed capital to invest as a sharer in the Lord Chamberlain's theatre company, which he had recently joined. If the actual amount was in fact less, or a loan rather than an outright gift, or just a profitable investment in so lucrative a talent, the young Earl would still be by far the likeliest known source, and the 1590s the likeliest period; and those manifest inferences further enhance his identification as the young lord of the Sonnets. He was extremely rich; his grandfather the 1st Earl had been Henry VIII's accomplice in plundering the monasteries). There is no reason to doubt that young Henry was fined the enormous sum of £5,000, or half a million modern pounds, by Lord Burghley for his five-year refusal to marry the Lady Elizabeth de Vere; but there is no record that he failed to pay that punitive penalty, or indeed found the least difficulty in doing so. Revealingly, the sole source of this information was the Jesuit Father Garnet, whose manuscript note endorsed 19 November [1594] is preserved in the Stonyhurst archives (Akrigg 1968, 39). Catholics often had to pay especially heavy fines (VII).

In the Sonnets, the young patron is not only noble, as 'Lord of my love' (26.1) implies and 'birth' (37.5) says; he is also 'fond on praise' (84.14). Rather predictably, therefore, writers vied for his favours as a patron;

there was more than one rival poet (Sonnets 78–87). This is demonstrably true of Southampton in the 1590s. Both Barnaby Barnes and George Peele offered poetical tributes to him in 1593; the former's volume of verse *Parthenophil and Parthenope* has a dedicatory sonnet to Southampton, and Peele's poem *The Honour of the Garter* bestows that honour on him, prematurely. At about the same time, Thomas Nashe inscribed his prose fiction *The Unfortunate Traveller* 'To the Right Honourable Lord Henry Wriothesley Earl of Southampton' who is called 'A dear lover and cherisher . . . of Poets' (205). Nashe also presented his pornographic poem *The Choice of Valentines* with a prefatory sonnet to 'Lord S.', sometimes identified as Lord Strange, Earl of Derby (Steane 1972, 458). But it was Southampton who was accused of lustfulness, e.g. in Clapham's *Narcissus*, and the young lord of the Sonnets is not only charged with 'wantonness' (86.1) but actually shares the poet's mistress (41.9; 144.14), in about 1593. Nashe has surely heard about this; hence the saucy allusion in his 1593 dedication partly cited above; Henry Wriothesley is 'a lover of the lovers of Poets'. No wonder he was publicly pilloried in the Parnassus plays (XVIII) as 'lewd Gullio' (presented as the patron of the Nashe character Ingenioso) and as the lubricious 'H.W.' in *Willobie* (XIX). Both of those characters are young, over-emotional, rich, vain, reluctant to marry and addicted to Italian phraseology; each source also refers to Shakespeare by name.

Further, Nashe ends his *Choice of Valentines* with a second sonnet, this time expressing the hope to 'please Apollo's eye' and containing the defensive comment 'Ovid's wanton Muse did not offend'. These are surely references to 'Apollo' in the dedication of *Venus and Adonis* and that poem's use of erotic material from Ovid, again with personal application to Southampton. Here too, incidentally, is one possible explanation of Spenser's 'Aetion' as a reference to Shakespeare (XVII). That name has remained otherwise unknown in any context. But 'Aethon' in Ovid's *Metamorphoses* (I, 153) was one of the horses that drew the chariot of the sun god Apollo, and hence a suitable name for a poetic devotee of the high-born auburn-haired 'flavus Apollo', well versed in Ovid.

Another member of the same team, it has been colourably claimed, was Marlowe, whose *Hero and Leander* was written for, and indeed about, the Earl of Southampton, at the same period (e.g. Rowse 1964, xxvi). Sonnets 4 to 14 show awareness of that poem, then available in manuscript (Kerrigan 1986, 175). So Marlowe remained among Shakespeare's rivals (XVI). His main identification marks are usually assigned to Sonnet 86: 'his great verse', 'his spirit, by spirits taught to write/Above a mortal pitch', 'his compeers by night/Giving him aid' and 'that affable familiar ghost/Which nightly gulls him with intelligence' (86.1, 5–10). But most of this applies much more plainly to Barnaby Barnes, whose volume of verse mentioned above contains plentiful evidence of obsession with the spirit world and its conjuration. No such tendencies are documented about Marlowe, whose Mephostophilis in *Dr Faustus* (*pace* Rowse 1964, 178) can hardly be that informative ghost, least of all after Marlowe's death in 1593. Further, Southampton's countenance had certainly filled up Barnes's line, literally: 'with your countenance grac'd/ . . . vouchsafe . . . with gracious eyes/(Those heavenly lamps which give the Muses light)' (86.13). It is generally held that all this is far outweighed by the phrase 'great verse' (86.1), which is regularly interpreted as sincere and true, and hence applicable solely to Marlowe (Rowse, *passim*); but this assessment remains essentially subjective.

Thus the patronage of Southampton, as a rich young enthusiast for literature and drama, was predictably sought after,* not to say fought over. It will hardly be coincidence that the names of Marlowe, Nashe, Peele and other University-trained writers including Barnaby Barnes (*c.* 1569–1609) appear in the lists of contenders; rivals indeed (XVI). In addition, Antonio Perez sent a presentation copy of his autobiography *Relations* in 1593 or 1594 (Akrigg 1968, 37) and Gervase Markham dedicated his poem *The Tragedy of Sir Richard Grenville* (1595) to Southampton among others. The Sonnets specify such a superfluity with the memorable phrase 'wild music burthens every bough' (102.11), which also implies more generally the proliferation of other sonnet-sequences in the early 1590s.

These productions also independently point to the same period for Shakespeare's Sonnets. His Senecan tragedies such as *Titus* and the early *Hamlet* are closely contemporary with Kyd's *Spanish Tragedy*, his English histories with those of Peele and Marlowe, his *Venus and Adonis* with Marlowe's *Hero and Leander*. So his Sonnets would predictably belong in the same lustrum as Sidney's *Astrophel and Stella*, which though written much earlier was not published until 1591, when it set the fashion. That volume also contained twenty-seven sonnets by Samuel Daniel, whose separate sonnet-volume *Delia* followed in 1592. So did Henry Constable's *Diana*. Thomas Watson's *Tears of Fancie*, Barnaby Barnes's *Parthenophil and Parthenope*, Thomas Lodge's *Phillis* and Giles Fletcher's *Licia* appeared in 1593; Richard Barnefield's *Cynthia* and *Affectionate Shepherd* in 1594; Michael Drayton's *Idea's Mirror* and Edmund Spenser's *Amoretti* in 1595. Thereafter the fashion fades and sonnets dwindle and cease. Shakespeare was an originator, not an epigone.

Shakespeare himself helps to confirm that his own contributions belong to the same brief period of the early 1590s. His first truly creative poetry to be published (the 'first heir of my invention') was *Venus and Adonis* in 1593. But he was also wielding a poetic 'pupil pen' in his

---

* The earliest applicant may be the author of *Edmund Ironside c.* 1588, which not only creates a brave and staunch Earl of Southampton but stages an imaginary wedding there, with the contrived exchange 'How far off are we from Southampton? . . . Why, we are in the town' (476–7).

opening sonnet-sequence (16.9); so that too may be assigned to the early 1590s. This dating, further, enables parallels to be drawn between individual sonnets and historical events.

Thus the imagery of a house (in both senses) left dilapidated and unrepaired, as in Sonnets 10 and 13 ('that roof to ruinate/Which to repair should be thy chief desire'; 'Who lets so fair a house fall to decay/Which husbandry in honour might uphold?' 10.7–8;13.9), recalls the 3rd Earl's letter of 26 June 1592 to Michael Hicks, chief secretary to Lord Burghley, asking for the release of funds to repair 'my manor house at Beaulieu . . . like to fall into great decay'. This letter (BL Lansdowne 71) is signed 'H. Southampton' but written by a secretary; the hand has been identified as Shakespeare's (XXXVI).

The 'great princes' favourite' and 'painful warrior' capriciously disgraced in Sonnet 25 has long been identified with Sir Walter Raleigh (*c.* 1552–1618), who though a well-established favourite of Queen Elizabeth's was recalled from a freebooting expedition in February 1592 and imprisoned in the Tower that July. His offence was courting Elizabeth Throckmorton, one of the Queen's maids of honour, whom he later married. Shakespeare himself was 'in disgrace with fortune and men's eyes' (Sonnet 30.1) because of 'vulgar scandal' (Sonnet 112.2) put about by Robert Greene and Thomas Nashe in 1592 to 1593, as expounded above (XVI); hence his request to 'o'er-greene my bad' (Sonnet 112.4), i.e. not be considered as black as Greene paints him. That verb was specially invented for, and used only in, this context. No doubt Southampton was among the 'divers of worship', various gentry, who (as Chettle tells us, **182**) vouched for Shakespeare's honesty, and hence his innocence of the charge brought against him, namely plagiarism for personal prestige and profit. In that event the young Earl was well rewarded; the two great poems dedicated to him and published in 1593 and 1594 are presumably 'my books' (Sonnet 23.9) and also 'this written embassage' (Sonnet 26.3) which Shakespeare sends in manuscript to plead his own cause.

The 'growing age' of sonneteering (Sonnet 32.10) was also the early 1590s. If (as seems likely) Marlowe was among the main rival poets, then the transition from present to (mainly) past tense in Sonnet 86 is well explained by his death on 30 May 1593. The conjunction of a queen's jewel with a stern wolf (96.5, 10) assorts aptly with the 1594 arrest and trial of Elizabeth's physician Dr Lopez [= wolf, Latin *lupus*] and her retention of his ruby ring. Similarly, Time's 'pyramids [= obelisks] set up with newer might' (123.2) have been plausibly related (I. Wilson 1993, 167–8) to the four flanking obelisks on the design for the Earl of Southampton's Titchfield tomb, commissioned in 1594. By that year, Shakespeare was thirty. As a countryman and a touring actor he had worked and walked out of doors in all weathers. There is no difficulty or contradiction in his calling himself old (138.10); on the contrary, it would be surprising if he were not 'beated and chopped with tanned antiquity' (62.10), where the word 'tanned' is especially telling.

By 1594, the rivalry and rift between poet and patron for the favours of a mistress (Sonnets 34, 35, 41, 133, 134, etc.) were apparently over, according to *Willobie his Avisa* (XIX). The 'fools of time/Which die for goodness who have lived for crime' (124.14) are fully conformable with the Catholic martyrs whose beliefs constrained them to crime in the sense of contravening the 1593 laws of a Protestant Parliament, leading to judicial executions in 1594 and 1595. If 'supposed as forfeit to a confined doom' (107.4) means what it seems to say, namely 'we thought you were going to stay in prison for ever', then it may be dated either 1598 or 1603, when Southampton was in prison. 'My love looks fresh' from the same sonnet (107.9) also suggests a recent release. All such unforced correlations between the poetic text and the historical record have evidential value.

Finally, the main parallels of thought and imagery between the Sonnets and other works relate preponderantly to the two narrative poems dedicated to Southampton and to *Love's Labour's Lost*, *Romeo and Juliet* (both of which have Dark Lady characters) and *Richard III*.* Again the relevant studies (e.g. Isaac 1884, Sarrazin 1895, Schaar 1962) are independent of each other. The most extended canonical parallel is that between Sonnet 127 and the passage in *Love's Labour's Lost*, written in the 1590s (IV.iii.247–65), about blackness in beauty. Also relevant is the manifest kinship (Kerrigan 1986, 292–5) of the Sonnets with *Edward III*, a play often attributed to Shakespeare (e.g. Slater 1988, Wells and Taylor 1990), first published in 1596 but no doubt written earlier in accordance with the standard pattern of performance first and publication later, perhaps much later.

There are other candidates for the recipient of the Sonnets, just as there are for their writer. But William Herbert, 3rd Earl of Pembroke (1580–1630), for the former is on the same astral plane as Bacon for the latter. 'Mr. W.H.', the only factual connection, was always a red herring; he was the publisher's dedicatee, not the poet's. A penchant for identifying this plain Mr with an exalted Earl, and then converting both together into the Fair Friend (104.1), exemplifies the anti-historical approach actively preferred by many literati (Chambers 1930, i, 567; Halliday 1964, 360; J. Wilson 1963, 1966), psycho-analysts (Padel 1981) and others (e.g. Callow 1994). Further fanciful identifications of 'W.H.' include 'William Himself'

---

* The *Edmund Ironside* parallels are worth noting, e.g.: 'sun . . . marigolds . . . spread . . . glory . . . cloudy look' (1093f), 'spread . . . marigold . . . sun frown . . . glory' (Sonnet 25.5–8); 'raze out . . . dishonourable blot . . . book of . . . fame' (748–9), 'from the book of honour razéd forth' (Sonnet 25.11); 'truth needs no colours' (1197), 'truth needs no colour' (Sonnet 101.6); and see XXII.

(Barnstorff 1862) and a misprint for 'W.SH', again meaning William Shakespeare himself (D. Foster 1987).

By contrast, Southampton was Shakespeare's only known patron, from 1593 onward, and the only person for whom he ever publicly declared his love. Each of those dear friends is separately linked by extant evidence to the Essex rebellion of 1603, while that rebel Earl himself (Southampton's fellow-conspirator and cousin-in-law) was the only living person to whom Shakespeare ever alluded anywhere in his work (*Henry V*).

From the historical viewpoint a likely candidate for Mr. W.H. would be Sir William Harvey, who in 1598 married Southampton's widowed mother. She usually referred to him, and to her second husband Sir Thomas Heneage, as 'Master' or 'Mr.'; it was the regular form of address 'for persons of recognised status', from an M.A. to a knight (Rowse 1964, xi). She left Master Harvey most of her possessions when she died in April 1607. Perhaps he took the Sonnets and *A Lover's Complaint* to their 1609 publisher. That would explain what Thorpe, who was noted for his flowery language, meant by calling Mr. W.H. their 'onlie begetter'. Thorpe also wished Harvey 'that eternity promised by our ever-living poet', which was most obviously the continuing life of one's progeny as promised in Sonnets 1 to 17, not (*pace* Kerrigan 1986, 169) 'the immortality assured the youth in sonnets like 81 and 107'. By 1609 Harvey had recently remarried the significantly named Cordelia Annesley, whose old father was losing his mind. It seems that Shakespeare was still in close touch with the Southampton circle; and he might well have consented to the publication of the Sonnets. Otherwise there would have been no question of any eternity for them or anyone. The misprints in that first edition (such as the involuntary repetition of 'my sinful earth', 146.1–2) certainly show that the poet had not read the proofs. There is however no reason to doubt that the original manuscript was holograph. On that basis, the printing errors permit interesting inferences about Shakespeare's handwriting. For example, his 'your' could be misread as 'you' (13.7) and conversely (16.7), while his 'thy' must have looked very like 'their' (27.10; 35.8; 43.11; 45.12; 46.3, 8, 11, 14; 69.5; 70.6) to at least one compositor. Again, the words printed in italics were presumably written thus by the poet, like foreign words or proper names in the plays. Other examples, such as *Rose* (1.2), need special explanation; perhaps Wriothesley was sometimes pronounced 'Roseley'? Similarly the line printed as 'A man in hew all *Hews* in his controwling' (20.7) seemed so evidently yet enigmatically meaningful as to persuade Oscar Wilde to postulate the existence of a boy-actor named Hughes with whom Shakespeare was in love. But perhaps the word refers to an embroidered or otherwise inscribed name-monogram, such as 'He. W', or

Henry   Wriothesley
Earl of   Southampton.

On any analysis, all the copious evidence confirms, and none denies, that this was indeed the name 'which from hence immortal life shall have' (81.5). But only historians (notably Dr A.L. Rowse) have honoured that promise; the modern literary establishment has mislaid name and life alike, among much else.

XXI

The Actor-Playwright of the 1590s

NO EVIDENCE LINKS the Sonnets, or any other single work by Shake-speare, with William Herbert (1580–1630), the 3rd Earl of Pembroke. But he and his brother Philip, the 4th Earl (1584–1650), received the dedi-cation of the first Complete Works in 1623 because 'your lordships have been pleased to think these trifles something heretofore, and have pros-ecuted them and their author, living, with so much favour . . . therefore, we most humbly consecrate to your highnesses these remains of your servant Shakespeare . . .'.

The manifest yet mainly unmentioned inference is that he had served in the 2nd Earl's theatre company. This was unknown before 1592, and reported as bankrupt in September 1593. But even a brief membership would qualify any Pembroke's Man as a servant of the young future earls; and there is no reason to doubt that their benevolence continued until Shakespeare's death in 1616, and their appreciation until their own. Further, such service neatly bridges a known gap, caused by the plague years. By 1592 the Queen's Men (XIV) were in terminal decline; by 1594 Shakespeare had joined the Chamberlain's company. No doubt the lead-ing Queen's Men would transfer to a new troupe as readily as it would recruit them. It is surely sensible to suppose (*pace* the universal but unevidenced academic assumptions about theatre companies' alleged rights) that an experienced and shrewd business-man like Shakespeare, with legal training (XI), would soon secure some control in the ownership and performance of his own plays and indeed take them with him. So the arguments about his original authorship of the Queen's plays he later rewrote (XIV, XXVI, XXVII) will also apply to certain Pembroke's plays of the early 1590s, especially when the facts are allowed to speak for them-selves after the removal of such gags as 'memorial reconstruction' theory (XXXI). Thus *The True Tragedy of Richard Duke of York* as published in 1595 with the affidavit 'as it was sometimes acted by the Right Honourable the Earl of Pembroke his servants', is prima facie a play by one such servant, William Shakespeare, just as its later title-page affirms. So therefore is its earlier companion piece, published in 1594 as *The First Part of the Conten-tion betwixt the two famous Houses of Yorke and Lancaster*. The same applies to another first version, *The Taming of A Shrew*, published in 1594 'As it was sundry times acted by the Right Honourable Earl of Pembrook his seruants'. It was prima facie with that company that Shakespeare had toured in 1592 or 1593, as recorded in the Sonnets: 'from you have I been absent in the spring' (98.1), 'large lengths of miles' away (44.10) from the friend, on horseback journeys (50), etc. Similarly the 1594 first edition of *Titus Andronicus* (**190**) refers to performance by the Earl of Pembroke's servants, thus offering a further justification for 'your servant Shakespeare'.

That play had also been performed by Sussex's Men and Derby's Men. The former company played 'Buckingham', perhaps an early version of *Richard III* (**189**), at the end of 1593. The latter's floruit can be definitely dated, since it existed only between September 1593, when Ferdinando Stanley, Lord Strange, became 5th Earl of Derby, and April 1594, when he died. Before then, Strange's company had also played an extensive repertory season at the Rose, including the popular *1 Henry VI* (**173**) in March and April 1592, as noted by Nashe later that same year (**XVI**). Also very popular was 'Tittus and Vespacia' (**175**), again repeatedly played by Strange's Men, which qualifies as an early version of *Titus Andronicus*.

During these plague years, separate theatre troupes are hard to find in the fog of reformation and amalgamation, further obscured by the closure of the London theatres for three months at the end of 1592 (**180**) and for well over a year in 1593 to 1594 (**185**). But as the health hazards abate, the scene clears. As companies reform or founder, playscripts are released for publication. One of them may well have been the earliest *Hamlet*, now lost; Gabriel Harvey's later mention of it (**XVII**) 'appears to refer to a work that could be read . . .' (Jenkins 1982, 6). That play figures in the best-documented account of any joint production from this period. At Newington Butts (**199**), in June 1594, the Admiral's Men and the Lord Chamberlain's Men together performed *The Taming of A Shrew*, *Hamlet* and *Titus Andronicus*. Presumably both companies had been depleted by deaths and defections. Shakespeare had joined Chamberlain's by December of that year (**198**), and he stayed with it for the rest of his life. Prima facie he was already a member by June, and had once again brought his early plays with him. Already, therefore, by 1592 or earlier, he was indeed a Shake-scene, who dominated the London and provincial theatre world as a competent actor and leading playwright. Such eminence would have taken time to attain. Next came a period of stability and prosperity, when Shakespeare would be widely known to readers as well as playgoers, readily recognisable and verifiable by his special style.

XXII

Early Style: the Noted Weed

SHAKESPEARE HIMSELF SURELY says in the 1590s that his sonnet style is readily identifiable:

> Why write I still all one, ever the same,
> And keep invention in a noted weed [well-known guise],
> That every word doth almost tell my name,
> Showing their birth and where they did proceed?
>
> (Sonnet 76.5–8)

Editors (Ingram and Redpath 1964, 91, 177; Kerrigan 1986, 221, 270) interpret these lines as a reflection of the prevailing aesthetic; the poet laments his lack of subject-matter, in the rhetorical procedure of *inventio*. Instead, the historian and biographer A.L. Rowse glosses: 'by this time his own style was readily recognisable . . . his name by now was well known for his plays . . .' (1964, 155).

Both viewpoints together provide a better perspective. An analysis of Kerrigan's apparatus identifies the salient stylistic features of the Sonnets: allusions to Tudor law, the Bible, and Ovid's *Metamorphoses*, by the dozen, and puns or quibbles by the score. Other overlapping characteristics noted by Kerrigan include bawdry, proverbs, echoes of Marlowe, Spenser or Sidney, and such technical devices as chiasmus. Exactly these same stylistic components are found throughout Shakespeare's earliest known plays.* These are mainly written in the same metre as the Sonnets, often with rhymes, and can even incorporate actual sonnets, as in *Love's Labour's Lost* (IV.iii.58–71) or the Prologue to *Romeo and Juliet*. Both those plays have a dark lady named Rosaline, with apparent relevance to the sonnet story. The former has clear claims to the status of a *drame à clef* relating to the Southampton milieu and entourage; the same may apply to *The Two Gentlemen of Verona* (Rowse 1989, 61–4). Kerrigan (1986, 293–5) adds copious sonnet parallels with *Edward III* (published in 1596), and says that such links strengthen the case for its Shakespearean authorship.

Many other far closer connections between that play and the Sonnets have passed unnoticed, including such clear clues to identity as the

---

*   Cf *Edmund Ironside*: law, Bible, Ovid, puns, *passim*; bawdry, 1140, 1151f; proverbs, 498, 581, 773, 1059, 1112, 1136, 1261, 1386, 1547, 1550, 1555, 1634, 1637, 1737, 1869; Spenser ('Braggadochio'), 1070; chiasmus (bless/curse/curse/bless), 827, (plainly thus/thus plainly) 1319–20.

so-called 'blot cluster' of interlinked imagery. Its *Edward III* context (II.i.146–72) was described by its discoverer thus:

> The key-word, *blot*, is accompanied by *heaven, night, moon, constancy, disguise (mask), sovereign, eye, winter,* and *sun.* All these words, except *constancy* and *disguise,* appear also in a passage in *Love's Labour's Lost* (IV.iii.220ff); five of them, including *inconstancy, constant* and *disguise* appear in *The Two Gentlemen of Verona* (V.iv.107ff), seven of them in *Richard II* (I.iii.202ff), six of them in *Venus and Adonis* (773–816) and five in another passage in the same poem (154–93). There are traces of the same cluster in ten other plays and in *Lucrece.* (Muir 1960, 22)

Hence that passage in *Edward III* was written by Shakespeare, an attribution now generally accepted (most recently by Slater 1982, 1988, followed by Proudfoot 1985, Kerrigan 1986 and Wells and Taylor 1990). On any rational appraisal, the same evidence entails the same conclusion; in Academia, the preconceived conclusion invalidates the evidence. Exactly the same image-cluster, in the selfsame detail, was noted in *Edmund Ironside* by a researcher (Jackson 1963, 331) who thence inferred the opposite, namely that there must be something amiss with the whole notion of image-clusters, on the unspoken assumption that *Ironside* cannot possibly be by Shakespeare. The same *non sequitur* was soon repeated, and the same assumption explicitly avowed, in a book about authorship evidence (Schoenbaum 1966, 188–9).

The plays and the poem mainly invoked by Muir have all been separately identified as intersecting with the Southampton circle. Sonnet 33, addressed directly to him (XX), contains in its fourteen lines the key synonyms *stain . . . staineth* (14), together with *heavenly* (4) and *heaven's* (14), *masked* (12) and *his visage hide* (7), *sovereign* (2), *eye* (2), *sun* (9, 14) and *suns* (14). Constancy is, in a word, the theme of the sonnet. The darkness of night and the coldness of winter are both caused by the clouds that occlude the source of light and warmth; thus the associations are further illuminated. 'Face' (33.3, 6) also appears in the canonical passages cited. Further traces occur elsewhere in the Sonnets (e.g. 18; 35). This new evidence deserves close and unbiased attention.

The avowedly deep significance of links between *Edward III* and the Sonnets, admitted even by the anti-biographical school (Kerrigan 1986), concedes that style is the man, or at least that the two overlap, like life and works in general. The artist and his personality stride forward together in step, with increasing experience and maturity. Both should thus be readily recognisable, at any given stage, from the very first, exactly as suggested or stated by Marlowe, Nashe, Greene, Spenser, the *Parnassus* playwright, the *Willobie* author, and indeed Shakespeare himself.

Yet among all the oceans of modern Shakespeare commentary, hardly a drop has ever touched upon this topic, because his art is eccentrically seen as a sudden sunburst in his late twenties, after ten lost years spent stumbling about in the dark. In his case, and his alone, Academia admits no gradual process of artistic development. The dawn never arises; the first light is high noon.

It is surely more sensible, as well as better-attested, to accept that Shakespeare 'did not simply burst into life as a fully-fledged dramatist' (Wilders 1986) in his late twenties but began early, with popular plays. Once they had run their course upon the stage, they would be published, because that too was profitable. But where are they now? At the leisurely rate of two a year, the so-called 'Lost Years' (lost by literary theory, not by Shakespeare himself) would contain at least twenty of them, all utterly unknown to the present-day reading and playgoing public. Prima facie, they might well exemplify successive stages of the 'noted weed' well known to its wearer and his contemporaries. But there are no specialists in style. The accredited experts not only failed to recognise *King Lear* 1608 as a mature masterpiece but actually condemned it as a corrupt 'memorial reconstruction', *for most of this century* (Taylor 1988, 509). What chance of recognition, then, does Shakespeare's *early* style now stand?

None, unless from the vantage-point of the 1590s instead of the 1990s. When the savage menagerie of Shakespeare's early imagery was first specifically indicted (Greene 1592), no work of his had ever been printed under his own name. Yet the 'tiger's heart' allusion to Queen Margaret of England was readily recognisable; literary London would already know which dramatist treated queens as tigers, and in which plays. Greene was prophetic. Three years later, the line he chose to parody appeared in print, albeit anonymously, in *The True Tragedy of Richard Duke of York*. The equally anonymous *Titus Andronicus* had been published a year earlier. Here too every word almost told its author's name; for example, Queen Tamora of the Goths is twice called a 'ravenous tiger' (V.iii.5, 195), among other fierce animals. The same style recurs throughout the two long narrative poems *Venus and Adonis* and *The Rape of Lucrece*, which despite their deep differences of theme and treatment continue to bristle with beasts and birds of prey, and venomous reptiles, all emblematic of villains and wickedness. Each such source also copiously exemplifies the special style of the young countryman still obsessed (not too strong a word) by animal and plant life. One name scoffingly awarded by the satirical Nashe in 1589 was 'Pliny', the most famous classical writer on natural history. Here surely, in all those crows, owls, peacocks, falcons, vipers, bees, pines, cedars and many other such flora and fauna, including lions, tigers, and basilisks,* is one aspect of Shakespeare's style that was instantly identified

---

* As also throughout *Edmund Ironside*: crow (1362), peacock (283), falcon (480–81), viper (167), bees (1336), pines and cedars (1341), lions (1448), tigers (1349), basilisk (1652) owls (637).

and imitated, in sport or spite, and is now all but forgotten, even by his most expert editors (thus Kerrigan 1986 makes no mention of it despite dozens of such allusions throughout the Sonnets).

Yet Shakespeare was the only lyric or dramatic poet ever to be thus identified. So all his early histories, tragedies and comedies ought to have remained recognisable from their ideas and imagery springing from close observation of tame or wild animals against a background of weather and seasons, growth and decay, varied with the homely wisdom of proverbs and sayings.* The student of Shakespeare also expects copious if not always accurate reference to the Bible (as pilloried by Greene in 1587, and perhaps also by *Willobie*'s marginalia) and classical or Italianate sources such as Ovid, Seneca, Plutarch† and Ariosto (as instanced by Nashe in 1589) together with occasional deliberate allusions to those contemporary colleagues whom Greene in 1592 openly accused him of plagiarising, namely Marlowe, Nashe, Peele and Greene himself.

The many other idiosyncrasies noted in documentary sources already cited include not only the obvious insistence on puns and quibbles, and constant legal or financial allusion, but the occasional contrast of red and white, and references to the power of fire, frost, storm and oratory. More general poetic style is described by detractors as over-rhetorical, with 'tragicall speeches' and so forth. It is especially stigmatised for its naive classical personifications, and banal Latin quotations.‡ Other plain evidence, which can be examined afresh as soon as the distorting lens of 'memorial reconstruction' is removed, includes the fact that Shakespeare, and always and only he, in Tudor times or any other, is the dramatist who on copious title-page and manuscript evidence regularly rewrites and revises and reworks his own plays. There are many other such early pointers and indications, which only a few scholars (notably Everitt 1954 and Feuillerat 1961) have ever attempted to describe in detail. Obvious examples are the ceaseless alliteration and antithesis found throughout Shakespeare, especially in the earlier work. All such characteristics can be combined into a complex fingerprint showing typical touches which would surely help to discriminate among the many juvenilia and apocrypha.

---

*   See also *Edmund Ironside* for weather and proverbs *passim*.
†   *Edmund Ironside* contains Biblical and Ovidian references by the dozen; Senecan style and incident *passim*; and Plutarch (777, 1551–5).
‡   Cf *Edmund Ironside*: 'his colour comes and goes' (1306), allusions to the power of fire, frost and storm, passages about the powers of oratory (1179f, 1275f), personifications including Boreas, a Latin quotation (1555–6), etc. as already exemplified, together with alliteration, repetition and antithesis *passim*. Many such ideas and phrases are echoed or repeated in canonical plays; some fifty in *Titus Andronicus*, forty in *1–3 Henry VI*, thirty in *Richard II* and *Richard III*, twenty in *Henry IV* and *Henry V* and another fifty elsewhere in the canon.

Another pointer is verbal invention, expressed in new coinages or usages, and duly recorded in the Oxford English Dictionary as first citations, or indications of Shakespearean provenance. Thus the painstaking analysts of vocabulary (Hart 1934, 1942; Slater 1988) are in full agreement with each other, and with all academic commentators who have specialised in the subject (e.g. Kerrigan 1986; Wells and Taylor 1990) that *Edward III* is a Shakespeare play in its entirety; it has 'in proportion to its length the largest vocabulary* of any play belonging to the last decade of the sixteenth century that I have examined' (Hart 1934, 222), i.e. almost all that have survived.

Pending new editions of the plays that bear these hallmarks, in varying proportions, for which there is other evidence of Shakespearean authorship (before 1594, the period here under review) the following chapters set out in summary form all the relevant arguments and a selection of textual data, in the hope of stimulating and assisting further research.

---

* The same can be said of *Edmund Ironside* in the previous decade, and its ratio as defined is even higher than that of *Edward III* (Sams 1985f, 346–7).

XXIII

Ur Hamlet

NASHE ATTACKED A popular play called *Hamlet*, and its author, in 1589 (160; XVI). That playwright, even though no *Hamlet* text was printed until 1603, was the young Shakespeare, on the following grounds among others (see also Sams 1988c, 1993b, 1995):

1 Nashe was writing under the aegis of his mentor Greene, who famously attacked Shakespeare (179; XVI) and no other known or named playwright.

2 Shakespeare was writing popular plays in the 1580s (137).

3(a) He is the only playwright known to have rewritten or revised his own work in Tudor times;

 (b) conversely, there is no evidence that he ever rewrote or revised anyone else's work (XXXII, XXXIII). So

 (c) economy of reasoning (also known as Ockham's Razor) and common sense say that the same revising author wrote and rewrote all the various versions of *Hamlet* as of any other multiple-text play (e.g. *King Lear*).

4(a) The Danish prince is called Amlethus (Saxo Grammaticus 1514) or Amleth (Belleforest 1570), never Hamlet, in the only known sources; so

 (b) that name was changed to Hamlet by the early dramatist, for some personal reason. But

 (c) this was the name of *Shakespeare's only son* (1585–96), after the Stratford friend Hamlett (so spelt in Shakespeare's will) Sadler, who was prima facie related to the Katherine Hamlett whose drowning in the Avon had been the subject of a 1580 Stratford inquest verdict relevant to the famous fate of Ophelia.

5(a) Both *Hamlet* and Kyd's *The Spanish Tragedy* were indebted to Seneca (e.g. *Thyestes*) for the idea of a vengeful ghost which initiates the action;

 (b) both are identified in Nashe's 1589 attack on Seneca-plagiarists, the former by a mention of its title and the latter by a typical sly allusion to its author ('the *Kidde* in Aesop'). But

 (c) Nashe's repeated plurals ('companions' 'they', 'followers [of Seneca]' etc.) entail at least two playwrights, who both have to be recognised by Nashe's readers; so

(d)   if one was Kyd, the other was not; hence

(e)   the obvious and clear candidacy is Shakespeare's.

6   Again, the non-Stratfordian Kyd is independently eliminated by 4 (a)–(c) and 5 (a)–(d) above; again, that leaves Shakespeare.

7(a) Nashe's reference inculpates 'English Seneca'; and

(b)   the only dramatist ever thus associated in any contemporary source was Shakespeare (Meres 1598: 'As . . . *Seneca* [is] accounted the best for . . . Tragedy among the Latines: so *Shakespeare* among the English . . .)'

8(a) Nashe's reference implies a known actor as well as a playwright: 'he will afford you . . . tragical speaches';

(b)   only Shakespeare was a known actor-playwright.

9(a) Nashe's reference implies the actual actor of the Ghost: 'if you entreat him fair on a frostie morning';

(b)   the Ghost in his own *Hamlet* was Shakespeare's best-remembered role.

10(a) Nashe says that the early *Hamlet* was written by a noverint or lawyer's clerk;

(b)   the extant evidence (XI) entitles Shakespeare far more than Kyd to such a description.

11(a) Nashe also pillories playwrights who borrowed from Cicero's *Tusculan Disputations*;

(b)   the first dialogue is about life after death, and hinges on 'id aut esse aut non esse', *anglice* 'to be or not to be'; hence

(c)   Shakespeare.

12(a) An early *Hamlet* had been played by the Admiral's Men and the Chamberlain's Men jointly in June 1594, together with *Titus Andronicus c.* 1589; but

(b)   *Hamlet* does not figure in later Admiral's repertory, hence

(c)   it was a Chamberlain's play in 1594, when Shakespeare was a Chamberlain's Man; and

(d)   like *Titus Andronicus*, it was a Shakespeare play, *c.* 1589.

13(a) An early *Hamlet* was performed at the Shoreditch Theatre in or before 1596, as Lodge recalled in *Wit's Miserie* of that year; and

(b)   the theatre was then the playhouse of Shakespeare's own company, the Chamberlain's Men.

14(a) The *Hamlet* quoted by Lodge was not the First Quarto text, which does not contain the words 'Hamlet, revenge'; hence

(b)   it was prima facie the 1589 version.

15(a) Lodge's tone is scoffing (Hibbard 1987, 13);

(b)   he was associated with Greene, who complained of Shakespeare's plagiarism;

(c)   *Venus and Adonis* seems indebted to Lodge's 1589 volume of poetry *Scilla's Metamorphosis* (Halliday 1964, 284); so

(d)   Lodge 1596 is hitting at Shakespeare (XVI).

16(a) Gabriel Harvey attributed *Hamlet* to Shakespeare, in a source which (Boas 1923, 256–60) there is no reason to date later than 1598; but

  (b) the only *Hamlet* known to have existed then was the play named by Nashe in 1589.

17(a) Harvey seems to be writing about a published *Hamlet* (Jenkins 1982, 6) which he knew to be by Shakespeare;

  (b) *Hamlet* was performed jointly with *Titus Andronicus* and *The Taming of A Shrew*, both of which were published in that same year, 1594; so

  (c) perhaps *Hamlet* was also published, though no copies now remain.

18(a) Experts (e.g. Jenkins 1982, 96f) have demonstrated that Shakespeare must have been deeply indebted to the 1589 *Hamlet* for scores of detailed ideas (summarised in Sams 1988c, 23–4) which he incorporated in his later masterpiece; but

  (b) in the real world, Shakespeare could hardly have plundered so much of *Hamlet* from someone else.

The other pan of the scales has stayed down for a century or so. Yet its sole contents are the personal opinion that 1589 was too early for Shakespeare, so Nashe's phrase 'the *Kidde* in Aesop', though a full fifty words after the reference to *Hamlet*, nevertheless identifies Kyd as its author, whether 'quite possibly' (Barton 1980, 15) or 'highly probably' (Jenkins 1982, 84). This notion is not only unevidenced but counter-factual. Nashe repeatedly refers to two or more people (5 above); believers in 'Kyd's *Hamlet*' have to assert that this plethora of plurals must refer solely to one singular person, namely Kyd, because 'all together the items listed are conclusive of identity' (Jenkins 1982, 84). But this deduces the evidence from the verdict. Of course Nashe could be, and indeed obviously was, talking about two people. Nor should anyone silently assume that Shakespeare blatantly plagiarised a known and named colleague, least of all without a word of comment, let alone censure, from any of his critics (XVI). Further, the Kyddites have to reject Shakespeare not only as the author of *Hamlet* ('too early') but also as a reviser of his own work (3 above); otherwise 'late start', 'Bad Quarto', 'memorial reconstruction' and the rest (XXXI–XXXIII) are sacrificed along with 'Kyd'. Hence the typically subjective assurance that 'my conception of Shakespeare is of a supremely inventive poet who had no call to rework his previous plays when he could always move on to a new one', and 'if it comes to be accepted that the Quarto and Folio texts of *King Lear* represent two Shakespearean versions, the exception will be of a kind, I think, to prove the rule' (Jenkins 1982, 5). Rationally speaking, however, that revision would prove the rule *wrong*.

Similarly, argument 5 above has encountered entrenched opposition, again on no evidence save the unshakeable preconviction, cited from scholars (such as Schoenbaum 1971, Wells 1994), that Mr and Mrs

Shakespeare called their only son 'Hamnet' (Nye 1993, Freeman 1993) not its alternative spelling Hamlet. Another authority, while apparently accepting the facts, nevertheless wonders whether Kyd too might not have had good reason to amend Amleth to Hamlet (Jackson *ShS* 1991, 267–8). In other words, let's stick with our 'Kyds' as with our 'Hamnets', evidence or not. Again, all argument about *Hamlet* can always be dismissed as insufficiently polite (Jackson *ShS* 1991) or even 'polemical' (Ward 1992). But the facts and the arguments far outweigh the feelings and opinions, as would soon be seen if the empty pan of the scales were ever released.

XXIV

Hamlet *1603*

THE AUTHORSHIP OF this much maligned text should be assigned to Shakespeare, not 'memorial reconstruction by pirate-actors' (XXXI), on the following grounds among others (see also Sams 1983, 1988c, 1989a, 1991a, Bains 1993, Urkowitz 1988a, 1992, Sprinchorn 1994a–c):

1   Economy of reasoning (also known as Ockham's Razor) or common sense far prefers one known person and process, i.e. Shakespeare the reviser, to dozens of hypothetical entities and circumstances.

2   Those effective instruments of thought are further sharpened by the attribution of the unpublished 1589 *Hamlet* to Shakespeare, for the eighteen basic reasons set out above (XXIII).

3(a)   Shakespeare revised even his masterpieces, such as *King Lear*; hence

(b)   the stylistic disparities for which this first edition (Q1) is notorious are best explained by revision. Further,

4(a)   of course some of the 1589 text might have been retained; so

(b)   the dates themselves would serve to explain any stylistic disparities. Besides,

5(a)   there is no reason to doubt that Q1 was the publication licensed by the registration to James Roberts in July 1602 of 'A booke [= playscript] called the Revenge of Hamlett Prince Denmarke as yt was latelie Acted by the Lord Chamberlayne his servantes', i.e. Shakespeare's own company; but

(b)   that registration was formally granted by two masters of the Stationers' Company; so

(c)   the text was prima facie genuine. Further,

6   Q1 is announced, on its 1603 title-page, by its readily identifiable publishers 'N.L. [i.e. Nicholas Ling] and John Trundell' as a play

(a)   written by William Shakespeare and

(b)   acted by his company (the King's Men, as they had been renamed after the accession of James I); so again, on both counts by double testimony,

(c)   that text was prima facie genuine. Further,

7(a)   in 1598, the same James Roberts (5 above) had already registered *The Merchant of Venice*, which he printed in 1600 together with *Titus Andronicus* Q2;

(b)   also in 1600, he had registered other 'Lord Chamberlens mens plaies' including 'As you like yt, Henry the Fift, and the Commedie of much A doo about nothing'; so

(c)   the printed texts were authentic, and there is no reason to impugn the registrations.

8   In 1607, the same Nicholas Ling (6 above) owned the rights in *Love's Labour's Lost* and *Romeo and Juliet* as well as in *Hamlet*; again there is no reason to doubt their or his *bona fides*, then or ever.

9(a)   The incontestably authentic *Hamlet* Q2 was printed by James Roberts for Nicholas Ling, who had also published Q1; hence again

(b)   Q1 was also authentic.

10(a)   Q2 (*c.* 3700 lines) was announced on its title-page as 'Newly imprinted and enlarged to almost as much again as it was, according to the true and perfect copy';

(b)   in other words, it was a revision of Q1 (2500 lines) which as readers could readily check was also 'by William Shakespeare'.

11(a)   Text-editors have argued that 'the compositors of Q2 made use of an exemplar of Q1'; if so

(b)   Q1 was prima facie regarded as a reliable and authentic text in its own right.

12   Gabriel Harvey's *c.* 1598 allusion to Shakespeare's *Hamlet* may well refer to Q1 as well as the 1589 play.

13(a)   The Q1 title-page refers to its performances by the Chamberlain's Men in Cambridge and Oxford; but

(b)   no Cambridge performances can be traced after the mid-1590s; so

(c)   they occurred in 1594, soon after Shakespeare had joined that company and brought his plays with him.

14   On strong textual evidence (J. Wilson 1918), Q1 derived from a Shakespeare manuscript.

15   Q1 contains otherwise unknown lines which are deemed authentically Shakespearean by some modern editors (e.g. Spencer 1980).

16   Given that an early *Hamlet* alluded to Cicero's 'id aut esse aut non esse' (XXIII, argument 11), Nashe may well have heard the Q1 words 'To be or not to be, ay, there's the point'; that latter phrase neatly translates 'id' in this context, far better than the more familiar 'that is the question'.

Again the rest is silence. There are no factual counter-arguments to show that Shakespeare did not write *Hamlet* Q1, or that anyone else did, least of all amnesiac actors. Yet such phantoms haunt edition after edition (e.g. Spencer 1980, Jenkins 1982, Edwards 1985, Wells 1986, Hibbard 1987, Taylor 1988) and still defy exorcism (Vickers 1993, 1994, Jenkins 1994, Wells 1994, 199). Even the explicit concession (Taylor 1988, 398) that the unfamiliar style found in Q1 might be very early Shakespeare is rejected without discussion (idem) in favour of the preconviction that Q1 is a 'report', not a play.

Such reticence has long been standard procedure. No further thought is needed; we must all just believe 'what we are required to suppose' (Jenkins 1982, 20). But recently the case has been reopened, because an edition of Q1 (Holderness and Loughrey 1992) has rejected 'memorial reconstruction'. A rasping review (Vickers 1993) sought to reimpose orthodoxy, thus incurring a grave responsibility. The laity follows the clerisy, which follows its leaders. Detailed analysis of their current claims is therefore essential; for if they are as mistaken about *Hamlet* 1603 as they confessedly were about *King Lear* 1608, yet another Shakespeare play will be wrongly rejected for decades as a botched corruption by pirate-actors. But the claim that *King Lear* 1608 was a 'memorial reconstruction', once made just as confidently, was later grudgingly withdrawn by its own inventor (Duthie 1949, 1960), who had also earlier asserted just as absurdly (XXV) that *The Taming of A Shrew* was a 'memorial reconstruction' (Duthie 1943). No literary theorist has ever been more thoroughly discredited. Even Duthie's own candid descriptions of his practices (1960, 131) are self-condemnatory, thus: 'In my 1949 edition [of *King Lear*] I adopted . . . a theory which had already been advanced to explain Q *Richard III*, namely that the text is a memorial reconstruction made by the whole company. I thought of the company as being in the provinces, temporarily deprived of its prompt-book, and desirous of producing a new one; and I imagined its personnel gathered round a scribe . . . I was forced to suggest . . . that the scribe wrote down (as best he could) all that he heard (or thought he heard) in a very hasty manner . . .'. In other words, Duthie defines his function as baseless invention.

On whose infallible findings about *Hamlet*, then, does the latest apologist (Vickers 1993, 1994) rely? On Duthie's (1941). He has 'irrefutably confirmed' (Vickers 1993) that *Hamlet* 1603 is a piracy by actors who had 'probably performed' the better-known version, 'may have had access to one or more of the "parts" (separately copied roles) and put the text together from memory, maybe for performances in the provinces or abroad'. But of course no literary theory imagined by Duthie could possibly confirm what may have happened in Tudor theatre history. Nor is it really likely that the alleged bad and bizarre behaviour of forgetful actors remained unmentioned for some 340 years. What *is* still unmentioned by Duthie's disciples after fifty-three years, conversely, is the fatal fact that every single component of his 1941 theory of *Hamlet* 1603, exactly as with his 1949 theory of *King Lear* 1608, is a figment of his fantasy. A pre-existing version of the play, its performances, its actors, their lack of a prompt-book, their desire to produce a new one, the way their memories worked, and so forth, are all mere chimaerae for which no trace of evidence has ever existed.

The extant documentary evidence (such as 'by William Shakespeare' on the 1603 title-page) completely contradicts the theory. True to the literary tradition, Vickers (1993) ignores it altogether. Instead, he invokes other professors of literature. Thus not only Duthie (1941) but also Hart (1942) are both 'independently' credited with a conclusive but unspecified proof that *Hamlet* Q1 was a 'memorial reconstruction'. But, firstly, they were not in the least independent. They are readily traceable to the same source, namely Peter Alexander (1929), on whose dogmas Hart's book is avowedly based from its first page (XXXI). Next, Vickers defers to his literary colleagues' opinions even about such technical topics as Elizabethan shorthand. His claim that 'Duthie and Hart... conclusively demolished' the theory that stenography could have contributed to such texts as *Hamlet* 1603 is uninstructed and wrong; the question is one of individual contemporary competence (Butler 1951, 37; Sams 1990a, 63), not editorial theories about the existence or the adequacy of Tudor shorthand systems. Next, Vickers announces that 'Bad Quartos' cannot be 'first drafts, for they contain so many garbled reminiscences of the authentic texts (some 407 lines of fustian verse interpolated by actors whose memories had failed them) that we cannot imagine Shakespeare patiently rearranging all his lines into a coherent order while simultaneously eliminating the dross, which often runs quite counter to his conception of character and motive.' This just assumes that Shakespeare had only one conception of character and motive – with which modern experts are infallibly familiar. Unfamiliar lines however are dismissed as 'fustian', or 'dross', just as Duthie and his followers had previously dismissed the marvellous but unfamiliar lines of *King Lear* 1608, also freely attributed to 'actors' or 'reporters', or 'pirates' or any combination of all three. All the actual questions at issue, such as whether the resemblances to other versions are 'reminiscences' or not, are still blatantly begged, for example thus: 'the fact [*sic*] that the actor-reporters regularly echoed lines from other plays is another sign of how their memories (having to retain a large number of roles) contaminated a text' (Vickers 1993).

Again, does Q1 'drastically cut the authentic text' from Q2's 3,762 lines to 2,514 of which only 591 verse lines are retained unchanged? Did the supposed 'pirates', also called 'inept actors', really 'reduce many passages to confusion', 'conflate and rearrange scenes' and 'omit several key entrances for major characters', as Vickers (1993) also asserts? As usual, the vicious circle shamelessly starts at its own conclusion, namely that some undefined and unknown version of *Hamlet* had actually been written and performed earlier than 1603, in good time for hypothetical 'pirates' to board and despoil it.

Even on that unproven assumption, how can 'memorial reconstruction' explain such massive variation and such huge gaps? That awkward posture would sit so much more comfortably the other way round; the expansion of a short Shakespeare play into a much longer one is exactly what their two title-pages describe (argument 9 above), and exactly what he is known to have done. Equally self-destructive is the intended knock-down blow with which Vickers begins, thus: 'Suppose you were locked up in a room and made to write out from memory "To be or not to be". What would you come out with? Something like this, perhaps:

> To be or not to be, I there's the point,
> To Die, to sleepe, is that all? I all:
> No, to sleepe, to dreame, I mary there it goes,
> For in that dream of death, when wee awake,
> And borne before an everlasting Iudge
> From whence no passenger euer return'd,
> The undiscovered country, at whose sight
> The happy smile and the accursed damn'd.'

But the answer is surely 'no', unless the room was not only locked but padded. 'Aye' was often written 'I' in Tudor playscripts; but even so, how could any actor conceivably have *remembered* Hamlet's famous soliloquy thus, even if it was already there to be remembered and even if any actor was trying to remember it? Yet this combination of assumption and opinion about a few actual lines is regularly advanced as a compelling argument about an entire hypothetical play. Thus 'there's the point' is denounced as a corruption of 'the original', although that is the question (Wells 1986, xxx). Again, 'those tempted to believe that the 1603 *Hamlet* is authentic, if early, Shakespeare' would 'do well to read that text' (Wells 1987, 15). Lastly 'how anyone could believe that Shakespeare, even as a schoolboy, could have intentionally written lines such as these passes my understanding' (Wells 1994, 213, still following Duthie 1941). But the real puzzle is why literary opinion is vaunted so far above documentary evidence and simple explanations. 'In the realm of rational discourse', errors or corruptions in any Tudor play-text are 'attributed not to actors and egregiously bad memories but to compositors whose eyes skip to the wrong line or whose ears mishear the assistant who is reading aloud the copy; to the messiness of the author's foul papers or of a heavily marked up prompt-book; or simply to the author's wish to revise his own text' (Sprinchorn 1994a). The same noted authority on the theatre helpfully explained that the observed textual differences between successive versions of *Hamlet* clearly exemplify the well-documented process of authorial revision from Tudor times onward, not a hypothetical 'recon-struction' by hypothetical 'pirates'.

This demonstration was brusquely brushed aside by accusations of 'fallacious argument and inaccurate scholarship' (Vickers 4 Feb. 1994a) as well as failure to understand the issues involved (Vickers 29 April 1994c), which had been 'lucidly' defined thus (Jenkins 1994): 'What memorial reconstruction supposes is that actors who lacked a playbook created one for themselves out of their memory of a play in which they had minor roles . . .'. This 'desperate attempt to recreate the play by actors who had never actually learnt more than their own small parts' naturally entailed guessing and invention. 'So it need not surprise anyone, except Sprinchorn and the author of the article he quotes [sc. Bains *N&Q* 1993] that in Ophelia's reply to Laertes (I.iii.45–51) the reporting actor, while recalling the general sense, "got only seven words right out of fifty-three and added sixty-one of his own". This is how the speech was reproduced not by an actor who had played Ophelia but by one who had not.'

In other words, what we now have to suppose is that the theory of 'memorial reconstruction by actors' actually and admittedly includes a theory of non-memorial non-reconstruction by a non-actor of the role in question. So this theory ends there, inadvertently slain by its own champion. No sane historical hypothesis about actual events in a real world could conceivably invoke causes A, B and C etc. for effects which could also arise in the total absence of A, B or C etc. This concedes that not only those first three terms but the whole series are unnecessary, and therefore misconceived, because by definition and consent the hypothetical actors had played hardly any of the two dozen roles in question. So the entire theory should now at last be officially and formally abandoned.

The attempt to resuscitate it at its last gasp calls for an especially close examination. Here are the two texts defended by Professor Jenkins and Professor Vickers as excellent examples of their 'memorial reconstruction' theory:

A. from the First Quarto. 1603

> *Ofel.*   Brother, to this I have lent attentive eare
> And doubt not but to keepe my honour firme.
> But my deere brother, do not you
> Like to a cunning Sophister,
> Teach me the path and ready way to heaven,
> While you forgetting what is said to me,
> Your selfe, like to a carelesse libertine,
> Doth give his heart, his appetite at ful,
> And little recks how that his honour dies.
>   (Holderness and Loughrey 1992, 47)

B. from a conflation of the Second Quarto, 1604–5 and the Folio, 1623

> *Oph.*   I shall th'effect of this good lesson keep
> As watchman to my heart. But good my brother,
> Do not as some ungracious pastors do,
> Show me the steep and thorny way to heaven
> Whiles like a puff'd and reckless libertine
> Himself the primrose path of dalliance treads
> And recks not his own rede. (Jenkins 1982, 201)

Who else, apart from believers in the theory, will not be surprised, or indeed stupefied, at the assertion that *B was written earlier and reproduced as A by an actor who had never had to learn any of the B lines, let alone speak them?* This same 'actor' was also familiar with the modern sense of 'cunning', recorded in the OED (adj. 5) as first introduced into the language by Shakespeare, in *Henry V*; so prima facie he was more like the actual author of A than the hypothetical 'reporter' of B as A. No wonder that 'theories of memorial reconstruction have sometimes come under attack in recent years' (Jenkins 1994). They are doughtily defended, often by default. When Professor Sprinchorn (1994b) wrote to the *Times Literary Supplement* in response to the charges of failing to understand the theory, his letter was not accepted for publication. But his points were surely pertinent and persuasive; and his field of expertise is drama and theatre practice, i.e. the actual topic of the theory. His letter (1994c) is accordingly reproduced verbatim as an appendix to this section. It is high time that the garrison registered the fact that its main fortress has fallen.

Many other weakly defended areas are thereby exposed. Take for example what is seriously described as Duthie's 'greatest triumph', namely,

> to show that these passages of non-Shakespearean blank verse [i.e. in the First Quarto, assumed to be non-Shakespearean] were often put together from remembered scraps of Shakespeare's play [i.e. the Second Quarto or the First Folio, both assumed to be extant and available] and occasionally of other plays as well . . . An invention which is helped out by words and phrases rising in the mind from a previous contact with the play must be that of the actor-reporter himself. (Jenkins 1982, 26)

Alternatively (Vickers 1993), the First Quarto includes phrases also found in 'fifteen plays by Shakespeare, including *Othello*'. Thus the standing army of assumptions is massively reinforced. The 'actor-reporter', though confused, forgetful and dishonest, must have been employed by other companies in all the plays thus identified, which can accordingly be redated, thanks to the theory. Further, this same bit-part player obligingly turns into a dramatic poet and writes verse of his own. Outside Academia, what obvious and economical inference would be drawn from these data? In the real world, in whose mind would Shakespearean words and phrases be most likely to arise? Which actor in Shakespeare's company would be the likeliest to write dramatic blank verse?

Instead, the vicarious power and prestige of baseless speculations have sufficed to sink *Hamlet* Q1 with hardly a trace in serious scholarship. Before long, however, this scuppered Quarto will be raised and its treasures rediscovered, like those of *King Lear* Q1. Then at last students will see how Shakespeare rewrote his scripts, with consequent new insights into his compositors' occasional confusions, especially in printings which he had not personally authorised, and also into his stylistic development. *Hamlet* Q1 will prove of permanent interest and value in both respects.

Among its variants of nomenclature are Voltemar for Voltemand, Leartes for Laertes, Corambis for Polonius, Montano for Reynaldo, Ofelia for Ophelia, Braggart Gentleman for Osric and Player Duke and Duchess for Player King and Queen. Its characterisation is different (thus the Q1 Hamlet is a young man, and the Queen denies her complicity in her husband's murder). So is its structure (thus Q1 contains a unique dialogue between the Queen and Horatio about Hamlet's return, its nunnery scene precedes the players' performance, and the sentries appear in reverse order). All these startling differences, incidentally, provide further obvious but evaded evidence that Q1 cannot possibly be a 'memorial reconstruction'.

The following Q1 lines, among many others, have no counterpart in any other *Hamlet* text (cited here verbatim from the 1603 text by reference to page numbers in Holderness and Loughrey 1992): 'Yet something is there whispers in my hart' (p. 41, i.e. Laertes's longing for France); The King says to Hamlet, 'What meanes these sad and melancholy moodes?'; as for the latter's wish to return to Wittenberg, 'Wee hold it most vnmeet and vnconvenient,/Being the Ioy and halfe heart of your mother' (p. 42).

Here already are typical stylistic signs* including the noun-verb discord of 'means' and 'moods' (Abbott 1869, 234f), the compound 'half heart' (Everitt 1954, 162), and the prefix 'un-'; cf also the coinage 'unclasp' infra.

Hamlet wishes that 'the vniuersall globe of heauen would turne al to a Chaos!' (p. 43); Leartes warns Ofelia to 'keepe a loofe/Lest that he trip thy honor and thy fame' (p. 47); Corambis adds an injunction to 'receiue none of his letters/For louers' lines are snares to intrap the heart' (p. 48); note here the countryman's bird-snaring metaphor (Spurgeon 1935, 105–6) and the pun on 'lines'; further, 'Come in *Ofelia*, such men often proue/Great in their wordes, but little in their loue' (p. 48); cf 'We men . . . still we prove/Much in our vows, but little in our love' (*Twelfth Night*, II.iv.117–18), again with typical antithesis. Ofelia in her pity for the apparently insane Hamlet laments that,

> The Iewell that adorn'd his feature most
> Is filcht and stolne away, his wit's bereft him
> . . . [he] gripes me by the wrist
> And there he holdes my pulse till with a sigh
> He doth vnclaspe his holde, and parts away
> Silent, as is the mid time of the night: (p. 56)

Hamlet instructs the players:

> and then you have some agen that keepes one suit of jeasts, as a man is known by one sute of apparel, and gentlemen quotes his jeasts downe in their tables, before they come to the play, as thus: Cannot you stay till I eate

---

* As also in *Edmund Ironside* e.g. 'so comes these Danes' (1337); *c.* forty words in 'un-' and *c.* fifty compounds, each group including several coinages.

my porrige? and, you owe me a quarters wages: and, my coate wants a cullison: and, your beere is sowre: and, blubbering with his lips, and thus keeping in his cinkapase of jeasts, when, God knows, the warme clowne cannot make a jest unless by chance, as the blind man catches a hare; maisters tell him of it. (pp. 71–2)

Note here the noun-verb discord 'some keeps', the pun on 'suit' associated with 'apparel' (Whiter 1794, 83), the lively use of 'cinquepace', the special collocation 'warm clown' (i.e. one whose jests are spontaneous) and the amusing application of a proverb deriving from country and animal life.* Further, two of the jests later attributed to Richard Tarleton (*Tarleton's Jests* 1844) concern beer and a 'cullison' (i.e. a badge of arms), and he was a Queen's comedian whose association with *Hamlet*, as the prototype of Yorick, and with Shakespeare, has already been discussed (XIV). Again, the Player Duke mourns that,

> Now the blood that fill'd my youthfull veines
> Runnes weakly† in their pipes, and all the straines
> Of musicke, which whilome pleasde mine eare
> Is now a burthen that Age cannot beare . . . (p. 74)

Hamlet tells the Queen

> here is your husband,
> With a face like *Vulcan*.
> A looke fit for a murder and a rape,
> A dull dead hanging look and a hell-bred eye
> To affright children and amaze the world. (p. 80)

The Shakespeare-lover will know, e.g. from *Titus Andronicus*, why a damned villain should resemble the harmless Vulcan, who is eccentrically portrayed as black-faced as Satan from the smoke of underground furnace-fires. Hence the evocative neologism 'hell-bred', which parallels the other 'hell-' compounds first cited by the Oxford English Dictionary from Shakespeare. On the same authority, 'hanging look' was a Shakespeare coinage (*Measure for Measure*, IV.ii.34). 'So dull, so dead in look' appears in *2 Henry IV* (I.i.71), 'affrights our children' in *1 Henry VI* (I.iv.43) and 'amazes the world' in *Venus and Adonis* (634). All four passages relate to the physical appearance of faces, just as in Q1. Here prima facie is the playwright jeered at by Nashe and Greene in 1589 for describing demigods like Boreas as real people with recognisable facial features and physical presence.‡ The need is now for a new edition of *Hamlet* 1603 identifying and analysing its early Shakespearean features.

---

* All as in *Edmund Ironside*: antitheses, quibbles or country proverbs 'e.g. rich as new-shorn sheep' (1550) *passim*; 'apparel' (1219), 'suit' (1240).

† Cf the converse in *Edmund Ironside*: 'youthful blood . . . springs through every vein . . .' (1798–9) and the deliberately archaic use of 'whilom' (869).

‡ Cf *Edmund Ironside*, 'Aeolus's boisterous northern breath' (1347).

Appendix

April 27, 1994

Editor
Times Literary Supplement
66–68 East Smithfield
London E1 9XW

Dear Sir:

In his letter to *TLS* (April 15), Harold Jenkins joins Brian Vickers in saying that my "defence of professional actors and their powers of memorization is . . . quite beside the point." The ability to remember lines accurately is irrelevant to the theory of the memorial reconstruction of *Hamlet* First Quarto, Professor Jenkins argues, because those actors who made "a desperate attempt to recreate the play . . . had never actually learnt more than their own small parts but had a fitful recollection of the rest." In his introduction to the Arden *Hamlet*, Jenkins elaborates on this, saying that "passages of non-Shakespearean blank verse were often put together from remembered scraps of Shakespeare's play (and occasionally of other plays as well)." When the actor-reporter tried to recreate *Hamlet*, "widely separated parts of the play were present in the reporter's mind at the same time" [pp. 26, 29]. One of the troupers, the boy assigned the role of Ophelia, had, according to Jenkins, never before acted the part!

There are two points to be considered here. The first has to do with the composition of the troupe of players that Jenkins has in mind. He maintains that *Hamlet* Q1 was created by minor actors for the purpose of performing the play. The odd thing about this imaginary company is that it is made up entirely of supporting players, even though it was a large company with at least twelve actors (the number required for the last scene in the play). In fact, however, every troupe, large or small, had one or more leading actors, of which the First Player in *Hamlet* and the player of interludes in *Sir Thomas More* are good examples. The repertoire of the company was determined by these chief players, and common sense dictates that the repertoire would be made up of plays for which they possessed the roles and not of plays in which every one of a dozen actors had had only "small parts."

The second point concerns the "desperate attempt" these minor actors made to recreate a play of which they had only scattered memories. In the hope of skirting my argument that professional actors remember their lines quite faithfully or not at all, Professor Jenkins would like to make a distinction in this regard between leading actors and supporting players. Only the latter, says Jenkins, would be the culprits guilty of trying to pirate *Hamlet*. In the theatrical profession, however, an excellent memory is no respecter of rank and may be found in a bit player as well as in a leading actor. Some rather poor actors are notorious as quick studies, while some great actors have difficulty in remembering their lines, as did Ellen Terry, by general consent the finest English actress of her time, in the latter half of her career, when she would often have to signal the prompter for her line. But in all instances actors remember what is set down for them, and that is what they recall days or weeks later, as the case may be. That is why the evidence I provided in my first letter (*TLS* January 21), which Vickers and Jenkins would like to dismiss as irrelevant, is absolutely central to the argument.

It must be kept in mind that Jenkins's scholarly knowledge of the play is quite different from what actors would know about it, especially those actors he imagines as engaged in this task of reconstruction. With his incomparable command of the *Hamlet* material, he can range over the whole of it, scavenging for scraps of verse to feed his theory, patching together speeches for his bit players. Yet no evidence is offered that this is how actors ever reconstructed half-forgotten plays. Theatre historians, however, do know how a team of actors might, on rare occasions, put together a script from their collective memories. I gave an example in my first letter. More familiar is the method employed by John Bernard when he reconstructed Sheridan's *School for Scandal*, having on various occasions played three of the leading parts [Bernard, *Retrospections of the Stage*, Boston, 1832, 127–8]. In other words, the script was assembled in much the same way as an orchestral score can be reconstituted from the various instrumental parts.

But in his burlesque of what actors are known to have done, Jenkins supposes that a group of provincial actors who had played only minor roles in it, and who had such a poor recollection of it that they could not even remember the proper sequence of scenes, took it upon themselves to do *Hamlet*. Why would they bother? Why not choose a play that they or their fellow strollers knew better? And if they didn't know the play very well but still persisted in reconstructing it, why wouldn't they do what sensible actors like Bernard and his company did? Why? Because, says Jenkins, they were "desperate."

Clearly, when those who believe in the theory of memorial reconstruction fall back on this line of defence, it is they who are desperate, not those inept, unheard-of actors their imaginations have conjured up.

Sincerely,

Evert Sprinchorn
Professor Emeritus of Drama
Vassar College
New York

XXV

The Taming of A Shrew

THIS PLAY TREATS the same theme, with the same basic plot, characters and episodes, and often in the same language, as *The Taming of the Shrew*. The characters Sly and Kate are common to both. But the other names are different; so is the poetic style; and *A Shrew* is located in Athens, not Padua.

This very short play (only some 1,500 lines as against its Folio counterpart's *c.* 3,000) was registered (**194**) in May 1594 and published in the same year by the printer Peter Short and the bookseller Cuthbert Burby. They jointly issued a second edition in 1596. In that year, Sir John Harington published *Ajax*, which says 'Read the book of Taming a Shrew, which hath made a number of us so perfect, that now everyone can rule a shrew in our country, save he that hath her.' The composition of *A Shrew* can be assigned to *c.* 1588, because it quotes and parodies Marlowe's *Tamburlaine* (1587), and is in turn ridiculed by both Greene and Nashe in *Menaphon* (1589).

The reasons for assigning *A Shrew* to Shakespeare are:

1   He was an originator, and *A Shrew* is the first modern comedy in English.

2   He was writing popular plays (such as *Hamlet*) in the 1580s; *A Shrew* was a favourite, as its prompt reissue shows and its citation by Harington confirms.

3   He was a reviser, even of his masterpieces (*Lear, Hamlet*); so the relationship of *A Shrew* to the far longer, better known and more sophisticated Folio play *The Shrew* (1623) is prima facie one of authorial revision.

4   Economy of reasoning again requires that the same revising author wrote both plays on the *Shrew* theme, like all other such counterpart versions.

5   Shakespeare was no mere exploitative plagiarist; so the close dependence of the 1623 on the 1594 version confirms that he wrote both.

6   So does the fact that both were governed by the same copyright, which would be a sensible rule for treatments of the same theme by the same dramatist (but not otherwise).

7   The 1594 printer and bookseller have strong Shakespearean connections: Short went on to print the second edition of *Lucrece* and

the first of *1 Henry IV* in 1598 and the fifth of *Venus and Adonis* in 1599. Burby sold the first known edition of *Love's Labour's Lost* in 1598 and the second edition of *Romeo and Juliet* in 1599.

8(a) The Nashe-Greene method of satirical attack was identification by allusive quotation;

(b) their main butt in *Menaphon* and its preface was Shakespeare; so

(c) the play that Nashe alludes to ('get Boreas by the beard') and Greene quotes ('white as the haires that grow on father *Boreas* chinne'), namely *A Shrew* ('icy hair that grows on *Boreas* chin', II.i. 150), was by Shakespeare. Similarly

(d) Nashe's references to Ovid, Pliny, Plutarch, Ariosto and Athens are also prima facie identificatory.*

9   By the same token, if Greene and Nashe jointly wrote the play which quotes from *A Shrew*, namely the anonymous comedy *A Knack to Know a Knave*, then those excerpts too (*pace* Thompson 1982) are flouts at the young Shakespeare's work and style; and *Knack* has often been attributed to that collaboration, of which Greene wrote in *Groats-worth* (1592) 'Juvenal [Nashe] that lastly with me together wrote a comedy'.

10(a) *A Shrew* quotes and parodies Marlowe (*Dr Faustus*,† *Tamburlaine*) so extensively and disrespectfully as to explain if not justify a malicious charge of plagiarism;

(b) no other known play does anything of the kind;

(c) the only dramatist ever accused of plagiarising Marlowe was Shakespeare (by Greene 1592).

11   Such evidence (see also *Troublesome Reign*, XXVI) of Shakespeare's irreverence towards Marlowe assorts well with Greene's 1592 appeal to the latter as a fellow graduate and natural ally against the grammar-school boy Shakespeare.

12   *A Shrew*'s 1594 title-page announces its performance by Pembroke's Men, a company to which Shakespeare may well have belonged (XXI).

13(a) *A Shrew* was performed in June 1594, together with *Titus Andronicus* and *Hamlet*, by the Admiral's and the Chamberlain's men jointly (**203**); but

(b) none of these three plays figures in the Admiral's later lists; and *Hamlet* was acted by Chamberlain's. Further,

(c) by the end of 1594 Shakespeare was certainly a member of Chamberlain's company, which included ex-Pembroke's players after their 1593 bankruptcy. So

---

* Cf also the personified north wind (1347), Ovid (*passim*), Pliny (natural history *passim*) and Plutarch (777, 1551–2) in *Edmund Ironside*.

† Which is thus also datable *c.* 1588, though the point is often overlooked (e.g. by Roma Gill 1990).

(d)   prima facie he had joined Chamberlain's by June and brought three
      of his own early plays with him, including *A Shrew*.

14   To reinforce point 13:

(a)   in June 1594 Shakespeare's *Hamlet* and *Titus Andronicus* were per-
      formed by the company he had just joined, together with *The
      Taming of A Shrew*; so

(b)   the third of that trio was also a Shakespeare play.

15   The Oxford editors (Wells 1986, 60–61), who cannot tell who
      wrote *A Shrew*, rate its structure superior to Shakespeare's Folio
      play, and include excerpts from the former in their text of the latter,
      exactly as if both are authentically Shakespearean.

16   The same editors later explicitly concede (Taylor 1988, 169) that *A
      Shrew* may indeed be Shakespeare's own first attempt at a comedy
      on the Shrew theme.

17   The latest editors (Holderness and Loughrey 1992, 16) note that 'in
      many ways *A Shrew* is a more interesting text than *The Shrew*' and
      indeed even 'more complex and sophisticated' in its structure. Of
      whom, other than Shakespeare himself, could that have been true
      in 1588?

There are many other detailed arguments, as set out below. As with
Hamlet, there are no reasons whatever against Shakespeare's authorship
of *A Shrew*, or in favour of anyone else's, least of all amnesiac actors (Sams
1985c, 1986f and pp. xii–xiii above). Yet here too confusion and prejudice have prevailed for decades. Their source, as with the Henry VI plays
(XXVII), was the daunting combination of John Smart and Peter Alexander, who persuaded themselves, and each other, that *A Shrew* 1594 was
the work of a 'plagiarist' who 'attended performances of Shakespeare's
comedy' (meaning *The Shrew*, unknown before 1623), and 'incorporated
portions of Shakespeare's dialogue which had lodged in his memory'. This
baseless invention is an exact counterpart to the equally imaginary pirate
of *Hamlet* 1603 (XXIV). It appeared among Smart's posthumous papers
(1928, 172–8) edited by his close colleague Alexander from 'pencilled
chapters and notes' which had 'never received the author's final revision'
(ibid., xxiii). Sadly, Smart had no chance of thinking again before publication or (like Greg and Duthie) recanting afterwards. Alexander (1926)
eagerly espoused and announced *A Shrew* 1594 as a 'memorial reconstruction' of Shakespeare, a view to which he still adhered thirty-nine
years later (1965) and which is still being reaffirmed as fact to this
day (Hibbard 1968, Morris 1981, Oliver 1982, N. Alexander 1983,
Thompson 1984), although it is unrelated to any recorded fact whatever
(Sams 1985c). It was robustly rejected from the first by the leading
authority, who wrote: 'I am quite unable to believe that *A Shrew* had any
such origin' a view he justified from the facts (Chambers 1930, i, 327).
The notion of a 'memorial reconstruction' which is textually entirely

different from its supposed original has understandably caused consider-able confusion.

Thus the Oxford editors Taylor and Wells contradict not only the separate Oxford edition of *The Shrew* (Oliver 1982) but also each other. Both of them subscribe (argument 16 above) to Shakespeare's possible authorship of *A Shrew*, which one of them had already rejected out of hand (Taylor 1988, 85) in the same volume. The latest contribution is that the relationship between the two plays is 'one of the great unsolved problems of Shakespeare scholarship' (Wells 1994, 52). But editorial opinion, whatever it may be, has long been final. 'I find it difficult to believe that Shakespeare' rewrote *A* as *The Shrew* (Bond 1904, xlii); 'even in his earliest plays [Shakespeare's] blank verse is not so monotonously end-stopped as in *A Shrew*' (Boas 1908, xxxv). Similarly 'we can be entirely confident that' Shakespeare could not have written *A Shrew*, because of mathematical tests (XXXIV) which must somehow be incontrovertibly valid even though confessedly devised and operated by non-mathematicians (Taylor 1988, 81, 85) whose methods have been slated by actual mathematicians (M. Smith *N&Q* 1991).

Such confidence can cause over-confidence. Thus some editors claim that the impresario Henslowe, when he wrote down 'the tamynge of A shrowe' together with *Hamlet* and *Titus Andronicus* in his still extant diary for 1594, must really have meant the 1623 Folio play *The Taming of the Shrew*. Sometimes Henslowe's words are falsely given as 'The Taming of the Shrew' (Harrison 1956, 137), or else his phrase 'A shrowe' is twisted into meaning 'either *A* or *The Shrew*' (Halliday 1964, 483). More subtly, Taylor insinuates (1988, 110) that 'Henslowe's carelessness about titles makes it difficult to repose complete confidence in his use of the indefi-nite article'. The separate Oxford edition (Oliver 1982, 32) even claims that 'since Shakespeare's company is somehow involved' *A Shrew* would have been 'the genuine Shakespeare play [i.e. *The Shrew*] and not what we mean by *A Shrew*'. But the unprejudiced inference from the same facts is the exact opposite; *A Shrew* was itself a genuine Shakespeare play, as set out at argument 13 above.

The argument at 5 above has been similarly obfuscated by the Cambridge *Taming of the Shrew* (Thompson 1984, 1). In 1607, *A Shrew*, *Romeo and Juliet* and *Love's Labour's Lost* were jointly re-registered, with the written consent of the master stationer Burby (who owned rights in all three), for republication by Nicholas Ling, who duly issued a Third Quarto of *A Shrew* in that same year. Ling then transferred his rights to John Smethwick, who in 1631 (and perhaps earlier) printed a quarto edition 'not of *A Shrew* as one might expect, but of *The Shrew*'. The Cambridge editor (idem) curiously concludes from these admitted facts that neither Smethwick nor Burby discriminated between the two plays (and nor, though this is not mentioned, did Ling). They, like Henslowe, supposedly had no notion what they were writing or signing or licensing, and could not tell one play from another. But again a more balanced stance would take the opposite view. Tudor impresarios, editors and publishers were not stupid. Henslowe wrote down *A Shrew* because that was the play's name; not only its title but its text says so, twice (Holderness, p. 45). Burby, Ling and Smethwick dealt with copyright in *A Shrew* as with *Romeo and Juliet* and *Love's Labour's Lost* because all three were Shakespeare plays. Smethwick published *The Shrew* by virtue of his *A Shrew* copyright because that was his entitlement; which permits the inference that plays on the same theme by the same author were subject to the same copyright. In other words, *A Shrew* was known as a Shakespeare play to all concerned, from 1594 to 1631. In 1603 its 1594 first edition was listed by the Exeter bookseller Christopher Hunt among his available stock (Baldwin 1957) together with *The Merchant of Venice*, *Love's Labour's Lost* and *Love's Labour's Won* (still unidentified, but named by Francis Meres in 1598 as a Shakespeare play). So here is a third different and independent group of canonical plays plus *The Taming of A Shrew*, as though that early version also belonged in the same category. But even this evidence has been irrationally denied and reversed with the flat statement that this title at this time meant *The Taming of the Shrew* (Wells 1994, 70).

In 1602, *A Shrew*'s first printer Peter Short apprenticed the son of George Badger, a Stratford draper well known to Shakespeare's father, from whom he had purchased Henley Street land in 1597. From the first, its publishing background and credentials are thus those of an authentic Shakespeare play, not an anonymous anomaly and still less a botched corruption; and least of all a 'memorial reconstruction' of a play with which it has no single line in common (see pp. xii–xiii). Its authenticity has also been avouched by earlier commentators (e.g. Courthope 1903, Bullough 1957–75), whose assessments have been generally forgotten or set aside.

All this interconnects with the argument already adduced about *Hamlet* and reinforces the conclusion that Nashe, like Greene, was hitting out at the hated Shakespeare as early as 1589, which further confirms the latter's status at that stage. Satirical shadow-boxing would be boring; the clues are meant to clinch and strike. The beard of Boreas inculpates *The Taming of A Shrew*. So it is not mere coincidence that Nashe also derides those who 'borrow invention of Ariosto', given that the underplot of *A Shrew* was drawn entire from George Gascoigne's *Supposes* (1566), the English version of Ariosto's *I Suppositi*. No other play of the period is thus indebted, save the Folio text of *The Shrew*; but (*pace* all modern authorities, e.g. Wells 1985–94) there is no evidence that the latter was an early play, and much evidence that it was not (Sams 1985c, 1986f).

Such impudent plagiarism, Nashe says, had never been noted before in all 'the descending yeares from the Philosopher's *Athens*', which is the actual location of *The Taming of A Shrew* and no other play of the period.

Its main action begins with the words, 'Welcome to Athens, my beloved friend,/To Plato's schools and Aristotle's walks'.

So *A Shrew** was prima facie among the plays that Nashe attributed to 'Italianate pens' which also 'in disguised arraie, vaunts *Ouids* and *Plutarchs* plumes as their own'. How like an upstart crow. And indeed *A Shrew* jauntily sports Ovid's feathers, by the dozen, diversified by a plume or two from Plutarch. Thus Polidor describes 'two lovely dames' as '. . . far more lovely than the Terean plant/That blushing in the air turnes to a stone' (p. 55). This description of coral, as the graduate classicists Greene and Nashe no doubt knew, comes from Book IV (750–54) of the *Metamorphoses*; 'nunc quoque curaliis eadem natura remansit,/duritiam tacto capiant ut ab aere quodque/vimen in aequore erat, fiat super aequora saxum' [to this day, the same nature has remained in coral, so that it hardens in the air, and what was a twig below the sea becomes a stone above]. The same thought recurs in Book XV (416–17): 'sic et curalium quo primum contigit auras/tempore, durescit: mollis fuit herba sub undis' [so coral too hardens at the first touch of air although it was a soft plant while under the waves].

The opposite softening of Kate herself is amusingly called a 'wonderful metamorphosis' (p. 86). In another early play, 'Ovid's *Metamorphosis*' [*sic*] is quoted and alluded to *passim*; and there it is even brought on stage as a property, this time as a tragic symbol of the heroine's change by mutilation. This is *Titus Andronicus* (IV.i.42), written at the same time (*c.* 1588) as *A Shrew*, performed on the same stage (Newington Butts) by the same company (Shakespeare's)† and published in the same year (1594).

Then what might Nashe have meant by *Plutarch*'s plumes? In *A Shrew*, marriage is amusingly compared to the Gordian knot, which Alexander undid at a swordstroke or with one deft twist, as recounted in Plutarch's *Age of Alexander* (section 18). Again, the Tudor playwright best known, then and now, for using Plutarch‡ sources was Shakespeare, for example in *1 Henry VI* (I.ii.138–9) which alludes to the *Life of Caesar* (published 1579 in North's translation). This same play, again from the same period as *Titus Andronicus* and *A Shrew*, was also touched upon by Nashe in *Pierce Penniless*; and it too refers (I.i.55–6) both to Ovid's *Metamorphoses*, again Book XV (843–5), where Julius Caesar is turned into a bright star, and to Plutarch, *Life of Fabius Maximus* (I.v.21).

---

*   Exactly like *Edmund Ironside*: see footnote on p. 137.

†   Like the early *Hamlet*, the 1603 version of which may also contain Ovidian allusions, e.g. to Vulcan (XXIV), though other sources are possible. Only a very few Tudor plays are demonstrably indebted to the *Metamorphoses*, notably the anonymous *Edmund Ironside*, *Edward III* and *The Troublesome Reign of King John* (XXVI).

‡   Again as in *Edmund Ironside* where Plutarch is cited at lines 776–7 and 1551–82 (*Life of Fabius Maximus*).

'Whole sheetes and tractacts *verbatim* from the plenty of *Plutarch* and *Plinie*'; thus Nashe continues his charge-sheet in 1589. The dramatist who above all others relied on a whole anthology of fierce or tame fauna, and harmful or wholesome flora, as in the *Historia Naturalis* of Pliny the Elder, was Shakespeare. Before long, Greene would be famously flouting him for treating a woman as a tiger. This happens not only in *The True Tragedy of Richard Duke of York* but also, as we have seen, in *Titus Andronicus*, where Tamora is twice a 'ravenous tiger'. In *A Shrew*, the heroine twice becomes a hungry hawk (Holderness, p. 68), while her tamer is a lion, thrice in three lines (p. 61). There is also a hunting scene where a winged horse surprisingly runs over unexplained plains in free association with pride and fierce beasts and their prey: '. . . winged Pegasus . . . pride . . . ran . . . o'er the plains . . . hounds . . . roe . . . tiger' (pp. 46–7), again just as in *Titus Andronicus*: 'proudest panther . . . horse . . . run like swallows o'er the plain . . . hound . . . doe . . .' (II.ii.21, 23–6).

Other canonical links are even closer and more curiously wrought. Armstrong (2/1963, 210–11) notes that 'venison pasty', 'shillings' and 'pie' appear in *A Shrew* (pp. 63–4) and *Merry Wives* (I.i.195, 198, 303); but he omits to mention the even more striking circumstance to which each scene also alludes: 'I gat a broken shin the other day' (p. 64) and 'I bruised my shin t'other day' (line.283). There are other shared words, such as 'boy' and 'married'. The subconscious sources are presumably the insistent ideas of an impending marriage and a delayed wedding feast in both contexts. Their economical explanation is surely not (*pace* Armstrong ibid.) that Shakespeare 'read, saw or acted in *The Taming of A Shrew*', but that he wrote it. There are other clear traces of just such an image-cluster in the canon: thus *Romeo and Juliet* moves from 'bride' to a 'broken shin' (I.ii.11, 52), within the context of a thrice-mentioned 'feast' (I.ii.20, 82, 98). The trains of thought may have started from Shakespeare's own wedding and its associations with venison and violence (XII), as also in the opening scene of *The Merry Wives*.

There are equally clear interconnections between *A Shrew c.* 1588 and *The Shrew* first published in 1623. Thus Christopher Sly is plainly one and the same character in both. In the later version, he is a Warwickshire man who immediately establishes his connections with Burton Heath (where Shakespeare's uncle Edmund Lambert lived) and Wincot, also in the vicinity of Stratford (Induction, ii. 18, 22). But he is the same Sly in *A Shrew* also; and hence from the same locality, by way of the same hand. There is no real reason (*pace* Morris 1981, 62–3) why the more explicit place-names should belong to the earlier version (as *The Shrew* is feigned to be); Shakespeare might well have reserved his local allusions for the time when he was a famous son of Stratford, not when he had only just fled thence under a cloud.

These two plays contain over 100 phraseological parallels. But only two or three are exact repetitions. The manifold differences consist in either

(a) significant verbal variation or (b) complete change of thought and expression. Most of the repeated phrases are allotted to the same character, though under a different name (the hero Ferando becomes Petruchio, and so on). On a dozen occasions, however, the same thought in much the same words is uttered by a quite different personage. Thus in *A Shrew* it is one of the suitors who says of the girls' father that 'his eldest daughter first shall be espoused before he grants his youngest leave to love' (p. 49), whereas in *The Shrew* the father himself announces his decision 'not to bestow my youngest daughter/Before I have a husband for the elder' (I.i.50–51). Sometimes, the parallel passages are hundreds of lines apart. In *A Shrew* for example Kate pretends to take the travelling Duke for a lady 'as glorious as the morning washed with dew' (p. 78), late in the play, while in *The Shrew* the same idea is rehearsed by Petruchio for his first meeting with Kate: 'I'll say she looks as clear as morning roses newly washed with dew' (II.i.173). Other verbatim echoes may be tabulated thus:

A Shrew 1594	*The Shrew* 1623
item, a loose-bodied gown. Master, if ever I said loose body's gown, sew me in a seam	Imprimis, a loose-bodied gown. Master, if ever I said loose-bodied gown, sew me in the skirts of it,
and beat me to death with a bottom of brown thread the note lies in his throat thou hast braved many men, brave not me . . . thou hast faced many men, face not me: I'll neither be faced nor braved.	and beat me to death with a bottom of brown thread (IV.iii. 136) the note lies in's throat (ibid. 134) Thou hast faced many things, Face not me. Thou hast braved many men, brave not me. I will neither be faced nor braved (ibid. 123–6) that fac'd and brav'd me (V.i.121)
take it up for your master's use. Zounds, villain, not for thy life; touch it not. Zounds, take up my mistress' gown to his master's use? Well, sir, what's your conceit of it? I have a deeper conceit in it than you think for. Take up my mistress' gown to his master's use? (p. 74)	go, take it up unto thy master's use. Villain, not for thy life: take up my mistress' gown for thy master's use. Why, sir, what's your conceit in that? O sir the conceit is deeper than you think for. Take up my mistress' gown to his master's use. O fie, fie, fie (IV.iii.158–64)

The reviser visibly reverses the flow of discourse, so as to end with the gown. He has an entirely free hand. But note which points, out of thousands, he rates worth retaining; quibbling word-play (on 'face' and 'brave') and bold bawdry (about lifting up a gown). Both are typically Shakespearean (the gown jest is also allotted to coarse Jack Cade in *Contention*). So are allusions to animals and birds; and these too are retained. Thus the bawdy chat between Ferando and Kate about 'an ass' and 'the woodcock' (p. 52), chosen for cheeky comment by the servant Sander ('you spoke like an ass . . . and you talk of woodcocks', p. 53) is remembered by the latter in his new incarnation as Grumio: 'o this woodcock, what an ass it is!' (I.ii.160). The tamer Ferando says 'I'll mew [Kate] up as men do mew their hawks' (p. 68); in *The Shrew*, a different character in a different context is asked 'will you mew her up?' (I.i.87). Similarly Kate becomes an unbroken colt in both plays, at the mercy of the master of the taming-school (p. 69; IV.ii.53–6).

If all this had occurred in different versions of *Hamlet*, it would be hailed as proof of 'memorial reconstruction' with so-called 'anticipations' and 'recollections' (Jenkins 1982, 29, Vickers 1993). Rationally considered, however, such appearances result from authorial revision here, just as in *Hamlet* (Sprinchorn 1994a). Even without such amplification the voice of the young Shakespeare, with its characteristic tones and overtones, is surely already audible in *A Shrew*. This very early comedy has its moments of lyric grace ('golden summer sleeps upon thy cheeks'), fin-de-siècle touches of decoration ('richly powdered with precious stones/Spotted with liquid gold, thick-set with pearl'), Ovidian eloquence ('Where Phoebus in his bright equator sits,/Creating gold and precious minerals'), all contrasting most effectively with farcical malapropisms ('abusious', 'imperfectious', 'supernodical'), the racily rhythmical prose of low-life comedy ('there's two shillings for thee, to pay for the healing of thy left leg, which I mean furiously to invade, or maim at the least') and the movingly simple evocation of married love ('why, thus must we two live, one mind, one heart and one content for both'). As with *Hamlet* Q1, the need is now for modern performances and a new edition setting out in detail, line by line, all the hundreds of forgotten Shakespearean affinities. Here, in that interest, is a summary synopsis of salient features.

First, the quotations from Marlowe have been well (though not ex-haustively) documented by F.S. Boas in his 1908 edition (91–8). In addition, the by-play of Ferando's feeding of Kate from his dagger's point (p. 70) is a palpable thrust at *Tamburlaine* (IV.iv.43f) where the prisoner Bajazeth is thus taunted. The intention is parodistic and provocative, *passim* from *A Shrew*'s opening lines, where the dark nightfall invoked by Faustus for his conjuration of the Devil is allotted to a Lord as a reason for calling a halt to his own hunting of game. No wonder that Greene, if not Marlowe himself, complained. No comparable use was ever made of parody save by Shakespeare, for example in the Pyramus play presented in *A Midsummer Night's Dream* (V.i.126f). That work is also anticipated in Sly's dream (p. 89), which is as rare a vision as Bottom's (IV.i.203f). Similarly *Hamlet* has a play within a play, and a scene where a troupe of travelling actors is affably received by a nobleman. *A Shrew's* induction structure is often accounted superior to its canonical counterpart (Wells 1986, 29, 60–61; Holderness and Loughrey 1992, 13; Sams 1994a); its style blends typical ingredients in typical proportions. Some sample flavours, in alphabetical order of key-words, are: alliteration, 'leagues of lasting love' etc.; antithesis, 'blunt . . . sharp' etc.; bawdry, as above; Bible, e.g. 'put forth thy hand' (p. 47), 'my ten commandments' (p. 52) (= finger-nails, cf the same words in *Contention*), and details from Genesis (p. 87); classical personification, e.g. Boreas (p. 62), Aeolus (p. 77); compound words, e.g. 'sun-bright' (p. 75), 'eye-trained' (p. 78); fauna and flora, some thirty types; law, 'deeds of land', again in association with 'father' (p. 69); many parallels with canonical plays* including the idiosyncratic conceit that 'in [her] bright looks sparkles the radiant fire/Wily Prometheus slily stole' (p. 59), cf 'women's eyes . . . sparkle still the right Promethean fire' (*Love's Labour's Lost*, IV.iii.347–8); 'ifs and ands' (Nashe 1589), cf four and five lines beginning with 'And' (pp. 44–5); Latin tags, 'omne bene' (p. 43), 'ecce signum' (p. 55); Marlowe imitations, as well as quotations, *passim*; noun-verb discord, even in the noble Lord's usage, e.g. 'is all things ready' (p. 46); Ovid, in detail, *passim*; Plutarch, Gordian knot (p. 77); proverb, 'as the proverb says' (p. 79); pun and word-play, e.g. pp. 55, 58, 74, 87. The elaborate wedding language, after a whirlwind wooing and before an abrupt departure (XIII), is worth quoting *in extenso*: 'when our nuptial rites be once performed' (p. 52), 'espoused . . . wedding-day' (p. 65), 'solemnise with joy your nuptial rites', 'knit themselves in holy wedlock band', 'marriage rites performed', 'nuptials . . . celebration of his spousal rites' (p. 72), 'marriage rites performed', 'great solemnity' (p. 79), 'celebrate and solemnise this day' (p. 80).

The same remarkable mixture recurs in *The Troublesome Reign of King John* (XXVI).

---

* And with *Edmund Ironside*, *Edward III*, etc.

XXVI

The Troublesome Reign of King John

TROUBLESOME REIGN (AS it is often called) was written c. 1588 and published in 1591 by Sampson Clarke, of whom little else is known. Its structure is the same as Shakespeare's King John (first published in 1623), but its language is very different. So, experts assume, one must be deeply indebted to the other. Either order will do; both theories are respected as scholarly, though at least one of them must be wrong; neither is evidenced, and one entails decades of antedating. The first explanation to investigate, especially by anyone who avows that Shakespeare started much earlier than is generally realised (Honigmann 1982, 1985) or that he completely rewrote Troublesome Reign (Smallwood 1974), is authorial revision. All that is needed is an acceptance of artistic development and the admission that Shakespeare may have been a master of structure before he was a master of language. In practice, however, it is Honigmann and Smallwood who head the opposing factions. Both have fallen silent on the subject for the past six years (since Sams 1988a); it is long overdue for general re-examination in the light of some fifty arguments so far (XXIII, XXIV, XXV) to show that Shakespeare was indeed an early starter who rewrote nobody's plays but his own, in the two John versions as in their Hamlet and Shrew counterparts. Here are some arguments for assigning The Troublesome Reign of King John (cited from the latest edition, Everitt 1965) to the young Shakespeare.

1   Alexander Pope (1723) could recognise Shakespeare's hand in it.

2(a) It was a popular play of the 1580s, performed by the Queen's Men and written in the entirely new genre of English history-drama;

  (b) it remained popular for another thirty years (as witness two further editions in that time);

  (c) the popular dramatist with the Queen's Men in the 1580s, and the originator of new forms, was Shakespeare.

3(a) He was thus a predecessor of Marlowe, writing (often with frequent interspersed rhyme, as in Troublesome Reign) for a mass audience, and hence the plainest of identifiable targets for Marlowe's blank-verse shafts about 'rhyming mother-wits'; so

  (b) Shakespeare is the likeliest source of the only known rejoinder, namely the Prologue to Troublesome Reign.

4(a)   That rejoinder is headed 'To the Gentlemen Readers', alluding to the other University Wits' snobbish practice of addressing their supposedly élite audience thus, like Nashe and Greene in *Menaphon* 1589, which hits at the noverint (law-clerk) who wrote the early *Hamlet*, i.e. (XI, XVI, XXIII–IV) Shakespeare; so

(b)   he is also the '*Noverint*' who 'comes off with a long *circumquaque* to the gentlemen readers', i.e. in *Troublesome Reign* (XVI).

5(a)   Among that play's broad comic effects is a rhyme to the Ovid quotation 'tempus edax rerum' noted by Nashe in his 1589 satire on Shakespeare;

(b)   this tagging device parallels Greene's identificatory quotation of the 'tiger's heart' line from *True Tragedy* (XXVII).

6(a)   'tempus edax rerum' (far less hackneyed a tag then than now) comes from Ovid's *Metamorphoses* (XV.234);

(b)   Nashe in his 1589 Preface attacking Shakespeare's early *Hamlet* inveighs against those who borrow plumes from Ovid;

(c)   Shakespeare later espoused and enshrined this same dictum in his Sonnets (e.g. 19.1), which led Francis Meres (1598) to identify him with Ovid.

7(a)   Arguments 5 and 6 are on lines parallel with *A Shrew*; it too flouts Marlowe and is in turn scoffed at in *Menaphon*; so

(b)   both plays were written by the same playwright at much the same period; and

(c)   there are seventeen reasons for (and none against) ascribing *A Shrew* to Shakespeare (XXV).

8(a)   *Troublesome Reign* was published in two separate parts, in blatant imitation of Marlowe's *Tamburlaine c.* 1587;

(b)   the only known writer ever accused of imitating Marlowe (by Greene, in 1592) was Shakespeare.

9(a)   The fourth line of *Troublesome Reign* is 'clad this land in stole of dismal hue', which borrows its last five words from George Peele's *Arraignement of Paris*;

(b)   the speech of Philip (260ff) is in Peele's poetic style;

(c)   the only known poet ever accused of exploiting Peele was Shakespeare, by Greene in 1592.

10   *Troublesome Reign* may well be the tragedy named as *King John* in Meres's Shakespeare work-list of 1598; there is no reason to date the 1623 Folio text of *King John* thus early.

11(a) The earlier play is however the basis of the later, which deliberately replicates the structure of *Troublesome Reign* in detail, scene by scene, in both plotting and character-drawing; so

(b)   this is Shakespeare revising his own play, not thieving someone else's, just as with the *Hamlet, Shrew* and *Henry VI* counterpart plays (XXIII–V, XXVII).

12(a)   The second edition of *Troublesome Reign*, 1611, says 'Written by
         W.Sh.', which obviously means William Shakespeare, who still had
         another five years to live; there is no record of any demurrer from
         any quarter;

  (b)   its publisher was Valentine Simmes, who had brought out the first
         three editions of *Richard II* (1597–8), and the first of *Richard III*
         (1597), *2 Henry IV* and *Much Ado* (both 1600).

13   Its third edition, 1622, says 'Written by W. Shakespeare'. This time
         the publisher was Augustine Matthews, who would issue the first
         edition of the same author's *Othello* in 1630.

14   Exceptionally, the Folio publication of *King John* was not entered in
         the Stationers' Register; and the simplest explanation of this
         anomaly is that (again as in the case of the *Shrew* plays, XXV) the
         rights already vested in *Troublesome Reign* still applied, i.e. these two
         were also treatments of the same theme by the same writer.

This last point is worth stressing. It is much enhanced by the parallels
already noted with *A Shrew* which, as Chambers says (1930, i.323), was
clearly regarded as 'commercially the same' as *The Shrew*. Commerce
sharpens rather than blunts perception, so the inference is that the two
John plays also were the same for financial purposes. No common factor
other than authorship has ever been suggested; but that factor suffices.
The only other known example of a play found in the First Folio yet not
separately copyrighted is *King John*; and Chambers (ibid., 365) draws the
evident inference that this too was covered by a previous copyright,
namely that of *Troublesome Reign*. Again the common factor required by
common sense would be that of authorship, again supported by the same
independent evidence, notably that the two John plays, like the two
Shrew plays, flesh out a shared skeleton of plot and character.

There is no objective reason to assume that Shakespeare did not write
Troublesome Reign or that anyone else did. Its usual contemptuous rejection is mere personal opinion, though often presented as universal
modern expertise, e.g. 'No one now takes the idea of Shakespearian
authorship seriously' (Smallwood 1974, 365). The only factual counter-
argument, which no one has so far offered, is that *Troublesome Reign* is
overtly anti-Catholic, contrary to Shakespeare's upbringing. But there is
no reason to suppose that he was himself a devout or practising Catholic
c. 1588. On the contrary, such a background might have provoked just
such a reaction, especially in so patriotic a playwright at a time of threatened or actual invasion from Catholic Spain. Indeed, that very patriotism
arguably offers further evidence of Shakespeare's authorship. The closing
lines of *Troublesome Reign*, 'If England's peers and people join in one/Not
Pope, nor France nor Spain can do them wrong', not only voice the same
sentiment as the far more famous final lines of *King John*, 'Come the three
corners of the world in arms/And we shall shock them! Naught shall

make us rue/If England to itself do rest but true!', but also explain, as the later text does not, what the imagined 'three corners' actually were. So they remained throughout Elizabeth's reign, with ceaseless threats of aggression, and the equally constant fear of disloyalty and defection on the part of English Catholics* (Wernham 1994, 407–15).

When Shakespeare wrote *King John*, he surely had a copy of *Troublesome Reign* at his elbow, just as he wrote *The Shrew* from *A Shrew*. Again the structure and the characters are in close conformity, scene by scene. So, in this play, are the mistakes of historical fact. Sometimes the earlier words seem to creep into the later text along subconscious paths; thus the *Reign* stage direction 'Enter the Sheriff, and whispers the Earl of Salisbury in the ear' reappears in *John* as Queen Eleanor's image 'So much my conscience whispers in your ear', which is instantly followed by 'Enter a Sheriff'. Some lines and ideas are repeated verbatim, thus:

Troublesome Reign	*King John*
[the King of France claims] the kingdom of England with the lordship of Ireland, Poitiers, Anjou, Toraine, Maine (51–2)	lays most lawful claim to this fair island . . . to Ireland, Poitiers Anjou, Toraine, Maine (I.i.10–11)
Then King of England, in my master's name . . . I do defy thee . . . prepare for bloody wars (61–6)	. . . fierce and bloody war take my King's defiance from my mouth (I.i.18–21)
thy brother and thine elder, and no heir (136)	Is that the elder, and art thou the heir? (I.i.57)
Philip kneel down . . . Rise up Sir Richard Plantagenet (318–20)	Kneel thou down, Philip . . . Arise Sir Richard (I.i.161–2)
ungracious youth, to rip thy mother's shame (150)	rude man, thou dost shame thy mother (I.i.64)
my father was ambassador in Germany unto the emperor . . . The king lay often at my father's house (180–82)	in an embassy to Germany, there with the emperor the king . . . sojourned at my father's (I.i.99–100,103)
I never saw so lively counterfeit of Richard Coeur de Lion as in him (211–20)	he hath a trick of Cordelions face (I.i.85)

---

* Cf the equally anachronistic fears of a fifth column within England in *Edmund Ironside* 375–80.

Next them a bastard of the king's deceased (512)	With them a bastard of the king's deceas'd (II.i.65)
I can infer a will that bars the way he urges . . . a will indeed, a crabbed woman's will (542–4)	I can produce a will that bars the title . . . a woman's will, a cank'red grandam's will (II.i.191, 194)
You men of Angiers, and . . . my loyal subjects (638)	You men of Angiers, and my loving subjects (II.i.203)
thirty thousand marks of stipend coin (837)	full thirty thousand marks of English coin (II.i.530)
I Pandulph Cardinal of Milan (1010)	I Pandulph, of fair Milan Cardinal (III.i.138)
never an Italian priest of them all shall either have tithe, toll . . . out of England (1022–4)	no italian priest/ Shall tithe or toll in our dominions (III.i.153–4)
will [you] upon your wedding day . . . follow dreadful drums? (1082–3)	Upon thy wedding day? . . . loud churlish drums (III.i.300, 303)
issue suddenly forth . . . set [Arthur] in this chair (fast bound) (1395–8)	rush forth and bind [Arthur] fast to the chair (IV.i.3–5)

These examples are drawn solely from Part One of *Troublesome Reign*; and they could be copiously supplemented. Taken in conjunction with the continuous parallelism of stage directions, they surely show that Shakespeare was deliberately reworking the text from a printed copy, not dimly recalling stray phrases. For those who believe (with Boyce 1990, 46) that *Troublesome Reign* was 'probably' a Bad Quarto, or memorial reconstruction of *King John* (a view fully as preposterous as its Shrew equivalent), these examples too will be 'anticipation', 'recollection' and so forth, and acclaimed as proof positive of the theory, despite all demonstrations that they are in fact characteristic of authorial revision (cf Sprinchorn on *Hamlet*, 1994a). But common sense insists that all three cases are themselves parallel. Note too the features that Shakespeare chooses to preserve from his source, namely a pun, a ribald allusion and one line almost *verbatim*, exactly as in the Shrew plays, together with an abrupt departure after a whirlwind wooing and wedding. But it was just as easy for him to change all the many parallels as to retain them; the two plays are essentially different, again as in the Shrew pair. It is strange to assume, without question, that Shakespeare should treat someone else's work exactly as if it were his own personal property to exploit as he pleased. That assumption becomes odder still when it entails the unchanged continuance of unhistorical inventions and errors from one history play to another on the same reign.

Troublesome Reign was not merely a historical source, like Holinshed's *Chronicles*. It is commonly called 'the old play'; but its author could perfectly well have been younger than Shakespeare. On any analysis the two kept very close company; prima facie, they were both Queen's Men. So the principle of economy independently proposes that the relationship was one of identity. The words used by R.L. Smallwood, the doyen of *King John* studies, inadvertently suggest this self-evident solution, throughout his Commentary (1974, 155f). First, 'Shakespeare seems to have worked more closely with this play than with any other source he used . . .'. In other words, he made more free with a fellow writer's adaptation of the chronicle sources than ever he did when dealing directly with those sources themselves. How puzzling and peculiar a procedure on his part; how strange that it occasioned no known protest, even from inveterate detractors such as Greene and Nashe who accused him of plagiarising his fellow writers. The depredations were such that every character in the 1591 play has some counterpart in the 1623 version. Here are some further detailed examples, all avouched by Smallwood (ibid.), of Shakespeare's so-called borrowings (a euphemism for the thefts that this theory requires) from a forgotten work which he admired enough to base his own upon. The Folio play is woven, strand by strand, from the original inventions found in the Quarto playwright. It is therefore the latter who confused the town Poitiers with the province Poitou, and added the following gratuitous inventions and errors which Shakespeare unquestioningly retained in his Folio version: the arrival of the Faulconbridge brothers; the imaginary character of the pompous Robert; the bastardy trial and its consequences; the equally imaginary character of the ebullient Bastard (announced as a special attraction on the Quarto title-page), who influences events despite his non-existence; the anachronistic addition of a will and testament; the equally anachronistic title of 'Dauphin'; the exaggerated concessions allegedly made by John at Le Goulet; the telescoping of two separate enemies of Richard I into one minor character; Blanche's siding with the Bastard against Austria; the Angiers spokesman's suggestion of reconciling the warring factions by intermarriage; the creation of Arthur as Lord of Brittany, Richmond and Angiers; the sudden mention of Stephen Langton immediately followed by John's excommunication; the equally sudden clash between John and Pandulph; the misnomer of the latter as Cardinal of Milan; the fusion of two papal legates into that one character; the references to a warrant for Arthur's blinding; and many another plastic remodelling of historical material from Holinshed. Such data are collectively called 'Shakespeare's creation of great drama from the inert material of *Troublesome Reign*' (Smallwood ibid., 249); but what would that play's author have thought of all these depredations had he been anyone other than Shakespeare himself?

Such arguments are often disparaged as 'Bardolatry'. But that word means the uncritical adoration of Shakespeare's art, not his morals. It is not idolatrous to deny that Shakespeare was a thief; and it is sheer fantasy to claim (D. Foster 1988) that plagiarism was rife in Tudor times, so that *Edmund Ironside* with its hundreds of parallels and affinities with the canon may colourably be claimed as another result of Shakespeare's pilfering practices. On the contrary, it was precisely such an accusation from Greene ('dressed in our feathers') that Shakespeare found so offensive, as Chettle tells us (182) and contemporary witness (191) confirms. These same considerations also apply to the Shrew and Hamlet plays, where the original versions are the earliest known modern comedy and tragedy respectively. *Troublesome Reign* is the first modern history play. Are not all three the apprentice works of the playwright whose complete comedies, tragedies and histories were collected in the 1623 First Folio?

Not only the similarities but also the differences between the John plays also present the same surprising pattern as the Shrew (and the Henry the Sixth) plays. In each pair, the Folio text shows that Shakespeare has looked again not only at the so-called 'source-play' but also at that play's own sources such as Holinshed or Ariosto. Again, as analysis shows, he behaves exactly like a reviser, not like a second writer. Even without such evidence, the voice of the young Shakespeare is already audible *per se* in *Troublesome Reign* just as in *A Shrew*, *Hamlet* 1603, *Contention* and *True Tragedy*. To the typical and overt word-play, proverbs, bawdry, Biblical and classical (especially Ovidian) allusion, highspeed wooing and wedding, and other such characteristics (XXV), *Troublesome Reign* adds dozens of other strands woven in the same pattern,* as exemplified in the following list, arranged in alphabetical order of key-word, and again designed to assist future researchers and facilitate new studies and editions.

Alliteration, 'harmful and harsh, hell's horror to be heard' (I.1422), 'dark and direful guerdon for their guilt' (I.1501), 'frown, friends, fail, faith' (I.1736), etc.; antithesis, 'contented uncontent' (I.29), 'right . . . wrong' (I.111–12, 527–9), 'shadow . . . substance' (I.536–7), etc.; bawdry, (I.834–5, 1306–8), etc.; Bible, hairs on head numbered (I.1646–7), motes and beams (I.559), revenge is God's (II.88, 497–9), longest home (II.169), flight from Egypt (II.1020), fiery furnace (II.1091–2), etc.; chiasmus (I.1146, II.679–80), etc.; compounds, 'black-spotted' (I.919), 'ease-bred' (I.1581) 'peace-breaking' (II.239); flattery (II.333, 853); flora and fauna, viper (I.160–61), falcon (I.280–81, II.486), whale (I.740), fox (I.1046), buzzard (II.163), eagle (II.983); 'if and ands' (Nashe 1589), three consecutive lines begin with 'And' (I.44–6); Latin, 'atavis regibus' (I.260), 'quo me rapit tempestas?' (I.262), etc.; imagery, 'this bitter wind must nip somebody's spring . . . harvest weather' (I.507–8), 'pruned . . . branch . . . stock' (I.1559–60), 'northern wind' (I.1758), etc.; law (I.540f, II.1211–13)

---

* Again as in *Edmund Ironside*, where such characteristics are on copious display, together with many phraseological parallels.

etc.; noun-verb discord, 'thy fortunes stands' (I.1365); Ovid, Phaeton/ Merop (I. 357-8), Icarus (I. 553), cave of Morpheus (I.686-7), 'tempus edax rerum' (I.1350), Io/Juno (II.876); proverb (I. 308-9, 1046, II.1047-50); pun, on 'will' (I.542-4), internal/eternal (I.1466-7), trump/triumph (I.1452), etc.; rhyme, couplets *passim*; stichomythia (I.1470f); wooing and wedding, 'marriage rites . . . presently', 'holy nuptial rites' (I.836, 892-3, 975, 1603), 'upon your wedding day forsake your bride' (I.1081-2); 'un-' prefix, over forty examples including two (unfitting, unhallowed) recorded as first known usages by the Oxford English Dictionary. There are also frequent references to such typical motifs as oath-taking and unburied bodies (IV), as well as dozens of parallels with canonical plays, chiefly *Titus Andronicus*.

As close comparison shows, the 1623 John and Shrew plays omit all the Biblical and Ovidian references found in the Quarto versions but replace them with different allusions from the same sources, like a reviser thoroughly familiar with such texts and not at all like any imaginable exploiter of earlier anonymous plays. As with *Hamlet* Q1, and *A Shrew*, *Contention* and *True Tragedy*, the chief need now is a new edition of *Troublesome Reign* setting out in detail, line by line, all the hundreds of forgotten Shakespearean affinities.

XXVII

Contention *and* True Tragedy

THESE TWO PLAYS are taken together because they are the first and second parts of a drama about King Henry VI. The former (*Contention* for short) was published in 1594 as *The first part of the Contention betwixt the two famous houses of Yorke and Lancaster, with the death of the good Duke Humphrey,* etc.; the latter (*True Tragedy* for short) in 1595 as *The True Tragedie of Richard, Duke of Yorke, and the death of good King Henrie the Sixt, with the whole contention between the two Houses Lancaster and Yorke.* Each is a version of a much longer play first published in 1623 as the second or third part respectively of *King Henry VI.*

The reasons for assigning these early versions to Shakespeare, as well as the later, are:

1   He began as a writer of popular plays; and these two were relished enough to be republished separately in 1600 and jointly (as *The Whole Contention* etc.) in an undated third edition.

2   That edition was specifically announced on its title-page as 'Written by William Shakespeare, Gent[leman],' an honorific to which he had become entitled after the death in 1601 of his armigerent father.

3   That edition was also 'newly corrected and enlarged', prima facie by its author; the process of radical improvement and enlargement was typical of Shakespeare and not identifiable in any other dramatist.

4   The inference of his original authorship is further enhanced by the evidence above that

  (a)   the earliest mentioned or published texts of the Hamlet, Shrew and John plays, for over sixty reasons, also represent rewritings (and not 'memorial reconstructions');

  (b)   *Hamlet* was also revised and enlarged, while *A Shrew* and *Troublesome Reign* were completely rewritten;

  (c)   all the plays that exist in variant versions always have one component known to be by Shakespeare and never have any component known to be by anyone else.

5(a)   As in the case of the Hamlet, Shrew and John variants, either Shakespeare wrote their first versions or he stole their ideas, characters, plots, and lines, i.e. exploited an unknown contemporary colleague for his own profit and prestige; but

(b) there is no reason to believe that he ever even contemplated any such underhand dealing, about which, further, there is no trace of criticism or indeed comment from any quarter, not even from his detractors such as Greene and Nashe who complain of his alleged plagiarisms.

6(a) Robert Greene in 1592 says in effect that the play which contains the line 'O tiger's heart wrapped in a woman's hide' is a play by the young Shakespeare;

(b) that line occurs in *True Tragedy* 1595, which on any rational appraisal identifies it, and not the 1623 Folio text of its counterpart *3 Henry VI*, as Greene's source.

7 So *True Tragedy*'s first part, *Contention*, was also a Shakespeare play.

8 *True Tragedy* 1595 (and hence prima facie *Contention* 1594) was 'sundry times acted by' Pembroke's Men, a company with which Shakespeare may well have been associated in the early 1590s (XXI; George 1981) between his earlier membership of Queen's and later membership of Chamberlain's. Pembroke's are also recorded as having performed *Titus Andronicus* and *A Shrew*, with the same implication.

9(a) *Contention* was printed by Thomas Creede and *True Tragedy* by Valentine Simmes; both were sold by Thomas Millington. Their connections with Shakespeare's known plays, his known company, Chamberlain's, and his likely first company, Queen's, are well worth recording. Only modern theory impugns their reputation.

(b) Creede printed the second to fifth editions of *Richard III* 1598–1612 (advertising all but the second as 'newly augmented'), the second of *Romeo and Juliet* 1599, the first and second of *Henry V* 1600–1602, and the first of *The Merry Wives of Windsor* 1602; all of these volumes specify Chamberlain's, and the first four and the last give Shakespeare's name.

(c) For Simmes see XXVI above, argument 12b;

(d) Millington sold the first edition of *Titus Andronicus*, 1594 and (with Creede as printer) the first of *Henry V*.

10(a) Shakespeare concludes his *Henry V*, written by June 1599, with these lines:

Henry the Sixth, in infant bands crowned King
Of France and England, did this King succeed,
Whose state so many had the managing
That they lost France, and made his England bleed:
Which oft our stage hath shown; and, for their sake,
In your fair minds let this acceptance take.

(b)   as editors* acknowledge (e.g. Wilson 1947, 185; Gurr 1992, 210), this is a deliberate reference to his own three plays about Henry VI; but

(c)   the only three plays on that subject ever recorded as having been played at all, let alone often, by 1599, were *1 Henry VI* (acted in 1592), *Contention* (published in 1594) and *True Tragedy* (published in 1595 'as acted by' Pembroke's Men, and quoted by Greene in or before 1592, see argument 8); so

(d)   those were the Shakespeare plays to which his *Henry V* epilogue refers.

11   Millington owned the rights in *Contention* (and hence in *True Tragedy*, issued by the same publisher without further entry). In 1602 he transferred them to Thomas Pavier, who on that authority republished them together as *The Whole Contention* Divided into two Parts: and newly corrected and enlarged. Written by William Shakespeare, Gent (arguments 2 and 3 above). The same authority presumably covered the First Folio publication of the longer versions *2–3 Henry VI*; that is, the same rule was applied as to the Shrew and John versions, namely that treatments of the same theme by the same author are covered by the same copyright.

12(a)   The Oxford editors, Wells and Taylor, have gratuitously bestowed the titles *Contention* etc. and *True Tragedy* etc. on their texts of *2* and *3 Henry VI* respectively (1986, 63–140; 1988, 111–12, 175–208 *et passim*), on the ground that the early wording sounds authentically Shakespearean; but

(b)   if it is, the rather obvious reason (not noted in the Oxford edition) is that those were indeed his own titles which he himself devised and applied to his own original versions as published in 1594–5.

13   The Oxford editors include passages from both early versions in their Complete Works texts of *2–3 Henry VI* (1986, 101, 140), exactly as if the 1594–5 plays were also authentic Shakespeare, and indeed contained his 'original draft' (ibid., 101).

There are no grounds, *pace* the entire profession, most recently represented by Montgomery and Taylor (Taylor 1988, 175–216) and Hattaway (1991, 216 and 1993, 203) for supposing that Shakespeare did not write these plays, or that anyone else did, least of all 'pirate-actors' with abysmal memories (see e.g. Sams 1983, 1988c, 1989a, 1991a, 1994a, b, and c, 1995; Urkowitz 1988b, Bains *N&Q* 1993; and XXXI). On the contrary, their style is entirely consonant with his early manner as parodied by Greene and pilloried by Nashe. The latter's obscure 1589

---

*   Including Taylor (1982, 281), although he later became convinced that *1 Henry VI* was not wholly Shakespeare's own (Taylor 1988, 217) and also felt that the second and third parts might well also be collaborative (ibid., 112).

reference to 'those, that . . . haue not learned so long as they haue liued in the spheares, the iust measure of the Horizon without an hexameter' may perhaps allude to the scansion or measure of 'horizon' in *True Tragedy*: 'And then as early as the morning sun/Lifts up his beams above the horizon . . .'. But the clear and certain allusion is Greene's famous quotation from that play of York's line that treats a woman in terms of tigers, an idea which he emphasises by repetition in that same speech: 'But you are more inhumane, more inexorable,/O ten times more than Tigers of Arcadia.'

That latter location sufficed J.S. Smart (1928, 171) as a justification for concluding that *True Tragedy* must be a 'memorial reconstruction', because 'any poet must have known' that Arcadia was a tiger-free zone. But many a Tudor poet, if not every modern commentator, would have known it was more like Africa; it teemed with tigers, and lions too. This can be readily inferred from Ovid (*Metamorphoses*, I.216f, 304–5). When Jupiter visited Lycaon, King of Arcadia, he traversed a terrain 'bristling with the lairs of wild beasts'. That evil monarch was duly transformed into an Arcadian wolf; the ensuing flood swept away wolves, lions and tigers galore. Perhaps it was the same student of Ovid who twice called another hated queen a 'ravenous tiger' in *Titus Andronicus* (V.iii.15, 195).

Smart's claims were posthumously published by his close colleague Peter Alexander. They suited Alexander's book; and he would soon command such awestruck respect that his reputation sustained and enhanced Smart's. To this day, no one knows or cares about their Shrew absurdities (XXV), which are less like joint scholarship than *folie à deux*. Their thoughts on *Contention* and *True Tragedy*, however, have been even more epidemically influential.

Their main method was to juxtapose parallel passages from the counterpart texts, denounce one of them as corrupt, and announce their own memorial reconstruction theory as the only possible explanation, while ignoring all the actual well-documented causes of textual confusion. Thus Alexander (1929, 64–5) claims that what he calls the corruption in *Contention* 1594 cannot conceivably be attributed to any writer (this 'may be dismissed without further consideration'), nor indeed to any 'compositor or transcriber or abridger, or to their combined efforts; to account for it we require to postulate a factor not found in the normal method of transmission', namely his own theory. Thus the Alexander method exactly exemplifies the approach castigated by A.E. Housman (1892, 2) as 'conclusion first, reasons afterwards . . . you write down at the outset the answer to the sum; then you proceed to fabricate . . . the ciphering by which you can pretend to have arrived at it'. And the sphere in which, according to Housman, these deceptions are routinely practised is editorial and textual criticism.

Alexander begins by transporting two five-act plays, *2–3 Henry VI* 1623, back to about 1590, in good time to be 'reconstructed'. Not only is

Shakespeare deemed to have written them by then; his company is required to have accepted, rehearsed, copied and performed them, without however leaving any trace of any such activity. Then, just as silently, they suddenly disappeared, not to resurface anywhere before being published verbatim in the First Folio. So before the theory can even begin, it furnishes itself with two whole history plays and dozens of other documents, people, places and activities all invented *ex nihilo* and conveniently left unmentioned by anyone but Alexander throughout recorded history.

That is just the overture. As the curtain rises, the theory has been left playless in 1590, as the entire hypothetical cast of the hypothetical *2–3 Henry VI* has departed somewhere else for some unknown reason, taking their copies with them, or perhaps just petulantly throwing them away. But, somehow, one or two players were left behind, to become an independent rump of 'actors who, like Bottom, attempted to play the parts of all the characters' (Taylor 1988, 26). Bottom indeed; a fundamental yet asinine fallacy from a literary dream world. These actors had decided to reconstruct the vanished play from memory, an activity for which they had made no preparation and possessed no talent. Indeed, they were so hopelessly unfitted for their self-imposed task that they could recall very little of the text they had just been acting and had to make up new words of their own. So although recruited as actors, because of their memories of their supposed performances, they are now discovered to be suffering from severe amnesia. Uniquely in the long history of hypothesis, these imaginary entities actually lack their own *raison d'être*. With great versatility therefore they obligingly transform themselves into writers instead of actors, a role which surprisingly suits them rather better. Next, despite their incompetence at their own professional task, they managed to persuade a full supporting cast of strolling hypotheses which happened to be passing to join with them in illicit performances of their botched corruptions. These were duly passed off as genuine Shakespeare plays, to the delight of obtuse audiences and the profit of the pirate-actors and then of equally dishonest publishers and booksellers.

Fortunately for Smart and Alexander, and for Duthie, who would later accept the same eccentric conclusions about *Hamlet*, also still hailed as 'proved', no actual evidence was ever needed. Before long, the leading expert had announced his conversion, thus: 'I formerly accepted [revision], but a recent study [of Greg and Alexander] has convinced me that it is wrong' (Chambers 1930, i, 281). That conviction in favour of memorial reconstruction by actors then became a whole profession's preconviction.

So it remains, to this day. Forty years on, the same theory, still without any factual evidence or rational argument, had become 'commonly accepted' (Evans 1971, 229). Four years later it was hailed as 'demonstrated' and true 'in fact' (Schoenbaum 1975, 123). So it stayed;

Contention 1594 and *True Tragedy* 1595 had been 'shown' (Jackson 1986, 164) to be memorial reconstructions of the 1623 plays *2–3 Henry VI*. Some believers at last felt safe in explaining what Alexander's arguments actually were, as follows. First, a passage in *Contention* about York's descent from Edward III contains a genealogical error which leaves 'no dramatic reason for the speech to continue after its fifth line; yet it does continue, and for another twenty-one lines. No . . . author could have made this error [*sic*] but . . . a reporter easily could. Once having established [*sic*] that part of *Contention* is clearly [*sic*] a report, it is natural [*sic*] to suppose that the rest of the text is also a report.' These assertions are called a 'central argument', which is also applied to *True Tragedy*. This too contains a historical inaccuracy, so again the only conceivable cause is faulty memory and again the entire text must be the result of 'memorial reconstruction by actors' (Montgomery and Taylor in Taylor 1988, 175 and 197). On such grounds, two early plays are denied to Shakespeare and two others are dated thirty years earlier than their first recorded appearance in print or performance (with equally calamitous consequences considered later, XXXI–XXXIII). These are indeed Alexander's arguments; and thus the emperor's clothes are held up for approval by the emperor's tailors.

Even the Oxford editors so far cited seem to find such arguments barely adequate. What they treat as revealed truth in one paragraph becomes mere 'hypothesis' or 'plausible' in the next (idem). So they feel the need for extra supports, and they offer three. First, Alexander also says that *Contention* 'contains a number of echoes of other plays, by Shakespeare and others, which are absent from [*2 Henry VI*]', which 'in the context of the bad quarto hypothesis' are 'easily explained as the reporters' interpolations from other plays they knew'; otherwise the explanation would have to be 'deliberate excisions from [*2 Henry VI*]', which is 'less probable'. In other words, yet again, conclusions first and reasons afterwards. In reality, the 'reporters' are not people but hypotheses, just like their knowledge of other plays, and their peculiar practice of interpolation, and the existence of *2 Henry VI* at the time. These are just further samples of invention, regularly vaunted over the simple sensible explanation of authorial revision, which as in Alexander is never even considered. That kicks away the second proposed prop, namely that the theory is, of all things, 'economical'. The Oxford editors' third claim, that Alexander's argument has 'never been plausibly refuted', is justified solely by omitting any mention of all known refutations readily available to them (e.g. Greer 1933, 1956, 1957, Craig 1961, Sams 1983). The Cambridge editor of *1–3 Henry VI* is also content to echo Oxford, thus: 'Peter Alexander demonstrated' (*sic*) how the same passages in *Contention* and *True Tragedy* 'could only have been written by a reporter who did not understand the facts of the case' (Hattaway 1991, 216; 1993, 203). But he is bolder about this supposed reporter's 'echoes of plays by Shakespeare and others'; this 'supports the case for memorial reconstruction and almost certainly destroys the case of those who see the play as an early draft'. Again the hypothetical reporter is treated as a real historical person instead of a literary theory, while the young Shakespeare's well-documented and much-discussed propensity to echo himself and others is hailed as proof of his irrelevance to the question.

In reality, such Shakespearean parallels undermine 'memorial reconstruction', which leaves authorial revision of early plays as the only rational alternative. Again all refutations of Alexander (which by 1993 included Sams 1989a) remain unmentioned, except one (Urkowitz 1988a, b, and c) which is dealt with thus: 'Alexander's assumptions and conclusions are challenged but not convincingly overthrown.' That is fortunate for the New Cambridge editions concerned; but only in Academia would Alexander's assumptions, or anyone's, need to be overthrown, especially when they actually also are the so-called conclusions, exactly as in the parallel *Hamlet* theories (XXIV).

However, they demand more detailed analysis because of their fatal influence on all modern Shakespeare studies. Alexander's first chapter, called 'The Argument', states as a fact that Greene in 1592 was quoting *3 Henry VI* 1623, i.e. the rightness of the theory about to be announced is silently assumed from the outset. The same assumption is then reiterated, still as a fact, in the heading of the first substantive chapter, namely 'Greene's quotation from *3 Henry VI*', a play produced with a flourish from the top hat of Tudor history. The same assumption is affirmed three more times on the same page (39): 'for *3 Henry VI* we have Greene's important reference in 1592', 'Greene's reference to *3 Henry VI*', '[that reference is] the natural and indeed the only interpretation which the passage will bear'. *3 Henry VI* is then explicitly identified as Greene's target *seven* more times in the same chapter. For the first fifty-four pages, no attempt of any kind is made to justify this settled assumption. Then readers are told that 'to see how limpingly the Quarto writer [i.e. *Contention* 1594] halts after Shakespeare [i.e. *2 Henry VI* 1623] one has only to compare the two versions' of the Duke of York's pedigree. In other words, 1594 is 'after' 1623, as the basic assumption requires. The two passages are duly set forth, and readers are instructed that 'all the hopeless confusion in the details of the pedigree and the mechanical repetition of phrases found in the [1623 version] indicate that we have in the [1594 version] nothing more than someone's attempt to reconstruct from memory [in 1594] one of [the 1623] scenes'. Again time obligingly flows backwards, as the basic assumption requires, and drowns any possibility that 1594 is actually earlier than 1623. In its torrential course, it throws up 'mechanical repetition' by 'someone', and his 'attempt' to 'reconstruct' by 'memory'; by leaving 'nothing more' in its wake. It also obliterates Shakespeare himself and his known practice of revision. In fact, the whole theory is nothing more than Alexander's attempt to justify his own *idée fixe*. He then applies the same techniques to the other pair of plays (p. 63f). He further describes other textual variants as 'transposition of phrases' or 'additional material' or 'confusions' which must also mean a memorial reporter (p. 67), who must have been the actor who played Warwick, because that part is reported best, again exactly as in the corresponding *Hamlet* theories. The Bad Quarto/memorial reconstruction blinkers continue to shut out the obvious and unitary explanation of all such appearances, namely authorial revision in which some parts are changed less than others.

As we have seen, one Tudor author above all wrote in a known style, for example about wicked queens who imitated the action of the tiger; hence Greene's unkind parody. Some fifty different animals, wild or tame, are named in *Contention* and *True Tragedy*. So are a dozen plants. Here is Pliny in plenty, together with Ovid and Plutarch, just as Nashe says. As soon as the early strata are separated out, their constituents are seen to match those of *Hamlet*, *A Shrew* and *Troublesome Reign*,* as in the list that follows (again set in alphabetical order of key-word; lineation from Morgan 1892, with *Contention* called C. and *True Tragedy* T.): antithesis, 'swords . . . words' (C. 149), 'fall . . . rise' (C. 266–7); bawdry (C. 1765, 1825, T. 1247–50); blood drinking (T. 969); Bible, God pouring vengeance (C. 798); compounds, 'big-swolne' (C. 98), 'thrice-valiant' (C. 197); country imagery, 'lime-twigs . . . will intangle them' (C. 346); flattery (C. 381); flora and fauna, hawk (C. 459–60), lizards (T. 874), etc.; Greene (*Menaphon* 1589), 'Abradas, the great Macedonian pirate' (C. 1498–9); Latin, 'et tu, Brute' (T. 1935); law (C. 400); Marlowe, 'Furies . . . masks . . . black Cocytus' (a conflation of notions found in *I Tamburlaine* IV.iv.17–18, V.ii.155); noun-verb discord, 'is all our labours then spent in vain' (C. 87), 'thousands . . . dreads' (C. 1043), 'subjects owes . . . laws commands' (T. 1261–2); Ovid, 'Pluto in his fiery wagon' etc. (C. 499–503, cf. *Metamorphoses* V. 355f), 'tigers of Arcadia' (C. 515, cf *Metamorphoses* I. 305f); country proverb, 'the fox barks not when he would steal the lamb' (C. 1091), 'if we slack this fair bright summers day, sharp winter showers will mar our hope for hay' (T. 2032–4); pun, usurer/usurper (C. 297–8); rhyming couplets (C. 1164–5, 1176–7, T. 2033–4); 'un-', unlade (C. 1449), ungrateful (T. 1479); quick wooing and wedding, 'sudden marriage' (T. 1536).

Here incidentally are further disproofs of 'memorial reconstruction'. Only one Tudor actor, namely Shakespeare himself, was likely to have written thus, and also added historical and topographical details not found in the supposed sources (*2–3 Henry VI*), such as Long Melford

---

*   Again, as exemplified throughout *Edmund Ironside*.

(C. 314), Maidstone (C. 1543), O'Neil (C. 1104) and even a legendary Earl of Southampton* (Bevis, C. 858). But he would hardly have forgotten thousands of his own Folio lines in the process. Again, what is now needed is a new edition of these two pioneering early histories, showing the forgotten affinities with their canonical versions and other plays.

---

* Another equally legendary Earl of Southampton is introduced as a staunch bluff English hero in *Edmund Ironside*, together with gratuitous references to that location (I.i. and 476).

XXVIII

Faire Em *and* Locrine

THERE ARE TWO other extant plays for which there is some evidence of Shakespearean authorship within the time span covered by this volume, up to 1594: *Faire Em*, and *Locrine*. The former is, beyond doubt, the play attacked by Greene in 1587 (see also XVI). His words, from the Preface to his *Farewell to Folly* (a work registered in 1587, but unknown in print before 1591), are as follows:

> Others will flout and ouer read euerie line with a frumpe [= sneer], and say tis scuruie [= scurvy], when they themselves are such scabd Iades that they are like to dye of the fazion [ulcerated throat]; but if they come to write, or publish anie thing in print, it is either distild out of ballets, or borrowed of Theological poets, which, for their calling and grauitie being loth to haue anie prophane pamphlets pass under their hand, get some other *Batillus* [Bathyllus, a poet who claimed a verse by Virgil as his own] to set his name to their verses. Thus is the asse made proud by this vnder hande brokerie. And he that cannot write true Englishe without the help of Clearkes of parish Churches will needes make himself the father of interludes [= stage plays]. O tis a iollie matter when a man hath a familiar stile, and can endite a whole year, and neuer be beholding to art? but to bring Scripture to proue any thing he sayes, and kill it dead with the text in a trifling subiect of loue, I tell you is no small peece of cunning. As for example two louers on the stage arguing one an other of unkindness, his Mistris runnes ouer him with this canonicall sentence, *A man's conscience is a thousand witnesses*; and hir knight againe excuseth him selfe with that saying of the Apostle, *Loue couereth the multitude of sinnes*. I thinke this was but simple abusing of the Scripture.

Those words are quoted from *Faire Em*, which in turn alludes to 1 Peter 4:8, 'for charity shall cover the multitude of sins'.

Among much that remains obscure, Greene's typical attack on poorly educated playwrights ('dunces' here and again in 1592) who are carping critics, and plagiarists, yet have their own all too familiar style, is clear enough. His only named target was Shakespeare, known in 1592 as the 'tiger's heart' playwright, who had himself written *c.* 1592 that his style was readily recognisable and indeed recognised (XX). Nashe too inveighs against playwrights, identified above as Shakespeare and Kyd (XVI), who are censurers, borrowers, and Latinless dolts. Both Greene and Nashe also complain of a playwright who consorts with and consults a churchman (XVI); the Parnassus plays present a parallel pair, identified above as Shakespeare and Kyd (XVIII). Nashe further inveighs against playwrights who are so blasphemous that they 'repose eternity in the mouth of a player' (XVI), i.e. write such awesome words for mere actors to speak on the stage; cf 'eternal' once each in *Contention* and *True Tragedy*, twice in *Troublesome Reign* and thrice in *The Taming of A Shrew*.*

Furthermore, Greene's first target apparently had some throat trouble, yet was the 'father of interludes', i.e. the popular entertainments (OED 1) presented between the acts of mystery or morality plays. This assorts well with the unnamed writer of and actor in a mystery and a morality play, reported as the 'absolute Interpreter to the puppets' [= actors], whose voice Greene thought 'nothing gracious'. It may not be coincidence that Nashe in *Pierce Penniless* (Steane 1972, 69) speaks of a 'puling accent . . . like a feigned treble, or one's voice that interprets to the puppets'.

So the principle of economy proposes that Greene's *Farewell to Folly*, unknown in print before 1591, is aimed at Shakespeare, who may be further identified as the writer whose subject-matter was 'distilled out of ballets' [= ballads, OED 3]; for *Titus Andronicus c.* 1589 seems to have been based on a ballad (Maxwell 1953, xxvii). Shakespeare was certainly the Tudor dramatist most given to quoting the Bible, sometimes with arguably blasphemous results (II). Further, a dramatist accused of abuse of scripture, and blasphemous rhetoric, by the two Protestants Greene and Nashe respectively, is likely to have a Catholic background, like Shakespeare (V, XI, etc.). Again, Greene disparages his victim as a love-poet, a category also despised by Nashe in *Pierce Penniless* (XVI); Shakespeare is specifically described thus in the Parnassus plays (XVIII) and also by Meres in 1598 ('one of the most passionate among us to bewaile and bemoane the perplexities of Loue'). Finally Greene employs exactly the same methods of style-criticism, namely direct quotation, as in his known attack on Shakespeare.

That early style is now far less familiar, because it has been written off for decades. For those who believe that Shakespeare could not possibly have written anything until he was nearly thirty, least of all a play not accepted by the authorities, it remains merely 'wild' to suggest that 'Greene's attack of 1592 was only the last shot of a five-year pamphlet campaign', which 'probably nobody now believes' (Chambers 1930, i, 69, on the assumption that *Farewell to Folly* was in fact finished in 1587). But the premiss of a much younger Shakespeare attacked by name, or at least nickname, as the author of *True Tragedy* (not *3 Henry VI*) and perhaps much earlier than 1592 (which on any analysis represents the *terminus ad quem* of Greene and his *Groats-worth*, not a definite date) places all such

---

* And once in *Edmund Ironside* (1019), together with the actual word 'eternity' (652) of which Nashe complains.

easy assumptions in a new perspective, where it looks very much as if the authorship of *Faire Em* is being attributed to Shakespeare by someone who was exceptionally well placed to know.

That play was first published in an anonymous and undated text *c.* 1592 as 'A Pleasant Commodie, of faire Em the Millers daughter of Manchester, With the loue of William the Conqueror: As it was sundrie times publiquely acted in the honourable citie of London, by the right honourable the Lord Strange his seruants'. It proved popular and durable enough to be reissued in 1631. Lord Strange's Men were later known as the Earl of Derby's because Ferdinando Stanley, Lord Strange bore that title from September 1593 until his death in April 1594; as Derby's Men, they performed *Titus Andronicus*. The possible connections between Shakespeare and Strange's have been explored in detail (Honigmann 1985, 59–76). *Faire Em* was included among 'Shakespeare, Vol. 1' in the library of Charles II; and that attribution has been argued in depth (Simpson 1875–6, 155–80), with interesting suggestions about characterisation, for example that Valingford is intended to represent Shakespeare himself. That might explain why the rustic actor-playwright also attacked by Greene (XIV) allegedly grew rich enough to build a windmill; Valingford marries Em the miller's daughter.

The second extant play which may be attributed to Shakespeare on evidence dated 1594 or earlier is *Locrine*, which was registered for publication to Thomas Creede on 20 July 1594 and printed by him in 1595 as 'The Lamentable Tragedie of Locrine, the eldest sonne of King Brutus, discoursing the warres of the Britaines, and Hunnes, with their discomfiture: The Britaines victorie with their Accidents, and the death of Albanact. No less pleasant than profitable. Newly set foorth, ouerseene and corrected, by W.S.' Creede's Shakespearean credentials are summarised above (XXVII, argument 9). There is no reason to doubt that 'W.S.' means William Shakespeare, or that the whole play, not merely its editing and correction, is intended to be assigned to him by those initials (like 'W. Sh.' on the second edition of *Troublesome Reign* in 1611, also in Shakespeare's lifetime). It was partly on the strength of that assurance, if not indeed on independent knowledge, that *Locrine* was included as authentic in the Third Folio of 1664 and the Fourth of 1685.

An additional item of evidence is that Nashe, speaking in 1589 of two Senecan dramatists identifiable as Shakespeare and Kyd, says scoffingly that they 'thrust *Elisium* into hell', with the implication that this is sheer ignorance on their part, as one might expect from mere grammar-school boys who lack Latin and classical learning in general. Kyd certainly commits this supposed solecism, in the Prologue to *The Spanish Tragedy* (I.i.73), where the Senecan ghost of Andrea announces that he met Pluto in a stately tower standing in 'the fair Elysian green'. Similarly the Senecan ghost of Albanact in *Locrine* (IV.v.43–4) says 'Back will I post to hellmouth Taenarus/And pass Cocitus, to the Elysian fields'. In some sources, Elysium was indeed part of the infernal regions, and ghosts had unrestricted travel facilities. But Nashe was seeking to score a point, by reference to some play that his Tudor readers could recognise.

That ability has atrophied. *Locrine* is 'rejected by scholars' (Bartlett 1922, 59). 'It is fustian in the manner of Pistol, certainly not Shakespeare's work' (Halliday 1964, 283), even though Pistol *was* his work.

Its general style belongs to the mid-1580s. But its final speech, as follows, is datable to 1595, the thirty-eighth year of Elizabeth's reign:

> Lo here the end of lawlesse trecherie,
> Of vsurpation and ambitious pride;
> And they that for their priuate amours dare
> Turmoile our land, and set their broiles abroach,
> Let them be warned by these premisses.
> And as a woman was the onely cause
> That ciuill discord was then stirred vp,
> So let vs pray for that renowned mayd,
> That eight and thirtie years the scepter swayd,
> In quiet peace and sweet felicitie;
> And every wight that seekes her graces smart,
> Wold that this sword wer pierced in his hart!

These lines were presumably among the matter advertised as 'newly set forth' in 1595 by 'W.S.' But they are quite typical of the entire text, which the original author would be best qualified to revise, in the same style. This is readily analysable into such components as alliteration, antithesis, bawdry, Biblical and classical allusion (especially to Ovid), compounds, noun-verb discord, country imagery, puns, proverbs, words beginning with 'un-', whirlwind wooing and wedding, and so forth, as already categorised (XXIV–XXVII).* Here too, as with *Faire Em*, new editions are needed. They will show that the 'familiar style' of both these plays is entirely conformable with the early Shakespeare style.

* And in *Edmund Ironside*.

XXIX

Man's Wit *and* The Dialogue of Dives

THESE TITLES WERE attributed by Greene (XV, 179) to his actor-play-wright X, equated above with Shakespeare, in the 1580s. They sound like two separate works. The first is called a 'Moral', i.e. a morality play (OED 4, first recorded in 1578); the latter was presumably a mystery play dramatising the Bible story. Neither text is now known. But both genres were still flourishing in the early 1580s; any young stage talent of the time would be acquainted with them (VI), first as a spectator and then if possible as an author and actor.* Of course (*pace* Schoenbaum 1975, 115) the young Shakespeare would have written and performed them, as required; that was his métier. *Man's Wit* has remained unrecorded; but *The Marriage of Wit and Wisdom* and *Dives and Lazarus* were among the reper-tory of the travelling company of 'four men and a boy' that entertains the Lord Mayor of London and his lady at the feast made for them by Sir Thomas More in the play of that name. Part of it was certainly written by Shakespeare (Wells 1986, 889f); the whole text has been cogently attrib-uted to him, on detailed evidence (Mills 1993). *The Marriage of Wit and Wisdom*, incorporating lines by the *More* playwright, was enacted in full; its genre and provenance are well explicated by Gabrieli and Melchiori (1990, 143–60). The story of Dives and Lazarus, the rich man and the beggar, and the former's dialogue with father Abraham, is found in Luke 16: 19–31; it was of course familiar to Shakespeare, who often refers to it whether directly (*1 Henry IV*, III.iii.31f) or obliquely (*Henry V*, II.iii.9–10). In the play of *Histriomastix*, printed in 1610 for Thomas Thorpe (who had published the Sonnets in the previous year), the character 'Posthaste' the playwright, often interpreted as a caricature of Shakespeare, has *The Devil and Dives* in his repertory.

Greene's actor-playwright (X, 179) also played three scenes of the Devil in the highway to Heaven, and 'terribly thundered' the twelve labours of Hercules on the stage. Again, no text of either entertainment is now extant. But some reminiscence of the former may survive in 'the steep and thorny way to Heaven' (*Hamlet*, I.iii.48); and the labours of Hercules form leitmotifs in Shakespeare's works. He is so familiar with some of

---

* Like the author of *Edmund Ironside*, where the Judas-figure Edricus is dressed in black as in mystery plays and shares Shakespearean Judas allusions (792–3, 1362, 1847).

them that he relies on one relevant epithet to convey their full heroic power, as when Hamlet's fate 'makes each petty artery in this body/As hardy as the Nemean lion's nerve' (I.iv.82–3). It helps to know, whether from classical learning, Lemprière or an editorial footnote, that the lion of Nemaea, which had ravaged the environs of Mycenae, was slain by the young Hercules with a club after a fierce struggle. Many of the Twelve Labours, including this one, occur allusively in *Love's Labour's Lost* (IV.i.83) where Hercules is presented as a character in a pageant. There are many other clear echoes of past declamations, such as Bottom's claim that Hercules ('Ercles') was a tyrant (*Midsummer Night's Dream*, I.ii.26–36). 'This may allude to a ranting role in a particular play, now lost' (Wells 1967, 129); for example, the terrible thundering of Greene's actor-playwright (X).

XXX

Early Start and Revision

THE NEW TERRAIN explored in the last seven chapters was always accessible to the approach that Shakespeare (like most other comparable geniuses) started early and (like many of them) regularly revised or rewrote his own work. These two viewpoints together are needed for a proper perspective; but the profession at large has ignored or denied them both for most of this century. Here and there however an expert eye has caught a glimpse of lost horizons. Professor Honigmann has endorsed 'early start', which means that 'the dramatic history of the Elizabethan age will have to be rewritten' (1982, 90). Nearly as long ago, Professor Wells (1983, 20) was persuaded that the 1623 *King Lear* was an authorial revision of the 1608 version, with implications fully as far-reaching, yet still equally unnoticed or unaccepted.

All extant editions need to be rewritten in the light of these two complementary perceptions. 'Early start' is readily inferable from the facts up to 1594. Authorial revision needs later data, as follows: 1598, *Love's Labour's Lost* 'newly corrected and augmented'; 1599, *Romeo and Juliet*, 'newly corrected, augmented and amended' and *1 Henry IV*, 'newly corrected by W. Shakespeare'; 1599, *The Passionate Pilgrim*, containing early versions of Sonnets 138 and 144; 1601, *Richard II* acted with a new episode portraying the King's deposition (IV.i.154–319); 1602, *Richard III*, 'newly augmented'; 1604, *Hamlet*, 'enlarged to almost as much again as it was'; 1608, *Richard II* printed 'with new additions of the Parliament Sceane, and the deposing of King Richard'; 1616, *The Rape of Lucrece*, 'newly revised'; 1623, the First Folio, where each one of the eighteen plays already published now has textual variants, which are often very striking (*Titus Andronicus* for example has a whole new scene, III.ii.).

This plain evidence is regularly ignored or misinterpreted. Thus the *Richard II* abdication scene, unmentioned before 1601 and unpublished before 1608, is feigned to have been already written at the time of the first edition in 1597 but 'omitted' from it, 'most probably for political reasons' (Wells 1969, 269). If it were generally admitted that Shakespeare was a thoroughgoing reviser, then the obvious explanation for all his counterpart plays, such as the strikingly different variations on the Hamlet, Shrew, John, or Henry VI themes would be authorial revision. Then 'early start' would also become an irresistible inference, and modern scholarship would be completely discredited.

A typical credo or *cri de coeur* is worth recalling in this context: 'My conception of Shakespeare is of a supremely inventive poet who had no call to rework his previous plays when he could always move on to a new one' (Jenkins 1982, 5). But inventive reworkings *are* new works. Take the arguably comparable case of Schubert's song-writing, as set out in the latest work-list (Sams 1980). Of his over 600 lieder he completely rewrote 35, often more than once, and revised 100 others into some 150 different new versions; all this, in one single genre between the ages of thirteen and thirty-one. His motivation was surely the sense of service, even servitude, to his art and its chosen themes. Like Shakespeare, he was a performer who could learn from performance. No one has yet proposed that any of Schubert's rewritings and revisions were really memorial reconstructions made by piratical pianists or singers who had supposedly performed the allegedly extant later versions; but exactly this is universally asserted and believed about Shakespeare.

The rationally predictable pattern of his early start and habitual revision is fully confirmed by the factual record up to 1594, when his first canonical play, *Titus Andronicus*, was published. That fact implies previous popularity, and hence continuing profitability. But commercial considerations would delay a play's appearance in print until it had run its course on the stage. *Titus* had been acted by three or four different companies, which took time; so did its original rehearsal and its final printing. The plague had closed the theatres and inhibited business for part of 1592 and 1593. So the play was written earlier, and perhaps much earlier, than 1594, which like all publication dates is a *terminus ad quem* for composition. Even in that year, when Shakespeare became thirty, neither he nor his playwriting had attained the status of real respectability. Actors were still vagabond hirelings; the new drama was still not an attributable art-form. Authors were either left anonymous, as with *Titus*, or designated by initials, like 'W.S.' on the *Locrine* title-page in the following year. But popular plays were financially viable, and indeed lucrative. The notion that their rights were invariably vested in the theatre company concerned is unfounded, while the equally widespread notion that Shakespeare was 'notoriously unconcerned to preserve in stable form the texts of most of his plays' (T. Hawkes 1986, 75) is just another academic fantasy.

In reality, his business acumen and experience impose the opposite inference, which the facts firmly support; by 1616, the year of his death, *eighteen* of his plays had already appeared, in over *forty* editions. He would be expected to profit from performance as well as publication, and to retain appropriate rights as a matter of equity. The fact that *Titus* was performed in 1594 by the company that Shakespeare had just joined implies that he had literally brought its text with him. As a reviser, he was always ready to incorporate new ideas and theatrical experience. So prima facie the previously unknown scene (III.ii) contained in the 1623 Folio text of *Titus Andronicus* was the result of just such a revision, perhaps made during his Stratford retirement, when the oeuvre was being prepared for definitive publication. No doubt certain apprentice plays would be omitted, especially those which had themselves been reworked or reused.* By parity of reasoning, extended to the beginning of the same process, the 'Tittus and Vespacia' (**175**) acted in 1592 was a first version of *Titus Andronicus*, an inference further confirmed by the fact that the character Lucius is called Vespasianus in a German version printed in 1620 (Halliday 1964, 497). That first version was written earlier still; it is apparently the play whose writer was jeered at by Nashe in 1589 for 'taking the heavenly Bull by the dewlap', a notion which still looks recognisable enough in the 1594 text (IV.iii.72f). And there is contemporary confirmation that *Titus* was remembered as a very early play, in an early style. In *Bartholomew Fair* (1614) Jonson plainly implies that it was then twenty-five or thirty years old, i.e. it had been written between 1584 and 1589.

In his *Ode to Myself* (1629) Jonson proceeds to include *Pericles* among old plays, by calling it 'mouldy', that is, outmoded and stale in style. This is later explicitly confirmed by Dryden, whose actual words are well worth recording:

> Your *Ben* and *Fletcher* in their first young flight
> Did no *Volpone*, no *Arbaces* write . . .
> *Shakespear's* own Muse her *Pericles* first bore,
> The Prince of *Tyre* was elder than the *Moore* . . .
> A slender Poet must have time to grow,
> And spread and burnish as his Brothers do.

Dryden wrote this *c.* 1680 about a play by a very young author. By 'the *Moore*' he means not Othello but Aaron in *Titus Andronicus*, well-known to him as Shakespeare's first published play. *Pericles*, says Dryden, was *even earlier* than that. If he is wrong, then his apologia is pointless. So he had some reason for his assurance; and his likeliest informant would have been his late friend and collaborator William Davenant, who was Shakespeare's godson and also the father of the young playwright in question. There are no objective grounds for disparaging Davenant (*pace* Schoenbaum 1975, 133) and still less for dismissing Dryden (*pace* M. Smith *CHum* 1988, 35); quite the contrary. On historical testimony, *Pericles*, in its first version, was even earlier than *Titus Andronicus*, which itself dates back to 1589 and beyond. So even the canonical Shakespeare started early; and the actual Shakespeare earlier still. But both plays were

---

* E.g. *Troublesome Reign* as *King John*, or *Edmund Ironside* in *Titus Andronicus*.

revised; the 1609 *Pericles* is well-known for its stylistic discontinuity, like the 1603 *Hamlet*, and prima facie for the same reason, namely authorial revision, for which there is abundant evidence, not memorial reconstruction, for which there is none at all.

XXXI

'Bad Quartos' (BQ) and 'Memorial Reconstruction by Actors' (MRA)

SOME SEVENTY REASONS, together with dozens of source-references, have already been given (XXIV–XXVI) for rejecting the trumped-up charges of 'Bad Quarto' (BQ) or 'memorial reconstruction by actors' (MRA) made against *Hamlet* 1603, *A Shrew*, *Troublesome Reign*, *Contention* and *True Tragedy*, and restoring these plays to their previous Shakespearean status (as e.g. in Furnivall 1880 for *Hamlet* or Courthope 1903 for the other four). The same restitution is long overdue for other so-called BQ/MRA texts (Boyce 1990, 46), such as *Romeo and Juliet* 1597, *Henry V* 1600, *The Merry Wives of Windsor* 1602, *King Lear* 1608 and *Pericles* 1609. Those texts fall largely outside the scope of this volume; but the same basic considerations apply to them as to all BQ/MRA theories, which begin with early plays *c.* 1590. This section therefore addresses the general question of all such theories, their antecedents and their advocates, with special reference to two particular cases: *Merry Wives* 1602 because that was the first to be falsely accused of corruption, and *King Lear* 1608 because that was the first (and so far the only) one to be officially pardoned.

The essential prelude to any such investigation is to establish what a BQ/MRA actually is; and the first daunting discovery is that nobody knows or much cares. This fact is sometimes disguised by a pseudo-definition of BQs, thus: 'bad not because they were, necessarily, badly printed, but because they did not descend in a direct line of written transmission from their author's manuscript' (Wells 1986, xxx). All such formulae are unverifiable and merely assume what they feign to know. No wonder, therefore, that the BQ list varies with fashion and feeling. But the rusted weathervane of editorial opinion veers with creaking reluctance. Twenty years after Hardin Craig (1961) had pointed out that the category of BQ/MRA was itself a category mistake, which misclassified Shakespeare's own first versions, Academia at last agreed (without any acknowledgement to Craig then or since) to restore *King Lear* 1608 from its century of exile as a botched BQ/MRA to full enthronement as an authentic Shakespeare masterpiece. This amazing volte-face is still far from universal, because those concerned 'are likely to experience a sub-conscious resistance . . . a mental adjustment that may prove painful . . . we must . . . ask ourselves whether our resistance is logical or whether it proceeds, perhaps, from mental inertia, from mere dislike of change' (Wells 1983, 20).

Yet soon after this particular resistance was finally overcome, fellow editors were rebuked for having found it possible for so long 'to attribute the discrepancies between Shakespearean texts to corruption rather than revision' (Wells 1987, 12). The reason is the persistence of editorial attitudes such as those still adopted and promulgated world-wide by the Oxford Shakespeare (Wells 1986, Taylor 1988, *passim*), which regularly attributes exactly such discrepancies in all other so-called Bad Quartos to corruption rather than revision, just as inertly and illogically as in the case of *King Lear* 1608. The actual credit for the review and release of that martyr belongs to those who from 1920 onwards have seen and said that the BQ/MRA theory maltreats all its victims, not just one.

Not only was Shakespeare thereby robbed of his masterly first version of *King Lear*; his revision of it was taken to be his *first* treatment of that theme and preposterously dated the *earlier* of the two. Further, the two distinct texts have been crassly conflated, also for most of this century (Taylor 1988, 509–42; 1990, 356–62). Exactly the same is still happening to other first versions, and indeed to *King Lear* 1608 itself, which is still being obstinately misclassified in some quarters (e.g. Boyce 1990, 46) as a BQ/MRA.

Nor is the damage confined to these texts. One aspect of the theory has hoodwinked even its opponents. An entire profession, with one voice, proclaims that Greene's parody of Shakespeare's 'tiger's heart' line by 1592 'proves' the prior existence of *3 Henry VI* by that date. In reality, it proves no such thing; it is merely what Alexander assumed and repeatedly asserted just to suit his own 1929 BQ/MRA theory (XXVII). Yet it has been ceaselessly cited as a famous fact ever since, in edition after edition of book after book, year after year, thus: Chambers 1930, i, 287, 1933, 39, 1946, 49; Attawater 1941, 223; J. Wilson 1952 2/1968, 142; Harrison 1959, 15; Cairncross 1964, xli; Rowse 1973, 1988, 52; Schoenbaum 1975, 116, 1977, 2/1987, 151, 1971, 2/1991, 24, 1986, 5; Wells 1978, R/1985, 75, 1986, 201; Sanders 1981, 192, 285–6; Honigmann 1982, 24; Levi 1988, 65; Taylor 1988, 201; Urkowitz 1988c, 232; Boyce 1990, 226; Hattaway 1993, 53; I. Wilson 1993, 124; Wells 1994, 24. This selection, which could have been extended for pages, shows that those who agree about nothing else share this one certainty.

But it is only an invention. The point, however painful or deflating, has to be pressed home. Only the false belief of BQ/MRA requires a text unknown before 1623 to be inserted into history *c.* 1590. Remove it, and Greene's 1592 book (XV) attributes to Shakespeare, as the source of the 'tiger's heart' line, the known extant early version not the unknown non-existent late one, the actual printed Tudor play not the modern literary theory, i.e. *The True Tragedy of Richard Duke of York* 1595 not '*3 Henry VI*' 1623.

Let *King Lear* 1608 serve as a warning. It shows that professional editors, for most of this century, as one of them has admitted (Taylor 1988, 509), 'have most often described [it] as a reported text'. In other words, they could not distinguish between an actual Shakespeare master-piece and a hypothetical memorial corruption. Worse still, this confusion still persists, at the highest professional level. The latest edition of *King Lear* 1608 (Halio 1994, 1–2) begins by saying that 'earlier scholars' believed it was a 'memorial reconstruction', and that 'a number of distinguished textual scholars and editors, such as Kenneth Muir, G. Blakemore Evans, David Bevington and G.K. Hunter, uphold the older orthodoxy', a polite way of saying that they were and are mistaken.

But an inability to tell the canon from Anon. plainly applies to all BQ/MRA lore, not just one sample; so it undermines confidence in all such editorial notions and procedures, not just some. The establishment's own admitted responsibility over the whole field of BQ/MRA theory is to demonstrate in each case that 'the original documents seriously mis-represent Shakespeare's intention' (Wells 1983, 20). Yet no attempt whatever has been made to do so, whether by Wells or his colleagues or anyone else. On the contrary; the inclusion of *Pericles* 1609 for example as a BQ/MRA (Taylor 1988, 556, with Jackson and Wells; Boyce 1990, 46) is merely frivolous; there is not even an alternative text to compare it with, even if such comparisons were valid. Nor is 'Shakespeare's inten-tion' retrievable, except in the one respect where it is known yet ignored, namely his intention to revise and rework his plays and themes, even to the extent of rewriting and reshaping masterpieces.

In the light of revision, a new pattern leaps to the eye. All the texts ever to have been stigmatised as BQ/MRA are shorter and arguably inferior versions of later (often very much later) Shakespeare plays. All of them, furthermore, are dated between the early 1590s and 1609, which is the known floruit of Shakespeare himself, not of hypothetical pirates or reporters. Further, their relation to their canonical counterparts is very variable, from strikingly similar to diametrically different; and this feature is far more rationally explained as the result of different kinds of revision or rewriting, just as in the case of Schubert songs (XXX), not different kinds of piracy or reportage. The obvious inference is that all of them, not just *King Lear* 1608, represent Shakespeare's own first versions.

The leading canard of BQ/MRA theory can be shot down thus: who could really know, pretence and pretension aside, how the hypothetical memories, motives and methods of hypothetical actors in hypothetical plays actually functioned, four centuries ago? Further, who can believe in a 'reconstruction' from the 'memory' of 'actors' which also seeks to explain scores of unknown lines as the invention (hence neither recon-struction nor memory) of writers (hence not actors)? The absurdity of this assumption is well if unwittingly demonstrated by its own latest apolo-gists. Thus fifty-three words from Ophelia were 'reproduced' (meaning forgotten apart from seven words, with sixty-one invented), it is claimed, 'not by an actor who had played Ophelia but by one who had not' (Jenkins 1994). Similarly a long verse passage in the so-called BQ/MRA version of *The Merry Wives of Windsor* 1602 was 'entirely the invention of the reporter, being typical of a reported text' (Craik 1989, 52).

Thus the Bad Quarto theory goes from Bad to worse; it admittedly relies on invention. The pre-existing plays needed for its 'reconstruction', and their availability, and their performances, and the various parts and exits and entrances of their actors, are all just so many (already far too many) inventions which are not only unsupported by any recorded fact but instantly overturned by all the facts there actually are, such as registration, copyright, and title-page documentation. Even the basic MRA procedure of juxtaposing parallel passages from BQs *c.* 1590 and Folio versions 1623, and then treating the earlier as the later (as e.g. in Jackson 1986, 172–3 or Craik 1989, 62, or Vickers 1993 among scores of others from Alexander in 1929 onwards) is just an *a priori* assumption required by the theory, not any kind of argument. It silently stifles the plain possibility that only the BQ version existed at the material time. The same applies to the supposed identification of certain players as the 'pirates' or 'traitors' or 'actor-reporters', solely because some short speeches correspond more closely than others in the two different versions. This also assumes that the BQ/MRA was not the only extant version at the material time, although that is the actual question at issue. Similarly all attempts to turn modern textual theories into living Tudor actors, and the assignment of such names as 'recollections' and 'anticipations' to their supposed activities, are also mere elaborations of the theory, and nothing like proofs of it (*pace* Vickers 1993 among many others). They also rely on further assumptions, for example that actors' memories regularly muddle up roles and texts and scenes as well as words and names and action. But most general readers will see that the only mind which could really range over an entire playscript, and also apparently quote other Shakespeare plays as yet unwritten (Honigmann 1982, 81, Vickers 1993, refuted by Sprinchorn 1994c) was that of Shakespeare himself, and that this alone is the rational explanation of all the appearances without remainder or contradiction.

BQ/MRA may also postulate 'communal reconstruction' made by the entire company (Taylor 1988, 229–30), or a 'book-keeper' (Chambers 1930, i, 283) or 'reporters' and/or 'abridgers' (Taylor 1988, *passim*), or 'disaffected players' or suppliers of 'un-Shakespearean verse' (both Hoppe 1948), or 'spectators' (Wells 1986, xxx), or shorthand writers (Harrison 1923 and Padhi 1990, or Alexander 1929, 65–7), or pages preserved from a transcript, or 'smaller fragments which have become detached in some way from the original mass' (Alexander, 86–7). All this is calmly called a 'single, simple hypothesis' (Taylor 1988, 27), which is then vaunted as far preferable to what actually is a single simple inference from known facts, covering all cases, namely Shakespeare's own revising hand.

The entire establishment, heedless of the *King Lear* lesson, feels safe in assuming and asserting these bizarre fantasies as fact, without evidence, argument or discussion (Wells 1985, 1986, xxx). This happens partly because text-editors, in an age of specialisation, are likely to be closely concerned only with one or two BQ/MRAs, and will thus never have occasion to consider the anomalies and absurdities inherent in the general theory. That powerful grip, therefore, will not be readily relaxed or released, after nearly a century.

Its tragic history needs to be told. Immediately after the bibliographer Alfred Pollard had divided Quartos into 'Good' and 'Bad' (1909), the bibliographer Walter Greg took one of Pollard's 'Bad' texts, *The Merry Wives of Windsor* 1602, and elaborated an ancient notion (Daniel 1888, ix) that its 'badness' was due to the bad memory of a 'literary hack'. Greg (1910) preferred the even more damaging libel of a 'traitor-actor' who at some time before 1602 had supposedly played one part in a supposed performance of the supposedly extant 1623 text. Pandora's Box was thus officially declared open. By the time the lifter of the lid was ready to close the case, forty years on (Greg 1951, 1955), it was already too late; BQ/ MRA had 'slowly passed into critical orthodoxy' (F. Wilson 1945, 114, repeated in 1970, ed. Gardner, 81). The intended inference is 'because it was true'; but the real reason is that another quite different version of it, in different plays (P. Alexander 1929) had been instantly accepted by an influential authority (Chambers 1930) and further puffed as 'The New Bibliography' (Wilson 1945), although no aspect of MRA was either new or bibliographical. As Smart's confused notes were published posthumously (1928, ed. Alexander) so too was Wilson's 1945 essay (1970, ed. Gardner).

This Oxbridge orthodoxy overrode all opposition. Cogent criticism (such as Albright 1927, 300ff, and Bracy 1952, both unmentioned by Craik 1989) strove to bring Greg back to earth; but his theory was already launched, and in orbit. Greg himself (1951, 70–72 and 1955, 354, again unmentioned by Craik) later unobtrusively withdrew his 'Host' theory and substituted 'an independent reporter', who was able to 'draw on the recollection' of 'the actor who played the Host', thus adding yet another unevidenced agent, forty years on, rather than relinquish the 1910 theory he had borrowed from thirty years earlier (Daniel 1888). Similarly Alexander's Greg-based theory of the Henry VI plays (1929) was soon annihilated (Greer 1933). Yet nothing happened.

The American and other voices raised against 'memorial reconstruction' over the years should certainly be recorded, and if possible heard. Here is a selected roll-call: Hubbard 1920, Albright 1927, Rubenstein 1950, Bracy 1952, Richardson 1953, Everitt 1954, Prouty 1954, Craig 1961, Feuillerat 1961, Weiner 1962, Smidt 1964, Burkhardt 1970, Schamp 1974, Sams 1983, Urkowitz 1986, Bains 1990, Werstine 1990, M. Foster 1991, Shiras 1991, Sprinchorn 1994. These and many others are treated by the current British orthodoxy as non-existent or negligible. The best they can hope for is unsubstantiated condemnation, e.g. of Craig 1961 as 'eccentric textual theories' (Jenkins 1982, 19) or of Sprinchorn 1994 as 'a hopeless mixture of irrelevant anecdote, fallacious argument and inaccurate scholarship' (Vickers 1994, 4 Feb. supported as 'fair comment' by Jenkins 1994). No wonder, then, that the first British professionals ever to have rejected 'memorial reconstruction' in any edition of any play (Holderness and Loughrey 1992) were themselves anathematised by a devotee of that doctrine (Vickers 1993), which has degenerated into a mystic cult.

In any other field calling itself a discipline, at least some actual argument would have been advanced in favour of the philosophical foundations on which everything else has been built. Yet the only semblance of argument ever offered in favour of BQ/MRA in general (Taylor 1988, 27) begins with exactly the same blatant built-in bias as all the earlier special theories. The BQs concerned must be MRA because their quality 'soars and plummets', which is typical of MRA. As a result, they 'cannot be convincingly assigned to any one period of Shakespeare's career' (ibid.); in other words, they are unfamiliar to modern specialists. Furthermore, if he wrote them 'they have to be relegated to an earlier period than any of the extant authoritative texts' (ibid.); in other words, they are too early for modern specialists. Such subjective reasoning is so circular in all directions as to be positively spherical.

There is, finally, the desperate defence of MRA that it must have been what the 1623 Folio editors meant by their often-excerpted phrase 'stolne and surreptitious copies'. This is invoked, by Jackson (1986, 171), Wells (1987, 12), Taylor (1988, 26), Boyce (1990, 46) and Vickers (1993), among many others, as basic to their own beliefs. It was chosen by Alfred Hart (1942) as the title of a book advocating BQ/MRA which typically begins with the very assumption it pretends to prove: 'I have included *Contention* and *True Tragedy* among the bad quartos . . . I firmly believe' they are 'corrupt abridgements derived from the acting versions of' *2–3 Henry VI* 1623.

At least these various invocations of the 1623 Folio concede that some historical evidence might be helpful. But that source is regularly ignored or rejected in other respects; thus its clear and repeated assurances that all its contents are authentically Shakespearean is anathema to modern editors (e.g. Taylor 1988, *passim*), whose theories of 'collaboration' are thereby annihilated. On any analysis, the relevant remarks from the Folio editors, Heminges and Condell, should have been quoted verbatim and *in extenso*, thus:

> It had bene a thing, we confesse, worthie to have bene wished, that the Author himself had liu'd to haue set forth, and ouerseen his own writings; But since it hath bin ordain'd otherwise, and he by death departed from that right, we pray you do not envie his Friends, the office of their care, and

paine, to have collected & publish'd them, and so to have publish'd them, as where (before) you were abus'd with diuerse stolne, and surreptitious copies, maimed and deformed by the frauds and stealths of injurious imposters, that expos'd them: even those, are now offer'd to your view cur'd, and perfect in their limbes; and all the rest, absolute in their numbers, as he conceiued them.

Remove the BQ/MRA blinkers, and Heminges and Condell are seen to be addressing actual readers, many of whom would be unborn when the first alleged BQ/MRAs appeared in the 1590s. That address must surely have referred to some much more recent circumstances and in particular to a recent commercial rivalry. Nor do the Folio editors deny, but rather seem to assert, that the shortened, unauthorised and unreliable versions they indict were nevertheless plays by Shakespeare. Their point is that their own Folio texts are longer and better than others recently published as his. Thus construed, their 1623 targets can be readily identified. In 1619, the publisher Thomas Pavier was associated with the printer William Jaggard in the publication of ten Shakespeare plays, prima facie intended as the first volume of a collection. Among Pavier's contributions was the undated *Whole Contention betweene the two Famous Houses, Lancaster and Yorke*. Divided into two Parts: and newly corrected and enlarged. Written by *William Shakespeare*, Gent. These were the plays *Contention* and *True Tragedy* issued in 1594 and 1595, now absurdly classified as BQ/MRA but then sensibly described by their publisher, who had acquired their rights and knew what he had paid for, as Shakespeare plays. Hence the indignation of Heminges and Condell, who themselves owned rights in the revised versions *2–3 Henry VI*. They might well have been unaware, seven years after Shakespeare's death and some thirty-five years after the Quarto texts were written, that these were indeed his own first versions, just as Greene's 1592 reference had indicated.

Rationally considered, therefore, their 1623 reference to 'stolne and surreptitious copies' disproves rather than proves the BQ/MRA theories; and that removes the last vestige of any supposed historical evidence for them. Their logical grounds, under attack for decades, have never been, and cannot be, defended by anyone. Their impending collapse, demolition and clearance will open wider and clearer views everywhere. The need now is for new performances and editions rehabilitating all the rejected and forgotten BQ/MRA versions and reassessing the text-genesis of all the Folio plays concerned in the light of a rational appreciation of their dating and development.

XXXII

'Source-plays' (SP), 'Derivative Plays' (DP) and Plagiarism

AS WITH BQ (XXXI), nobody quite knows what these are either. Plays allegedly plagiarised *by* Shakespeare are called SP; *from* Shakespeare, DP. Three nominations for the latter category are *Troublesome Reign* (published in 1591), *The Taming of A Shrew* and *The True Tragedy of Richard the Third* (both published in 1594), of which 'none can be regarded as a Bad Quarto' (Honigmann 1982, 57). But some experts certainly classify the first two thus (Boyce 1990, 46; Taylor 1988, 26), and all three are freely treated as SP. So Tudor plays can belong to either of two exclusive opposite categories; it all depends on the expert. The record is currently held by *A Shrew*, which is variously described by Oxford Shakespeare editors as a derivative of *The Shrew* (Wells 1982), or an MRA of it (Oliver 1982, 22), or (ibid., back cover) as a probable adaptation of it, or an imitation of it (Wells 1986, 29), or a 'Bad Quarto' of it, or conversely and self-contradictorily a possible source of it, or even Shakespeare's own first version of it (all Taylor 1988, 169) which however he could not possibly have written (ibid., 85). All this amounts to 'one of the great unsolved problems of Shakespeare scholarship' (Wells 1994, 52).

The only definite fact is that several of Shakespeare's Folio plays, though none of anyone else's, exist in two or more very different versions, including totally different treatments of the same theme. The simple and obvious explanation, now universally overlooked, is that the earlier publications were his first versions; and thus each supposed example of 'BQ', 'MRA', 'SP', 'DP' and so forth can be instantly and economically accounted for. Dozens of specific arguments point to that conclusion about individual examples (XXIV–XXVII). The same would also apply, by parity of reasoning, to other instances such as *King Leir* and *The Famous Victories of Henry V*, now universally labelled as 'SP'. Every editor would accept such conclusions without question if everything about the early versions had been lost except their titles. But their extant texts fail to conform with the various modern editorial opinions of how, when and what Shakespeare must have written. So all these plays are relegated to limbo by obscure literary theories, and removed from the oeuvre.

All remaining problems are explained away as 'plagiarism', whether by or from Shakespeare (again, either will do). If the former, the victim is called a 'Source Play', meaning the victim of Shakespeare's shameless exploitation. This hypothetical theft is then called anything but theft, such as adaptation, rewriting and so forth, which are then disguised as respectable and indeed praiseworthy activities. But how would they have looked to each Tudor playwright thus exploited, had he really been someone other than Shakespeare?

Alternatively, the exact opposite must be the case, a contretemps common in Academia. Just make *King John* (1623) precede *Troublesome Reign* (1591) and, handy-dandy, the anonymous author of the latter becomes the thief. There is then no need to be polite about him; he is the merest 'hack-writer' (Honigmann 1982, 58), with a 'memory-box filled with scraps from other men's plays'; his 'literary talent may be described as essentially derivative or parasitic; he attempted blank verse, rhymed pentameters, fourteeners, Skeltonics and other forms of doggerel, as well as prose. He was an imitator of popular styles, as well as phrases, and this makes it all the more likely that he also imitated another man's plot' (ibid., 81). He has 'minimal literary talent'. The same is freely alleged of the author of *A Shrew* and the rest. So if the alleged imitator is Shakespeare, he is hailed as a genius; if anyone else, he is denounced as a dolt.

Exactly these same incompatible opposites are also freely invented to explain such apocrypha as *Edmund Ironside*. This contains (Sams 1986d) literally hundreds of close and undeniable parallels to canonical Shakespeare. But academic commentators are certain that it cannot possibly be his. This personal opinion, which has also relegated all the other counterpart plays to limbo (including Shakespeare's own *King Lear* 1608, for most of this century), is then subconsciously used as an argument. If *Ironside* demonstrably contains an image-cluster previously identified as Shakespearean, then so much the worse for all image-clusters as pointers to authorship; out they go instanter (Jackson 1963). It takes only half-a-dozen such authorities to constitute an infallible consensus (Honigmann 1987). So the explanation of *Ironside*, as of all other rejected texts, must be the favourite one of 'plagiarism'. The plagiarist had better not be Shakespeare, despite the supposed 'Source Plays'. So suitable *Ironside* dates are freely invented; it must have been written 'circa 1590 or so' (Wells), or '1592 or 1593 or something like that' (Wilders), or 'the early or mid 1590s' (Jones) or '1595–1599' (Proudfoot) or '1595–1600' (Kerrigan), or indeed any unspecified date permitting plagiarism from Shakespeare (Honigmann); all in reviews of 1986 and 1987. The same authorities also automatically assume that the authentically Shakespearean sources were freely available for the required plagiarisms at the dates in question. No factual confirmation is required.

Again however there is academic dissent and denial; the opposite assumptions are also freely made and stated as facts. These too begin from the same subjective supposition that Shakespeare cannot conceivably have written *Ironside*. But many scholars can infer readily enough from its style that it must be an early play, *c.* 1588, and hence on current theory pre-Shakespearean. So Shakespeare himself must be the plagiarist of all such hopeless plays, in phrase after phrase during year after year, for hundreds of parallels. For this purpose plagiarism must be treated as the Tudor norm, and entirely exempt from reproach or complaint (D. Foster, review 1988); any special treatment for Shakespeare would be mere Bardolatry.

But it was never the norm, and there was indeed complaint, and 'vulgar scandal' (Sonnet 112.2) as well. The historical record shows that the charge levelled by both Nashe and Greene against Shakespeare was indeed one of plagiarism. Greene's words were later interpreted thus by a contemporary (191): '... the men, that so Eclipst [Greene's] fame/ Purloynde his Plumes, can they deny the same?' One of them, namely Shakespeare, could not. Yet he found the accusation offensive; so did another eye-witness and personal participant, Henry Chettle (182). Now, not even the envious Greene could have taken serious umbrage at an actor's use of a playwright's words, though his attack is still regularly interpreted thus. This is yet another legacy from Alexander (1929, 39–50), which is just as invalid as all the rest. Greene was surely saying something which he thought serious. The purloining of plumes, to which Nashe also animadverts, manifestly implied illicit or improper profiteering from other writers' ideas.

There is no doubt at all that Shakespeare helped himself. One of the first facts that anyone learns about him, for example, is that very few of his plots or sub-plots are original. But the inference is that he saw stories, whether histories as in Holinshed or *Histoires* as in Belleforest (the source of *Hamlet* and other plays), as common stage properties, like Ovid; for him, the play was the thing. Again Schubert provides a possible parallel. He created modern song just as Shakespeare created modern drama. That was surely sufficient proof of their artistic seriousness and originality. If more is needed, it may be found in their tireless revision and rewriting within both genres, as if their aim was a perfection of treatment; they wished to do the best they could for their chosen subject-matter. But it was just as natural for them, in their respective eras, to dramatise a story from any source as to set any poet's words to music, without seeking prior formal permission or paying subsequent royalties. Their sources were their debtors.

Conversely, however, there is no possible ethical or aesthetic justification for the present automatic assumption (again required by BQ, MRA, SP and DP lore) that Shakespeare stole non-stop from the actual texts as well as the plots of such plays as the early *Hamlet*, *A Shrew*, *Troublesome Reign*, *Famous Victories of Henry V*, or *King Leir*, any more than Schubert stole his melodies from his predecessors. Modern commentators call these Shakespeare sources 'old plays' to conceal or extenuate what are thought to be his verbal borrowings. But in fact those works were performed in his heyday, by actors and companies well known to him; he must have known who had written them. On any objective economical appraisal, *he* had.

At least none of them has any association with Greene, Nashe, Peele or Marlowe. Yet those are the writers from whom Shakespeare allegedly purloined plumes, which ruffled their feathers. But he must have felt they were fair game. Such phraseological allusions, as already illustrated (XIV–XX), were the everyday ammunition of Tudor writers, whether fired in anger or used for a salute. Greene's own 'tiger's heart' line was after all itself a plucked plume, used as satirical identification of the bird in question. Within that context, to which works might Greene's strictures have been intended to apply?

No doubt his own grievances were uppermost. He would surely have been furious to realise that *The Winter's Tale* takes its plot from his novel *Pandosto* (1588). So an early version of that play, always a possibility for a revising author, would offer one obvious explanation. So would an early *Pericles*, as described by Dryden; its plot seems indebted to Greene's *Menaphon* (1589). More specifically, *The First Part of the Contention* borrows the phrase 'Abradas, the great Macedonian pirate' (1568–9) from Greene, who uses those same words in both *Penelope's Web* and *Menaphon*; as we have seen (XVI), there are independent reasons for inferring Shakespeare's familiarity with both those books.

Snippets from Nashe are so discernible in *I Henry VI* that one theorist attributed its entire first act to his hand (J. Wilson 1952, xxiif). Another would-be disintegrator (Taylor 1988, 217) awards Nashe several scenes of the same play. Similarly the first act of *Titus Andronicus* has been attributed to Peele (J. Wilson 1948, a theory now aptly dumped in the litter-bins of literature). But the Peele parallels are clear; so again this is the obvious and, in a sense, justified ground of Greene's gravamen. Peele's plumes are indeed purloined, for what they are worth; so perhaps were Nashe's.

Marlowe provides the most manifest example of all. The copious citations and imitations of Marlowe throughout *A Shrew* go far beyond the common change of Tudor stage parlance; they are undoubtedly deliberate and parodistic, so much so indeed as to provide an argument for Shakespeare's authorship. Here is a play deliberately festooned with Marlowe's plumes, like a bower-bird's nest.

Greene also mentions other authors, presumably also University Wits: 'I might insert two more'. Perhaps they were also victims of these depredations. If so, one of them may well have been the Oxfordians Lodge or Lyly, for reasons already given (XVI).

Shakespeare remained unrepentant and resentful. His unique coinage 'o'er-greene' in the context of 'vulgar scandal' (Sonnet 112.4) has already been noted. A further citation from the same source sounds equally relevant. The poet has been 'vile esteemed', criticised for bad behaviour. But 'On my frailties why are frailer spies/Which in their wills count bad

what I think good?' (Sonnet 12.1, 7–8). That can hardly refer to Shakespeare's admitted adultery; there is no reason to suppose either that it was
spied upon, or that he defended it as morally good. The allusion is surely
to some other known practice of which two views might be taken, and
which is claimed as a God-given right:

> No, I am that I am, and they that level
> At my abuses reckon up their own:
> I may be straight, though they themselves are bevel;
> By their rank thoughts my deeds must not be shown.

The writer of those words believed himself guiltless as charged; and
posterity agrees with him. Influence or allusion are venial; only plagiarism properly so-called is venal, because practised for prestige or profit.
Shakespeare could properly protest that he did neither; his art and his
morals were unaffected thereby. He could certainly distinguish between
meum and *tuum*; it is not Bardolatrous but rational to refrain from treating
him as a common thief and cheat. But he could hardly have justified his
putative treatment of *Troublesome Reign*, *A Shrew*, etc., in such terms; so
they were indeed his own property to exploit as he pleased.

XXXIII

Dating and 'Collaboration'

THE THEORY OF BQ/MRA (XXXI) is directly responsible for the wrong dating of Shakespeare plays. The various incompatible errors of the Oxford Shakespeare and the Oxford Dictionary (Sams 1992a) have now been compounded by the latest Chambers Dictionary (1993, 2059), which offers a third wrong chronology. The main mischief is Alexander's mistaken MRA theory (1929) which falsely identifies *3 Henry VI* 1623 as the Shakespeare source alluded to by Greene in or before 1592, and hence misdates every word of it. The result is that a play containing many lines unknown until long after their author's death at fifty-two in 1616 is arbitrarily assigned to his later twenties, thus sabotaging any planned survey of his style and development. Yet so ingrained has Alexander's MRA become that even the first and so far sole professional commentator with the wit to see and the nerve to say that Shakespeare must have started his theatre career early, *c.* 1585 (Honigmann 1982, dedicated to the memory of Alexander, and 1985) cannot countenance the clear corollary that *True Tragedy* not *3 Henry VI* was the early play. In consequence he has to antedate the accepted canon, assigning for example *The Two Gentlemen of Verona* to 1587 and *The Taming of the Shrew* to 1588 on no evidence at all (1982, 88; 1985, 128). The former play, unrecorded in performance until the Restoration, unpublished until 1623, and unmentioned even as a title before Meres in 1598, is allocated to 1590–91 in one Oxford volume (Taylor 1988, 109) or 'probably the late 1580s' in another (Wells 1986, 1), mainly because of thirty-year-old admittedly unprovable notions (Wells 1963 and 1994, 40) about the supposed defectiveness of its dramatic structure. Similarly *The Taming of the Shrew* 1623 is dated '1590–1' (Taylor idem) on 'stylistic criteria', a phrase not further defined. Again, *The Comedy of Errors* 1623 is assigned to '1594' (ibid., 116), when it 'may well have been new' (Wells 1986, 291), although there is no reason to suppose that the 'comedy of errors' then performed at Gray's Inn was the 1623 Folio text, except that 'it seems quite likely' (to Wells 1972, 10). But, now that Shakespeare is acknowledged (Wells 1986, 1987) as an assiduous reviser, neither the play's newness in 1594 nor its survival unchanged for three decades has any prima facie probability at all. And the same principle must inexorably apply to the entire oeuvre. The date of any work by a revising artist, whether Shakespeare or any other, must be either the date printed on its first extant edition or else the earlier day of its author's death, considered as *termini ad quem*. The latter alternative applies to all the many Shakespeare texts which remained unpublished until the 1623 First Folio, a fact confirmed by the explicit testimony of his earliest named editors that 'wee haue scarse receiued from him a blot in his papers'. *Pace* his modern editors, this means that he had sent them certain plays in holograph fair copy; and of course he would continue his practice of revision, like any conscientious artist, especially for incorporation in his Collected Works. Hence no doubt his special bequest in his 1616 will to those same editors, 'my fellows John Hemynges . . . and Henry Cundell, twenty-six shillings eight pence apiece, to buy them rings' as mourning mementos and also admonitory reminders. Shakespeare, like his own Ghost, says 'Adieu, adieu, adieu. Remember me'. The individualistic entrepreneur whose works were published in some sixty separate editions in his own lifetime, including much substantive revision, would naturally also prepare revised manuscript copies for collected publication, as necessary, and would sensibly use his Stratford retirement years for that purpose. It follows that texts known only from that 1623 collection (such as *The Two Gentlemen of Verona, The Comedy of Errors, 1 Henry VI*, and any lines in *2–3 Henry VI, King John, The Taming of the Shrew, Titus Andronicus, Richard III, Henry V, The Merry Wives of Windsor* or any other play, which are not found in any earlier edition or version) cannot be rationally dated save as 'not later than April 1616'.

The same principles and caveats perforce apply to all theories or opinions or calculations about 'collaboration'. These too are all-pervasive, though entirely unevidenced and imaginary. They are also theories about dating, though the point is never noticed, because the supposed collaborator has to be alive and active at the material time. Instead, literary theory takes precedence over historical actuality, which is assumed as required, just as with the BQ/MRA/SP/DP theories outlined above (XXXI–XXXII). The theory builders sometimes seek to prepare the ground by such flat assertions as 'Certainly, it would have been difficult for any young playwright, trying to establish himself in the professional public theatre of the late 1580s and early 1590s, to avoid writing collaborative plays . . . It therefore seems likely that some of Shakespeare's earliest works, like some of his latest, were written in collaboration' (Taylor 1988, 73). Here again, invention is typically advanced as its own evidence. In reality, no supporting fact is anywhere on record before 1634, with the registration and publication of *The Two Noble Kinsmen*, by John Fletcher and William Shakespeare. There is no earlier recorded reason to suppose that Shakespeare ever collaborated with anyone; the notion that such practices were rife and he was unlikely to have been the exception is wholly illogical and disingenuous, like BQ, MRA, SP, DP and the rest. But 'collaboration' has acquired mana and power. So it too is freely applied to any unfamiliar or unadmired text; and it too is empowered to take Shakespeare's plays away from him. Thus the 1623 Folio's prefatory assurances that these texts are 'absolute in their numbers, as he conceived them' are treated as deliberate lies, despite the pious claim that 'When the Folio speaks, we must echo it' (Taylor 1988, 71). In practice there is a compulsion to contradict it. *1 Henry VI* for example is imagined as exceedingly collaborative; Shakespeare had the assistance of 'X', 'Y', 'Y? (or X)', 'X? (or Y?)', '?' and 'Thomas Nashe', with the proviso that 'the identities of X and Y are unknown', though Y 'has particular links with *Locrine*' (Taylor 1988, 217), and one of these assistants may have been the author of *Edmund Ironside* or of *Edward III* (Taylor 1986). Each of those last three plays has been attributed to Shakespeare – the first on its title-page, the second in a full edition (Sams 1986d), and the third eventually by Stanley Wells and Gary Taylor themselves (1990), after previous rejection (Wells 1986, Taylor 1988, 136–7). So perhaps some of Shakespeare's earlier stylistic strata were indeed present in *1 Henry VI*, a text unknown in print until 1623. Nothing justifies the overweening assumption that he could manage only one style per play, which modern commentators can infallibly identify by 'tests'. This too is in flat contradiction to the simultaneous assertion that he was a revising author. Revision normally entails the juxtaposition of two or more separate styles, as extant manuscripts and editions of the Brahms Op. 8 piano trio for example fully corroborate. Shakespeare scholarship, lacking these resources, substitutes misconceived and useless speculations, freely announced as fact. Thus *Titus Andronicus* is also disintegrated (Taylor 1988, 115) on 'stylistic evidence' into Shakespeare and a collaborator, 'either Peele or an imitator of Peele', who obligingly contributed the first scene. The rather obvious possibility that this 'collaborator' might be the only Tudor dramatist who remains on record as being publicly accused of indebtedness to Peele, namely Shakespeare himself, remains unmentioned and unconsidered despite its obvious relevance. A reason is offered for this neglect: 'the rest of the play seems' to have been written by someone else. As so often, 'seems' supersedes observed and admitted stylistic variety. The same applies to the editorial disintegration, whether by 'tests' or intuition, of *The Taming of the Shrew*, *2 Henry VI*, *3 Henry VI*, *Timon of Athens*, *Macbeth*, *Henry VIII* and many other plays including *Pericles* (ibid., 111–12, 128–30, 133 and *passim*). Here is a whole congeries of imaginary collaborators.

Pericles in particular is worth special study in this connection, since it is prejudged by the same bias as *Titus*. Here too the beginning of the play appears to stylists to be, and therefore was in fact, they feel, written by a different author, as their tests predictably confirm. In *Titus* Shakespeare's documented and admittedly plausible indebtedness to Peele, an admired master and an available model, is questioned on the ground that it concentrates on the long first scene; yet again, the uneconomical and unevidenced theory of 'collaboration' is far preferred to the simple and admitted explanation of revision, which might very well have had the observed result. Stylistic differences, even if they are real and demonstrable, would naturally seem less detectable and significant to Shakespeare then than to specialists now. In the first two acts of *Pericles*, similarly, the stylistic resemblances (Jackson 1990–93, 1993) allegedly inculpate one George Wilkins. Here again the plain possibility of Shakespeare's own early authorship is steadfastly ignored, like his name on the *Pericles* title-page, although George Wilkins is remembered only as a plagiarist of Shakespeare, and may have been far too young for any possible question of collaboration at the time of composition. The fact is that until the stylistic tests and testers are themselves tested, and supplied with reliable dates, all their results will remain unverifiable and worthless. Meanwhile it is vain in every sense to vaunt 'reasonable scholars', 'serious scholars' and so forth as infallible guides, as in the *Oxford Companion* (Taylor 1988 *passim*). The same applies to stylometry (XXXIV).

XXXIV

'Stylometry'

THE WORD ITSELF assumes that styles can be objectively measured and identified. In reality, that proposition remains utterly unproven, despite loud claims of infallibility (such as N. Hawkes 1986 on the Merriam-Morton method, Taylor 1988, 69–109 on some forty plays, and M. Smith 1988 and 1993 on *Pericles* and *Ironside* respectively). In the intervals of vaunting their own methods and results, the same authorities regularly reject each other's (e.g. M. Smith v. Merriam and Morton from 1983 onwards, and v. Taylor *N&Q*, 1991; Taylor v. Slater 1988, 100–101; M. Smith v. Slater *N&Q*, 1989, 338–9; Merriam v. Taylor 1989; Merriam v. M. Smith *N&Q*, 1992). Thus the stylometrists attain collective disagreement while claiming individual certainty, exactly like the equally tiny coterie of text editors. Only a very few names (e.g. Jackson, Taylor) are found in both groups. Yet stylometrists accept modern literary assumptions about dating and attribution, which they are accordingly reinforcing, not testing at all. Thus the Shakespearean authorship of *Ironside c.* 1588, which had received some measure of stylometric support (Ranson 1986; Slater 1983, 1988) has now been 'tested' and rejected by comparison with the allegedly contemporary *3 Henry VI* and *Richard III* (M. Smith 1993) in ignorance of the fact that neither of the Folio texts used was published until 1623. Dating each of them thirty-five years earlier than their first printing is a mere self-confessed BQ/MRA fantasy, which vitiates any validity Smith's latest method might have had (Sams 1994c). As Taylor admits (1988, 112), the Oxford date of '1591' for *3 Henry VI* 'presumes that [its Quarto version *True Tragedy*] represents a memorial reconstruction'; so does the allocation of *Richard III* to '1592–3', for which, as Taylor also confesses (ibid., 115), there is 'no documentary evidence or certain allusion'.

Even extant counter-evidence is elbowed aside by stylometrists eager to stand shoulder to shoulder with 'scholarship'. Thus Dryden's plain testimony to an early *Pericles*, before 1589, destroys the theory (Taylor 1988, 556f, with Jackson; Jackson 1990–93; M. Smith 1982–91; Hope 1994, 106–13) of collaboration with George Wilkins, a forgotten dramatist, victualler and brawling brothel-keeper who was then in his infancy (Prior 1972). This minor difficulty is either ignored (Taylor, Jackson, Hope) or else dealt with (M. Smith *CHum* 23, 1988, 35) by deciding that Dryden must have been wrong. The proffered proof, on the cited authority of

Grace Seiler (1951, 23), is that 'it is now known that [Dryden] was not an authority on Shakespearean chronology'. Again academic opinion is not investigated but perpetuated, often in the selfsame stock phrases such as 'scholars agree' (Taylor 1988 and M. Smith 1982–93, both *passim*).

One day, mathematicians may liberate 'stylometry' from its inverted commas by relying solely on objective historical fact and its immediate inferences, such as dating by recorded *termini ad quem*, as already recommended (XXXIII; Sams 1992a). Many new paths look promising. But they too will meet obstacles and opposition. A distinguished mathematician (Littlewood 1953) has argued that there is no permissible inference from probability theory to any human activity. Many serious readers will resent the notion that a computer operator, however mathematically gifted, can infallibly pronounce on style without being in the least literary or even literate, and indeed without having any need even to glance through the work in question. Further, the texts used are always modern printed editions, so the statistics analyse the habits of editors, compositors or copyists as well as playwrights. Above all, the assumption that Shakespeare had only one style at a time, which varied only with genre (comedy or tragedy) and medium (poetry or prose) needs to be explicitly avowed and defended, if that is possible. Even then, Shakespeare lovers will still wonder what might have happened if all the myriads of unmade tests had been applied, instead of the infinitesimal selection so far favoured. And surely rarities and idiosyncrasies of vocabulary (the Slater method) are a more rational criterion than the commonest words and collocations (Taylor, M. Smith, Merriam) which cannot even be clearly quantified. 'That', to cite only one example among dozens, is in fact three quite different words, used in some forty distinguishable senses, not an objective unit at all. The road from numbers to authorship is no broad thronged highway, least of all by such routes. The pioneering approach of A.Q. Morton has been crushingly discredited, apparently with its inventor's awareness, in a recent television interview (*Streetlegal* 1993). This same basic approach underpinned the confident claim that *Edmund Ironside* was written by Robert Greene, at odds of 890 trillion to one (Hawkes 1986); this has now been somewhat reduced to 'less than 0.1% significant' (Merriam 1992), though without any question of retraction. Earlier, analogous approaches had yielded the conclusion that *Sir Thomas More* was from Shakespeare's hand in its entirety (Merriam 1982, dismissed as 'inept' by M. Smith 1992) and also, less controversially, that the same applied to *Titus Andronicus* and *Pericles* (Metz 1985). Gary Taylor's 'function word' method (1988) disintegrated the latter play, among many others; but he and Stanley Wells have undermined their own mathematics and all its results by confessing that they are no mathematicians (1988, 81), a fact also apparent to a professional statistician (M. Smith *N&Q*, 1991, 73–8) and indeed to laymen (Sams 1988f, Merriam 1989). The disintegrator's logic is fallible too; thus the criticism (Sams 1991b, 68) that it is absurd to attribute *Pericles* I–II to 'Wilkins', who is remembered solely as a plagiarist of Shakespeare, has been noted by at least one literary expert (Woudhuysen 1992, 202). The repeated claims of significance, correctness or even infallibility (N. Hawkes 1986; Taylor, M. Smith, *passim*) may also serve to discredit current methods and attitudes.

The *Pericles* contretemps highlights yet another difficulty; even if 'stylometry' worked, how could the computer distinguish between a given style and its deliberate imitation or parody, or even its subconscious influence on a malleable creative mind? This may vitiate many another study, such as the claim for 'Marlowe's Hand in *Edward III*' (Merriam 1993). That play's composition date is unrecorded. But it was first published in 1596, three years after Marlowe's death. So here, as in *Pericles* (M. Smith 1992), stylometry hoists itself over the stile of possibly unfavourable fact; if the method finds for Marlowe or Wilkins then their availability, like the method's reliability, is taken for granted, despite any historical evidence to the contrary. Such *a priori* assumption is no doubt subconscious. But it often surfaces, e.g. in the reasoning (Merriam 1993) that certain ratios in various distributions are more like 'disassociation from Shakespeare' than 'association with *Tamburlaine*', and 'this fact alone casts doubt on the claim that one author wrote *Edward III*'. The rather more obvious doubt cast on the stylometrist is never even considered, throughout a paper which records some 3,000 calculations about thirty-six plays arranged in eighteen tabulations through ten pages of a learned journal devoted to literary and linguistic computing.

Not all its readers may have noted that this complex apparatus in its turn has also been tacitly dismantled, and its products disowned, by the experimenter concerned, who has moved on to a new system called 'neural networks'. This 'suggests that *Edward III* was written by Shakespeare under considerable influence from Marlowe' (Matthews and Merriam 1994). Here is a total repudiation of an earlier method which supposedly showed that 'Shakespeare's share [in *Edward III*] was a small one' (Merriam 1982, 2).

None of this necessarily invalidates the mathematical approach as such. Indeed, 'neural networks' (Matthews and Merriam, idem) look rather promising, if they can truly distinguish between influence, imitation, parody or plagiarism on the one hand and actual authorship on the other, as their proponents claim. Then they could perhaps 'cast light on the origin of the anonymous play *Edmund Ironside*'. The same applies to other statistical methods and researches (such as Thisted and Efron 1986, Elliott and Valenza 1991, D. Foster 1991). Meanwhile, most students of Shakespeare will perforce continue to rely on language rather than on numbers for their appreciation of style; and all investigators should depend upon historical documentation rather than literary theory for their allocation of dates and authorship. On that basis, 'stylometry' may well be developed into a powerful instrument of authorship attribution, and for this reason the bibliography below includes detailed documentation of that topic.

As to verbal stylometry, some attempt has already been made above to define Shakespeare's style up to 1594, from sources including contemporary witness. It has been well said by a front-rank style critic (Robinson 1988, 41) that 'the only way to make a case [for attribution] is to be exhaustive' about 'details any one of which could have come from writers other than Shakespeare, but the more of them there are the more they suggest Shakespeare'. Only this method of cumulative detail (as successfully practised by R. Chambers 1939 in the attribution of scenes in *Sir Thomas More*) has so far achieved any consensual success, and even then many professionals (such as Gurr 1985) remain perplexed or unpersuadable. Among the most promising of modern developments is the identification of characteristic imagery, especially complex image-clusters (e.g. Spurgeon 1935, Armstrong 1946). *Pace* Jackson (1963), there is nothing wrong with such criteria *per se*; as with mathematical methods, the main identifiable source of error lies in the a priori prejudice which unwittingly incorporates its own conclusions into its results.

XXXV

Handwriting

HANDWRITING, QUITE UNLIKE computer statistics, is well within everyone's reach. There are excellent primers on Tudor penmanship in general (e.g. Hector 1966), and stimulating studies of Shakespeare's in particular (E. Thompson 1916 and 1923, Everitt 1954, Hamilton 1985). Yet here too prejudice prevails. The evidence (XI) and common sense together proclaim that the young Shakespeare studied law and hence was practised in legal penmanship. But he is not allowed (Schoenbaum 1975, 87) to be a mere clerk, any more than a mere butcher. So we can securely scoff (Schoenbaum 1971–91, 533) at any suggestion that he learned various legal styles as well as the recently introduced italic script and the ordinary secretary hand written by all literate Englishmen in Tudor times. Even his treasured signatures, like his plays, are similarly scrapped to suit personal preconvictions. According to a Public Records Office handbook, it is 'unthinkable' that he did not develop a personalised signature. So experts can tell 'at a glance' that most of the six treasured specimens must be fakes (Cox 1985, 33). Alternatively, the 1616 will signatures must be genuine, so 'it needs no expert knowledge' (Shapiro 1986) to see that the will itself must have been written by someone else. But the phantoms conjured up for that purpose, such as 'Francis Collins', or his 'clerk', (e.g. Schoenbaum 1975, 242; 1991, 19–20) are mere wisps o' the will. The former arises from the assumption that the writer could not have been Shakespeare, and the latter from the corrective expert opinion that the hand is in fact quite unlike that of Francis Collins. Similarly the world-famous words 'by me' prefixed to the final will signature are freely deemed to mean nothing at all, or anything but their actual well-known meaning at the time, namely 'in my own hand'.

Ordinary readers may rate it rather obvious that an ex-law-clerk might very well write his own will. Anyone prepared to stop glancing and assuming and start looking and analysing would do well to begin by consulting the archives (see also Sams 1993e). Many of the main relevant items are reproduced in Hamilton 1985. Here are six selected addenda, all from Shakespeare's first thirty years, 1564–94.

In October 1579, when he was fifteen and a half years old, his impoverished and illiterate parents sold their land-holdings (his own patrimony) to raise cash. The detailed deed of sale, to which they both appended their marks, is still extant. Such skilled and specialised penmanship was necessary but expensive. Its legal style is not clearly paralleled elsewhere in the Stratford archives. Excerpts have been published in facsimile (Catalogue 1944, 25–8; Schoenbaum 1975, 38). They strikingly resemble the legal hand of the playscript *Edmund Ironside c.* 1588 (BL Egerton 1994), which has been assigned to Shakespeare (Everitt 1954, Sams 1986d). That latter autograph attribution is generally rejected without even a glance (Nye 1993), despite explicit confirmation from the New York documents expert Charles Hamilton (30 June 1986; and see Corathers 1986, Ezard 1986), whose competence is acknowledged (e.g. by Taylor 1988, 138). Yet facsimile pages are available for study and comparison (Boswell 1928, Everitt 1954). Ideally, the actual documents should be consulted, rather than reproductions. On both the early playscript (Greg 1931, 206) and the 1579 deed (Bearman 1993) the right-hand margins have been pricked and ruled with an impressed stylus.

The third sample may well prove even more contentious, because it relates to speculations such as the young Shakespeare's possible connection with the Lancashire Catholic clans of Houghton and Hesketh in the early 1580s (Honigmann 1985). The Pedigree Roll of Sir Thomas Hesketh (BL Add. MS. 44026, excerpted in Keen and Lubbock 1954, 36) is penned in a style very like that of the 1579 deed of sale and the *Ironside* MS. That 1954 book (anticipated in Wadman 1941 and McLaren 1949) is about a copy of Hall's *Chronicle* 1550 with annotations identified as Shakespeare's, as also on different and independent grounds by Pitcher (1961); this volume too is now housed in the British Library. These ascriptions have never been contested by any accredited expert; on the contrary, close and informed analysis (H. Rhodes in Keen and Lubbock 1954, 151–63) supports them.

But argument is no match for prejudice, as the history of the fifth item confirms. This has been known since 1939, when the inscription 'W. Shakespere' was found on the Folger Library copy of a 1568 legal textbook, William Lambarde's *Archaionomia* (Knight 1973; Schoenbaum 1981). But Schoenbaum (1981, 109) feels that *Archaionomia* 'seems an odd choice for Shakespeare's library'. This opinion is echoed from the Folger palaeographer's report on the original discovery (Dawson 1942), which concludes that the poet himself indeed signed the volume 'perhaps because he owned the book – a strange volume indeed for his library'. Thus pundits decide, up to 400 years after the event, what books Shakespeare ought not to read – exactly as they determine what plays he ought not to write, and even how he ought not to sign his own name (Cox 1984). But here prima facie is a seventh signature for comparison, as Professor W. Nicholas Knight (1973) has been saying, hardly heeded, for twenty years. It has been obscured only by opinion. Its location, a law book which Shakespeare should not have owned, served as a source (Proudfoot 1982; Sams 1986, 210–12) for *Ironside c.* 1588, a play which he should not have written. However, the respected senior authority Giles Dawson has recently announced a change of mind, fifty years after his own original report. He now (1992) sees the signature's authenticity as not just probable but provable. On that basis, the many underlinings and annotations throughout this copy of *Archaionomia* might also now be profitably studied and reported upon, for the first time ever.

Last comes a letter dated June 1592 signed but not written by the 3rd Earl of Southampton. This too is penned in an analogue of the *Ironside* hand, though in a rather less formal style. It is literally a secretary hand, which deserves detailed comparison, for example with the *Sir Thomas More* manuscript additions which have at last (a century or so after the ascription was first argued) been accepted as Shakespeare's. This Southampton letter, also preserved in the British Library (Lansdowne 72), received some publicity (Grice 1981) but elicited no response, although it was written at a time when Southampton was Shakespeare's patron and the recipient of sonnets on the same theme, namely the young lord's unwillingness to spend his own money on necessary repairs to his manor house: cf 'Seeking that beauteous roof to ruinate/Which to repair should be thy chief desire' (10. 7–8) and 'Who lets so fair a house fall to decay' (13. 9). These references (*pace* Kerrigan 1986, 185, 190) might just as well be allusions as imagery, and are surely at least as likely to derive from personal experience as from echoes of Marlowe, Spenser and Erasmus.

Further, the New York documents expert Charles Hamilton again added his own explicit affidavit (30 June 1986), thus: 'the handwriting in the body of the [Southampton] letter appears to me to be that of William Shakespeare. The "feel" or general appearance of the writing, which includes the size of the script, slant, space between lines and words, configuration of letters, stroke pattern, speed of the writing, is the same as in Shakespeare's will . . . and the three pages in *Sir Thomas More*.'

Thence other interesting inferences follow. On the evidence of overt errata in the 1609 first edition, Shakespeare could not have corrected the Sonnet proofs. But there are no rational grounds for doubting that their publisher, Thomas Thorpe, had access to an authoritative or indeed authorial manuscript. If the latter, then the 1609 printing permits clear but largely undrawn conclusions about Shakespeare's ordinary handwriting at the relevant time: thus his 'your' could be misread as 'you' (13.7) and conversely (16.7); his 'due' as 'end' (69.3); his 'One' or 'one' as 'Our' or 'our' (99.9, 120.8); and, most characteristically and consistently of all, his 'thy' as 'their' (27.10; 43.11; 46.3, 8, 11, 14; 69.5; 70.6; 128.11, 14). Other characteristics, identified from the *More* pages, include wilful spacings after the letter o and before r, such as fo rbid (line 96), o ffyc (98) th offendo r (123) count ry (126). Urkowitz thus compellingly explains the allegedly memorial errors in *King Lear* Q1 (1980). Similarly *More* contains idiosyncratic spellings such as 'gotte', 'dogge', 'don' and 'offyc'.

Although palaeography has become a dead letter (Sams 1993e), like much else in Shakespeare scholarship, some students of these specialised subjects might feel inspired to make objective comparisons among the manuscripts mentioned.

The Documents 1500–1594

1. Before 1501: a Shakespeare ancestor [great-great-grandfather] was granted lands and tenements by King Henry VII.
2. 1501: Thomas Arden [maternal great-grandfather] of Wilmcote [a village three miles north-west of Stratford] and his son Robert [grandfather] buy land in Snitterfield [a village three miles north of Stratford].
3. 1528–60: Robert Arden recorded as a landowner and farmer in Snitterfield.
4. C. 1529: John Shakespeare born [father, d. 1601].
5. October 1535: Richard Shakespeare [grandfather], a tenant farmer in Snitterfield, fined for keeping too many cattle on the common pasture. The name sometimes appears in the form 'Shakstaff'.
6. 1538: Richard Shakespeare ordered to mend his hedges between his land and Thomas Palmer's.
7. C. 1540 Mary Arden born [mother, d. 1608].
8. 21 October 1543: R. Shakespeare bequeathed a team of oxen by Thomas Attwood.
9. 21 April 1548: the widower Robert Arden married Agnes Hill, née Webbe, a farmer's widow.
10. 29 April 1552: John Shakespeare's first mention in the Stratford records. He was fined one shilling, together with Humphrey Reynolds and Adrian Quiney, for making a dunghill [fecerunt sterquinarium] in Henley Street.
11. 17 June 1556: the husbandman Thomas Suche of Armscote, Worcestershire seeks recovery of £8 from 'Johannem Shakyspere . . . glover'.
12. 2 October 1556: John Shakespeare buys property and land in Stratford, a house with garden and croft in Greenhill Street from George Turnor and a house with garden in Henley Street from Edward West.
13. 19 November 1556: John Shakespeare sues Henry Field for the detention of eighteen quarters of barley.
14. 24 November 1556: Robert Arden's testament bequeaths his soul 'to Allmyghtye God and to our bleside Ladye Sent marye and to all the holye compenye of heven'. Among his property were several woven and painted tapestries; his livestock included

cattle, horses and pigs; he also kept bees. His youngest daughter Mary [mother] was bequeathed 'all my land in Wilmcote, cawlide Asbyes, and the crop apone the grounde sowne and tyllide as hitt is'; and '£6.13.4 of money to be paid ere my goods be divided'.

15. *C.* 1556: Anne Hathaway born [wife] (d. 1623).

16. *C.* 1557: John Shakespeare marries Mary Arden.

17. 3 June 1557: 'John Shakyspeyr', borough ale-taster, fined 8d for absence.

18. 6 May 1558: order of *distringas* [to compel an appearance in court or the surrender of goods] awarded against 'Johannem Shakspeyr' at the suit of Adrian Quiney and Thomas Knight.

19. 15 September 1558: 'Jone Shakspere daughter to John Shakespeare' christened. The incumbent was the Catholic priest Roger Dyos (**25**). The child presumably died in infancy, although there is no record of her burial; the name was used again (**51**).

20. 30 September 1558: 'The xii men have orderyd ther trysty and wellbelovyd Humfrey Plymley, Roger Sadler, John Taylor and John Shakespeyr constabulles' [officers of the peace].

21. 1 October 1558: John Shakespeare serves as a juror.

22. April 1559: John Shakespeare, Master Clopton of New Place, and others, fined 'for not kepynge ther gutteres cleane'.

23. 6 October 1559: John Shakespeare appointed affeeror [an assessor of fines not prescribed by statute] and reappointed as petty constable. He signs by making his mark.

24. 3 October 1560: Richard Shakespeare fined for neglecting to ring his swine and for keeping his animals on the common pasture.

25. 1560: Roger Dyos (**19**) ousted from Stratford.

26. 10 February 1561: administration of the estate of Richard Shakespeare granted to his son 'Johannem Shakespere de Snytterfield agricolam' [farmer].

27. 4 May 1561: John Shakespeare, affeeror, witnesses the court meeting, and signs with a mark (if indeed it is his – it is widely separate from the clerk's record of his name) said to represent a pair of glover's compasses.

28. 1 October 1561: John Shakespere (as his late father's assign), Margery Lyncecombe and William Rounde each fined a shilling for not keeping their hedges in order.

29. 3 October 1562: John Shakespeare described as chamberlain [= borough treasurer].

30. October 1562: John Shakespeare fined for neglecting his Snitterfield hedges [he had inherited part of his father's smallholding].

31. 2 December 1562: 'Margareta filia Johannis Shakespere' christened [sister, d. 1563].

32. 24 January 1563: John Taylor and John Shakespeare present their accounts as Stratford chamberlains; the latter signs with a mark said to represent a glover's clamp.

33. 30 April 1563: 'Margareta filia Johannis Shakespeare' buried [sister, b. 1562].

34. 10 January 1564: John Taylor and John Shakespeare, chamberlains, present their 1563 accounts, including three shillings paid to the latter for a piece of timber. In this period 'images' were 'defaced' in accordance with Protestant directives.

35. 26 April 1564: William Shakespeare, 'Gulielmus filius Johannis Shakespeare', christened (d. 1616). His exact date of birth is not recorded.

36. 11 July 1564: the plague struck Stratford, claiming some 200 victims, none named Shakespeare.

37. 30 August 1564: John Shakespeare paid three shillings towards the relief of the poor, with another sixpence on 6 September.

38. 27 September 1564: John Shakespeare recorded as witness to a corporation order.

39. 20 December 1564: John Shakespeare recorded as attending a corporation meeting.

40. 1 March 1565: John Shakespeare presents the 1564 accounts.

41. 4 July 1565: 'At this Hall [= council meeting] John Shakspeyr is appwynted an alderman'.

42. Before Michaelmas 1565: 'peyd to [John] Shakspeyr for a rest of old debt £3.2.7'.

43. 15 February 1566: John Shakespeare presents the 1565 accounts, prepared by William Tyler and William Smith, chamberlains.

44. September 1566: John Shakespeare goes bail for Richard Hathaway [future father-in-law] (117).

45. 13 October 1566: 'Gilbertus filius Johannis Shakespeare' christened [brother, d. 1612].

46. September 1567: John Shakespeare is called 'Mr. Shakespeyr', a title of dignity, for the first time on record.

47. 4 September 1568: 'The names whereof one to be balyf [mayor], Mr. John Shakspere, Mr. Robert Perrot, Robert Salusbury'. John Shakespeare was duly elected and presided over the council on 1 October and the Court of Record on 6 October.

48. 1 October, 10 October 1568: John Shakespeare presided over the council and the Court of Record respectively.

49. 4 November 1568: John Shakespeare sells five hundredweight of wool to John Walford of Marlborough; the debt was still outstanding thirty-one years later.

50. 1568–70: John Shakespeare recorded as tenant of Ingon Meadow, a fourteen-acre estate some two miles north-east of Stratford, in the parish of Hampton Lucy.

51. 15 April 1569: 'Jone the daughter of John Shakspere' christened [sister, d. 1646].

52. *C.* August 1569: the Stratford council paid nine shillings for dramatic performances to the Queen's players and one shilling to the Earl of Worcester's players.

53. 1569: John Shakespeare was 'Baylife, A Justice of peace, the Queenes officer & cheffe of the towne of Stratford vppon Avon', as stated in the application on his behalf for a coat of arms.

54. 1569–99: 'His Father . . . was a considerable Dealer in Wool' (Rowe 1709). 'For this we [also] have . . . the tradition of Stratford' (Jordan *c.* 1790). 'Mr. John Shakespeare Wool Stapler' (Oldys *c.* 1750). 'The landlord of the [hostelry into which the Henley Street birthplace was later converted] . . . assured the writer, that, when he relaid the floors of the parlour, the remains of wool, and the refuse of wool-combing, were found under the old flooring, imbedded with the earth of the foundation . . .' (Phillips 1818). Part of the Henley Street house was 'known, from far back, as the Woolshop' (Schoenbaum 1975, 27).

55. 1570: 'Johannes Shappere alias Shakespere de Stratford upon Haven in comitatu Warwicensi glover' twice accused of breaking usury laws by making loans of eighty and one hundred pounds to Walter Musshem or Mussum (probably a sheep farmer) of Walton D'Eiville near Stratford, and charging twenty pounds interest on both sums.

56. September 1571: John Shakespeare elected Chief Alderman (Lord Mayor) and Justice of the Peace for the coming year.

57. 28 September 1571: 'Anna filia magistri Shakspere' christened [sister, d. 1579]. The title 'magister' [master] denotes substance and status in the community.

58. 10 and 24 October 1571: John Shakespeare present at council meetings.

59. 29 October 1571: Simon Hunt (**75**) appointed by the Bishop of Worcester as Stratford schoolmaster.

60. *C.* 1571: the seven-year-old Shakespeare becomes eligible for Stratford grammar [= Latin grammar] school.

61. 1571: John Shakespeare accused of illegal wool-dealing, in that he had purchased 200 tods (5600 lb) in Westminster and a further 100 tods at Snitterfield, for a total of £210, in contravention of a law forbidding such purchases by private individuals. He was fined forty shillings.

62. 18 January, 7 February, 2, 9, 18 April, 28 May, 3 September and 4 October 1572: John Shakespeare presides at council meetings.

63. 1572: John Shakespeare awarded fifty pounds, a debt from a glover.

64. 18 January 1572: Stratford council resolve that John Shakespeare and his close associate Adrian Quiney should go to London and report on parliamentary matters affecting Stratford.

65. 7 February 1573: the council receives their report.

66. *C.* September 1573: Leicester's Men, led by James Burbage, perform in Stratford.

67. 1573: John Shakespeare, 'whyttawer' [= dresser of hides and skins] and Walter Musshem jointly sued for £30 by Henry Higford of Solihull.

68. 1573: the will of Alexander Webbe, farmer, of Snitterfield, appoints 'John Shackespere of Stretford-upon-Avon' and 'John Hill of Bearley' as executors.

69. 11 March 1574: 'Richard sonne to Mr. John Shakspeer' christened [brother, d. 1613].

70. 1574–96: Henry Shakespeare [uncle, d. 1596], recorded as a tenant farmer in Snitterfield.

71. 9–27 July 1575: Elizabeth I was entertained by Robert Dudley, Earl of Leicester, at Kenilworth, some twelve miles from Stratford.

72. *C.* August 1575: the Earl of Warwick's Men perform in Stratford, for the unusually high fee of seventeen shillings.

73. 20 September 1575: 'John Shakespere, yeoman' [= a freeholder of land].

74. October 1575: John Shakespeare buys two Stratford houses with gardens and orchards from Edmund and Emma Hall of Grimley near Worcester.

75. 1575: Simon Hunt (59) leaves Stratford for the Catholic seminary at Douai; he later became a Jesuit in Rome. He is replaced as schoolmaster by Thomas Jenkins.

76. 1576 or earlier: John Shakespeare applies for a grant of arms.

77. *C.* January 1576: the Earl of Worcester's Men perform in Stratford.

78. 5 September 1576: John Shakespeare's last council meeting for some years.

79. 1576–7: Leicester's Men perform in Stratford for fifteen shillings, Worcester's Men for three shillings and fourpence.

80. March 1577: twenty-five shillings 'paid to my Lord of Leyster's players' from the Stratford accounts.

81. Throughout 1577: John Shakespeare fails to attend Stratford council meetings.

82. *C.* 1577: William removed from school. Cf 'rude groom', 'such peasants' (Greene 1592); my 'heavy ignorance', 'rude ignorance' (Sonnet 78 *c.* 1595); 'how farr sometimes a mortal man may goe/ By the dimme light of Nature' (Beaumont *c.* 1615); he 'wanted art' (Jónson 1619); 'thou hadst small Latine, and lesse Greeke' (Jonson 1623); 'fancy's child ... native woodnotes wild' (Milton 1632);

'That Latine Hee [Jonson] reduc'd and could command/That which your Shakespeare scarce could understand' (in *Ionsonus Virbius* 1638); 'Without art', 'Nature onely helpt him' (Digges 1640); 'his Learning was very little', 'Master *Jonson* . . . was built far higher in Learning . . .' (Fuller *c.* 1650); punning anecdotes about the giving of latten spoons at christenings 'and you [i.e. Shakespeare, with the implication that he had little Latin] shall translate them' (Nicholas L'Estrange, before 1655; Thomas Plume *c.* 1657); 'I have heard that Mr. Shakespeare was a natural wit, without any art at all' (John Ward, vicar of Stratford, *c.* 1660, when Shakespeare's daughter Judith was living there); 'the pride of Nature, and the shame of Schools/Born to create, and not to Learn from Rules' (Sedley 1667); 'taught by none' (Dryden 1669); 'untaught, unpractised' (Dryden *c.* 1670); 'natural wit', '. . . as Ben Johnson says of him, he had little Latine and lesse Greek' (Aubrey *c.* 1681); '[His father] had bred him, 'tis true, for some time at a free-school, where 'tis probable he acquir'd that little Latin he was master of; but the narrowness of his circumstances, and the want of his assistance at home, forc'd his father to withdraw him from thence, and unhappily prevented his further proficiency in that language', 'hearing Ben [Jonson] frequently reproaching him [Shakespeare] with the want of Learning and Ignorance of the Antients' (Rowe 1709); 'His being imperfect in some Things, was owing to his not being a Scholar . . .' [Anon 1728]; etc., etc.

83.   *C.* 1577: 'His father was a Butcher, and I have been told heretofore by some of the neighbours, that when he was a boy he exercised his father's Trade, but when he kill'd a Calfe he would do it in a high style, and make a Speech. There was at this time another Butcher's son in this Towne that was held not at all inferior to him for a natural wit, his acquaintance and coaetanean [contemporary], but dyed young' (Aubrey *c.* 1681); 'The clarke [William Castle] that shew'd me this Church is above 80 yrs old; he says that this *Shakespear* was formerly in this Towne [Stratford] bound apprentice to a butcher . . .' (Dowdall 1693).

84.   29 January 1578: 'Mr. Plumley, Mr. Shakespeare Aldermen' and five others exempted from payment towards the maintenance of three pikemen, two billmen, and one archer.

85.   12 November 1578: John and Mary Shakespeare and George Gibbes transfer seventy acres of land to Thomas Webbe and Humphrey Hooper, apparently on receipt of cash.

86.   14 November 1578: in the will of Roger Sadler, baker, proved 17 January 1579, 'Item, of Edmonde Lambert [uncle: mother's brother-in-law] and . . . Cornishe for the debt of Mr. John Shakspere', five pounds.

87.   19 November 1578: John Shakespeare exempted from weekly tax for the poor, levied on aldermen.

88.   1578: Henry Higford (67) again sues John Shakespeare for thirty pounds.

89.   Throughout 1578: John Shakespeare absent from all eight recorded meetings of the Stratford council.

90.   *C.* 1579–*c.* 82: young William continues to work on the homestead smallholding; 'Upon his leaving School, he seems to have given intirely into that way of Living which his Father propos'd to him' [Rowe 1709].

91.   11 February 1579: Lord Strange's Men are paid for a performance in Stratford.

92.   11 March 1579: John Shakespeare's levy of three shillings and fourpence for arms listed as 'unpaid and unaccounted for'.

93.   4 April 1579: Anne Shakespeare buried [sister, b. 1571]; the chamberlain's accounts include 'item for the bell and pall for Mr. Shaxper's daughter, 8d'.

94.   Easter Term 1579: John Shakespeare mortgaged his wife's property Asbies (a house and some sixty acres in Wilmcote) to his brother-in-law Edmund Lambert, yeoman (the husband of Mary Shakespeare's sister Joan) of Barton on the Heath [a village some fifteen miles south of Stratford] for forty pounds cash, to be repaid in 1580 (**104, 157**).

95.   *C.* August 1579: the Countess of Essex's players perform in Stratford.

96.   10 August 1579: Richard, son of the Stratford tanner Henry Field [d. 1592 (**178**)], apprenticed to a London printer for seven years (**186**).

97.   15 October 1579: the interest of John and Mary Shakespeare in two messuages at Snitterfield (her ninth share of her father's property and land, two houses and *c.* 100 acres) is sold to Robert Webbe for four pounds. John is again styled 'yeoman'; he and his wife both sign with marks, in the presence of Nicholas Knolles, Anthony Osbaston and William Meades, witnesses.

98.   December 1579: Katherine Hamlett drowned in the Avon at Tiddington.

99.   1579: the Stratford schoolmaster Jenkins is replaced by John Cottam, whose brother was put to death in 1582 for his Catholic faith.

100. Throughout 1579: John Shakespeare absent from all recorded council meetings.

101. February 1580: a Stratford inquest jury finds that Katherine Hamlett's death was *per infortunium* [accidental].

102. 3 May 1580: 'Edmund, sonne to Mr. John Shakespeare' christened [brother, d. 1607].

103. Summer 1580: John Shakespeare of Stratford, yeoman, fined twenty pounds as pledge for the hatmaker John Audeley of Nottingham.

104. 29 September 1580: John Shakespeare (as he later deposed) offered Edmund Lambert the forty pounds due to him (**94**), and was refused. Lambert said that he would retain possession of the Asbies estate until other outstanding debts were discharged (**157**).

105. 29 December 1580: Agnes Arden [mother's stepmother], described as 'aged and impotent' in July 1580, is buried.

106. By October 1580: Earl of Derby's Men perform in Stratford.

107. 1580: John Shakespeare fined forty pounds for his failure to appear before a London court to give security that he would keep the peace towards the Queen and her subjects.

108. 1580: Henry Shakespeare involved in a dispute about paying tithes on crops.

109. Throughout 1580: John Shakespeare absent from the eight recorded council meetings.

110. 1580–81: Worcester's Men in Stratford.

111. *C.* 1581: John Shakespeare's will, beginning. 'In the name of God, the father, sonne, and holy ghost, the most holy and blessed Virgin Mary, mother of God, the holy host of archangels, angels, patriarchs, prophets, evangelists, apostles, saints, martyrs and all the celestial court and company of heaven, I John Shakspear, an unworthy member of the holy Catholick religion . . . calling to mind . . . that I may be possibly cut off in the blossome of my sins . . . and that I may be unprepared for the dreadful trial . . . make and ordaine this my last spiritual will . . . and confession of faith . . . IV. *Item,* I John Shakspear doe protest that I will also pass out of this life, armed with the last sacrament of extreme unction: the which if through any let or hindrance I should not then be able to have, I doe now also for that time demand and crave the same; beseeching his divine majesty that he will be pleased to anoynt my senses both internall and externall with the sacred oyle of his infinite mercy, and to pardon all my sins . . . IX. *Item,* I John Shakspear do heere protest that I do render infinite thanks unto his divine majesty for . . . the benefit of my . . . vocation to the holy knowledge of him & his true Catholike faith . . . X. *Item,* I John Shakspear do protest, that I am willing, yea, I doe infinitely desire and humbly crave, that of this my last will and testament the glorious and ever Virgin mary, mother of god, refuge and advocate of sinners (whom I honour specially above all other saints) may be the chief Executresse, togeather with these other saints, my patrons, (saint Winefride) all whome I invocke and beseech to be present at the hour of my death, that she and they may comfort me with their desired presence . . . XII.

Item, I John Shakspear do in like manner pray and beseech all my dear friends, parents and kinsfolks . . . least by reason of my sinnes I be to pass and stay a long while in purgatory, they will vouchsafe to assist and succour me with their holy prayers and satisfactory workes, especially with the holy sacrifice of the masse, as being the most effectual meanes to deliver soules from their torments and paines . . . XIV. *Item*, . . . blessed be he also a thousand thousand times; into whose most holy hands I commend my soul and body, my life and death; and I beseech him above all things that he never permit any change to be made by me John Shakspear of this my aforesaid will and testament. Amen' (full text in Malone 1790, i. ii. 161–2, 330–31; Schoenbaum 1975, 41–2).

112. ?*C*. 1581: 'though [Shakespeare] . . . had little Latine and lesse Greek, he understood Latine pretty well: for he had been in his younger years a scholmaster in the country' (Aubrey *c*. 1681, on the authority of the actor William Beeston, d. 1682, whose actor father had belonged to the Chamberlain's company).

113. 1581: *Seneca, His Tenne Tragedies translated into English.*

114. Throughout 1581: John Shakespeare absent from council meetings.

115. 1581–2: Berkeley's Men and Worcester's Men perform in Stratford.

116. Summer 1582: John Shakespeare craves 'sureties of the peace against Ralph Cawdrey [then bailiff of Stratford], William Russell, Thomas Logginge and Robert Young, for fear of death and mutilation of his limbs'.

117. 9 July 1582: will of Richard Hathaway [father-in-law (**44**)] probated; his farmland is left to his eldest son Bartholomew.

118. 27 November 1582: special licence granted by the Bishop of Worcester for marriage 'inter Wm. Shaxpere et Annam Whateley [*sic*] de Temple Grafton' [five miles west of Stratford].

119. 28 November 1582: 'Fulconem Sandells de Stratford in Comitatu warwicensi agricolam et Johannem Rychardson ibidem agricolam' [farmers from Shottery, one mile west of Stratford, friends of Richard Hathaway] enter into a bond to exempt the Bishop of Worcester from all liability in the forthcoming marriage of 'William Shagspere and Anne Hathwey of Stratford in the Dioces of Worcester maiden'.

120. 28 November 1582: bond executed for grant of marriage licence between William Shakespeare and Anne Hathwey of Stratford on Avon.

121. 1582: John Shakespeare cited as witness before a special commission in a Chancery suit about the Arden estates.

122. 1582: John Shakespeare present (for the first time since 1576) at a council meeting, where he voted for John Sadler as bailiff.

123. *C.* 1582: by 14 January 1583 Edward Alleyn had joined Worcester's Men.

124. 1582–3: Berkeley's Men, and Lord Chandos's Men, perform in Stratford.

125. *C.* 1582–3: 'He run from his master to London' (Dowdall 1693); 'This William . . . came to London I guesse at about 18 . . .' (Aubrey *c.* 1681); [William Shakespeare was] 'much given to all unluckiness [= mischief] in stealing venison & Rabbits particularly from Sr [blank] Lucy who had him oft whipt & sometimes Imprisoned & at last made Him fly his Native Country to his great Advancement' [R. Davies *c.* 1700]; 'One stanza of it [= the ballad, much as given by Oldys *c.* 1750, *infra*], which has the appearance of genuine, was put into the editor's hands many years ago by an ingenious gentleman (grandson of its preserver) with this account of the way in which it descended to him. – Mr Thomas Jones, who dwelt at Tarbick [Tardebigge] a village in Worcestershire a few miles from Stratford on Avon, and dy'd in the year 1703, aged upwards of ninety, remembered to have heard from several old people at Stratford the story of Shakespeare's robbing sir Thomas Lucy's park; and their account of it agreed with Mr. Rowe's [*infra*], with this addition – that the ballad written against sir Thomas by Shakespeare was stuck upon his park gate, which exasperated the knight to apply to a lawyer at Warwick to proceed against him: Mr Jones had put down in writing the first stanza of this ballad, which was all he remembers of it, and Mr Thomas Wilkes (my grandfather) transmitted it to my father by memory, who also took in writing, and his copy is this:

> A parliemente member, a justice of peace,
> at home a poor scare-crowe, at London an asse,
> if lowsie is Lucy, as some volke miscalle it,
> then Lucy is lousie whatever befall it.
> He thinks himself great, yet an Asse in his State
> We allowe by his ears but with Asses to mate.
> If Lucy is Lowsie as some volke miscalle it
> Sing Lowsie Lucy whatever befalle it.
>
> (Jones, before 1703, recorded by Capell in 1780)

'In this kind of Settlement [i.e. his father's employment, after prematurely leaving school *c.* 1577] he continu'd for some time, 'till an Extravagance that he was guilty of, forc'd him both out of his Country and that way of Living which he had taken up . . . He had, by a Misfortune common enough to young Fellows, fallen into ill Company; and amongst them, some that made a frequent practice of Deer-stealing, engag'd him with them more than once in robbing a Park that belong'd to Sir *Thomas Lucy* of *Cherlecot*, near

Stratford. For this he was prosecuted by that Gentleman, as he thought, somewhat too severely; and in order to revenge that ill usage, he made a Ballad upon him. And tho' this, probably the first Essay of his Poetry, be lost, yet it is said to have been so very bitter, that it redoubled the Prosecution against him to that degree, that he was oblig'd to leave his Business and Family in *Warwickshire*, for some time, and shelter himself in *London*' (Rowe 1709). 'Tis a tradition descended from old Betterton [the actor: Rowe's informant, after enquiry in Stratford] that [Shakespeare] was drawn into a company of deer Stealers & concernd with them in robbing Sr. Thos. Lucy's Park at Charlecot, wch drove him to London so among the Players where he became the Great Genius we read him in his Plays' (Oldys *c.* 1750). 'There was a very aged gentleman living in the neighbourhood of Stratford (where he died fifty years since) who had not only heard, from several old people in that town, of Shakespeare's transgression, but could remember the first stanza of that bitter ballad, which, repeating to one of his acquaintance, he preserved it in writing; and here it is, neither better nor worse, but faithfully transcribed from the copy which his relation very curteously communicated to me [as above, with six extra quatrains]. Contemptible as this performance must now appear, at the time when it was written it might have sufficient power to irritate a vain, weak and vindictive magistrate; especially as it was affixed to several of his park-gates, and consequently published among his neighbours. – It may be remarked likewise, that the jingle on which it turns, occurs in the first scene of *The Merry Wives of Windsor*' (Oldys *c.* 1750). Other verses were also recorded, e.g. by Professor Barnes *c.* 1690 (as reported by Chetwood, before 1766):

> Sir Thomas was too covetous
> to covet so much deer
> when horns enough upon his head
> most plainly did appear.
> Had not his worship one deer left?
> What then? He had a wife
> took pains enough to find him horns
> should last him during life.

A *Biographia Britannica* article refers to 'two shafts [whether in ballad or other form] which [Shakespeare] let fly against his persecutor, whose anger drove him to the extreme end of ruin . . . how long the knight continued inexorable is not known, but it is certain that Shakespeare owed his release at last to the Queen's kindness' (Nichols 1763). Further, '[Sir Thomas Lucy] had at the time also another park at a place called Fullbroke, two miles distant from the other [Charlcote]; and there tradition reports it was that Shakspeare and his companions made a practise of following their favourite diversion; which they did so often, that the knight's resentment was raised, and he commenced a prosecution against them, but desisted upon their making an abject submission; but which so hurt the high spirit of our poet that he could not repress his indignation. A satirical song went abroad, which inflamed Sir Thomas to the utmost pitch, and he renewed the prosecution with redoubled vigour. His power was too great for poor Shakspeare to contend with, and he now saw, perhaps with horror, that his youthful levity obliged him to quit his father, his fond wife, his prattling babes, and his native place' (Jordan *c.* 1790). The place was 'the old park, now deparked, from which it is said William Shakespeare stole Mr. Lucy's deer' . . . adjoining a farm 'at Ingon containing now about 200 acres of land' (Cooper 1788). 'It was in this [Fulbrook] park our bard is said to have been, in a youthful frolic, engaged in stealing deer, and thereby to have drawn upon himself a prosecution from the then owner, Sir Thomas Lucy . . . Within this park is now standing, on a spot called Daisy Hill, a farm house, which was antiently the keeper's lodge. To this lodge it is reported our Shakspeare was conveyed, and there confined at the time of the charge, which is supposed to have been brought against him' (Ireland 1795). 'At Stratford, the family maintain that Shakspeare stole Sir Thomas Lucy's buck, to celebrate his wedding-day [1582] and for that purpose only' (Phillips 1818). 'Charlecote is in high preservation, and inhabited by Mr Lucy, descendant of the worshipful Sir Thomas. . . . He told me that the park from which Shakspeare stole the buck was not that which surrounds Charlecote, but belonged to a mansion at some distance, where Sir Thomas Lucy resided at the time of the trespass. The tradition went that they hid the buck in a barn, part of which was standing a few years ago, but now totally decayed. This park no longer belongs to the Lucys' (Sir Walter Scott 1828). 'My best thanks are due to Mrs Lucy, of Charlecote Park, for valuable information, which is a key to the whole history of Shakespeare . . . The proof of the [deer-stealing] story is a note in a manuscript pedigree of the Lucys, made about ninety years ago by an old man named Ward, who derived his information from the family papers then in his hands. This version of the incident has been obligingly communicated to us by Mrs Lucy, of Charlecote . . . The note by Ward in the manuscript pedigree of the Lucys informs us that [Shakespeare's] friends interested in his behalf the most important man in Warwickshire, no less a person than Robert, Earl of Leicester; and this great magnate, now interceded with Sir Thomas Lucy, and prevailed on him to abandon the prosecution . . . The note by Ward agrees with Rowe as to the course [Shakespeare] pursued. The ballad was nailed on the park-gates at Charlecote . . . The Lucy note reports that the satiric ballad obliged him to quit Stratford – at least for a time' . . . (Fullom 1862).

126. 26 May 1583: 'Susanna, daughter to William Shakespere' chris-tened [d. 1649].

127. 1583: the local acting troupe of 'Davi Jones and his company' were paid thirteen shillings and fourpence 'for his pastyme at whitsontyde'.

128. Throughout 1583: John Shakespeare absent from all fourteen recorded council meetings.

129. C. 1583: 'a naturall witt . . . liv'd in Shoreditch' (Aubrey c. 1681); 'Recd Into the playhouse as a serviture [= servant], and by this meanes had an oppertunity to be wt he afterwards prov'd' (Dowdall 1693); 'It is at this Time, and upon this Accident [i.e. because of the Lucy deer-stealing, which] (tho' it seem'd at first to be a Blemish upon his good Manners, and a Misfortune to him, yet it afterwards happily prov'd the occasion of exerting one of the greatest *Genius's* that ever was known in Dramatick Poetry) that he is said to have made his first Acquaintance in the Play-house. He was receiv'd into the [London] Company then in being [prima facie the Queen's Men at the Theatre], at first in a very mean Rank . . .' (Rowe 1709). 'Sir William Davenant, who has been call'd a natural son of our author, us'd to tell the following whim-sical story of him; – Shakespear, when he first came from the country to the play-house, was not admitted to act; but as it was then the custom for all the people of fashion to come on horseback to entertainments of all kinds, it was Shakespear's employment for a time, with several other poor boys belonging to the company, to hold the horses and take care of them during the representation; – by his dexterity and care he soon got a good deal of business in this way, and was personally known to most of the quality that fre-quented the house, insomuch that, being obliged, before he was taken up into a higher and more honourable employment within doors, to train up boys to assist him, it became long afterwards a usual way among them to recommend themselves by saying that they were Shakespear's boys' (Anon. 1748). 'Here I cannot forbear relating a story which Sir William Davenant told Mr Betterton, who communicated it to Mr Rowe; Rowe told it Mr Pope, and Mr Pope told it to Dr Newton, the late editor of Milton, and from a gentleman, who heard it from him tis here related. Concerning Shakespeare's first appearance in the play-house. When he came to London, he was without money and friends, and being a stranger he knew not to whom to apply, nor by what means to support himself. – At that time coaches not being in use, and as gentlemen were accustomed to ride to the playhouse [the Theatre

in Shoreditch was across fields, outside the City] Shakespear, driven by the last necessity, went to the playhouse door, and pick'd up a little money by taking care of the gentlemens horses who came to the play; he became eminent even in that profession, and was taken notice of for his diligence and skill in it; he soon had more business than himself could manage, and at last hired boys under him, who were known by the name of Shakespeare's boys: Some of the players accidentally conversing with him, found him so acute, and master of so fine a conversation, that struck therewith they recommended him to the house' (Shiels 1753). '. . . his persecutor [Sir Thomas Lucy]'s anger drove [Shakespeare] to the extreme end of ruin, where he was forced to a very low degree of drudgery for a support' (Nichols 1763). '[Shakespeare] came to London a needy adventurer, and lived for a time by very mean employments' (Dr Johnson 1765). 'Many came on horse-back to the play, and when *Shakespeare* fled to *London* from the terrour of a criminal prosecution, his first expedient was to wait at the door of the play-house, and hold the horses of those that had no servants, that they might be ready again after the performance. In this office he became so conspicuous for his care and readiness, that in a short time every man as he alighted called for *Will. Shakespear*, and scarcely any other waiter was trusted with a horse while *Will. Shakespear* could be had. This was the first dawn of better fortune. *Shakespear* finding more horses put into his hand than he could hold, hired boys to wait under his inspection, who when *Will. Shakespear* was summoned, were immediately to present themselves, *I am* Shakespeare's *boy, Sir.* In time *Shakespear* found higher employment, but as long as the practice of riding to the play-house continued, the waiters that held the horses retained the appellation of Shakespear's *Boys*' (Dr Johnson 1765). 'Mr J.M. Smith said, he had often heard his mother [née Hart] state that Shakespeare owed his rise in life, and his introduction to the theatre, to his accidentally holding the horse of a gentleman at the door of the theatre, on his first arriving in London. His appearance led to enquiry and subsequent patronage . . .'. (Phillips 1818).

130. 1583–4: Oxford's, Worcester's and Essex's Men perform in Stratford.

131. April 1584: Shakespeare returns to Stratford for a time.

132. November 1584: Sir Thomas Lucy elected Member of Parliament for Warwickshire.

133. 17 December 1584: Sir Thomas Lucy appropriates the Fulbrook estate of a Catholic exile.

134. *C.* 1584: 'There is a stage tradition that [Shakespeare's] first office in the theatre was that of *Call-boy*, or prompter's attendant; whose employment it is to give the performers notice to be ready to enter,

as often as the business of the play requires their appearance on stage' (Malone 1790, ii. 107).

135. January 1585: *Felix and Philiomena* acted at Court by the Queen's Men.

136. 2 February 1585: the twins 'Hamnet [d. 1596] and Judeth [d. 1662] sonne and daughter to William Shakspere' christened. They were named after the Stratford friends Hamlet and Judith Sadler.

137. C. 1585: 'He began early [= soon after he became an actor] to make essays at Dramatique Poetry, which at that time was very lowe [= before Marlowe's *Tamburlaine, c.* 1587], and his Playes took well [= were popular]' (Aubrey *c.* 1681). 'In the playhouse [he] had an oppertunity to be what he afterwards prov'd' (Dowdall 1693). '. . . the Playhouse . . . prov'd the occasion of exerting one of the greatest *Genius's* that ever was known in Dramatick Poetry . . . his admirable Wit, and the natural Turn of it to the Stage, soon distinguish'd him, if not as an extraordinary Actor, yet as an excellent Writer' (Rowe 1709).

138. 19 January 1586: writ issued against John Shakespeare; but he had no goods on which distraint could be made.

139. 6 September 1586: 'At this Hall William Smythe and Richard Cowrte are chosen to be aldermen in the places of John Wheeler and John Shaxspere'; 'Mr. Shaxpere dothe not come to the halles when they be warned, nor hathe not done of longe tyme'.

140. 1586: mention of 'Johannes Shakespere . . . glover'.

141. 1586–7: the Queen's, Essex's, Leicester's, Stafford's and an unnamed theatre company perform in Stratford; the Queen's Men received twenty shillings.

142. 8 January 1587: action against John Shakespeare by Nicholas Lane to recover ten pounds owed by 'Henricus Shakspere frater dicti Johannis' [Henry, brother of the said John].

143. 23 April 1587: 'Edmund Lambarte, senior' [uncle by marriage (86)] buried at Barton on the Heath.

144. 26 September 1587: John Lambert [cousin] is told by John Shakespeare and his wife Mary together with their son William ('Johannes Shackespere et Maria uxor eius, simul cum Willielmo Shackespere filio suo', 157) that they will confirm the Asbies estate as his property in return for the payment of another twenty pounds.

145. 1587: Richard Field, son of the Stratford tanner Henry Field, completes his apprenticeship as a London printer.

146. 1587: Robert Greene, *Farewell to Folly* and *Penelope's Web* published.

147. By 1588: the first version of *Pericles*: 'Shakespeare's own Muse her *Pericles* first bore,/The Prince of *Tyre* was elder than the *Moore*' (Dryden, between 1677 and 1684).

148. 3 September 1588: burial of the comedian Richard Tarleton.

149. 19 September 1588: Thomas Nashe, *The Anatomy of Absurdity*, registered (attacks certain unlearned translators and writers as having only 'a little country grammar knowledge').

150. 1588: many court actions with John Shakespeare as either plaintiff or defendant.

151. 1588: Robert Greene, *Perimedes the Blacksmith* and *Pandosto* published.

152. *C.* 1588: the name 'W Shakespeare' written on the legal text-book *Archaionomia* (1568) compiled by William Lambarde.

153. *C.* 1588: in that same volume appears a note: 'Mr. Wm. Shakespeare/Lived at No. 1 Little Crown St./Westminster/N.B. near Dorset steps/St. James's Park'.

154. 1588–90: the Marprelate controversy, in pamphlets attacking and defending the power of churchmen, especially John Whitgift, Archbishop of Canterbury.

155. By 1589?: Shakespeare learns legal penmanship [the style of Hand D in *Sir Thomas More* 'certainly does convey the impression of training at least in some degree, in the formal style of the scrivener' (E. Thompson 1916)].

156. By 1589: Thomas Kyd's *The Spanish Tragedy* (also known as *Hieronimo*) and the first version of *Titus Andronicus*, written and acted. 'He that will sweare, *Ieronimo*, or *Andronicus*, are the best playes yet, shall passe unexcepted at, heere, as a man whose Iudgement showes it is constant, and hath stood still, these five and twentie, or thirtie yeeres' (Jonson 1614).

157. Early 1589: a bill of complaint heard at Westminster against John Lambert (son of Edmund, **86**) on behalf of John Shakespeare jointly with his wife Mary and his son William. They declared that on 26 September 1587 (**144**) they had been promised another twenty pounds by John Lambert; he denied it. The suit for restoration of property was unsuccessful.

158. 26 February 1589: 'Thomas sonne to Richard Quiney' christened (future son-in-law, d. *c.* 1655).

159. By August 1589: (?) the first versions of *Hamlet, The Taming of A Shrew, The Troublesome Reign of King John*, and other plays (**160**, **163**) written and acted.

160. 23 August 1589: Robert Greene, *Menaphon* entered to Sampson Clarke and published in that year with a Preface 'To the Gentlemen Students of Both Universities' by Thomas Nashe:

> I am not ignorant how eloquent our gowned age is growen of late; so that euerie moechanicall mate abhorres the english he was born too, and plucks with a solemne periphrasis, his *ut vales* from the inkhorne: which I impute not so much to the perfection of arts, as to the seruile imitation of vainglorious tragoedians, who contend not so seriouslie to excell in action, as

to embowell the clowdes in a speach of comparison; thinking themselves more than initiated in poets immortalitie, if they but once get Boreas by the beard and the heavenly Bull by the deaw-lap. But herein I cannot so fully bequeath them to follie, as their idiote art-masters, that intrude themselves to our eares as the alcumists of eloquence; who (mounted on the stage of arrogance) think to outbrave better pens with the swelling bumbast of a bragging blank verse. Indeed it may be the ingrafted overflow of some kilcow conceipt, that overcloyeth their imagination with a more than drunken resolution, beeing not extemporall in the invention of anie other meanes to vent their manhood, commits the disgestion of their cholerick incumbrances, to the spacious volubilitie of a drumming decasillabon.

Mongst this kinde of men that repose eternity in the mouth of a player, I can but ingrosse some deepe read Grammarians, who hauing no more learning in their scull, than will serue to take up a commoditie; nor Art in their brain, than was nourished in a seruing mans idlenesse, will take upon them to be the ironicall censors of all, when God and Poetrie doth know, they are the simplest of all. To leave them to the mercie of their mother tongue, that feed on nought but the crummes that fal from the translators trencher, I come . . .

But least I might seeme with these night crowes, *Nimis curiosus in aliena republica*, I'le turn back to my first text, of studies of delight; and talke a little in friendship with a few of our triviall translators. It is a common practice now a daies amongst a sort of shifting companions, that runne through euery arte and thrive by none, to leave the trade of *Noverint* [= law-clerk] wherto they were borne, and busie themselves with indeuors of Art, that could scarcelie latinize their neck-verse if they should haue neede; yet English Seneca read by candle light yeeldes manie good sentences, as *Bloud is a begger*, and so foorth: and if you intreat him faire in a frostie morning, he will afford whole *Hamlets*, I should say handfulls, of tragical speaches. But o griefe! *tempus edax rerum*, where's that will last alwaies? The sea exhaled by droppes will in continuance be drie, and *Seneca* let bloud line by line and page by page, at length must needes die to our stage: which makes his famisht followers to imitate the Kidde [no doubt a reference to Thomas Kyd] in Aesop, who enamored with the Foxes newfangles, forsooke all hopes of life to leape into a new occupation; and these men renowncing all possibilities of credit or estimation, to intermeddle with Italian translation: wherein how poorlie they haue plodded, (as those that are neither prouenzall men, nor are able to distinguishe of Articles,) let all indifferent Gentlemen that have trauiled in that tongue, discerne by their twopenie pamphlets: & no meruaile though their home-born mediocritie be such in this matter; for what can be hoped of those, that thrust *Elisium* into hell and have not learned so long as they lived in the spheres the iust measure of the Horizon without an hexameter. Sufficeth them to bodge vp a blank verse with ifs and ands, & other while for recreation after their candle stuff, having starched their beards most curiouslie, to make a peripateticall path into the inner parts of the Citie, & spend to or three howers in turning ouer French *Dowdie*, where they attract more infection in one minute, than they can do eloquence all dayes of their life, by conuersing with anie Authors of like argument. But least in this declamatorie vaine, I should condemne all and commend none, I will propound to your learned imitation, those men of import, that haue laboured with credit in this laudable kinde of translation.

161. 12 November 1589: 'the Privy Council instructs the Archbishop of Canterbury to join the Lord Mayor of London and the Master of the Revels to scrutinise all books of plays then being used by the players, and to compel them to strike out improprieties towards Divinity and State or be made for ever incapable of their professions'.

162. 1589: Ovid's *Metamorphoses* printed by Richard Field.

163. By 1589: Shakespeare studies Ovid (the *Metamorphoses* mentioned in *Titus Andronicus*, IV.i.42, a play which Jonson in his *Bartholomew Fair* of 1614 implies was written between 1584 and 1589).

164. *C.* 1589: George Peele, *Edward I*: 'Shake thy speres in honour of his name/Vnder whose roialtie thou wearst the same.'

165. 6 March 1590: 'Thomas Green alias Shakespeare' buried (the degree of kinship is uncertain).

166. 29 December 1590: Spenser, *The Teares of the Muses* registered; published in 1591:

> And he the man, whom Nature selfe had made
> To mock her selfe, and Truth to imitate,
> With kindly counter vnder Mimick shade,
> Our pleasant *Willy*, ah is dead of late:
> With whom all ioy and iolly merriment
> Is also deaded, and in dolour drent.
>
> In stead thereof scoffing Scurrilitie,
> And scornfull Follie with Contempt is crept,
> Rolling in rymes of shameles ribaudrie
> Without regard, or due Decorum kept,
> Each idle wit at will presumes to make
> And doth the Learneds taske vpon him take.

But that same gentle Spirit, from whose pen
Large streames of honnie and sweete Nectar flowe,
Scorning the boldness of such base-borne men,
Which dare their follies forth so rashly throw;
Doth rather choose to sit in idle Cell,
Than so himself to mockery to sell.

167. *C.* 1590: Shakespeare under the patronage of a young kinsman of the Ardens (his mother's family), Henry Wriothesley, the Catholic 3rd Earl of Southampton.

168. ?1590–1600: '[Shakespeare] had the honour to meet with many great and uncommon marks of favour and friendship from the Earl of Southampton . . . There is one instance so singular in the Magnificence of this Patron of Shakespear's, that if I had not been assur'd that the story was handed down by Sir William D'Avenant, who was probably very well acquainted with his Affairs, I should not have ventur'd to have inserted, that my Lord Southampton, at one time, gave him a thousand pounds, to go through with a purchase which he heard he had a mind to. A Bounty very great, and very rare at any time' (Rowe 1709).

169. 1591: '*The Troublesome Reign of Iohn King of England*, with the discoverie of King Richard Cordelions Base sonne (vulgarly named, the Bastard Fawconbridge): also the death of King Iohn at Swinstead Abbey. As it was (sundry times) publikely acted by the Queenes Maiesties Players, in the honourable Citie of London. Imprinted at London for Sampson Clarke, and are to be solde at his shop, on the backe-side of the Royall Exchange.'

170. 1591: 'The Second part of *the troublesome Raigne of King John*, conteining the death of Arthur Plantaginet, the landing of Lewes, and the poysning of King Iohn at Swinstead Abbey. As it was (sundry times) publikely acted by the Queenes Maiesties Players' [etc., as above].

171. 1591: Spenser, *Colin Clout's Come Home Again*:

And there though last not least is *Aetion*,
A gentler shepherd may no where be found:
Whose *Muse* full of high thoughts inuention,
Doth like himself heroically sound.

172. *C.* March 1592: John Shakespeare listed as a recusant, i.e. one who 'refused obstinately to resort to the church', with eight other names, annotated; 'Wee suspect theese nyne persons next ensuing absent themselves for feare of process' (see **181**).

173. 3 March 1592: 'Harey the vj £3.16.8' acted by the Admiral's Men at the Rose theatre, Bankside.

174. 7, 11, 16, 28 March, 5 April 1592, as **173**; the takings continue high.

175. 11 April 1592: 'Tittus & Vespacia' (? *Titus and Vespasian*, perhaps an early version of *Titus Andronicus*) performed by Strange's Men (? at Newington Butts), and again on 20 April, 3, 8, 15 and 24 May, and 6 June.

176. 13, 21 April, 4, 7, 14, 19, 25 May, 12, 19 June 1592: further performances of 'Hary the vi' at the Rose.

177. 8 August 1592: Thomas Nashe, *Pierce Penniless* entered on the Stationers' Register and published in that year. 'How it would haue ioyed braue Talbot (the terror of the French) [that bracketed phrase occurs verbatim in *1 Henry VI*, I.iv.42, a text not published until 1623] to thinke that after he had lyne two hundred years in his Tombe, hee should triumphe againe on the Stage, and haue his bones newe embalmed with the teares of ten thousand spectators at least (at seuerall times) who, in the Tragedian that represents his person, imagine they behold him fresh bleeding . . . no immortalitie can be giuen a man on earth like unto plays . . . what a glorious thing it is to have Henry the Fifth represented on the Stage, leading the French king prisoner, and forcing both him and the Dolphin to swear fealty' [cf the final scene of *The Famous Victories of Henry the Fifth* (197)].

178. 21 August 1592: John Shakespeare helped to value the goods of 'Henry Feelde (**96**) late of Stretford vppon Avon . . . Tanner, now decessed'.

179. 3 September 1592: death of Robert Greene. His autobiographical *Groats-worth of Witte, bought with a million of Repentance*, 'published at his dyeing request' in that year, contains an epistle

> To those Gentlemen his Quondam acquaintance, that spend their wits in making plaies, R.G. wisheth a better exercise, and wisdome to preuent his extremities.
>
> If wofull experience may move you (Gentlemen) to beware, or unheard of wretchednes intreate you to take heed: I doubt not but you wil looke backe with sorrow on your time past, and indeuour with repentance to spend that which is to come.
>
> Wonder not (for thee wil I first begin) thou famous gracer of Tragedians [= Christopher Marlowe], that *Greene*, who hath said with thee (like the foole in his heart) There is no God, shoulde now giue glorie vnto his greatness: for penetrating is his power, his hand lyes heauie vpon me, hee hath spoken unto mee with a voice of thunder, and I have felt he is a God that can punish enemies. Why should thy excellent wit, his gift, bee so blinded, that thou shouldst give no glory to the giver? Is it pestilent Machiuilian pollicy that thou hast studied? O peevish follie! What are his rules but mere confused mockeries, able to extirpate in small time the generation of mankind. For if *Sic volo, sic*

iubeo, hold in those that are able to command, and if it be lawful *Fas & nefas* to do any thing that is beneficiall; onely Tyrants should possesse the earth, and they striuing to exceed in tyrannie, should to each other be a slaughter man; till the mightiest outliving all, one stroke were left for Death, that in one age mans life should end. The brocher of this Diabolicall Atheisme [= Machiavelli 1467–1527] is dead, and in his life had neuer the felicitie hee aimed at; but as he began in craft; liud in feare and ended in despaire. *Quam inscrutabilia sunt Dei iudicia?* This murderer of many brethren, had his conscience seared like *Caine*: this betrayer of him that gaue his life for him, inherited the portion of Iudas: this Apostata perished as ill as Iulian: and wilt thou my friend be his disciple? Looke but to me, by him perswaded to that libertie, and thou shalt find it an infernall bondage. I knowe the least of my demerits merit this miserable death, but wilfull striuing against knowne truth, exceedeth all the terrors of my soule. Defer not (with me) till this last point of extremitie; for litle knowst thou how in the end thou shalt be visited.

With thee I ioyne young Iuvenall [= Thomas Nashe], that byting Satyrist, that lastly with mee together writ a Comedie [? *Knack to Know a Knave*]. Sweet boy, might I aduise thee, be aduisde, and get not many enemies by bitter words: inveigh against vaine men, for thou canst do it, no man better, no man so well: thou hast a libertie to reprooue all, and name none; for one being spoken to, all are offended; none being blamed no man is iniured. Stop shallow water still running, it will rage, or tread on a worm and it will turn: then blame not Schollers vexed with sharpe lines, if they reproue thy too much liberty of reproofe.

And thou [= George Peele] no lesse deseruing than the other two, in some things rarer, in nothing inferiour; driuen (as my selfe) to extreme shifts, a little haue I to say to thee: and were it not an idolatrous oth, I would swear by sweet S. George, thou art vnworthy better hap, sith thou dependest on so meane a stay.

Base-minded men all three of you [Marlowe, Nashe, Peele], if by my miserie you be not warnd: for vnto none of you (like mee) sought those burres to cleaue: those Puppets (I meane) that spake from our mouths, those Anticks garnisht in our colours. Is it not strange, that I, to whom they all haue beene beholding: is it not like that you, to whome they all haue beene beholding, shall (were yee in that case as I am now) bee both at once of them forsaken?

Yes trust them not: for there is an vpstart Crow, beautified with our feathers, that with his *Tygers hart wrapt in a Players hyde,* supposes he is as well able to bombast out a blanke verse as the best of you: and beeing an absolute *Johannes factotum*, is in his owne conceit that onely Shake-scene in a countrey. O that I might intreat your rare wits to be imploied in more profitable courses: and let those Apes imitate your past excellence, and neuer more acquaint them with your admired inuentions. I knowe the best husband of you all will neuer prove an Vsurer, and the kindest of them all will neuer prove a kind nurse: yet whilest you may, seeke you better Maisters: for it is pittie men of such rare wits, should be subject to the pleasure of such rude grooms.

In this I might insert two more [? e.g. Thomas Lodge], that both haue writ against these buckram Gentlemen: but lette their owne workes serue to witness against their owne wickednesse, if they perseuere to maintain any more such peasants.

For other new-commers, I leaue them to the mercie of these painted monsters, who (I doubt not) will drive the best minded to despise them: for the rest, it skils not though they make a ieast at them.

But now returne I againe to you three, knowing my miserie is to you no newes: and let me hartily intreat you to be warned by my harms. Delight not (as I haue done) in irreligious oathes; for from the blasphemers house, a curse shall not depart. Despise drunkennes, which wasteth the wit, and maketh men all equall vnto beasts. Flie lust, as the deathsman of the soule, and defile not the Temple of the holy Ghost. Abhorre those Epicures, whose loose life hath made religion lothsome to your eares: and when they sooth you with tearms of Maistership, remember *Robert Greene*, whom they haue often so flattered, perishes now for want of comfort. Remember Gentlemen, your liues are so many lighted Tapers, that are with care deliuered to all of you to maintaine: these with wind-puft wrath may be extinguisht, which drunkennes put out, which negligence let fall: for mans time is not of it selfe so short, but it is more shortned by sinne. The fire of my light is now at the last snuffe, and for want of wherewith to sustain it, there is not substance left for life to feede on. Trust not then (I beseech ye) to such weake staies; for they are as changeable in mind, as in many attyres. Well, my hande is tyred, and I am forst to leaue where I would begin: for a whole booke cannot containe their wrongs, which I am forst to knit vp in some few lines of words.

Desirous that you should liue, though himselfe be dying:

Robert Greene

Now to all men I bid farewel in like sort, with this conceited Fable of that old Comedian *Aesope*.

An Ant and a Grasshopper walking together on a
Greene . . . the Grashopper yeelding to the wethers extremitie,
died comfortles without remedy. Like him my selfe: like me,
shall all that trust to friends or times inconstancie.

An earlier anecdote runs thus:

With this lament, Roberto, [i.e. Greene] laid his head on his
hand, and leant his elbow on the earth, sighing out sadly, *Heu
patior telis vulnera facta meis!*

On the other side of the hedge sate one that heard his sorrow:
who getting ouer, came towards him and brake off his passion.
When approached, hee saluted *Roberto* in this sort.

Gentleman quoth hee (for so you seeme) I haue by chance
heard you discourse some part of your greefe; which appeareth
to be more than you will discouer, or I can conceipt. But if you
vouchsafe such simple comforte as my abilitie may yeeld, assure
your selfe, that I wil indeuour to doe the best, that either may
procure you profite, or bring you pleasure: the rather, for that I
suppose you are a scholler, and pittie it is men of learning should
live in lacke.

Roberto wondring to heare such good wordes, for that this iron
age affoordes few that esteeme of vertue; returnd him thankfull
gratulations, and (vrgde by necessitie) vttered his present griefe,
beseeching his aduise how he might be imployed. Why, easily
quoth hee, and greatly to your benefite: for men of my profession gette by schollers their whole living. What is your
profession, said *Roberto*? Truly sir, saide hee, I am a player. A
player, quoth *Roberto*, I tooke you rather for a Gentleman of
great liuing, for if by outward habit men should be censured,
I tell you, you would be taken for a substantiall man. So am I
where I dwell (quoth the player) reputed able at my proper cost
to build a Windmill. What though the world once went hard
with me, when I was faine to carry my playing Fardle a foote-
backe; *Tempora mutantur*, I know you know the meaning of it
better than I, but thus I conster it, its otherwise now; for my very
share in playing apparell will not be sold for two hundred
pounds. Truly (said *Roberto*) tis straunge, that you should so
prosper in that vayne practise, for that it seemes to mee your
voice is nothing gratious. Nay then, saide the Player, I mislike
your judgement: why, I am as famous for Delphrigus, & the King
of Fairies, as euer was any of my time. The twelue labors of
Hercules haue I terribly thundered on the Stage, and plaid three
Scenes of the Deuill in the High way to heauen. Haue ye so?
(saide *Roberto*) then I pray you pardon me. Nay more (quoth the
Player) I can serue to make a pretie speech, for I was a country

Author, passing at a Morrall, for twas I that pende the Morrall of mans witte, the Dialogue of Diues, and for seuen yeers space was absolute Interpreter to the puppets. But now my Almanacke is out of date:

> The people make no estimation
> of Morrals teaching education.

Was not this prettie for a plaine rime extempore? if ye will ye shall haue more. Nay its enough, said *Roberto*, but how meane you to vse me? Why sir, in making Playes, said the other, for which you shall be well paid, if you will take the paines.

Roberto perceiuing no remedie, thought best in respect of his present necessitie, to try his wit, & went with him willingly: who lodgd him at the Townes end in a house of retayle, where what happened our Poet [= Greene] you shall after heare. . . .

180. 20 September to 8 December 1592: the London theatres closed because of plague.

181. 25 September 1592: the Privy Council commissioners for Warwickshire, headed by Sir Thomas Lucy, again name the same nine recusants (**172**) including John Shakespeare, with the marginal annotation 'it is said that these laste nine coom not to Churche for feare of processe for debte'. The others were 'Mr, John Wheeler. Iohn Wheeler his sonne. Mr. Nycholas Barnehurste. Tho: James alias Gyles. William Bainton. Richard Harington. William Fluellen. George Bardolphe'. A supplementary list includes 'Julian Coorte'.

182. December 1592: Henry Chettle, *Kind-Hart's Dream*:

To the Gentlemen Readers

It hath beene a custome Gentlemen (to my mind commendable) among former Authors (whose works are no lesse beautified with eloquente phrase, than garnished with excellent example) to begin an exordium to the Readers of their time, much more convenient I take it, should the writers in these daies (wherein that grauitie of enditing, by the elder exercised, is not obseru'd, nor that modest decorum kept, which they continued) submit their labours to the favourable censures of their learned ouerseers.

For, seeing nothing can be said, that hath not been before said, the singularitie of some mens conceits (otherwayes exellent well deseruing) are no more to be soothed, than the peremptorie posies of two very sufficient Translators commended.

To come in print is not to seeke praise, but to craue pardon: I am vrgd to the one, and bold to begge the other; he that offends being forst, is more excusable than the wilful faultie, though both be guilty, there is difference in the guilt. To observe

custome, and auoid as I may, cauill, opposing your fauors against
my feare, Ile shew reason for my present writing, and after
proceed to sue for pardon.

About three moneths since [on 3 September] died M. *Robert
Greene*, leaving many papers in sundry Booke sellers hands,
among other his Groats-worth of wit, in which a letter written to
divers play-makers, is offensively by one or two of them taken,
and because on the dead they cannot be avenged, they wilfully
forge in their conceits a liuing Author: and after tossing it to and
fro, no remedy, but it must light on me, How I haue, all the time
of my conuersing in printing, hindred the bitter inueying against
schollers, it hath been very well knowne, and how in that I dealt
I can sufficiently prooue. With neither of them that take offence
[Shakespeare and Marlowe] was I acquainted, and with one of
them [Marlowe] I care not if I never be: The other, whome at
that time I did not so much spare, as since I wish I had, for that
I haue moderated the heate of liuing writers, and might haue
vsde my owne discretion (especially in such a case) the Author
beeing dead, that I did not, I am as sory, as if the originall fault
had been my fault, because my selfe haue seene his demeanor
no lesse ciuill than he exelent in the qualitie he professes [as
actor or playwright]: Besides, divers of worship [= highly-placed
personages] haue reported his vprightnes of dealing, which
argues his honesty, and his fa[ce]tious grace in writing, which
aprooues his Art. For the first [Marlowe], whose learning I
reverence, and at the perusing of *Greenes* Booke, stroke out what
then in conscience I thought he in some displeasure writ: or had
it beene true, yet to publish it, was intollerable: him I would
wish to vse me no worse than I deserue. I had onely in the copy
this share, it was il written, as sometime *Greenes* hand was none
of the best, licensd it must be, ere it could be printed which could
neuer be if it might not be read. To be breife I writ it over, and
neare as I could, followed the copy, only in that letter [i.e. in
Greene's section entitled 'To those Gentlemen', etc.] I put something out, but in the whole booke not a worde in, for I protest it
was all *Greenes* not mine nor Maister *Nashes*, as some uniustly
haue affirmed. Neither was he the writer to an Epistle to the
second part of Gerileon, though by the workemans error *T.N.*
were set to the end: that I confesse to be mine, and repent it not.

Thus Gentlemen, hauing noted the priuate causes, that made
me nominate my selfe in printe: being aswell to purge Master
Nashe of that he did not, as to justifie what I did, and withall to
confirm what M. *Greene* did; I beseech yee accept the publike
cause, which is both the desire of your delight, and common
benefite: for though the toye bee shadowed vnder the Title of

Kind-hearts Dreame, it discouers the false hearts of diuers that wake to commit mischiefe. Had not the former reasons been, it had come forth without a father: and then should I haue had no cause to feare offending, or reason to sue for fauour. Now am I in doubt of the one, though I hope of the other; which if I obtaine, you shall bind me hereafter to bee silent, till I can present yee with some thing more acceptable.

Henrie Chettle.

183.　1592: John Shakespeare again recorded as a glover.

184.　6, 15 and 25 January 1593: *Titus Andronicus* performed by Strange's Men.

185.　2 February 1593 to June 1594: the London theatres closed because of plague.

186.　18 April 1593: Richard Field, 'Entred for his copie under thandes of the Archbisshop of Canterbury and master warden Stirrop, a booke intituled, Venus and Adonis'; published that September, 'Imprinted by Richard Field, and are to be sold at the signe of the white Greyhound in Paules Church-yard' with the epigraph:

Vilia miretur vulgus: mihi flavus Apollo
pocula Castalia plena ministret aqua
[let the common herd marvel at cheap things; for me, let golden Apollo pour full cups from the Castalian springs]

and the dedication:

To THE RIGHT HONOURABLE
Henry Wriothesley, Earle of Southampton,
and Baron of Titchfield.

Right Honourable, I know not how I shall offend in dedicating my unpolisht lines to your Lordship, nor how the world will censure mee for choosing so strong a proppe to support so weake a burthen, onelye if your Honour seeme but pleased, I account myself highly praised, and vowe to take advantage of all idle hours, till I have honoured you will some graver labour. But if the first heire of my invention prove deformed, I shall be sorie it had so noble a god-father: and never after eare so barren a land, for feare it yield me still so bad a harvest. I leave it to your Honourable suruey, and your Honor to your hearts content, which I wish may alwaies answere your own wish, and the worlds hopefull expectation.

Your Honors in all dutie,
William Shakespeare.

187.　20 June 1593: 'Thomas [future grandson-in-law, d. 1647] filius Anthonij Nash generosi' [= gentleman] christened.

188. 30 June 1593: Thomas Nashe *Terrors of the Night* registered.

189. 30 December 1593, 1, 10 and 27 January 1594, *Buckingham* [? a version of *Richard III*] played by Sussex's Men.

190. 23, 28 January, 6 February 1594: *Titus Andronicus* played by Sussex's Men.

191. 1 February 1594: 'R.B. Gent.' *Greenes Funeralls* contains the stanza:

> Greene, is the pleasing Object of an eie:
> Greene, pleasde the eies of all that lookt vppon him.
> Greene, is the ground of every Painters die:
> Greene, gave the ground, to all that wrote vpon him.
> Nay more the men, that so Eclipst his fame:
> purloynde his Plumes, can they deny the same?

192. 6 February 1594: *Titus Andronicus* entered for his copy by John Danter 'under thandes of bothe the wardens a booke intituled a Noble Roman Historye of Tytus Andronicus'; first edition published in quarto later that year 'The Most Lamentable Romaine Tragedy of Titus Andronicus: As it was Plaide by the Right Honourable the Earl of Darbie [as Ferdinando, Lord Strange had become on 25 September 1593], Earle of Pembrooke, and Earl of Sussex their servants. Printed by John Danter, and are to be sold by Edward White and Thomas Millington, at the little North doore of Paules at the signe of the Gunne'.

193. 12 March 1594: 'Thomas Myllington. Entred for his copie vnder the handes of bothe the wardens a booke intituled, the first parte of the Contention of the twoo famous houses of york and Lancaster with the death of the good Duke Humfrey and the banishment and deathe of the duke of Suffolk and the tragicall ende of the prowd Cardinall of winchester with the notable rebellion of Iack Cade and the duke of yorks first clayme vnto the Crowne', published that year with that title, 'Printed by Thomas Creede for Thomas Millington and are to be sold at his shop vnder Saint Peters Church in Cornwall'.

194. 2 May 1594: 'Peter Short. Entred to him for his copie vnder mr warden Cawoods hande a booke intituled A pleasant Conceyted historie called the Tayminge of a Shrowe', published that year under that title 'As it was sundry times acted by the Right honorable the Earle of Pembrook his seruants. Printed at London for Peter Short and are to be sold by Cutbert Burbie, at his shop at the Royall Exchange.'

195. 9 May 1594: Master Harrison Senior Entred for his copie vnder thand of Master Cawood Warden, a booke intituled the Ravyshement of Lucrece', published later that year, 'Printed by Richard Field (**96**), for John Harrison, and are to be sold at the signe of the white Greyhound in Paules Church-yard'. It is dedicated:

To the Right Honourable, Henry Wriothesley, Earle of
Southampton, and Baron of Titchfield.

The love I dedicate to your Lordship is without end: wherof
this Pamphlet without beginning is but a superfluous Moity. The
warrant I have of your honourable disposition, not the worth of
my untutored lines, makes it assured of acceptance. What I have
done is yours, what I have to do is yours, being part in all I have,
deuoted yours. Were my worth greater, my duety would show
greater, meane time, as it is, it is bound to your Lordship: To
whom I wish long life still lengthened with all happinesse.

Your Lordships in all duety.

William Shakespeare.

196. Early 1594: second edition of *Venus and Adonis* (**186**).

197. 14 May 1594: Thomas Creede. 'Entred for his copie vnder thand of
mr Cawood warden a booke intituled The famous victories of
henrye the ffyft conteyninge the honorable battle of Agincourt.'

198. *C.* May 1594: formation of a new theatre company, the Lord
Chamberlain's Men (**203**).

199. 3 June 1594: 'Beginning at Newington, my Lord Admiral's Men
and my Lord Chamberlain's Men, as followeth', including *Hamlet*
(9 June), *Titus Andronicus* (5, 12 June) and *The Taming of A Shrew*
(11 June).

200. 25 June 1594: rights in *Venus and Adonis* transferred from Richard
Field to John Harrison.

201. 20 July 1594: Thomas Creede. 'Entred for his Copie under thandes
of the wardens. The lamentable Tragedie of Locrine, the eldest son
of K. Brutus discoursinge the warres of the Brittans etc.', published
in 1595.

202. 3 September 1594: 'Master Windet Enterd for his copie vnder
thandes of master Hartwell and the wardens A book entituled
Willobye his avisa or the true picture of a modest maid and of a
chaste and Constant wife'; published anonymously that year 'In
Hexameter verse. The like argument wherof, was neuer heretofore
published./Read the preface to the Reader before you enter farther./A vertuous woman is the crowne of her husband, but she
that maketh him ashamed, is a corruption in his bones. Prouerb.
12.4/. Imprinted . . . by John Windet.'

The Preface to the Reader says that 'there is some thing under
these false names and showes that hath bene done truely'. A
prefatory poem contains the strophe:

> Though Collatine haue deerely bought
> to high renowne, a lasting life,
> and found, that most in vaine haue sought,
> to have a Faire, and Constant wife,

> yet Tarquyne pluckt his glistering grape,
> and Shake-speare, paints poore Lucrece rape.

This is the earliest known direct reference to Shakespeare (apart from his christening) found in any dated or datable source.

Canto XLIII is prefaced thus:

> Henrico Willobego.   Italo-Hispalensis.
> H.W. being sodenly infected with the contagion of a fantasticall fit, at the first sight of *A*, pyneth a while in secret griefe, at length not able any longer to indure the burning heate of so fervent a humour, bewrayeth the secresy of his disease vnto his familiar frend W.S. who not long before had tryed the curtesy of the like passion, and was now newly recouered of the like infection [i.e. the infatuation was at an end by 1594]; yet finding his frend let bloud in the same vain, he took pleasure for a tyme to see him bleed, & in steed of stopping the issue, he inlargeth the wound, with the sharpe rasor of a willing conceit, perswading him that he thought it a matter very easy to be compassed, & no doubt with payne, diligence & some cost in time to be obtayned. Thus this miserable comforter comforting his frend with an impossibilitie, eyther for that he now would secretly laugh at his frends folly, that had given occasion not long before vnto others to laugh at his owne, or because he would see whether an other could play his part better then himselfe, & in vewing a far off the course of this louving Comedy, he determined to see whether it would sort to a happier end for this new actor, then it did for the old [cf Sonnet 138.10 'I am old'] player [Sonnet 110.1 'made myself a motley to the view']. But at length this Comedy was like to have growen to a Tragedy, by the weeke & feeble estate that H.W. was brought vnto, by a desperate vewe of an impossibility of obtaining his purpose, til Time & Necessity, being his best Phisitions brought him a plaster, if not to heale, yet in part to ease his maladye. In all which discourse is liuely represented the unrewly rage of unbrydeled fancy, hauing the raines to roue at liberty, with the dyuers & sundry changes of affections & temptations, which Will [? another deliberate allusion to the Sonnets], set loose from Reason, can deuise, &c.'

There follows a long verse dialogue between 'H.W.' and 'Avisa', with contributions from 'W.S.'

203. 26, 27 December 1594: 'Willm. Kempe, Willm. Shakespeare, & Richarde Burbage seruantes to the Lord Chamberleyne' were paid for Court performances on those days.

204. 28 December 1594: a version of *The Comedy of Errors* performed at Gray's Inn.

205. 1594: Thomas Nashe, *The Unfortunate Traveller* is dedicated:

To the Right Honourable Lord Henry Wriothesley Earl of
Southampton, and Baron of Titchfield . . .
. . . Unretrievably perisheth that booke whatsoever to wast
paper, which on the diamond rocke of your judgement chanceth
to be shipwrackt. A dere lover and cherisher you are, as well of
the lovers of Poets, as of Poets themselves.

Bibliography

The following comprehensive list, which includes sources consulted as well as those cited, is designed to aid further research and reflection. Items prefixed[†] rebut, while those prefixed* exemplify, the attitudes against which this book is directed. None of the former has ever been disproved, or indeed seriously discussed; all of the latter (to which selected rejections, refutations, or recantations have been added in square brackets) incorporate unproved preconceptions about how, what or when Shakespeare must or must not have written. Dates given in the text are those of original publication, but page numbers cited there are those of the editions specified below.

CHum	*Computers and the Humanities*
HamS	*Hamlet Studies*
LLC	*Literary and Linguistic Computing*
LRB	*London Review of Books*
NYRB	*New York Review of Books*
N&Q	*Notes and Queries*
PMLA	*Publications of the Modern Language Association*
ShJ	*Shakespeare Jahrbuch*
ShN	*Shakespeare Newsletter*
ShS	*Shakespeare Survey*
SQ	*Shakespeare Quarterly*
TES	*Times Educational Supplement*
THES	*Times Higher Education Supplement*
TLS	*Times Literary Supplement*

Abbott, E. *A Shakespearean Grammar*, 1869.
Adams, J. 'A New Signature of Shakespeare?', *Bulletin of the John Rylands Library*, xxvi, 1942–3, 256–9.
Akrigg, G. *Shakespeare and the Earl of Southampton*, 1968.
†Albright, E. *Dramatic Publication in England*, 1927.
*Alexander, N. 'Once more unto the text', *TLS*, 29 July 1983, 815 [Sams 1985c].
*Alexander, P. '*2 Henry VI* and the copy for the *Contention*' and '*3 Henry VI* and *Richard Duke of York*', *TLS*, 9 Oct. and 13 Nov. 1924 [see 1929].
*——— 'The Taming of A Shrew', *TLS*, 16 Sept. 1926, 614 [Sams 1983, 1985c; Wells 1986, 29; Taylor 1988, 169]
*——— *Shakespeare's Henry VI and Richard III*, 1929 [Greer 1933, 1956, 1957; Richardson 1953; Prouty 1954; Craig 1961; Sams 1983, 1989a, etc.; Urkowitz 1986a; Jofen 1987; Urkowitz 1988c].
*——— *Shakespeare's Life and Art*, 1939.
*——— *A Shakespeare Primer*, 1951.
*——— 'A Case of Three Sisters', *TLS*, 8 July 1965, 588.
*——— 'The Original Ending of *The Taming of the Shrew*', *SQ* xx, 1969, 111–16 [Sams 1983, 1985c].

Anders, H. *Shakespeare's Books*, 1904.

Anon., *The Cobbler of Canterburie*, 1590.

Anon., '*Edmund Ironside* Performed and Debated at Virginia-by-the-Sea Festival', *ShN*, 38, 1988, 4.

Anon., in *Essay against too much Reading*, 1728, cited in Chambers 1930, ii. 270–71.

Anon., in MS notes, 1748, cited in Halliwell-Phillipps 1887, ii. 286.

Anon., *The Parnassus Plays* (1598–1601), ed. J. Leishman, 1949.

Arber, E., ed. *Transcript of the Registers of the Company of Stationers, 1554–1640*, 5 vols, 1875–94.

Arden, R. *A Nest of Ninnies*, 1608.

†Armstrong, E. *Shakespeare's Imagination*, 1946, 2/1963.

†Arnold, M. Sonnet, 'Shakespeare', by 1849.

*Attawater, A. 'Shakespeare's Sources', in *A Companion to Shakespeare Studies*, 1941.

†Aubrey, J. 'William Shakespeare', *c.* 1681, in *Brief Lives* ed. Dick, 1949, reissued 1972, 334–5; facsimiles in Schoenbaum 1975, 58 and 205.

B., C. *The Ghost of Richard the Third*, 1614, cited in Chambers 1930, ii. 219.

B., R. *Greene's Funeralls*, 1594, cited in Chambers 1930, ii. 190.

†Bains, Y. 'Shakespeare's Revision of *Hamlet*', Symposium on *Hamlet*, University of Arkansas, Fayetteville, 6–8 March 1987.

†———— 'The Bad Quarto of Shakespeare's *Romeo and Juliet* and the Theory of Memorial Reconstruction', the Sixth Citadel Conference on Literature, Charleston, South Carolina, 10–12 March 1988.

†———— 'The Bad Quarto of Shakespeare's *Romeo and Juliet* and the Theory of Memorial Reconstruction', *ShJ* 126, 1990, 164–73.

†———— 'The Bad Quarto of Shakespeare's *The Merry Wives of Windsor* and the Theory of Memorial Reconstruction', *ShN* 3, 1990, 36.

†———— 'The Bad Quarto of Shakespeare's *The Merry Wives of Windsor* and the Theory of Memorial Reconstruction', Malone Society Meeting, Shakespeare Institute, Stratford on Avon, 29 June–1 July 1991.

†———— 'Making Sense of some Passages in the 1602 Quarto of *The Merry Wives of Windsor*', *N&Q* ccxxxvii, 1992, 322–6.

†———— 'Assessing the Incidence of Corrupt Passages in the First Quarto of Shakespeare's *Hamlet*', *N&Q* ccxxxviii, 1993, 186–92.

†———— 'Problems of Sense and Nonsense in the 1600 Quarto of Shakespeare's '*Henry V*', conference on Literary Theory and the Practice of Editing, University of Liverpool, 10–12 July 1993.

†———— 'Loose Ends and Inconsistencies in the First Quarto of Shakespeare's *Hamlet*', *HamS* (forthcoming).

†———— *Making Sense of the First Quartos of Shakespeare's Romeo and Juliet, Henry V, The Merry Wives of Windsor and Hamlet* (forthcoming).

Baker, O. *In Shakespeare's Warwickshire and the Unknown Years*, 1937.

Bald, R. 'The Book of Sir Thomas More and its problems', *ShS* 2, 1949, 44–65.

*Baldwin, T. *Shakespeare's 'Small Latine and Lesse Greeke'*, 1944 [J. Thompson 1952, 154].

———— *Shakespeare's Love's Labour's Won*, 1957.

Bancroft, T. *Epigrammes*, 1639.

Barnes, J. in MS, *c.* 1690, attrib. W. Chetwood, q.v.

Barnfield, R. *Poems in Divers Humours*, 1598, cited in Chambers 1930, ii. 195.

Barnstorff, D. *A Key to Shakespeare's Sonnets*, 1862.

*Barr, J. personal communication, 8 Oct. 1990.

*Bartlett, H.C. *Mr. William Shakespeare: Original and Early Editions of his Quartos and Folios, his Source Books, and those containing Contemporary Notices*, 1922.

*Barton, A. in *Hamlet*, ed. Spencer 1980, 15 [Sams 1988c].

Bearman, R. letter, 29 Jan. 1993.
—— *Shakespeare in the Stratford Records*, 1994.
Beaumont, F. Ms poem, *c.* 1615, cited in Chambers 1930, ii. 224.
Bellamy, J. *The Tudor Law of Treason*, 1979.
†Bentham, J. *A Treatise on Judicial Evidence*, 1825.
*Boas, F., ed., *The Taming of a Shrew*, 1908.
—— *Shakespeare and the Universities*, 1923.
*Bond, R., ed., *The Taming of the Shrew*, 1904.
Borromeo, C. *The Testament of the Soule*, 1638.
*Boswell, E., ed., *Edmund Ironside*, Malone Society, 1928.
†Bowden, H. *The Religion of Shakespeare* (chiefly from the writings of the late Mr Richard Simpson, MA), 1899.
*Boyce, C. *Shakespeare A to Z*, 1990.
†Bracy, W. *The Merry Wives of Windsor*, 1952.
Broadbent, C. 'Shakespeare and Shakeshaft', *N&Q* cci, 1956, 154–7.
Bullough, G. *Narrative and Dramatic Sources of Shakespeare*, 8 vols, 1957–75.
†Burgess, A. 'Cygnet of Avon', *Observer*, 2 Feb. 1986.
†Burkhardt, R. *Shakespeare's Bad Quartos*, 1970.
Burton, S. *Shakespeare's Life and Stage*, 1989.
†Butler, E. *The Story of British Shorthand*, 1951.

*Cairncross, A., ed., *3 Henry VI*, 1964.
Caldiero, F. 'Shakespeare's Signature in Lambarde's *Archaionomia*', *N&Q* xxi, 1945, 162–3.
*Callow, S. Radio Three broadcast, promoting Padel, q.v., 8 April 1994.
†Calvert, H. *Shakespeare's Sonnets and Problems of Autobiography*, 1987.
†Campbell, J. *Shakespeare's Legal Acquirements Considered*, 1859.
Capell, E. in MS notes, 1780, cited in Chambers 1930, ii. 289.
†Carlyle, T. *On Heroes and Hero-Worship*, 1842.
Castle, W. source of Dowdall, q.v.
Catalogue of Books, MSS etc. in Stratford on Avon, compiled by F. Wellstood, 1944.
Chalmers, A. *Works of the English Poets*, 1810.
*Chambers, E. *William Shakespeare: A Study of Facts and Problems*, 2 vols, 1930.
*—— *A Short Life of Shakespeare*, 1933.
—— 'William Shakeshafte', in *Shakespearean Gleanings*, 1944.
*—— *Sources for a Biography of Shakespeare*, 1946.
†Chambers, R. 'Shakespeare and the Play of *More*' in *Man's Unconquerable Mind*, 1939, 204–49.
†Chambrun, C. de *Shakespeare Rediscovered*, 1938.
†—— *Shakespeare: A Portrait Restored*, 1957.
*Champion, L. '*The Noise of Threatening Drum*', 1990.
Chettle, H. in *Kind-Hart's Dream*, 1592, cited in Chambers 1930, ii. 189.
—— in *England's Mourning Garment*, 1603, cited in Chambers 1930, ii. 189.
?Chetwood, W. in lost MS, source for Barnes, J., cited in Chambers 1930, ii. 57f.
Cohn, A. *Shakespeare in Germany in the Sixteenth and Seventeenth Centuries*, 1865.
Cooper, S. 1788, cited in Halliwell-Phillipps 1887, ii. 379.
Corathers, D. 'Much Ado', *Dramatics* 88, 1986, 15–17.
†Courthope, W. *A History of English Poetry*, iv, 1903, rev. 1911, 1916.
*Cox, J. 'WS – his marks', *The Times*, 11 Oct. 1984, 13 [Sams 1984b, 1993e].
*—— Section on the will and signatures, in *Shakespeare in the Public Records*, 1985 [Sams 1993e].
†Craig, H. *A New Look at Shakespeare's Quartos*, 1961.
*Craik, T., ed., *The Merry Wives of Windsor*, Oxford 1989 [Sams 1990b, 1991c; Bains 1990 *ShN*, 1992].

*Daniel, P., ed., *The Merry Wives of Windsor*, 1888.

Davies, J. *Scourge of Folly*, 1610, cited in Chambers 1930, ii. 214.

Davies, R. in MS notes, *c.* 1700, cited in Chambers 1930, ii. 255–7.

*Dawson, G. 'Authenticity and Attribution of Written Matter', *English Institute Annual*, 1942 (pubd 1943), 97 [Sams 1993c].

——— 'Shakespeare's Handwriting', *ShS* 42, 1989, 119–28.

——— 'A Seventh Signature for Shakespeare', *SQ* 43, 1992, 72–9.

†Deckner, E. *Die beiden ersten Hamlet-Quartos, Normannia IV*, 1909.

De Groot, J. *The Shakespeares and 'The Old Faith'*, 1946.

De Luna, B. *The Queen Declined: An Interpretation of Willobie his Avisa*, 1970.

Diamond, J. *The Rise and Fall of the Third Chimpanzee*, 1991.

Digges, L. in Shakespeare's *Poems*, 1640, cited in Chambers 1930, ii. 232–4.

Dowdall, mentioned in MS letter, 1693, cited in Chambers 1930, ii. 259.

†Dryden, J. Prologue to *The Tempest*, *c.* 1669.

†——— Prologue to *Troilus and Cressida*, *c.* 1670.

†——— Prologue to *Circe, A Tragedy*, *c.* 1684.

Dugdale, T. *Antiquities of Warwickshire*, 1656.

*Duthie, G. *The 'Bad' Quarto of Hamlet*, 1941 [Craig 1961, 75–83; Weiner 1962; Sams 1983, 1988c; Urkowitz 1988a, 1988b, 1992].

*——— 'The Taming of A Shrew and The Taming of The Shrew', *Review of English Studies* xix, 1943, 337–56 [Sams 1983, 1985c; Wells 1986, 29; Taylor 1988, 169].

*——— , ed., *Shakespeare's King Lear*, Oxford 1949 [Duthie 1960; Urkowitz 1980, 1983; Taylor 1983; Wells 1983].

*——— , ed., with J. Wilson, *King Lear*, Cambridge 1960, 131–2.

Eccles, C. *The Rose Theatre*, 1990.

Eccles, M. *Shakespeare in Warwickshire*, 1961.

Edmund Ironside, see Boswell 1928, Sams 1985f, 1986d.

Edward III, see Wentersdorf 1960, Sams 1986j, Slater 1988, Wells and Taylor 1990.

*Edwards, P. ed., *Hamlet*, New Cambridge Shakespeare, 1985 [Taylor 1988, 400–401].

*Elliott, W. and Valenza, R. 'A Touchstone for the Bard', *CHum* 25, 1991, 199–209.

*Evans, G. 'Shakespeare's text: Approaches and Problems', in *A New Companion to Shakespeare Studies*, ed. Muir and Schoenbaum, 1971.

*——— , ed., *Romeo and Juliet*, 1984 [Bains 1988, Urkowitz 1988a, Bains *ShJ* 1990].

Evans, M., ed., *The Narrative Poems*, New Penguin Shakespeare, 1989.

†Everitt, E. *The Young Shakespeare: Studies in Documentary Evidence, Anglistica II*, 1954.

†——— *Six Early Plays Related to the Shakespeare Canon, Anglistica XIV*, 1965.

*Ewbank, I. 'Shakespearean Constructs', *TLS*, 25 April 1986, 451 [Sams 1986e].

†Ezard, J. 'Bard's play theory backed', *Guardian*, 4 Sept. 1986.

Farmer, R. *An Essay on the Learning of Shakespeare*, 1767 (also in Malone 1821, i. 300).

†Feuillerat, A. *The Composition of Shakespeare's Plays*, 1961.

*Foster, D. 'Master W.H. R.I.P.', *PMLA* 102, i, 1987, 42–54.

*——— review of *Edmund Ironside*: *SQ* 39, 1988, 118–23 [Sams 1988d].

*——— 'Donald Foster replies', *SQ* 39, 1988, 253.

——— 'Reconstructing Shakespeare', *ShN* 4, 1991, 58–9.

†Foster, M. *The Play behind the Play: Hamlet and Quarto One*, 1991.

Fraser, R. *Young Shakespeare*, 1988.

——— *Shakespeare: The later years*, 1992.

Frazer, W. 'Henslowe's "Ne"', *N&Q* ccxxxvi, 1991, 34–5.

*Freeman, A., ed., *2 Henry VI*, Signet 1967–86, 159–63 [see Alexander 1929].
—— *Thomas Kyd*, 1967.
*—— 'Mrs. Shakespeare' *TLS*, 12 March 1993 [Sams 1993c].
†Frey, A., ed., *The Taming of A/The Shrew*, 1888.
Fripp, E. Introduction and notes to *Minutes and Accounts of the Corporation of Stratford-upon-Avon*, 1553–1620, 1926–9.
—— *Shakespeare's Haunts*, 1929.
—— *Shakespeare: Man and Artist*, 2 vols, 1938.
Fuller, T. *Worthies of Warwickshire, c.* 1650.
Fullom, S. *History of William Shakespeare*, 1862.
†Furbank, P. and Owens, W. 'Stylometry and Defoe', Appendix to *The Canonisation of Daniel Defoe*, 1988, 176–83.
†—— 'Dangerous Relations', *The Scriblerian* 33, 1991, 242–4.
†Furnivall, F., ed., *Hamlet* Q1, 1880.

Gabrieli, V. and Melchiori, G., ed., *Sir Thomas More*, 1990.
*Gardner, H. Preface to F. Wilson 1970, q.v.
†George, D. 'Shakespeare and Pembroke's Men', *SQ* 32, 1981, 305–23.
*Gibbons, B., ed., *Romeo and Juliet*, 1980, 2–12.
Gildon, C. *Lives and Characters of the English Dramatic Poets*, 1694, cited in Chambers 1930, ii. 261–2.
—— *Remarks on the Plays of Shakespeare*, 1710, ibid.
*Gill, R., ed., *Dr Faustus*, 1990.
†Giroux, R. *The Book Known as Q*, 1982.
Godshalk, W. 'Shakespeare's Bad Quarto', *TLS* Letters, 17 June 1994.
*Gray, H. 'The First Quarto *Hamlet*', *Modern Language Review* x, 1915, 171–80.
*—— '*Hamlet* Q1 and Mr. Henry David Gray', *PMLA* 43, 1928, 578–82.
Gray, J. *Shakespeare's Marriage, his Departure from Stratford and other Incidents in his Life*, 1905.
Greene, R. *Farewell to Folly*, 1587.
—— *Penelope's Web*, 1587.
—— *Pandosto*, 1588.
—— *Perimedes the Blacksmith*, 1588.
—— *Menaphon*, 1589.
—— *Never Too Late*, 1590.
—— *A Groats-worth of Witte bought with a million of Repentance*, 1592.
—— *Greene's Vision*, 1593.
—— *Friar Bacon and Friar Bungay*, 1594.
—— *The Scottish Historie of James the Fourth*, 1598.
—— *George a Green, the Pinner of Wakefield*, 1599.
—— with Nashe, T. 'a comedy' (?*A Knack to Know a Knave*, 1594).
†Greer, C. 'The York and Lancaster Quarto-Folio Sequence', *PMLA* 48, 1933, 655–705.
†—— 'The Quarto-Folio Relationship in *2* and *3 Henry VI* once again', *N&Q* cci, 1956, 420–21.
†—— 'More about the actor-reporter theory in *Contention* and *True Tragedy*, *N&Q* ccii, 1957, 52–3.
†Greer, G. *Shakespeare*, 1986.
*Greg, W., ed., *The Merry Wives of Windsor, 1602*, Oxford 1910 [Albright 1927; Greg 1951, 1955; Bracy 1952; Craig 1961; Urkowitz 1986a, 1988a, Sams 1990b, 1991c; Bains 1990, *ShN*, 1992].
—— *English Literary Autographs, 1 Dramatists*, 1925.
*——, ed., *True Tragedy of Richard III*, Malone Society, 1929.
*—— *Dramatic Documents from the Elizabethan Playhouses*, 1931.
—— *A Bibliography of the English Printed Drama to the Restoration*, 1939.

*——— *The Editorial Problem in Shakespeare*, 1951.

*——— *The Shakespeare First Folio: Its Bibliographical and Textual History*, 1955.

Grice, E. 'Take a letter, Shakespeare', *Sunday Times*, 19 April 1981, 1, 3; *Toronto Sunday Star*, 26 April 1981, B7.

Gurr, A. 'Shakespeare's First Poem: Sonnet 145', *Essays in Criticism* 21, 1971, 427–9.

*——— 'Paying for Plays'. *TLS*, 15 Feb. 1985, 174.

*——— , ed., *Henry V*, New Cambridge, 1992.

†Halio, J., ed., *King Lear*, New Cambridge, 1994.

Hall, W. letter, 1694, cited in Chambers 1930, ii. 261–2.

*Halliday, F. *The Life of Shakespeare*, 1961.

*——— *Shakespeare in his Age*, 1956.

*——— *A Shakespeare Companion*, 1964.

Halliwell-Phillipps, J. *Observations on the Charlecote Traditions*, 1881.

——— *Outlines of the Life of Shakespeare*, 2 vols, 1887.

†Hamilton, C. *In Search of Shakespeare: A Reconnaissance into the Poet's Life and Handwriting*, 1985.

——— 'A Letter in Shakespeare's Hand', *ShN* 36 1986, 37.

——— personal communication, 30 June 1986.

*Harrison, G., ed., *Hamlet*, 1923 [Sams 1990a].

*——— , ed., *Hamlet*, Penguin, 1937–66.

——— *Elizabethan Plays and Players*, 1956.

*——— , ed., *1–3 Henry VI*, 1959.

——— , ed., *Willobie his Avisa*, 1966.

*Hart, A. *Shakespeare and the Homilies*, 1934.

*——— *Stolne and Surreptitious Copies*, 1942 [Urkowitz 1988a, 1992].

Harvey, G. MS notes, *c.* 1598, cited in Boas 1923, 27–8.

*Hattaway, M., ed., *1–3 Henry VI*, New Cambridge, 1990–93 [Sams 1994b].

*Hawkes, N. 'Computer finds new play by Shakespeare', *Observer*, 6 July 1980, 1.

*——— 'Play on words blanks out the Bard's drama', *Observer*, 12 Jan. 1986, 3.

*——— 'Discovering the truth in a word', *The Times*, 16 Aug. 1990.

*Hawkes, T. *That Shakespeherian Rag*, 1986 [Sams 1994a].

Heal, A. 'A New Shakespeare Signature', *N&Q* clxxxv, 1943, 263.

Hector, L. *The Handwriting of English Documents*, 1966.

Heywood, T. *The Hierarchie of the Blessed Angels*, 1635, cited in Chambers 1930, ii. 219.

*Hibbard, G., ed., *The Taming of the Shrew*, 1968.

*——— , ed., *Hamlet*, 1987.

*Holderness, G., ed., *The Shakespeare Myth*, 1988 [Sams 1989c].

†Holderness, G. and Loughrey, B., ed., *Hamlet*, 1603, 1992.

†——— , ed., *The Taming of A Shrew*, 1993.

†——— 'Shakespeare's Bad Quarto', *TLS* Letters, 4 Feb. 1994 [Vickers 1994, 4 Feb.]; 8 April 1994 [Vickers 1994, 4 March].

Holinshed, R. *The Chronicles of England*, 1577, 2/1587.

*Honigmann, E., ed., *King John*, New Arden, 1954 [Sams 1988a].

——— *The Stability of Shakespeare's Text*, 1965.

*——— , ed., *Richard III*, 1968 [Urkowitz 1986b].

*——— *Shakespeare's Impact on his Contemporaries*, 1982 [Sams 1988a].

*——— *Shakespeare: the 'lost years'*, 1985 [Sams 1985d].

*——— 'Fingerprinting Shakespeare', *NYRB*, 12 Feb. 1987, 23–4 [Sams 1987a].

*——— 'Ernst Honigmann replies', *NYRB*, 7 May 1987, 48.

*Hope, J. *The Authorship of Shakespeare's Plays*, 1994.

*Hoppe, H. *The Bad Quarto of Romeo and Juliet*, 1948.

†Housman, A. 'Introductory Lecture', 1892, in *Selected Prose*, ed. Carter, 1961.
†Hubbard, F. *The First Quarto Edition of Shakespeare's Hamlet*, 1920.

*Ingram, W. and Redpath, T., ed., *Shakespeare's Sonnets*, 1964, 3/1978.
Ionsonus Virbius, 1638.
*Irace, K. 'Origin and Agents of Q1 *Hamlet*', in *The Hamlet First Published*, ed. Clayton, 1992, 90–122 [Urkowitz 1992].
Ireland, S. *Picturesque Views on the Warwickshire Avon*, 1795, 152, cited in Chambers 1930, ii. 297.
Isaac, H. 'Die Sonett-Periode in Shakespeares Leben', *ShJ* xix 1884, 176–264.

*Jackson, McD. 'Shakespeare and *Edmund Ironside*', *N&Q* cviii, 1963, 331–2 [Sams 1986d].
*———— 'Edward III, Shakespeare and Pembroke's Men', *N&Q* ccx, 1965, 329–31.
*———— 'The Transmission of Shakespeare's Text', in *The Cambridge Companion to Shakespeare Studies*, 1986.
*———— 'Editions and Textual Studies', *ShS* 40, 1988, 226.
*———— '*Pericles*, Acts I and II: New Evidence for George Wilkins', *N&Q* ccxxxv, 1990, 192–6 [Sams 1991b].
*———— 'George Wilkins and the First Two Acts of *Pericles*: New Evidence from Function Words', *LLC* vi, 1991, 155–63.
*———— 'Editions and Textual Studies', *ShS* 43, 1991, 266–8.
*———— 'Rhyming in *Pericles*: More Evidence of Dual Authorship', *Studies in Bibliography* xlvi, 1993, 239–49.
*———— 'The Authorship of *Pericles*: The Evidence of Infinitives', *N&Q* ccxxxviii, 1993, 197–200.
*Jenkins, H., ed., *Hamlet*, Arden Shakespeare, 1982 [Sams 1988c, Urkowitz 1988b, 1992, Sprinchorn 1994].
*———— 'The Arden *Hamlet*: Some Reflections a Decade Later', *ShN* 41, 1991, 47.
*———— 'Shakespeare's Bad Quarto', *TLS* Letters, 15 April 1994 [Sprinchorn 1994 a,b,c].
Jofen, J. Foreword to Ule, 1987.
Johnson, G. 'Thomas Pavier, Publisher, 1600–25', *The Library*, March 1992, 12–50.
Johnson, S. *Works* of Shakespeare, 1765 i. clii.
*Jones, J. 'Naming the Bard', *Financial Times*, 1 Feb. 1986 [Sams 1986d].
Jones, T. before 1703, source of Capell, E. q.v.
Jonson, B. *Every Man Out of His Humour*, 1599.
———— *Bartholomew Fair*, 1614.
———— *Conversations with William Drummond*, 1619.
———— 'To . . . Mr. William Shakespeare', in First Folio, 1623.
———— *Ode to Myself*, 1629.
Jordan, J. MSS notes *c.* 1790, in *Original Memoirs and Historical Accounts of the Families of Shakespeare and Hart*, ed. H.P., 1865, etc., cited in Chambers 1930, ii. 293.

*Kay, D. *Shakespeare: His Life, Work and Era*, 1992.
†Keen, A. and Lubbock, R. *The Annotator*, 1954.
†Keeton, G. 'Shakespeare at Law', *Anglo-American Law Review*, April 1974.
*Kerrigan, J., ed., *Love's Labour's Lost*, 1982.
*———— 'Diary', *LRB*, 6 Feb. 1986, 21 [Sams 1986d].
*————, ed., *The Sonnets and A Lover's Complaint*, 1986.
†Knight, W. 'The Seventh Shakespeare Signature', *ShN* 3, 1971.
†———— 'Equity and Mercy in English Law and Drama', *Comparative Drama*, 1972, 51–66.

†——— *Shakespeare's Hidden Life*, 1973.

†——— 'Equity, *The Merchant of Venice* and William Lambarde', *ShS* 27, 1974, 93–107.

†——— 'Translation to Law Language to Stage', *Shakespeare Translation* 8, 1981, 9–15.

†——— 'Equity in Shakespeare and his Contemporaries', *Iowa State Journal of Research* 56, 1, 1981, 67–77.

†——— 'Is *Edmund Ironside* Shakespeare's?', paper to Missouri Philological Association, St. Joseph, Missouri, March 1983; *Missouri Law Review*, 1983.

†——— 'Shakespeare's Court Case', *Law and Critique*, 1991, 103–12.

Kyd, T. *The Spanish Tragedy*, c. 1588.

Lambarde, W. *Archaionomia*, 1568.

Laneham, R. *A Letter Wherein part of the entertainment unto the Queens Maiesty . . . in this Summer's Progress 1575 is signified*, c. 1575.

Lebrecht, N. 'Now, a New Play?', *Sunday Times*, 29 Dec. 1985.

*Lee, S. *A Life of William Shakespeare*, 1898, 7/1915.

*———, ed., *The True Chronicle History of King Leir*, 1900.

Leishman, J., ed., *The Parnassus Plays*, 1949.

L'Estrange, N. MS notes, before 1655; cited in Chambers 1930, ii. 243.

Levi, P. 'Something Useful in the New Shakespeare', *Literary Review* May 1988, 6.

*——— *The Life and Times of William Shakespeare*, 1988 [Sams 1989c].

*——— *A Private Commission: New Verses by Shakespeare*, 1988 [Sams 1993e].

†Littlewood, J. 'The Dilemma of Probability Theory', in *A Mathematician's Miscellany*, 1953.

Lodge, T. *Scyllas Metamorphosis*, 1589.

——— *Wit's Miserie*, 1596.

*Lull, J. 'Forgetting *Hamlet*: The First Quarto and the Folio', in *The Hamlet First Published*, ed. Clayton, 1992, 137–50.

*Mackail, D., ed., *Sonnets*, 1930.

Madden, D. *The Diary of Master William Silence*, 1897.

Maley, W. *A Spenser Chronology*, 1994.

Malone, E. *The Plays and Poems of William Shakespeare*, 1790.

——— 'An Inquiry into the Authenticity of Certain Papers . . .', 1796.

——— *The Plays and Poems of William Shakespeare* (Third Variorum), 1821.

Marder, L. 'Scholars Dispute *Pericles* Data', *ShN* 33, 1983, 38.

——— 'Stylometry: Possibilities and Problems', *ShN* 34, 1984, 4.

——— 'Shakespeare Signatures (?) Seven, Eight and Nine!', *ShN* 34, 1984, 1–2, 14.

——— 'Apologies', *ShN* 34, 1984, 46.

——— 'Eric Sams and Edmund Ironside', *ShN* 36, 1986, 26.

——— 'Thoughts on the "Shakespeare Revolution"', *ShN* 36, 1986, 22.

†——— 'Memorial Reconstruction – a Still-Unsolved Problem', *ShN* 41, 1991, 10.

Marlowe, C. *Tamburlaine*, Parts I and II, c. 1587 (pubd 1590).

——— *Dr Faustus* c. 1588 (pubd 1604).

——— and Nashe, T. *Dido Queen of Carthage*, c. 1592 (pubd 1594).

Matthews, R. 'Wordplay open to interpretation', *Sunday Telegraph*, 11 July 1993.

*Matthews, R. and Merriam, T. 'Neural Computation in Stylometry: An Application to the Works of Shakespeare and Fletcher', *LLC* viii, 1993, 203–9.

——— 'A bard by any other name', *New Scientist*, 22 Jan. 1994, 23–7.

*Maxwell, J., ed., *Titus Andronicus*, Arden Shakespeare, 1953.

McGee, A. *The Elizabethan Hamlet*, 1987.

*McKerrow, R. *Prolegomena for the Oxford Shakespeare*, 1939.

————, ed., *The Works of Thomas Nashe* V, 1966.

McLaren, M. *'By Me . . .'*, *a report upon the apparent discovery of some working notes of William Shakespeare in a sixteenth-century book*, 1949.

McManaway, J. 'John Shakespeare's "Spiritual Testament"', *SQ* xviii, 1967, 197–205.

Meres, F. *Palladis Tamia*, 1598.

Merriam, T. 'The Authorship of *Sir Thomas More*', *ALLC Bulletin* 10, 1982, 1–7 [M. Smith *ShN*, 1984 28, 33, 47, 1985, *Studies in Philology* 1992].

———— 'Taylor's Statistics in *A Textual Companion*', *N&Q* ccxxxiv, 1989, 341–2.

———— 'Chettle, Munday, Shakespeare and *Sir Thomas More*, *N&Q* ccxxxvii, 1992, 336–41 [M. Smith *Studies in Philology* 1992].

———— '*Pericles* I–II revisited and considerations concerning the literary medium as a systematic factor in stylometry', *N&Q* ccxxxvii, 1992, 341–6 [M. Smith 1994].

———— letter, 17 March 1992.

*———— 'Marlowe's Hand in *Edward III*', *LLC* viii, 1993, 60–72.

Metz, G. 'Disputed Shakespearean Texts and Stylometric Analysis', *Transactions of the Society for Textual Scholarship* 2, 1985, 149–71.

Mills, H. *Working with Shakespeare*, 1993.

†Mills, J. *The Authorship of Sir Thomas More* (forthcoming).

†Milton, J. *L'Allegro*, c. 1632.

†———— in Shakespeare's *Poems*, 1640.

†Milward, P. *Shakespeare's Religious Background*, 1973.

*Monsarrat, G. review of *Ironside*, *Etudes Anglaises*, 1987, 203–4.

*Montgomery, W. in Taylor 1988, 175–8, 197–9 [Sams 1989a].

*Morgan, A., ed., *True Tragedy of Richard Duke of York* and *3 Henry VI*, Bankside Shakespeare, 1892.

*Morris, B., ed., *The Taming of the Shrew*, 1981.

*Morton, A. *Literary Detection*, 1978.

*———— interviewed by Hugh Dehn on *Streetlegal* on Channel Four, 6 June 1993.

*Muir, K. *Shakespeare as Collaborator*, 1960.

*———— *Shakespeare's Sonnets*, 1979.

Nashe, T. Preface to Greene's *Menaphon*, 1589.

———— *The Anatomy of Absurdity*, 1589.

———— *The Choice of Valentines*, c. 1590.

———— Preface to Sidney's *Astrophel and Stella*, 1591.

———— *Strange News*, 1592.

———— *Summer's Last Will and Testament*, 1592.

———— *Pierce Penniless*, 1592.

———— *The Terrors of the Night*, 1593.

———— *The Unfortunate Traveller*, 1594.

Nashe, T. and Greene, R. A comedy, c. 1590 (?*A Knack to Know a Knave*, published anonymously in 1594).

Nichols, P. article in *Biographia Britannica*, 1763, cited in Chambers 1930, ii. 287.

Noble, R. *Shakespeare's Biblical Knowledge*, 1935.

*Nye, R. 'Mrs Shakespeare', *TLS* Letters, 12, 26 Feb., 12 March 1993 [Sams 1993b and c].

Oldys, W. from *Marginalia*, c. 1750, cited in Chambers 1930, ii. 281.

*Oliver, H., ed., *The Taming of the Shrew*, Oxford 1982, 2/1984 [Sams 1985c].

Onions, C. *A Shakespeare Glossary*, 1911.

*———— *A Shakespeare Glossary*, enlarged and revised by Robert Eagleson [Sams 1991d].

Ovid, P. *Metamorphoses*, 1502, trans. Golding, 1567, trans. Miller, 1916, trans. Innes, 1955.

*Padel, J. *New Poems by Shakespeare*, 1981.
*Padhi, S. 'Revenge-Plays and Editors', *Encounter* lxxiv/1, Jan.–Feb., 1990, 59–61 [Sams 1990a].
Parnassus Plays, The, see Anon.
†Pascoe, D. review of Oxford Shakespeare, *N&Q* ccxxxv, 1990, 341–2.
Peele, G. *Edward I, c.* 1589 (pubd 1593).
Phillips, R. in *The Monthly Magazine* 1818, xlv. 1. 152, cited in Chambers 1930, ii. 297.
†Pitcher, S. *The Case for Shakespeare's Authorship of 'The Famous Victories of Henry V'*, 1961.
Pliny, *Historia Naturalis*.
Plume, T. MS notes, *c.* 1657, cited in Chambers 1930, ii. 247.
Plutarch, *Lives*, trans. North, 1579.
—— *Makers of Rome*, trans. Scott-Kilvert, 1965.
—— *The Age of Alexander*, trans. Scott-Kilvert, 1973.
*Pollard, A. *Shakespeare's Folios and Quartos*, 1909 [Schamp 1974].
—— ed., *Shakespeare's Hand in the Play of Sir Thomas More*, 1923.
*—— 'Shakespeare's Text' in *A Companion to Shakespeare Studies*, ed. Granville-Barker and Harrison, 1941.
Pooler, C., ed., *Sonnets*, 1918.
†Pope, A., ed., *The Works of William Shakespeare*, 1725.
*Potter, L. 'Shakespeare's Life, Times and Stage', *ShS* 36, 1983, 172.
*——review of Taylor 1988, *TLS*, 11–17 Nov. 1988, 1251 [Sams 1988f].
*Powell, A. 'Shakespeare's Lost Years', *TLS* Letters, 3 May 1985, 495 [Sams 1985e].
Price, H. 'Shakespeare's Classical Scholarship', *Review of English Studies*, N.S. ix, 1958, 54–5.
Prince, F., ed., *The Poems*, 1960.
Prior, R. 'The Life of George Wilkins', *ShS* 25, 1972, 138.
*Proudfoot, R. 'Edmund Ironside', *TLS* Letters, 17 Sept. and 8 Oct. 1982 [Sams 1982b].
—— 'The Reign of King Edward III (1596) and Shakespeare', British Academy Lecture, 1985.
*—— 'Canon Fodder', *THES*, 27 June 1986 [Sams 1986h].
†Prouty, C. *The Contention and 2 Henry VI*, 1954.

†Ranson, N. '*Edmund Ironside*: A Re-Appraisal Appraised', *ShN* 1, 1986, 16.
†Razzell, P. *William Shakespeare: The Anatomy of an Enigma*, 1990.
Reynolds, E. *Campion and Parsons: The Jesuit Mission of 1580–1*, 1980.
†Richardson, A. *The First Part of the Contention* (diss., Yale), 1953.
†Robinson, I. *Richard II & Woodstock*, 1988.
Roe, J., ed., *The Poems*, 1992.
†Ronay, G. *The Lost King of England*, 1989.
†—— 'King Canute and the Princes in the Tower', *New Hungarian Quarterly*, 33, Spring 1992.
†Rowe, N. *The Works of Mr. William Shakespeare*, I. 1709.
†Rowse, A. *Shakespeare's Sonnets*, 1964.
†——*Shakespeare's Southampton*, 1965.
†——*Shakespeare the Man*, 1973, 2/1988.
†——*Discoveries and Reviews*, 1975.
†——*Discovering Shakespeare*, 1989.

*————'Over generous', *Spectator*, 14 June 1986 [Sams 1986g].
†Rubenstein, W. *Shakespeare's Bad Quartos*, 1950.
Ryan, R., ed., *Dramatic Table Talk*, 1825, ii. 156, cited in Chambers 1930, ii. 300.

Sams, E. 1980 Schubert work-list, in *New Grove Dictionary of Music and Musicians*, ed. S. Sadie, 1980.
———— 1981a 'Take a Letter, Shakespeare', *Sunday Times*, 19 April 1981 [see Grice 1981].
———— 1981b review of Schoenbaum 1981, *Sunday Times*, 10 May 1981.
———— 1982a '*Edmund Ironside*: a reappraisal', *TLS*, 13 Aug. 1982, 879.
———— 1982b 'Edmund Ironside', ibid., Letters, 24 Sept. and 29 Oct. 1982.
———— 1983 'Viewpoint: Shakespeare's Text and Common Sense', *TLS*, 2 Sept. 1983, 933–4.
———— 1984a 'Dating *The Shrew*', *TLS*, 3 Aug. 1984, 869.
———— 1984b 'WS His Marks', *The Times*, 18 Oct. 1984, 15.
———— 1985a 'Editing Shakespeare', *TLS*, 1 and 22 Feb. 1985.
———— 1985b 'Dramatically Different', *TLS*, 22 March 1985.
———— 1985c 'The Timing of the Shrews', *N&Q* ccxxx, 1985, 33–45.
———— 1985d 'The Shakespeare mystery', *Sunday Times*, 5 May 1985.
———— 1985e 'Shakespeare's Lost Years', *TLS*, 17 May 1985.
———— 1985f 'Shakespeare's Lost Play *Edmund Ironside*', 1985.
———— 1985g 'Cryptanalysis and Historical Research', *Archivaria* 21, 1985–6, 87–97.
———— 1986a 'The bard's play: Taylor's U-turn', *Sunday Times*, 16 Feb. 1986.
———— 1986b 'The "Lost" Shakespeare', *Sunday Times*, 2 Feb. 1986.
———— 1986c 'Shakespeare nods', *LRB*, 6 March 1986, 4.
———— 1986d *Shakespeare's Edmund Ironside: The Lost Play*, 2/1986.
———— 1986e 'Edmund Ironside', *TLS*, 9 May 1986.
———— 1986f review of *The Taming of the Shrew*, ed. A. Thompson, *N&Q* ccxxxi, 1986, 222–3.
———— 1986g 'Attrib. Shakespeare', *Spectator*, 21 June 1986.
———— 1986h 'Right playwright', *THES*, 1 Aug. 1986.
———— 1986i 'Shakespeare's Will', *TLS*, 21 Nov. 1986, 1311.
———— 1986j ed., *Edward III* (unpublished).
———— 1987a 'Edmund Ironside', *NYRB*, 7 May 1987, 48.
———— 1987b Where There's a Will: the Oxford or the Stratford Shakespeare?', *Encounter* lxix/1 June 1987, 54–7.
———— 1987c 'Revisionist Shakespeare', *Oxford Magazine* 25, 1987, 7; 27, 1987, 15.
———— 1988a 'The Troublesome Wrangle over King John', *N&Q* ccxxxiii, 1988, 41–4.
———— 1988b 'Oxford Shakespeare', *LRB*, 18 May 1988.
———— 1988c 'Taboo or not Taboo? The Text, Dating and Authorship of *Hamlet*, 1589–1623', in *HamS* 10, i–ii, Summer–Winter 1988, 12–46.
———— 1988d 'To the Editor', *SQ* 39, 1988, 25–2.
———— 1988e review of Ule, L. *A Textual Concordance to the Shakespeare Apocrypha*, *N&Q* ccxxxiii, 1988, 372–3.
———— 1988f 'William Shakespeare: A Textual Companion', *TLS*, 11–17 Nov. 1988, 1251.
———— 1988g 'Word-links in Shakespeare Authorship Studies', *LLC* iii, 1988, 205–6.
———— 1989a 'Shakespeare, or Bottom? The Myth of "Memorial Reconstruction"', *Encounter* lxxii/1, Jan. 1989, 41–5.
———— 1989b 'Aggro at Agincourt', *TLS*, 24 Feb.–2 March 1989, 196.

——— 1989c 'A Plague o' Both Your Houses', *Encounter* lxxii/4, April 1989, 58–60.

——— 1989d 'Shakespeare Studies', *TLS* Letters, 8–14, Sept. 1989.

——— 1989e review of McGee, A. *The Elizabethan Hamlet'*, *N&Q* ccxxxiv, 1989, 99–100.

——— 1990a 'Fatal Fallacy', *Encounter* lxxiv/1, Jan.–Feb. 1990, 62–4.

——— 1990b 'Mistaken Methodology', *LRB*, 14 June 1990, 4–5; 28 June 1990.

——— 1990c 'Prestige and Profit: Gary Taylor's Shakespeare', *Encounter* lxxv/1, July–Aug. 1990, 57–8.

——— 1990d 'Shakespeare Studies', *TLS*, 8–14 Sept. 1990.

——— 1990e review of essays on *Sir Thomas More*, *N&Q* ccxxxv, 1990, 464–5.

——— 1991a 'Assays of Bias', *N&Q* ccxxxvi, 1991, 60–63.

——— 1991b 'The Painful Misadventures of *Pericles* Acts I–II', *N&Q* ccxxxvi, 1991, 67–70.

——— 1991c review of *Merry Wives of Windsor*, ed. Craik, *N&Q* ccxxxvi, 1991, 219–20.

——— 1991d ' "If you have tears . . .": Onions and Shakespeare', *Connotations* 1, 1991, 181–6.

——— 1992a 'Shakespeare and the Oxford Imprint', *TLS*, 6 March 1992, 13.

——— 1992b 'The play's the thing', *THES*, 3 July 1992.

——— 1993a 'A Documentary Life' *TLS*, 12 Feb. 1993, 13.

——— 1993b 'Mrs. Shakespeare', *TLS*, 19 Feb. 1993, 5.

——— 1993c 'Mrs. Shakespeare', *TLS*, 19 March 1993.

——— 1993d 'Oldcastle and the Oxford Shakespeare', *N&Q* ccxxxviii, 1993, 180–85.

——— 1993e 'The hand of a lawyer's clerk?', *TLS*, 24 Dec. 1993, 14.

——— 1994a review of *Hamlet* 1603 and *The Taming of a Shrew* 1594, ed. Holderness and Loughrey, *N&Q* ccxxxvi, 1994, 93–4.

——— 1994b review of *1–3 Henry VI*, ed. Hattaway, *N&Q* ccxxxvi, 1994, 242–3.

——— 1994c 'Edmund Ironside and "Stylometry"' (forthcoming, in *N&Q*).

——— 1995 'Hamnet or Hamlet, That is the Question' (forthcoming in *HamS*).

Sanders, N., ed., *1–3 Henry VI*, New Penguin, 1981.

†Sarrazin, G. 'Die Entstehung von Shakespeares *Verlornener Liebesmühe*', *ShJ*, 1895, 219–30.

†——— 'Wortechos bei Shakespeare', *ShJ*, 1897, 120–65 and 1898, 119–69.

——— *Aus Shakespeares Meisterwerkstatt*, 1906.

†Schaar, C. *Elizabethan Sonnet Themes and the Dating of Shakespeare's Sonnets*, 1962.

†Schamp, D. 'Thesen zu Shakespeare', *Theater Heute* Nov.–Dec. 1974, 28–35.

*Schoenbaum, S. *Internal Evidence and Elizabethan Dramatic Authorship*, 1966.

*——— *Shakespeare's Lives* 1971, 2/1991 [Sams 1987a, 1993a and e].

*——— *William Shakespeare: A Documentary Life*, 1975 [Sams 1987b, 1993a and e].

*——— *A Compact Documentary Life*, 1977, 2/1987 [Sams 1987b, 1993a and e].

*——— *Records and Images*, 1981 [Sams 1981, 1993e].

——— 'A Detour into Lancashire', *TLS*, 19 April 1985.

*——— *Shakespeare and Others*, 1985.

*——— 'The Life of Shakespeare' in *The Cambridge Companion to Shakespeare Studies*, ed. Wells, 1986, 1–16.

Scott, W. 1828, in *Diaries*, ed. Lockhart, 1838 vii. 123, cited in Chambers 1930, ii. 301.

Sedley, C. *Antony and Cleopatra*, 1667.

*Seiler, G. Shakespeare's Part in *Pericles* (diss., Missouri), 1951, 19–20.

Seneca, *Ten Tragedies*, ed. Newton, 1581, reissued 1927.

——— *Tragedies*, trans. Miller, 1917.

—— *Four Tragedies and Octavia*, trans. Watling, 1966.

*Shaheen, N. 'Shakespeare and *The True Tragedy of Richard III*', *N&Q* ccxxx, 1985, 33–4.

—— *Biblical References in Shakespeare's Tragedies*, 1987.

*Shapiro, I. letter, *Guardian*, 12 Sept. 1986 [Sams 1993e].

Shiels, R. *The Lives of the Poets*, 1753, i. 130, cited in Chambers 1930, ii. 285–6.

†Shiras, A., ed., *Hamlet* 1603, 1991.

Simpson, R. 'On some plays attributed to Shakespeare', *Transactions of New Shakespeare Society*, 1875–6, 155–80.

—— *The School of Shakespeare*, ii, 1878; and see Bowden.

Slater, E. 'Shakespeare: word links between poems and plays', *N&Q* ccxvii, 1975, 157–63.

—— 'Word links with *The Merry Wives of Windsor*', *N&Q* ccxvii, 1975, 169–71.

†—— 'The vocabulary of *Edward III*' (diss., London) 1982.

†—— 'Edmund Ironside', *TLS*, 18 March 1983, 268.

†—— *The Problem of the Reign of King Edward III: A Statistical Approach*, 1988.

*Smallwood, R., ed., *King John*, New Penguin Shakespeare, 1974 [Sams 1988a].

*Smart, J. *Shakespeare* 1928, 2/1966.

†Smidt, K. *Injurious Impostors and Richard III*, 1964.

Smith, A. *Servant of the Cecils*, 1977.

*Smith, G. *A Classified Shakespeare Bibliography*, 1963.

*Smith, M. 'The Authorship of *Pericles*: an initial investigation', *The Bard*, iii, 1982, 143–76 and iv, 1983, 15–21 [Sams 1991b, Merriam 1992].

*—— 'An Initial Investigation of the Authorship of *Pericles*: Statistics Support Scholars: Shakespeare did not write Acts I & II', *ShN* 33, 1983, 32 [Sams 1991b, Merriam 1992].

*—— 'Critical Reflections on the Determination of Authorship by Statistics Part I', *ShN* 34, 1984, 4–5.

—— ibid., 'Part II: Morton, Merriam and *Pericles*', *ShN* xxiv. 3, 1984, 28, 33, 47.

*—— 'Stylometry: The Authorship of *A Lover's Complaint* – Was it Chapman?', *ShN*, xxxiv. 4, 1984, 44.

*—— 'Stylometrics '84 – A Workshop for Authorship Studies', *ShN* 34, 1984, 44–5.

*—— 'An investigation of Morton's Method to Distinguish Elizabethan Playwrights', *CHum* 19, 1985, 3–21, 144.

*—— 'An Investigation of the Basis of Morton's Method for the Determination of Authorship', *Style* xix, 1985, 341–68.

*—— A Critical Review of Word-Links as a Method for Investigating Shakespearean Chronology and Authorship', *LLC* vol. 1, no. 4, 1986, 202–6 [Sams 1988g].

*—— 'Eric Sams and *Edmund Ironside*', *ShN* 36, 1986, 1, 19.

*——'*Edmund Ironside* and Principles of Authorship Attribution', *ShN* 37, 3, 1987, 50.

*—— 'The Authorship of *Pericles*: New Evidence for Wilkins', *LLC* vol. 2, no. 4, 1987, 221–30 [Sams 1991b, Merriam 1992].

—— 'Merriam's Application of Morton's Method', *CHum* 21, 1987, 59–60.

*—— 'The Authorship of Acts I–II of *Pericles*: A New Approach Using First Words of Speeches', *CHum* 22, 1988, 23–41 [Sams 1991b, Merriam 1992].

*—— 'A Procedure to Determine Authorship Using Pairs of Consecutive Words: More Evidence for Wilkins's Participation in *Pericles*', *CHum* 23, 1988, 113–29 [Sams 1991b, Merriam 1992].

*—— 'Word-links and Shakespearean Authorship and Chronology', *N&Q* ccxxxiii, 1988, 57–9.

*———— 'Word-links and the Authorship of *Edmund Ironside*', *N&Q* ccxxxiii, 1988, 447–9.
*———— 'Statistics and Authorship', *TLS* Letters, 17–23 March 1989.
*———— 'Word-Links as a General Indicator of Chronology of Composition', *N&Q* ccxxxiv, 1989, 338–9.
*———— 'Function Words and the Authorship of *Pericles*', *N&Q* ccxxxiv, 1989, 333–6 [Sams 1991b, Merriam 1992].
*———— 'A Procedure to Determine Authorship using Pairs of Consecutive Words: More Evidence for Wilkins's Participation in *Pericles*', *CHum* 23, 1989, 113–29 [Sams 1991b, Merriam 1992].
*———— 'Counting Wilkins In: Stylometry Reveals Who Wrote Acts I and II of *Pericles*, *ShN* 40, 1990, 60 [Sams 1991b, Merriam 1992].
*———— 'Shakespearean Chronology: A New Approach to the Method of Word-Links', *N&Q* ccxxxv, 1990, 198–203.
*———— 'A Note on the Authorship of *Pericles*', *CHum* 24, 1990, 295–300 [Sams 1991b, Merriam 1992].
*———— 'The Authorship of *Timon of Athens*', *Transactions of the Society for Textual Scholarship* 5, 1991.
———— 'Statistical Inference in *A Textual Companion* to the Oxford Shakespeare', *N&Q* ccxxxvi, 1991, 73–8.
*———— 'Stylometry: Will the Computer Finally End Authorship Controversies?', *ShN* 41, 1991, 14–17.
———— 'The Authorship of *The Revenger's Tragedy*', *N&Q* ccxxxvi, 1991, 508–13.
*———— 'Shakespeare, Stylometry and *Sir Thomas More*', *Studies in Philology*, lxxxix. 4, 1992, 433–4.
*———— '*Edmund Ironside*', *N&Q* ccxxxviii, 1993, 202–5 [Matthews 1993, Sams 1994c].
*———— '*Sir Thomas More*, *Pericles* and Stylometry', *N&Q* ccxxxix, 1994, 55–8.
Sparshott, F. *The Structure of Aesthetics*, 1963.
*Spencer, T., ed., *Hamlet*, New Penguin, 1980.
Spenser, E. *The Teares of the Muses*, 1591.
———— *Colin Clout's Come Home Again*, 1591.
Spevack, M. *The Harvard Concordance to Shakespeare*, 1973.
———— *A Shakespeare Thesaurus*, 1993.
†Sprinchorn, E. 'Shakespeare's Bad Quarto', *TLS* Letters (a) 21 Jan. 1994 [Vickers 4 March 1994, Jenkins 1994] (b) 1 April 1994 [Jenkins 1994, Vickers 29 April 1994] (c) unpublished letter to *TLS*, 27 April 1994 (see Appendix to XXIV above, pp. 134–5).
†Spurgeon, C. *Shakespeare's Imagery*, 1935.
Stow, J. *Annales, or a Generale Chronicle of England*, 1580.
Steane, J., ed., Thomas Nashe, *The Unfortunate Traveller and Other Works*, 1972.
†*Streetlegal*. A. Morton, interviewed by Hugh Dehn on *Streetlegal* on Channel Four, 6 June 1993.

Tarleton's Jests: Tarletons News Out of Purgatory, ed. Halliwell, 1844.
*Taylor, G., ed., *Henry V*, Oxford 1982, pbk 1984 [Sams 1993d].
*———— 'Edmund Ironside', *TLS*, 1 April 1983, 328.
†———— '*King Lear*: the Date and Authorship of the Folio Version', in *The Division of the Kingdoms*, 1983, 351–468.
*———— 'Anticipating an Attack', *Sunday Times*, 9 Feb. 1986, 2 [Sams 1986a].
*———— , et al. *A Textual Companion to the Oxford Shakespeare*, 1988 (not '1987' as printed) [Sams 1988f, 1989a and e, 1990a and d, 1991a and b, 1992a; Merriam 1989, Pascoe 1990, M. Smith *N&Q*, 1991].
*———— *Reinventing Shakespeare*, 1989 [Sams 1990c].

——— reported in *ShN* 40, 1990, 28.

Thisted, R. and Efron, B. 'Did Shakespeare write a newly-discovered poem?', *Biometrika* 74, 1986, 445.

Thomas, D. *Shakespeare in the Public Records*, 1985.

*Thomas, S. 'On the Dating of Shakespeare's Early Plays', *SQ* 9, 1958, 187–94.

*——— '*Hamlet* Q1: First Version or Bad Quarto?' in *The Hamlet First Published*, ed. Clayton, 1992 [Urkowitz 1992].

*Thompson, A. 'Dating Evidence for *The Taming of the Shrew*', *N&Q* ccxxvii, 1982, 108–9 [Sams 1985c]

*——— , ed., *The Taming of the Shrew*, New Cambridge 1984 [Sams 1985c, 1986f].

†Thompson, E. *Shakespeare's Handwriting*, 1916.

†——— 'Special Transcript of the Three Pages', *Shakespeare's Hand in the Play of Sir Thomas More*, ed. Pollard, 1923.

†Thompson, J. *Shakespeare and the Classics*, 1952.

Tusser, T. *Five Hundred Points of Good Husbandry*, 1573, ed. Grigson, 1984.

*Twain, M. *Is Shakespeare Dead?*, 1909.

†Tylden-Wright, D. *John Aubrey: A Life*, 1991.

Ule, L. *A Concordance to the Shakespeare Apocrypha*, 1987.

†Urkowitz, S. 1980 *Shakespeare's Revision of King Lear*, 1980.

†——— 1983 'The Base Shall to th'Legitimate: The Growth of an Editorial Tradition', in *The Division of the Kingdoms*, ed. Taylor and Warren, 1983, 23–44.

†——— 1986a 'I am not made of stone': Theatrical Revision of Gesture in Shakespeare's Plays', *Renaissance and Reformation* 10, 1986, 79–93.

†——— 1986b 'Reconsidering the relationship of Quarto and Folio texts of *Richard III*', *English Literary Renaissance* 16, 1986, 442–6.

†——— 1988a 'Good News about "Bad" Quartos', in *"Bad" Shakespeare*', ed. Charney, 1988.

†——— 1988b 'Well sayd old Mole', in *Shakespeare Study Today*, ed. Ziegler, 1988, 37–70.

†——— 1988c ' "If I mistake in those foundations I do build upon": Peter Alexander's Textual Analysis of *2–3 Henry VI*', *English Literary Renaissance* 18, 1988, 230–56.

†——— 1989 'Memorial Reconstruction: Decline of a Theory', *ShN* 39, 1989, 10.

——— 1992 'Back to Basics: Thinking about the *Hamlet* First Quarto', in *The Hamlet First Published*, ed. Clayton 1992.

*Vickers, B. '*Hamlet* by Dogberry', *TLS*, 24 Dec. 1993 [Sprinchorn 1994a, Holderness and Loughrey 1994, 4 Feb.].

*———'Shakespeare's Bad Quarto', *TLS* Letters, 4 Feb. 1994 [Sprinchorn 1994b], 4 March 1994, 29 April 1994 [Sprinchorn 1994c, Godshalk 1994, 29 July 1994.

Wadman, H. 'Who Wrote in the Margin?', *Picture Post*, 26 April 1941, 27–9.

†Wait, R. *The Background to Shakespeare's Sonnets*, 1972.

*Ward, D. 'The King and *Hamlet*', *SQ* 43, 1992, 280–302.

Ward, J. in *Diary*, ed. Severn, 1839, 183, cited in Chambers 1930, ii. 249–50.

Warnicke, R. *William Lambarde*, 1973.

Waugh, E. *Edmund Campion*, 1935.

Weever, J. *Epigrammes*, 1599, cited in Chambers 1930, ii. 19.

†Weiner, A., ed., *Hamlet, the First Quarto*, 1962.

*Wells, S. 'The Failure of *The Two Gentlemen of Verona*', *ShJ* 99, 1963, 161–73.

*——— , ed., *A Midsummer Night's Dream*, Penguin, 1967.

*——— , ed., *Richard II*, New Penguin, 1969.

*——— , ed., *The Comedy of Errors*, 1972.

*———— , ed., *The Merry Wives of Windsor*, New Penguin, 1973.
*———— *Shakespeare: An Illustrated Dictionary*, 1978, 2/1985.
*———— letter in *TLS*, 29 Oct. 1982, 1193.
*———— on back cover of Oliver 1982, 2/1984.
*———— 'Introduction: The Once and Future King Lear', in *The Division of the Kingdoms*, ed. Taylor and Warren, 1983, 1–22.
*———— 'Editing Shakespeare', *TLS* Letters, 7 Feb. 1985 [Sams 1985a].
*———— BBC radio interview, 1 Jan. 1986 [Sams 1986d].
*———— *Complete Works*, 1986 [Sams 1987b, 1988b, 1992a].
*———— 'Revisionist Shakespeare', *Oxford Magazine* 24, 1987, 10–13; 26, 1987, 15; 28, 1987, 12–13 [Sams 1987c].
*———— contributions to *Textual Companion* (Taylor 1988, q.v.).
*———— reported in *THES*, 19 June 1992, 1, 20.
*———— *Shakespeare: A Dramatic Life*, 1994.
Wells, S and Taylor, G. reported in *ShN* 2, 1990, 28.
Wellsted, F. compiler of *Catalogue of Books* etc., q.v.
†Wentersdorf, K. 'The authorship of *Edward III*' (diss., Cincinnati), 1960.
Wernham, R. *The Return of the Armadas*, 1994.
†Werstine, P. 'Narratives about Printed Shakespeare Texts: "Foul Papers" and "Bad" Quartos', *SQ* 41, 1990, 65–86.
†Whiter, W. *A Specimen of a Commentary on Shakespeare*, 1794.
*Wilders, J. BBC radio interview, *Kaleidoscope*, 16 Feb. 1986 [Sams 1986d].
*Williams, W. review of *Edmund Ironside*, *N&Q* ccxxxii, 1987, 381–2.
Willobie his Avisa, see De Luna.
*Wilson, F. 'Shakespeare and the 'New Bibliography'', in *The Bibliographical Society: Studies in Retrospect* 1945, reprinted 1970.
*————*Marlowe and the Early Shakespeare*, 1953.
*Wilson, I. *Shakespeare: The Evidence*, 1993.
Wilson, J. *The Copy for Hamlet 1603*, 1918.
*———— , ed., *The Taming of the Shrew*, 1928, 2/1953, 3/1968.
*———— , ed., *Henry V*, Cambridge, 1947.
*———— , ed., *Titus Andronicus*, Cambridge, 1948, 2/1968.
*———— , ed., *1–3 Henry VI*, Cambridge, 1952, 2/1968.
*———— *Shakespeare's Sonnets: An Introduction for Historians and Others*, 1963.
*———— , ed., *Sonnets*, Cambridge, 1966, 2/1967.
Woudhuysen, H. *ShS* 44, 1992, 202.

Index